PSYCHIC

PSYCHIC

true paranormal experiences

HANS HOLZER

SMITHMARK

This edition published in 1999 by SMITHMARK Publishers,
a division of U.S. Media Holdings, Inc.,
115 West 18th Street, New York, NY 10011

SMITHMARK books are available for bulk purchase for sales promotion and premium use.
For details write or call the manager of special sales, SMITHMARK Publishers, 115 West 18th Street,
New York, NY 10011.

BOOK DESIGN AND COMPOSITION BY KEVIN HANEK

ISBN 0-7651-0953-0

LIBRARY OF CONGRESS CATALOGING-IN-PUBLICATION DATA
    Holzer, Hans, 1920-
        Psychic : true paranormal experiences / Hans Holzer.
        p. cm.
        Includes index.
        ISBN 0-7651-0953-0 (hardcover)
        1. Parapsychology.   1. Title.
        BF1031.H666   1999
        133—dc21   99-19444
                                                  CIP

Printed in the U.S.A.

10   9   8   7   6   5   4   3   2   1

To those seeking the truth about life, wherever it may lead them.

contents

INTRODUCTION introduction

"PSYCHIC" HAS BECOME PART OF OUR everyday language as a term denoting an ability that is somehow supernatural; but it is nothing of the kind. The psychic dimension is a fact of life—both this life, and yes, the next, and the ones thereafter.

The main purpose of this book is not to shock or surprise, or to tell strange stories usually associated with the tabloids, but to put emphasis on the psychic and give the reader a true understanding of what the psychic world is. Some of the case histories

Regis Philbin, medium Sybil Leek, and Hans Holzer on San Diego television in 1966, discussing the haunted Whaley House in that city.

included go back some years, but they are no less true today. In all cases we have the testimonials of both the principals and the witnesses.

For thousands of years, the phenomena and experiences we now associate with the term "psychic" have been cooped up in religious edifices, jealously guarded by the various priesthoods as a matter of prerogative and power.

While it is true that all religion bases its claim to verity and factuality on the track record and evidence of psychic phenomena, it does not hold true the other way around. The psychic is not an expression of religion, or of the supernatural, but rather part of all that is natural in man.

One can be religious and even orthodox in the pursuit of one's particular brand of religion, and deny the reality of proven psychic experiences; and one can be an atheist and still acknowledge the existence of psychic experiences, even though one would want to ascribe them to a bodily or mental function rather than as proof of other dimensions, such as the spiritual.

This book is an overview from the point of view of a middle-of-the-road observer, neither believer nor disbeliever, but a pragmatic searcher for evidence and truth.

Three words have no place in my scientific vocabulary: belief, disbelief, and supernatural. Truth is universal and applies to all. No exceptions, please.

— HANS HOLZER

the psychic dimension ONE

THE PSYCHIC DIMENSION IS NOT LIKE SOME outer planet or other tangible body, at least not tangible to our ordinary five senses. It is as real, and in some ways more real, than the physical world in which we live.

All this has to do with the "rate of speed," or what we popularly call "vibrations," at which the tiny particles that make up *both* worlds move. Everything in the universe is constantly in motion. The physical world or worlds move at a particular speed determined only by the density of their makeup. The physical world has particles of matter moving at a certain distance from one another—a little like Swiss cheese. The less "dense" psychic world (which includes what many call the spiritual dimension) has its particles strung out farther from one another and thus moves at a higher rate of speed than the denser physical world.

Think of this example: Polaroid light can exist in the same space as ordinary light without clashing with it because it moves on a different angle or plane. The same holds true of the psychic dimension, a world that the great medium Eileen Garrett once called "the world next door, so far and yet so near."

While the less dense world can interact freely with the denser physical world, it is more difficult the other way around: only when people in the physical world "travel" in their etheric or "inner" body can they penetrate the psychic world and experience it meaningfully. In their physical, heavier body-vehicles they can penetrate it, unknowingly or knowingly, and not make contact.

The motivating force, or power, that allows us to partake of the psychic around us used to be called "extrasensory perception," but is now more commonly referred to as psychic ability. Without understanding the nature of that *natural* component of our personality, the psychic remains a mystery. But it is not a mystery any more: it obeys specific laws and has substance and purpose in the overall scheme of existence.

THE EXTRA SENSE

Everyone has an extra sense beyond the five normally relied upon, but only a minority of people are aware of it. An even smaller percentage knows how to use this sixth sense to good advantage.

The problems of acknowledging this extra faculty are many. Prior to the nineteenth century, anything bordering on the occult was considered religious heresy and had to be suppressed or at least kept quiet. In the nineteenth century, with social and economic revolution came an overbearing insistence on material things, and science became a new god. This god of tangible evidence leaped into our present century invigorated by new technological discoveries and improvements. Central is the belief that only what is available to the ordinary five senses is real, and that everything else is not merely questionable but outright fantasy. Fantasy is not long for this world, as it does not seem to fulfill any useful purpose in the world of computers and computerized humans. George Orwell's *1984* is closer than we dare think, and the signposts are ominous.

Laboring under these difficult conditions, Dr. Joseph Rhine developed a new scientific approach to the phenomena of the sixth sense some fifty years ago, when he brought together and formalized many research approaches in his laboratory at Duke University. But pure materialism dies hard—in fact, it dies not at all. Even while Rhine was offering proof for the "psi factor" in the human personality—fancy talk for the sixth sense—he was attacked by exponents of the physical sciences for being a dreamer or worse.

Nevertheless, Rhine continued his work, and others came to his aid, and new organizations came into being to investigate and, if possible, explain the workings of extrasensory perception—ESP, for short.

To define the extra sense is simple enough. When knowledge of events or facts is gained without recourse to the normal five senses—sight, hearing, smell, touch, and taste—or when this knowledge is obtained in apparent disregard of the limitations of time and space, we speak of *extrasensory* perception. It is essential that the person experiencing the sixth-sense phenomena has had no access to knowledge, either conscious or unconscious, of the facts or events, and that his impressions are subsequently corroborated by witnesses or otherwise proved correct by the usual methods of exact science.

It is also desirable, at least from an experimental point of view, that a person having an extrasensory experience dealing with events in the so-called future should make this impression known at once to impartial witnesses, so that it can be verified later when the event does transpire. This is rarely possible because of the very nature of this sixth sense: it cannot be turned on at will, but functions best when there is an emergency and genuine need exists for it to operate. When ordinary communications fail, something within man reaches out and removes the barriers of time and space to allow for communication beyond the five senses.

There is no doubt in my mind that extrasensory phenomena are governed by emotional impulses and therefore present problems far different from those of the physical sciences. Despite the successful experiments with cards and dice conducted for years at the Duke University Parapsychology Laboratory, the core of ESP experiences are not capable of exact duplication at will.

Parapsychology, that is, the science investigating phenomena of this kind, has frequently been attacked on these grounds. Yet normal psychology, which also deals with human emotions, need not produce exact duplication of phenomena in the laboratory. Of course, psychology and psychiatry themselves were under attack from the previous establishment, and have found a comfortable niche of respectability only recently. It is human nature to attack all that is new and revolutionary, because man tends to hold on to his old gods. Fifty years from now, parapsychology will no doubt be one of the older sciences, and hence accepted.

It is just as scientific to collect data from "spontaneous phenomena," that is, in the field, as it is to produce them in a laboratory. In fact, some of the natural sciences could not exist if it were not for *in situ* observation. Try to reconstruct an earthquake in the lab, or a collision of galaxies, or the birth of a new island in the ocean.

The crux is the presence of competent observers and the frequency with which similar, but unrelated, events occur. For example, if a hundred cases involving a poltergeist, or noisy ghost, are reported from widely scattered areas, involving witnesses who could not possibly know of one another, have communicated with one another, or have had

access to the same information about the event they report on, it is proper scientific procedure to accept the reports as genuine and to draw certain conclusions from them.

Extrasensory-perception research does not rely entirely on spontaneous cases in the field, but without them it would be meaningless. The laboratory experiments are an important adjunct, particularly when we deal with the less complicated elements of ESP, such as telepathy, intuition beyond chance, and psychic concentration—but they cannot replace the tremendous impact of genuine precognition (the ability to foresee events before they occur) and other one-time events in human experience.

The nature of ESP is spontaneous and unexpected. You don't know when you will have an experience, you can't make it happen, and you can't foretell when and how it will happen. Conditions beyond your knowledge make the experience possible, and you have no control over it. The sole exception is the art of proper thinking—the training toward a wider use of your own ESP powers—which we will discuss later. But the events themselves are definitely not under your control, or under anyone else's, for that matter. The ESP experience can take the form of a hunch, an uncanny feeling, an intuitive impression, or it can be stronger and more definite, such as a flash, an image, an auditory signal, a warning voice, or a vision, depending on your own makeup and inborn talents as a receiver.

The first impulse with all but the trained and knowledgeable is to suppress the "message," or to explain it away, sometimes taking grotesque paths to avoid admitting the possibility of extrasensory experiences. Frequently, such negative attitudes toward what is a natural part of human personality can lead to tragedy, or, at the very least, to annoyance, for the ESP impulse is never in vain. It may be a warning of disaster or only an advance notice to look out for good opportunities ahead, but it always has significance, even though you may miss the meaning or choose to ignore the content. I have called this substance of the ESP *message cognizance*, since it represents instant knowledge without logical factors or components indicating time and effort spent in obtaining it.

The strange thing about ESP is that it is really far more than an extra sense. It is actually a supersense operating through the other five to get its messages across to the consciousness of man. Thus, a sixth-sense experience may come through the sense of sight—as a vision, a flash, or an impression; the sense of hearing—as a voice or a sound effect duplicating an event to be; the sense of smell—as strange scents indicating climates other than the present one or smells associated with certain people or places; the sense of touch—the hand on the shoulder, the furtive kiss, or the fingering by unseen hands; and the sense of taste—stimulation of the palate not caused by actual food or drink. Of these, the senses of smell and taste are rarely used for ESP communication, while by far the majority of cases involve either sight or sound or both. This must be so because these two senses have the prime function of informing the conscious mind of the world around us.

What has struck me, after investigating extrasensory phenomena for over 40 years, is the thought that we are not really dealing with an additional dimension as such, an additional sense like touch or smell, but a sense that is nonphysical—the psychic, which, to make itself known, must go through the physical senses. Rather than an extra sense, we really have here an extension of the normal five senses into an area where logical thinking is absent and other laws govern. We can compare it to the part of the spectrum that is invisible to the naked eye. We make full use of infrared and ultraviolet, and no one doubts the existence of these "colors," which are merely extensions of ordinary red and violet.

Thus it is with extrasensory perception, and yet we are at once at war with the physical sciences, which want us to accept only what is readily accessible to the five senses, preferably in laboratories. Until radio waves were discovered, such an idea was held to be fantastic under the same set of yardsticks, yet today we use radio to contact distant heavenly bodies.

Our normal human perception, even with instruments extending it a little, is far from complete. To assert that there is no more around us than the little we can measure is preposterous. It is also dangerous, for in teaching this doctrine to our children, we prevent their potential psychic abilities from developing unhampered. In a field where thought is a force to be reckoned with, false thinking can be destructive.

THE STRUGGLE FOR ACCEPTANCE

The notion still persists among large segments of the population that ESP is a subject suitable only for special people: the weird fringe, some far-out scientists perhaps, or those among the young people who are "into" the occult. Under no circumstances is it something that respectable average citizens get involved with. An interest in ESP does not stand up alongside such interests as music, sports, or the arts. Anyone professing an interest in ESP is automatically classified as an oddball. This attitude is more pronounced in small towns than it is in sophisticated cities like New York, but until recently, at least, the notion that ESP can be a subject for average people on a broad basis was alien to the public mind.

During the last few years this attitude has shifted remarkably. More and more, people discussing the subject of extrasensory perception are welcomed in social circles as being unusual people, and have become centers of attraction. Especially among the young, bringing up the subject of ESP almost guarantees one immediate friends. True, eyebrows are still raised among older people, especially business people or those in government, when ESP is raised as a serious subject. Occasionally, one still hears, "You don't really believe in that stuff, do you?" Occasionally, too, people will give me an argument trying to prove that it is all a fraud and has "long been proved to be without substance." It is remarkable how some of those avid scoffers quote "authoritative" sources, which they never identify by name or place. Even Professor Rhine is frequently pictured as a man who tried to prove the reality of ESP but failed miserably.

Of course, we must realize that people believe what they want to believe. If a concept becomes uncomfortable to a person, reasons for disbelief will be found even if they are sometimes dragged in out of left field. A well-known way of dismissing evidence for ESP is to quote only sources that are negative toward it. Several authors who thrive on "debunking books," undoubtedly the result of the current popularity of the occult subjects, make it their business to select a bibliography of source material that contains only the sort of proof they want in the light of their own prejudiced purpose. A balanced bibliography would yield different results and would thwart their efforts to debunk the subject of ESP. Sometimes people in official positions will deny the existence of factual material in order not to be confronted with the evidence, if that evidence tends to create a public image different from the one they wish to project.

A good case in point is an incident that occurred on a Chicago television broadcast emceed by columnist Irving Kupcinet. Among the guests were myself and Colonel "Shorty" Powers of NASA. I had just remarked that tests had been conducted among astronauts to determine whether they were capable of telepathy once the reaches of outer space had been entered, in case radio communications should prove to be inadequate. Colonel Powers rose indignantly, denouncing my statement as false, saying, in effect, that no tests had been undertaken among astronauts and that such a program lacked a basis of fact. Fortunately, however, I had with me a letter on official NASA stationery, signed by Dr. M. Koneci, who was at the time head of that very project confirming my statement.

The types of people who are interested in ESP include some very strange bedfellows: on the one hand, there are increasing numbers of scientists delving into the area with newly designed tools and new methods; on the other hand, there are laymen in various fields who find ESP a fascinating subject and do not hesitate to admit their interest, nor do they disguise their belief that it works. Scientists have had to swallow their pride and discard many cherished theories about life. Those who were able to do so and adjust to the ever-changing pattern of what constitutes scientific proof found their studies in ESP most rewarding.

The late heart specialist Dr. Alexis Carrel became interested in psychic phenomena, during his famous experiment that established the immortality of individual cells in a fragment of a chicken heart. After he had been working on the problem for years, someone asked him about his conclusions. "The work of a scientist is to observe facts," he said. "What I have observed are facts troublesome to science. But they are facts." Science still knows very little about the human mind, but researchers are now certain that the mind is much more powerful and complicated than they ever thought it was.

People accept theories, philosophies, or beliefs largely on the basis of who supports them, not necessarily on the facts alone. If a highly regarded individual supports a new belief, people are likely to follow him. Thus, it was something of a shock to learn, several years after his death, that Franklin Delano Roosevelt had frequently sat in séances during which his late mother, Sarah Delano, had appeared to him and given him advice in matters of state. It has been established that King George V of England also attended séances. To this day, the English royal family is partial to psychic research although very little of this is ever published. Less secret is the case of Canada's late prime minister William Mackenzie King. According to *Life* magazine, which devoted several pages to King, he was "an ardent spiritualist who used mediums, the ouija board, and a crystal ball for guidance in his private life." It is debatable whether this marks King a spiritualist or whether he was merely exercising his natural gift of ESP with an interest in psychic research.

Curiously enough, the number of people who will accept the existence of ESP is much larger than the number of people who believe in spirit survival or the more advanced forms of occult beliefs. ESP has the aura of the scientific about it, while, to the average mind at least, subjects including spirit survival, ghosts, reincarnation, and such require seemingly other facets of human acceptance than the purely scientific. That, at least, is a widely held conviction. At the basis of this distinction lies the fact that there is a pronounced difference between ESP and the more advanced forms of occult scientific belief. For ESP to work, one need not accept survival of human personality beyond bodily death. ESP between the living is as valid as ESP between the living and the so-called dead. Telepathy works whether one partner is in the great beyond or not. In fact, a large segment of the reported phenomena involving clairvoyance can probably be explained on the basis of simple ESP and need not involve the intercession of spirits at all. It has always been a debatable issue whether a medium obtains information about a client from a spirit source standing by, as it were, in the wings, or whether the medium obtains this information from his own unconscious mind, drawing upon extraordinary powers dominant within it. Since the results are the main concern of the client, it is generally of little importance whence the information originates.

It is comforting to think that ESP is merely an extension of the ordinary five senses as we know them, and can be accepted without the need for overhauling one's philosophy. The same cannot be said about the acceptance of spirit communication, reincarnation, and other occult phenomena. Accepting them as realities requires a profound alteration in the ordinary philosophy, at least among average people. With ESP, a scientifically oriented person need only extend the limits of believability a little, comparing the ESP faculty to radio waves and himself to a receiving instrument.

So widespread is the interest in ESP research and so many are the published cases indicating its reality that the number of out-and-out debunkers has shrunk considerably in the past years. Some years ago, a chemist named H. H. Pierce seriously challenged the findings of Joseph Rhine on the grounds that his statistics were false, if not fraudulent, and that the material proved nothing. No scientist of similar stature has come forth in recent years to challenge the acceptance of ESP; to the contrary, more and more universities, such as the University of Charlottesville in Virginia, are devoting departments or special projects to inquire

into the field of ESP. What little debunking goes on still is done by inept amateurs trying to hang on to the coattails of the current occult vogue.

EXTRA-ORDINARY SENSES

Less noticed or studied are seemingly *paranormal abilities* some people are capable of by the use of their *ordinary* five senses. When we use our ordinary five senses for purposes that transcend their usual applications, we are doing something paranormal. For instance, if by touching an object, as in psychometry, we get entire messages or pieces of information that the touch of the object would not be likely to give us, we are partaking of an extrasensory experience although actually using one of our ordinary senses.

A great deal of attention has been paid to instances where people have been able to "read" with their fingers. The *New York Times* devoted considerable space to this discovery, in an article by Robert K. Plumb:

The phenomenon of extra-ocular vision—the ability to detect color in the dark with the fingertips—has been confirmed in at least three Soviet citizens, according to reports from Moscow.

About a year ago, Russian scientists reported that 22-year-old, Rosa Kuleshova, had the ability to run her fingers over printed text and "read" a newspaper. She could also name colors after touching pieces of colored paper placed in opaque paper envelopes.

Kuleshova's ability has been further investigated and two other women have been found to have it. The new cases are a 9-year-old Kharkov schoolgirl, Lena Bliznova, and a 37-year-old, Nina Kulagina.

The most recent test of Kuleshova was done this way: She put her finger to the eyepiece of an instrument called a spectroanomaloscope, a device used for testing color vision.

The device generates all colors of the spectrum from red to violet.

Ordinarily, a person puts his eye to the eyepiece. Kuleshova was blindfolded, although this was "admittedly an unnecessary precaution," and she put her fingertip to the eyepiece.

The tests were conducted under Prof. Yefim Rabkin.

Kuleshova "named all colored circles presented to her for identification by pressing the tip of a finger to the eyepiece of the anomaloscope."

As far as is known, only one American scientist has worked with the phenomenon. He is Dr. Richard P. Youtz, a psychology professor at Barnard College. Youtz has found an American woman, Patricia Stanley of Flint, Michigan, and has tested her ability to identify colors with her fingers.

The Parapsychology Foundation became very interested in these initial reports, and under the personal guidance of Eileen Garrett, its president, further investigations were undertaken that yielded additional data and additional sensitives. If colors are a form of radiation—and most scientists will agree that they are—there is nothing so remarkable about a person being able to register

color or other touch radiation, in view of the fact that so many human beings, when properly observed, can register psychic radiation, which is far more complex and evidential. The experiments with "finger vision" were undertaken with otherwise normal subjects, who merely had this additional gift or extension of ordinary sensitivity.

However, unusual usage of ordinary sensory organs is frequently found among those who are by nature or accident deprived of one of their senses. It is common knowledge that the blind develop extremely acute hearing or touch at times, and manage to replace some of the functions of the sight organs with other sensory perceptions. This normally takes years, and the degree of alternate perception varies with the individual, but a Thai physician has used hypnosis to break through the delay barrier and teach the blind how to see with their inner eyes.

According to Dr. Vichit Sukhakarn of Bangkok, certain areas of the head are highly sensitive to light rays when the subject is hypnotized to so receive sight impressions. Sukhakarn has been experimenting in this field since 1954, and there is now a training center for blind children under his guidance. He has discovered that the left cheek is particularly sensitive to light rays and accordingly instructs his subjects to "see" from that area. He has been able to help regain consciousness of the sight world in many otherwise hopelessly blind people.

In general, extrasensory perception tends to be greater when ordinary sensory stimuli are shut out. This conviction is behind the yogi's deep meditation, when all ordinary stimuli are cut off and only his self is present. It is also the underlying idea of the witch's cradle, a device used by would-be practitioners over the centuries. It is nothing more than a kind of straitjacket into which the subject is placed. It deprives him completely of all movement, no matter how slight, and all sight and hearing, and thus suspends him in a limbo of total quietness in which his inner self is allowed to develop its powers freely.

There are also some stage magicians and mentalists who, although not blind, have genuine extra-ocular vision. A case in point is "Lady Rhoda" Koren, who was interviewed about her strange powers by the *New York Journal-American*'s Walter Bazar after she had been in trouble with the Ottawa police for driving blindfolded through the streets. "It was perfectly safe. I had biscuit dough stuck against my eyelids. On top of that was some surgical gauze, plus a three-inch bandage wound around my head to cover the eyes and three dish towels masking my eyes. I could see fine. I was driving through crowded Ottawa streets on Monday showing reporters how I do it at racetracks."

Prof. J. Walther, a geologist in Halle, Germany, undertook to evaluate 450 university students and their reactions over geophysical disturbances, commonly detected by sensitive dowsers. He found about 10 percent of all students able to obtain a reaction with a dowsing rod; all of them showed increased blood pressure and a higher pulse rate over reaction zones.

Prof. S. W. Tromp, a geologist in Holland and an adviser to UNESCO, investigated practicing dowsers with an electrocardiograph and obtained clear evidence of bodily reactions registered with this instrument.

Hundreds of carefully conducted experiments of geologists, biologists, physicists, and physicians all led to the same conclusion: the actual existence of force fields of a still unknown nature, and the response of plants, animals, and the human body in reference to these force fields.

Just before World War I, Dr. Walter Kilner published a book, *The Aura*, on his findings and experiments with the human magnetic field. Since then, the Kilner screen has enabled scientists to actually see and measure this electromagnetic field that emanates from the physical body. This "human atmosphere" discovered by Kilner is the personality. It remains at physical death to continue life in the nonphysical world, or it may be "hung up" in the atmosphere as a "ghost" personality. A great deal of psychic healing can be accomplished by studying the variations and changes in the individual aura. However, I will refer to these matters in discussing healing itself.

Whether a psychic person reads with his eyes blindfolded, or with his hands—such as a California student named Alan Ames demonstrated to the full satisfaction of his teachers at Spring Valley Junior High School—the technique is similar. These people have highly sensitive nerve endings in other parts of their bodies, and they perceive through them. If objects as well as living things give off radiation, the reading is accomplished by entering the radiation zone and interpreting the signal much in the way that a radio receiver intercepts, and transforms into words, the signals emanating at a distance from a radio transmitter. In the case of young Alan Ames, the *San Diego Union* reported his ability to read the serial numbers of a dollar bill while his eyes were completely covered and to identify correctly most objects placed between his hands without touching any of them.

No doubt there are hundreds of people with such abilities throughout the world. There is nothing miraculous about it. The extension of human senses is part of the ever widening quest into the nature of ESP.

psychic phenomena

THERE IS NOTHING IN THE UNIVERSE THAT does not obey natural laws of one kind or another, some known, some as yet not fully understood. But psychic phenomena and experiences are neither exceptions, miracles, nor unique with certain people. The fascination with the psychic has taken on many disguises, especially in the Middle Ages, when extrasensory ability was tantamount to witchcraft and the psychically gifted person had to be in fear of his or her life.

Today, more than ever, the psychic ability of man as almost a major part of daily life is much more accepted. Grudgingly, perhaps, grown men (and far more women) acknowledge the existence of a faculty in humanity that isn't covered in the schoolbooks. The explanation for the psychic gift, how it operates, and where it originates may differ depending on a person's attitude, philosophy, and prejudices, but few will deny its existence.

SCIENCE AND ESP: A DEVELOPING RELATIONSHIP

Sometimes a well-meaning reporter will ask me, "How does science feel about ESP?" ESP is part of science. Some scientists may have doubts about its validity or its potential, just as scientists in one area frequently doubt scientists in other areas. For example, some chemists doubt what some medical men say about the efficiency of certain drugs; some underwater explorers differ with the opinions expressed by space explorers; and some medical doctors differ greatly with what other medical doctors believe.

A definition of science is in order. Science is not knowledge or even comparable with the idea of knowledge; science is merely the process of gathering knowledge by reliable and recognized means. These means may change with time, and the means considered reliable in the past may fail the test in the future, while, conversely, new methods not used in the past may become prominent and be found useful. To consider the edifice of science an immovable object, a wall against which one may safely lean with confidence in the knowledge that nearly everything worth knowing is already known, is a most unrealistic concept. Just as a living thing changes from day to day, so does science and what makes up scientific evidence.

There are people within science representing the conservative or establishment point of view, who are not so much unconvinced of the reality of controversial phenomena and the advisability of including these phenomena in the scientific process, as they are unwilling to change their established concept of science. They are unwilling to learn new and startling facts, many of which are in conflict with what they have learned in the past, the ideas that form the foundation of their scientific beliefs. Science derives from the Latin *scire*, meaning "to know." *Scientia*, the Latin noun upon which our English term "science" is based, is best translated as "the ability to know," or perhaps as "understanding."

Knowledge as an absolute is another matter. I doubt that absolute knowledge is possible even within the confines of human comprehension. What we are dealing with in science is a method of reaching out toward it, not attaining it. In the end, the veil of secrecy will hide the ultimate truth from us, very likely because we are incapable of grasping it because of insufficient spiritual awareness. This insufficiency expresses itself, among other ways, in a determined reliance upon terminology and frames of reference derived from materialistic concepts that have little bearing upon the higher strata of information. Every form of research requires its own set of tools and its own criteria. To apply the purely materialistic empiric concepts of evidence to nonmaterialistic areas is not likely to yield satisfactory results. An entirely different set of criteria must be established before we can hope to grasp the significance of those nonmaterial concepts and forces around us that have been with us since the beginning of time, that are both within us and without us, and that form the innermost layer of human consciousness as well as the outer reaches of the existing universe.

The average scientist not directly concerned with the field of ESP and parapsychology does not generally venture into it, either pro or con. He is usually too much concerned with his own field and with the insufficiencies found in his own bailiwick. Occasionally, people in areas that are peripheral to ESP and parapsychology will venture into it, partly because they are attracted by it and sense a growing importance in the study of those areas that have so long been neglected by most scientists, and partly because they feel that in attacking the findings of parapsychology they are in some psychologically understandable way validating their own failures.

When Professor Joseph Rhine first started out at Duke University to measure what he called the "psi" force in man, critics were quick to point out the hazards of a system relying so heavily on contrived, artificial conditions and statistics. Whatever Rhine was able to prove in the way of significant data has since been largely obscured by criticism, some of it valid and some of it not, and by the far greater importance of observing spontaneous phenomena in the field when and if they occur. At the beginning, Rhine at his laboratory at Duke represented a milestone in scientific thinking. It was the first time that the area formerly completely left to the occultist was being explored by a trained scientist in the modern sense of the term. Even then, no one took the field of parapsychology very seriously; Rhine and his closest associate, Dr. Hornell Hart, were considered part of the department of sociology, as there had not as yet been a distinct department of parapsychology or a degree in that new science. Even today, there is no doctorate in it, and those working in the field usually have to have other credits as well.

But the picture is changing. A few years ago, Dr. Jule Eisenbud of the University of Colorado startled the world with his disclosures of the peculiar talents of Ted Serios, a Chicago bellhop gifted with psychic photography talents. This man could project images into a camera or television tube, some of which were from the so-called future while others were from distant places where Serios had never been. The experiments were undertaken under the most rigid test conditions; they were repeated, something the old-line scientists in parapsychology

stressed over and over again. Despite the abundant amount of evidence, produced in the glaring limelight of public attention and under strictest scientific test conditions, some of Eisenbud's colleagues at the University of Colorado turned away from him whenever he asked them to witness the experiments that he was then conducting. Today, even orthodox scientists are willing to listen a little more; still, it is a far cry from having an actual institute of parapsychology independent of existent facilities, which I have been advocating for many years. But there is a greater willingness to evaluate the evidence fairly, and without prejudice on the part of those who represent the bulk of the scientific establishment.

According to an interview in the *Los Angeles Times* on August 30, 1970, psychiatrist Dr. George Sjolund of Baltimore concluded, "All the evidence does indicate that ESP exists." Sjolund works with people suspected of having ESP talents and puts them through various tests in specially built laboratories. Scientific experiments designed to test for the existence of ESP are rare. Sjolund knows of only one other like it in the United States—in Seattle. He does ESP work only one day a week.

Evelyn de Wolfe, a *Los Angeles Times* staff writer, wrote: "The phenomenon of ESP remains inconclusive, ephemeral and mystifying but for the first time in the realm of science, no one is ashamed to say they believe there is such a thing." The writer quotes this observation by Dr. Thelma S. Moss, assistant professor of medical psychology at UCLA School of Medicine, who has been conducting experiments in parapsychology for several years: "In a weekend symposium on ESP more than six hundred persons in the audience learned that science is dealing seriously with the subject of haunted houses, clairvoyance, telepathy, and psychokinesis and is attempting to harness the unconscious mind."

It is not surprising that some more liberally inclined and enlightened scientists are coming around to thinking that there is something in ESP after all. Back in 1957, *Life* magazine editorialized on "A Crisis in Science": "New enigmas in physics revive quests in metaphysics. From the present chaos of science's conceptual universe two facts might strike the layman as significant. One is that the old-fashioned materialism is now even more old-fashioned. Its basic assumption that the only 'reality' is that which occupies space and has a mass is irrelevant to an age that has proved that matter is interchangeable with energy. The second conclusion is that old-fashioned metaphysics, so far from being irrelevant to an age of science, is science's indispensable complement for a full view of life. Physicists acknowledge as much; a current Martin advertisement says that their rocket men's shoptalk includes the physics (and metaphysics) of their work. Metaphysical speculation is becoming fashionable again. Set free of materialism, metaphysics could well become man's chief preoccupation of the next century and may even yield a worldwide consensus on the nature of life and the universe."

By 1971, this prophetic view of *Life* magazine had taken on a new reality. According to the *Los Angeles Times* of

February 11, 1971, *Apollo 14* astronaut Edgar D. Mitchell attempted to send mental messages to a Chicago engineer whose hobby is extrasensory perception. Using ESP cards, which he had taken aboard with him to transfer messages to Chicago psychic Olaf Olsen, Mitchell managed to prove beyond any doubt that telepathy works even from the outer reaches of space. The Mitchell-Olsen experiment has since become part of the history of parapsychology. Not only did it add significantly to the knowledge of how telepathy really works; it made a change in the life of Mitchell. According to a UPI dispatch of September 27, 1971, Mitchell became convinced that life existed away from earth, and more than likely, in our own galaxy. But he doubted that physical space travel held all the answers. "If the phenomenon of astral projection has any validity, it might be perfectly valid to use it in intergalactic travel." Mitchell said that he was paying additional attention to ESP for future use. Since that time, Mitchell has become an active experimenter in ESP.

The German physicist Dr. Werner Schiebeler gave a lecture on physical research methods applicable to parapsychology. The occasion was the conference on parapsychology held in Constance, Germany. Schiebeler, as well versed in atomic physics as he is in parapsychology, suggested that memory banks from deceased entities could be established independent of physical brain matter. "If during séances entities, phantoms, or spirits of the deceased appear that have been identified beyond a shadow of a doubt to be the people they pretend to be, they must be regarded as something more than images of the dead. Otherwise, we would have to consider people in the physical life whom we have not seen for some time and encounter again today as merely copies of a former existence." Schiebeler said that parapsychology has furnished definite proof for the continuance of life beyond physical death.

Professor R. A. McConnell of the department of biophysics and microbiology at the University of Pittsburgh wrote in the *American Psychologist* that in discussing ESP before psychology students, it was not unusual to speak of the credulity of the public, while he felt it more necessary to examine the credibility of scientists, including those who believe ESP exists and those who do not. Referring to an article on ESP by the British researcher G. R. Price published by *Science* in 1955, McConnell pointed to Price's contention that proof of ESP was conclusive only if one were to accept the good faith and sanity of the experimenters, but that it could easily be explained away if one were to assume that the experimenters, working in collaboration with their witnesses, had intentionally faked the results. McConnell pointed out that this suggestion of fraud by Price, a chemist by profession, had been published on the first page of the most influential scientific journal in America.

Professor McConnell pointed out the fallibility of certain textbooks considered bulwarks of scientific knowledge. He reminded his readers that until 1800, the highest scientific authorities thought that there were no such things as meteorites until the leaders of science found out that meteorites came from outer space; text-

books were rewritten accordingly. What disturbed McConnell was that the revised textbooks did not mention that there had been an argument about the matter. He wonders how many arguments are still going on in science and how many serious mistakes are in the textbooks that we use for study. In his opinion, we ought to believe only half the ideas expressed in the works on biological sciences, although he is not sure *which* half. In his view, ESP belongs in psychology, one of the biological sciences, and he thinks that ESP is something about which so-called authorities are in error. McConnell pointed out that most psychology textbooks omit the subject entirely, as unworthy of serious consideration, but that the books are wrong, for ESP is a real psychological phenomenon. He also showed that the majority of those doing serious research in ESP are not psychologists, and deduces from this and the usual textbook treatment of the subject as well as from his own sources that psychologists are simply not interested in ESP.

A long time has passed since 1955: the American Association for the Advancement of Science recently voted the Parapsychology Association into membership. The latter, one of several bodies of scientific investigators in the field of parapsychology, had sought entrance into the association for many years but had been barred from membership by the prejudices of those in control of the association. The Parapsychology Association itself, ironically, had also barred some reputable researchers from membership in its own ranks for the same reasons. Parapsychology became an accepted subject within the American Association for the Advancement of Science. Doing research in a reputable fashion in the field, they were invited to join.

The cleavage between the occult or mystically, emotionally tinged form of inquiry into psychic phenomena, and the purely scientific, clinically oriented way is apparent. That is not to say that both methods will not eventually merge into one single quest for truth. Only by using all avenues of approach to a problem can we truly accomplish its solution, but it seems necessary at this time when so many people are becoming acquainted with the occult, and parapsychology in general, to make a clear distinction between a tearoom reader and a professor of parapsychology, between a person who has studied psychic phenomena for twenty-five years and has all the necessary academic credentials and a Johnny-come-lately who has crept out of the woodwork of opportunism to start his own "research" center or society.

Those who sincerely seek information in this field should question the credentials of those who give them answers; well-known names are always preferable to names one has never heard of. Researchers with academic credentials or affiliations are more likely to be trusted than those who offer merely paper doctorates fresh from the printing press. Psychic readers purporting to be great prophets must be examined at face value—on the basis of their accomplishments in each individual case, not upon their self-proclaimed reputation. With all that in mind and with due caution, it is still heartwarming to find so many sincere and serious people dedicating themselves

to the field of parapsychology and scientific inquiry, which I find one of the most fascinating areas of human endeavor. Ever since Sir Oliver Lodge proclaimed, "Psychic research is the most important field in the world today, by far the most important," I have felt quite the same way.

At Washington University in St. Louis, a dedicated group of researchers with no funds to speak of has been trying to delve into the mystery of psychic photography. Following in the footsteps of Jule Eisenbud of the University of Colorado, and my own work—*Psychic Photography: Threshold of a New Science?*— this group, under the aegis of the department of physics at the university, is attempting to produce psychic photographs with some regularity under many kinds of situations. The group feels that since Ted Serios discovered his ability in this field by accident, others might have similar abilities. "Only when we have found a good subject can the real work of investigating the nature of psychic photography begin," they explain. The fact that people associated with a department of physics at a major American university even speak of investigating psychic photography scientifically is a novelty; one can only hope that a new age in unbiased science is dawning upon us.

Stanley Korn of Maryland, employed by the navy as an operations research analyst, has a degree in physics and has done graduate work in mathematics, statistics, and psychology. Through newspaper advertisements, he discovered the Silva Mind Control Course and enrolled in it, becoming acquainted with Silva's approach, including the awareness of the alpha state of brain-wave activity, which is associated with increased problem-solving ability and ESP.

"What induced me to take the course was the astonishing claim made by the lecturer that everyone taking the course would be able to function psychically to his own satisfaction or get his money back. This I had to see," Korn explained. Through the Silva method, which incorporates some of the elements of diagnosis developed by renowned psychic medium, Edgar Cayce, but combines them with newer techniques and what we call "traveling clairvoyance," Korn learned that psychic activities are not necessarily limited to diagnosing health cases, but can also be employed in psychometry, the location of missing objects and persons, and even the locations of malfunctions in automobiles. "After seeing convincing evidence for the existence of psi, and experiencing the phenomenon myself, I naturally wanted to know the underlying principles governing its operation. To date, I have been unable to account for the psychic transmission of information by any of the known forms of energy, such as radio waves. The phenomena can be demonstrated at will, making controlled experiments feasible."

But the mind-control approach is by no means the only new thing in the search for awareness and full use of ESP powers in man. People working in the field of physics are used to apparatus, test equipment, and physical tools. Some of these people became interested in the marginal areas of parapsychology and ESP research, hoping to contribute some new mechanical gadget to the field. One such device had been developed to utilize infrared light to pinpoint the location of an otherwise unseen intruder by the heat radiating from his body.

Time magazine of August 17, 1970, headlined in its science section, "Thermography: Coloring with Heat." The magazine explained that "infrared detectors are providing stunning images that were once invisible to the naked eye. The medium is called color thermography, the technique of translating heat rays into color. Unlike ordinary color photographs, which depend on reflected visible light, thermograms or heat pictures respond only to the temperature of the subject. Thus the thermographic camera can work with equal facility in the dark or light. The camera's extraordinary capability is built around a characteristic of all objects, living or inanimate. Because their atoms are constantly in motion, they give off some degree of heat or infrared radiation. If the temperature rises high enough, the radiation may become visible to the human eye, as in the red glow of a blast furnace. Ordinarily, the heat emissions remain locked in the invisible range of infrared light."

It is clear that such equipment can be of great help in examining so-called haunted houses, psychically active areas, or psychometric objects—in other words, to step in where the naked eye cannot help, or where ordinary photography discloses nothing unusual. The magazine *Electronics World,* in an article entitled "Electronics and Parapsychology" by L. George Lawrence, claims, "One of the most intriguing things to emerge in that area is the now famous *Backster Effect.* Since living plants seem to react bioelectrically to thought images directed to their overall well-being, New Jersey cytologist Dr. H. Miller thinks that the phenomenon is based upon a type of cellular consciousness. These and related considerations lead to the idea that psi is but a part of a paranormal matrix—a unique communications grid that binds all life together. Its phenomena apparently work on a multi-input basis which operates beyond the known physical laws."

By the 1990s science was no longer quite as hostile to serious inquiry into psychic phenomena. Although the media exploited the renewed interest by the public in anything paranormal—sometimes too sensationally—the interest is genuine, and more people are becoming curious about this elusive "sixth sense" that we are all supposed to possess. A new generation of serious researchers are no longer afraid of calling extrasensory perception research outside of science, and rightly so, as any research based on actual observation and careful study is part of scientific inquiry. Laboratory experiments are no longer as important, and the artificial re-creation in laboratories of the phenomena, which never really worked well or proved much, has taken a backseat.

When Joseph Rhine created the term "extrasensory perception," abbreviated as ESP, in the 1930s, it was a novelty for the time. The link to anything spiritual or pointing toward the existence of a hereafter world was being denied. The psychic talent was a natural component of the human personality, an extension of man's psychological makeup that somehow could pierce the curtains of time and space. It took many more years of exploration before parapsychology, as the new science was called, would come up with

the answers of its origin. Because psychic research was satisfied to deal with laboratory tests, such as the sequence of cards and dice falling, and derive statistical information from them, the orthodox scientific community did not particularly object to the new science, seeing that it employed familiar research patterns.

It was only many years and thousands of recorded tests with hundreds of subjects later that the futility of this method became clear. The observation and careful recording of actual phenomena, when they occurred, was deemed more significant in the search for the origin of this mysterious gift. But in the 1990s, communications have altered our image of the world we live in. What seemed science fiction twenty years ago is commonplace today. Dick Tracy's wrist telephone is a crude forerunner of our cellular telephones; wireless contact over vast distances in space is almost routine in today's technological age. Jules Verne's Martian balloon may have amused the turn-of-the-century readership, but as we approach the millennium, we already know a lot about the red planet, because our instruments have already been there.

Leonardo da Vinci actually designed a working submarine, but no one took him seriously when even a steamship had not yet been invented. Yet mankind tends to respect inventions of the material kind, machines and devices that promise us a better life: you design it, you get the components, and you build it, and if you've done it right, it will work. But when it comes to unusual human faculties that transcend the limits of our knowledge of human ability at the time, mankind is very cautious. We can easily cope with transmissions by electronic gear over huge distances in space, because we understand how the gadget works. After all, we built it. But extrasensory perception, the psychic—where does it originate? Can we control it? Is it dangerous?

More and more, we study the effects of the psychic gift, and try to deduce its system from the results. Only in recent years have serious professionals gotten into the work—parapsychologists who try to understand and control the gift. No more card and dice tests; instead, observation and experimentation, though the latter is not as fruitful in its results as the former. Clinical conditions tend to inhibit the performance of genuine psychics. The psychic gift does not conform to any of the rules and laws of empiric science. The phenomena cannot be duplicated at will in the laboratory. The psychic ability occurs randomly in people, and there is little evidence that it can be categorized, even though astrologers point to the preponderance of so-called water signs among people with unusual psychic ability.

We know a lot about the ordinary five senses, how they work, and through which bodily organ; we even know the biochemical processes that make the functions possible. But with the psychic gift, we know no such thing. There is that metaphysical talk about the third eye, and the various chakras or focal energy points of the body. But finding the actual organ, the seat of psychic power in man, has thus far eluded us.

We cannot even be sure whether psychic ability is a function of the personality, differing in quality and intensity from person to person, or whether it is merely a channel of sorts through which other intelligences communicate information that the psychic person then formulates into words, images, and sounds. Either way, the psychic gift is a positive factor in our personalities, because it supplements our perception and ability to observe immeasurably, even beyond what we usually perceive as the boundaries of time and distance. A large segment of the earth's population has the gift, and it may well be that being psychic is the norm, while not having developed the gift is deprivation.

It is not supernatural but perfectly natural, and there are ways to develop and enhance it, and to control it at will.

TELEPATHY AND OTHER FORMS OF ESP

Telepathy is probably the most common form of the psychic element in man, and often easier to understand by purely scientifically minded people because it reminds them of our world of electronic communications—and so it should. Strictly speaking, the term in Greek means "impression across a distance." To the parapsychologist, it represents the simplest form of extrasensory perception. Another name given to this faculty at times is "thought transference," but I prefer to describe the ability of telepathic communication—whether as sender or as receiver—as knowledge gained without the use of the ordinary five senses.

First, let me define "thought" as the image or set of conditions created in the mind of one person, or the observation of existing conditions by a person in which he takes note of what he perceives through his ordinary five senses. A thought is also an electric impulse, very much like a radio message, sent out by means of the brain (as opposed to the mind, which operates through the brain but is not identical with it). Since it is an electric entity, a thought must naturally have some body or substance, no matter how small. Therefore, one should be capable of registering, measuring, or—in some other neutral, nonsubjective way—tracing its existence.

What orthodox medicine likes to call "brain waves" have long been measured by the electroencephalograph, an apparatus capable of registering, through electrodes attached to the head, the tiny currents within a patient's brain. When a person has an "idea," it means that a thought wave has already been created and sent out by his brain. Ordinarily, man cannot control either the direction or intensity of this "broadcast." However, some particularly endowed people can be trained to use thought messages in a way that they will be received by a particular receiver on the other end of the invisible line. We then have a two-way experiment that is capable of being rigidly controlled by the simple method of examining the information received by the receiver. If he had no foreknowledge of the contents, or any access to the information contained in it, yet the material checks out as true in specific respects, we have a clear-cut case of successful "thought transference," or telepathy.

"It must be telepathy," the astonished person exclaims when someone has just "read his mind." Erroneously referred to by the public as "mental telepathy," telepathy signifies communication from mind to mind without recourse to sensory perception. The transfer of thoughts from one mind to another is accomplished at great speed and with almost no loss in time. There is a tiny fraction of time—elapsed time, that is—between the transmission of a thought or image and its reception on the other end in another mind, but the amount of elapsed time is so insignificant that, for all practical purposes, we can say that telepathy is an instant transmission of thoughts from one person to another. It works best in times of stress and when ordinary communications are down. It is particularly strong between people who have an emotional bond, such as relatives, friends, lovers, or people who in some fashion rely upon each other. The instances of mothers feeling the distress of a child, at a distance, are numerous; cases in which someone just has to get through to another person and uses his mind to send forth a message are also numerous and are well attested in the files of most reputable psychic research societies, such as the American Society for Psychical Research.

Stress telepathy is by no means the only way of communicating mind to mind. To a degree, telepathy can be induced experimentally as well. In experimental telepathy, sender and receiver should know each other to make the contact possible. It is extremely difficult to send out a thought message to someone you cannot visualize. By knowing the receiver, or potential receiver, no evidential material is being given away, since the message contains the evidence. It is immaterial whether the two parties are close by, such as in two different rooms in the same apartment, or whether they are a thousand miles away from each other: telepathy does not recognize any difference. It is important that both sender and receiver be in a calm state of mind, in good physical health, and comfortable. Noise and other distractions tend to interfere with the possible transmission. It is advisable to transmit, or try to transmit, relatively simple messages or thoughts. These may be sentences or they may be visual impressions, such as definite scenes. In a way, this resembles the card test devised by Rhine at Duke University, except that instead of artificial symbols, real ideas and scenes are being used for transmission. Also, sender and receiver are not merely separated by a piece of cardboard, creating an artificial wall between them, but are literally apart and cannot see each other.

Telepathy works a little like radio: small impulses, specifically programmed by the sender, are sent out to a known receiver; the receiver, in turn, decodes the message and allows his conscious mind to formulate it into words. Telepathy works equally well between living people and between incarnates and discarnates. However, experimentally speaking, adequate proof can be obtained only from telepathy between living people. Those wishing to try their hand at telepathy and who have a suitable partner should plan on regular sessions of perhaps half an hour each during which a number of ideas or images are transmitted. A record should be kept on each end as to what is being sent and what is being received. Afterward, the two should be compared and scored. Anything considerably above the law of averages is significant. Generally speaking, if a receiver identifies three

out of ten possible messages fully or nearly so, he will have breached the law of averages and scored in ESP. It is unlikely that ten out of ten are ever received. Some messages may be obscured in part or may be received out of sequence, for some reason. Thought transference is outside the conventional time stream; therefore, the sequence can be jumbled, since all messages sent are coexistent in the timeless dimension.

While the incentive of experimentally induced telepathy furnishes the emotional motivation so necessary for success, necessity is a much stronger inducing agent. When ordinary communication is impossible and the initiator of the telepathic message realizes this, forces are brought into play that make the message very strong. This may be in real crisis situations or it may be in only comparatively unimportant domestic or personal matters. As long as there is an element of urgency and the realization that there is no other avenue to get through, telepathy may succeed.

The famous Australian explorer Sir Hubert Wilkins and the Little Rock, Arkansas, psychic Harold Sherman conducted what amounted to classical experiments in telepathy during Sir Hubert's travels to the North Pole. He was to transmit information about himself daily from the Arctic, Sherman was to take down whatever he received, and the material would then be compared after Sir Hubert came back to New York. A team of researchers stood by whenever Sherman was getting messages telepathically. This happened in a New York hotel room under test conditions. On one such occasion, Sherman insisted that he saw, that is, telepathically, Sir Hubert dancing in evening clothes. This seemed particularly improbable, since, at the time, the explorer was due at the Arctic base of his expedition. But when Sir Hubert returned to New York and the matter was brought up, he related that en route to his Arctic base, his plane had been forced down in a snowstorm and had landed in Calgary. Such a dignitary as Sir Hubert naturally brought out top government people to greet him. It so happened that the governor of Alberta was being inaugurated that day, and shortly after Sir Hubert's unscheduled arrival, the inauguration ball took place. Naturally, the governor invited his distinguished guest to attend and, since Sir Hubert had no evening clothes of his own, lent him a suit to wear. Thus, what Harold Sherman saw thousands of miles away in New York was correct.

J.S. lives in California, and all her life, she has had ESP experiences, but the incident of particular interest here indicates a form of telepathy somewhat different from both experimentally induced telepathy and spontaneous urgency telepathy. This form of communication is between the unconscious mind of a sleeping person and the conscious mind of a person who is fully awake. Here is her report:

I remember vividly when I was in college, I went to the library to do some research. Suddenly, I heard my friend Brian call my name. I looked around for him but I could not find him. Then I heard him call my name again, as though he were standing next to me, and he asked if he could come in. I looked and realized that Brian was not in the library. I then went home and found Brian asleep on the couch. I asked him where he had been at 2:00 P.M., the time when I had the experience at the library. He replied that he had just gotten off work about one o'clock and had come to see if there was anyone home at our house. He had called my name outside the house, but when no one answered, he opened the door, called again, and asked if he could come in. No one was home, so he lay down on the couch."

"Cross correspondences" are controlled experiments, often long-distance, in which a psychic person gets impressions of situations while a scientific team of observers at the other end also records what it sees or what is happening. There are many well-documented cases of this.

Typical of this is an experiment which was undertaken in New York. At that time, a group assembled on the Lower West Side watched as a young man named Stanley went into a trance state, in which he was able to project himself to a designated location some distance away. Naturally, he knew nothing about that location beforehand. The other team had arranged a rose in a vase and a book opened at a certain page as markers in the apartment that Stanley was to visit telepathically. On his "return," Stanley described accurately what he had seen. He could not have obtained this knowledge from those around him, since they did not know the details of the other apartment. The question arises of whether Stanley received a picture of the place from the minds of those present in the apartment, which would be telepathy, or whether he was able to project his "etheric self," his own person, to the place—that is, leave his body temporarily, observe what he could, and then return.

This is called *astral projection,* and is quite common, both the voluntary and the involuntary kind. I am convinced that many telepathic experiments involve this kind of projection. "Pure" telepathy, where the receiver does not go anywhere, but merely concentrates on getting messages or impressions, is much more common in spontaneous cases, that is, cases not anticipated or experimentally induced. Simple thought transference, telepathy without the possibility of other explanations, works best when there is a compelling reason for it. If there is an emotional urgency in transmitting a message, or if normal means of communication are not feasible, it works even better.

Several years ago, I was attending a play rehearsal in New York when I suddenly remembered that I had made an appointment with lyricist John Latouche for 5:00 P.M. that day. Since the set was closed and there was no telephone nearby, I became increasingly unhappy at the thought of having to disappoint my distinguished friend. My preoccupation was noticed by one of the singers present, a psychically gifted woman named Future Fulton. I explained my inability to let Latouche know I would be late, and how I wished I could send him a message to that effect.

"Is that all?" she asked, closed her eyes for a moment, breathed deeply, and then, reopening her eyes, added, "The message has been delivered." I laughed a little uncertainly, and went on with the work at hand. When I returned home around six, I immediately telephoned Latouche and started to apologize for not having called him earlier.

"What are you talking about?" Latouche interjected. "You most certainly did. Why, my answering service tells me *someone* called at five to say you'd be delayed."

HOW TO DEVELOP TELEPATHY

Telepathy works best between people who know each other, and even better between people who are emotionally close to each other. Two radios tuned in to each other naturally yield better results than a random beam looking for a receiver and losing its energy while searching a very large field.

I have already stated that all extrasensory experiences are emotionally tinged in that they involve the whole personality. The emotions need not be love or hatred. Creative excitement is an equally strong emotional force. Many ideas seem to have been "in the air" only to be picked up simultaneously by a number of people. The same inventions are made in widely separated areas, and music is composed by people who don't know of one another, and yet duplicate one another's work. Some philosophers want us to believe that there is a "World Mind" whence all knowledge comes—a sort of a super public domain ready to be tapped by anyone with the right tools. But it may be just one mind, giving out strong thought waves, and another at a distance, receiving them without realizing that the new idea he has suddenly hit upon really originated in someone else's mind. Innocent plagiarism, perhaps, and the world is full of this kind of "coincidence." Practically speaking, telepathy is a faculty everyone may have deeply imbedded within his personality, but only those capable of being "good senders" or "good receivers" will make practical use of this most valuable talent.

Here are some hints for how you can achieve this, that is, if you are honestly interested and not scared of something that is perfectly natural. Fear inhibits all forms of extrasensory perception.

Learn to remove all prejudices on the subject; have no preconceived notions whether it will "work for you" or not. Your doubting will surely make you fail. Cautious optimism—that it may well work—is the best attitude. Relax and don't strain or force. Tension is your enemy. A carefree, unperturbed, and unhurried attitude is helpful. Don't restrict your experiments to rigid schedules. Don't insist that it must work by next week, or else! Let go of yourself, allow it to happen, and sooner or later, it may.

Visualize the person to whom you wish to transmit your thoughts, if you are to be the sender. Check with the other person at intervals to see if you have succeeded, but do not alert the other person. This is not a controlled scientific experiment, and if the other person is aware of your efforts, he or she may also tense up, making it twice as hard to get through. If the receiver does not know when and what will be transmitted telepathically, you have an open door on the other end.

The best telepathy occurs when the thought being sent out is conceived spon-

taneously, without trying. For instance, you have a sudden thought of how nice it would be to see your mother again. Your mother lives five hundred miles away. Just at that instant, she also suddenly thinks of you and how nice it would be to see you. Coincidence? Not when it happens in thousands of cases, many of them easy to verify. There is something about thoughts that is very much like radio waves. They travel, once emitted, in every direction until their energies have thinned out to such an extent that they are no longer capable of being received.

Since thought waves, very much like other radiation, give off tiny particles of themselves as they travel along, they gradually become weaker. However, this loss of energy potential is so slight that, for all practical purposes, thought waves can travel great distances without apparent loss of clarity. Thus, we have a disregard for the usual laws of space and time, inasmuch as thought waves do not respect solid objects and other hindrances, either. They pierce walls and, in some as yet not fully understood way, are caught or attracted by "tuned in" receivers. There may be more than one receiver. There may be none. Once the thought waves have been created by the sender and are on their way, he has no further contact with them. We know that thought waves originate in the mind, which uses the brain as its switchboard. The electricity required to make the process possible is derived from the network of nerve fibers within the human body, which has sufficient voltage for this. Much more research will have to be done to explore the mechanics of transmission, but I daresay that it is no different in concept from radio transmission, only on an infinitely finer and more sensitive scale.

Although thoughts originate in the mind and are sent out via the brain, they are received on the other end through the unconscious part of the mind. With trained experimenters, the conscious part of the mind can also be used on occasion to serve as receiver, but the vast majority of telepathic cases involve spontaneous reception that employs the unconscious (or, if you prefer, subconscious) part of the mind as its gateway. This eliminates the inhibiting factors of rationalization and rejection, which might otherwise come into play and destroy the message before it is properly evaluated. Since only a few people understand the workings of telepathy, the majority of those having such experiences will explain the thought that arises in them, possibly spurring them into action of one kind or another, as a hunch, or a sudden inspiration.

The shadings of telepathic communication run the gamut from vague feelings about distant people or events to clear-cut, sharp, and definite messages instantly capable of verification. It depends on both sender and receiver, their individual abilities to free themselves from inhibiting factors, their surroundings, their prejudices, their fears, and the nature or urgency of the message. The stronger the need, and the greater the emergency, the more likely will there be a strong reception. Trifling bits of information are less likely to create such remarkable impressions on the other end of the line. There are cases also where one sender reaches several members of the same family to let them know of an emergency. There are cases in which the message is nothing more exciting than a friendly hello from a distance. Telepathy has no hard and fast rules. But it works.

What can it do for you? Lots of things. If you are "aware"—that is, willing to accept messages of this kind—you may well be warned in times of danger by someone at a distance who wishes you well. Conversely, you may do this for someone yourself. It is a distinct thrill when two people who are close, such as a husband and a wife or good friends, manage to communicate without words— spoken words, that is. Not that it saves wear and tear on their speech mechanisms, but the spark of instant thought flying from mind to mind makes such relationships stronger, and when creative work is involved, this can be a blessing. Two partners working together, or two artists or writers—their separate thought processes can be fused into one creative effort.

On a business level, for the salesman or executive to catch a fleeting thought from the mind of the man opposite him can be very useful. This is not so much mind reading as merely being tuned in on what the other person wishes to put across. Just think how surprised your new boss would be if you would say the very things he has on his mind. On the other hand, if the person you are dealing with is likely to be unreliable, catching a thought wave might warn you to be careful.

I would like to point out that so-called stage mentalists who claim to read a person's mind are almost never doing this. The majority of mentalists are clever entertainers, whether they use stooges in the audience or not. Occasionally, some genuine ESP is involved, but the entertainer is most likely the first one to deny this. There is no evidence that anyone can read another person's mind. There is evidence that a person's thoughts can be caught by another person if the reader is close by. But this is somewhat like reading the record, since material from the person's past is generally also involved. "Mind reading" is not telepathy.

SPECIAL PHYSICAL CONDITIONS

It appears from the evidence that many blind people, drug addicts (alas!), and twins have a higher incidence rate of psychic ability. Twins are linked in special ways from their physical birth, and they often experience each other's events and feelings. Unusual physical conditions have always had an impact upon the presence or absence of ESP capabilities. We are yet not fully aware of the implications that certain birth defects may have on ESP. We do know that on occasion, accidents can sharply increase the presence of ESP.

A well-known case is the Dutch psychic Peter Hurkos, who had been a housepainter plying his trade without giving any thought to extrasensory perception. One day, he fell off a ladder and cracked his head. After this accident, he began to predict future events with great accuracy. Eventually, his talent came to the attention of the Utrecht Center of Parapsychological Studies, and he was asked to test as a psychic subject. He then came to the attention of American researchers and eventually wound up in the employ of Henry Belk, an amateur psychic researcher and part owner of the

Belk dry-goods stores in the southern states. Belk tried to make use of Hurkos's talents, including the use of them to discover thefts in his stores. However, Hurkos was restless with all this newly acquired attention and looked for greener pastures. He got involved in the case of the Boston strangler, but because of politics that he did not understand at the time, he inadvertently caused difficulties between the Boston police and the district attorney, who did not like the idea of using a psychic. He moved to California, where he became the protégé of motion-picture actor Glenn Ford, who was a star in the 1950s, and currently employs his talents in private readings.

Twins often know of each other's whereabouts intuitively; they tend to go through similar experiences though widely separated in terms of distance, and they frequently feel the same about individual causes or people. This is not surprising, since identical twins—those of the same sex who are the result of one divided ovum—are in essence still connected on an etheric level even though their physical bodies move apart from each other freely and without seeming connection. But it would appear from the evidence of paranormal material available that identical twins continue to be connected very closely at times in ways that suggest a common etheric body or, at any rate, a continuing and close system of communication between two halves of what must originally have been one etheric body. This does not go as far as the death of both twins at the same time, but one twin frequently goes through the death pangs of the other without being aware of it taking place. Illnesses of one are frequently felt by the other, and symptoms can be observed in one twin that actually belong to the other. These are by no means produced by hysteria or because of foreknowledge that the other twin is undergoing similar situations, but are produced innocently and involuntarily.

Marlene Rouse of California contacted me to make a statement concerning her ESP experiences and capabilities. "I am a twin. In fact, my ESP is so similar to that of Dr. N. in your book *Predictions—Fact or Fallacy?* that I thought you might like to hear a little about me." Dr. N., a California psychiatrist associated with a major hospital, who is also an identical twin, had reported a number of experiences between himself and his brother, proving that both partook of psychic events at the same time.

Rouse states, "As a twin, I always thought of my sister as my other half, or part of me divided at birth. I therefore didn't think it strange that I knew what she was thinking, knew where she might be, and that we would always be sick together. People didn't discuss ESP then, but I sensed my mother knew. Whenever my mother couldn't find my sister, she would call me and ask where she was. I always knew. As a child, I was always the sick one, but my sister complained of the same symptoms. When I had a ruptured appendix, we argued over who was the sickest. When I was pregnant, she told me I was pregnant, for she had had morning sickness, and as I telephoned the doctor to go to the hospital, my hand was still on the telephone when my mother called, telling

me that my sister was complaining of labor pains.

"In October 1963, I awoke in the middle of the morning with pains in my chest and arms. As a registered nurse, I knew the symptoms of a heart attack. I was rushed to the hospital for an examination. They found nothing wrong. While the doctor was examining me, the symptoms came again. He turned white and rushed out to do an EKG. The results were the most normal heart you could ever ask for. He passed the news to my doctor that I was faking. I then asked my sister if she was sick, and she said that she hadn't been feeling well, but she didn't want to talk about it.

"For the next year, I would be driving toward the highway time after time and think what I would do if my twin sister would die. One night, I woke up in the middle of the night gasping for breath with the same thought. On getting up, I saw my sister's light on and heard her gasping. I called her up and she denied it. Two weeks before her death, on the way to church, as I was driving toward this highway, that familiar feeling that I knew she was dead came again. Thoughts came such as, 'I just know she's dead, can't you drive any faster? Hurry! Darn, why did that car stop in our only path and block our way?' By this time, it was so real to me that I began to cry, speeding and acting out the real incident. Then I thought it was funny that there was no car in front of me when I complained of a car being stalled. As I passed the hospital turnoff, I stopped crying and thought of how silly I must be.

"When I arrived at church late, I immediately started running up the

27

PSYCHIC
PHENOMENA

church steps, flung the swinging doors open, and felt as though everyone turned and stared, but no one did. It was such an odd feeling that my head dropped in dismay. I sat down next to my sister and stared at everything she was wearing, not believing that she was really alive. I kept thinking that she was wearing a new dress, but it wasn't new. I sobbed all through church and she kept asking me what was the matter, but I wouldn't tell. Later that day, when I was with her at my mother's house, I asked my mother when she was going to buy the cemetery plot that she mentioned after my grandfather died. My sister usually cut in and thought me silly to discuss the matter, but not that day. She discussed her own feeling about how she would rather be buried. The following two weeks I tried to visit her every possible minute I could. During that time I saw that bony look on her face and said, 'You look dead even though I know you're alive.' She jumped out of her chair, balling me out for talking to her like that. In her rage, she blurted out something to the effect that she was the one who was really sick: not mother. I jumped up, saying, 'You're sick?' She clammed up, started breathing very fast, ordered me out of the house, claiming that her doctor didn't want her upset.

"On the night that she had the heart attack, my husband answered the phone. Because I was six months pregnant, they didn't want to tell me that she was dead on arrival until I got to the hospital. The thoughts I had had so vividly two weeks before came exactly as I had visioned. A car was stalled on the hospital turnoff in our way, which thus delayed our exit off the freeway. As I stopped the car at the

hospital, I ran to find out if she were dead. As I flung open the swinging doors (as in the church), all the nurses did turn to stare, wondering what to say to me. When one finally told me to go to the conference room, I dropped my head, knowing that this meant she was dead. As for the new-dress incident, my sister stared at me in church on that last day of her life, for I was wearing a new dress that she hadn't seen before and she kept feeling the material and admiring it."

Frank Farnsworth has a twin brother named Francis. Farnsworth's report follows: "We lived in a beat-up old brick house in the country in upstate New York. One late afternoon, my twin brother had gone to my aunt, Lester Grant, for supper. I had wandered off into the woods and got lost. There was a distance of about twenty miles between my aunt's house and the old brick house in which we lived. It became dark, and I still couldn't find my way out of the woods. At this time, needless to say, I became frightened. I was almost ten years old. At the same time, my brother was sitting down to dinner at my uncle's house with the rest of the family, when he began to cry. When he was asked what was wrong, he merely said, 'Something is wrong with Frank.' Eventually, I found my way out of the woods and came home. By this time, my family was upset over my whereabouts."

Experiments conducted by Professor H. N. Banerjee, an Indian parapsychologist, and others have shown that people deprived of their ordinary senses sometimes develop a keener ESP capability. Experiments have also been conducted in Russia by blindfolding sensitives; messages were read in books, objects were described, and "the inner eyes" used as if they were physical eyes. There is no doubt that man can train himself to use other organs to take the place of eyesight. Various researchers have proved that any sensitive surface of the body, from the fingertips to the elbows, can be used to transmit information to the sight center in the brain. With patience and training, such substitute organs can almost simulate the sight of human eyes. Almost any psychic, with his eyes closed, can give accurate descriptions of places, whether they are where he is or at a distance. All this suggests that there is a duplicate set of eyes in the makeup of man, just as there are duplicate organs for other functions. Since the etheric body is a complete duplicate of the physical body, although more sensitive than the latter, it stands to reason that it contains eyes as well. It is with those eyes that the blind see.

L. Donn of Pennsylvania reports the story of a blind chemist who lived at a hotel in New Jersey between 1960 and 1964. The chemist had been blinded in an accident in his laboratory and had taken to sitting in the lobby of the hotel by himself, telling those who would listen what was going on in the various rooms of the hotel. Many confirmed that the chemist could "see" what was going on in their rooms.

The question of drugs and ESP goes back to the beginning of public discussion of drug taking, when Aldous Huxley recommended mescaline as a desirable way of opening the door to the unconscious.

Undoubtedly, drugs have been taken since the beginning of time, but in terms of modern scientific observance we are dealing with perhaps the last seventy-five years. When mescaline was followed by lysergic acid number 113, later known as LSD, and in turn by peyote, the drug of the Indians, the field seemed wide open for experimentation with various drugs, especially those called "hallucinogens." Dr. Andrija Puharich, in his book *The Sacred Mushroom*, was the first to discuss the relationship between certain drugs and ESP experiences. Celebrated mediums like Eileen Garrett decided to experiment with drugs under strictly controlled conditions and with the supervision of their psychiatrists.

The full impact of the drug scene had not yet dawned upon man. It was a novelty, something the avant-garde did, and was said to produce far-out sensations. As the years went on, the dangers of drug taking became apparent. Those mediums who had taken even small amounts of LSD in the hopes of having extraordinary psychic experiences became ill and had to discontinue even so slight a use as they had subjected themselves to. Doctors were as yet divided concerning the dangers of drug taking, some saying that only the heavier drugs were habit-forming and damaging to body and mind, while "grass," or marijuana, was not. Today, there are very few doctors who will omit even marijuana from their list of undesirable drugs, since the effects are cumulative, and may not manifest themselves for many years.

From the psychic-research point of view, and my own conviction, drug taking is utterly useless. Not only does it cause serious disorientation in the long run, if not in a shorter period, but the results obtained under drugs do not seem to be related to any kind of reality remotely comparable with the realities of genuine ESP experiences. I have gone into this in greater detail in a recent work entitled *Psycho-Ecstasy*, in which I suggested that ESP and its variants were a better way of getting "high" than the taking of drugs, and explained certain techniques that would lead to that desirable state. True, the fantasies encountered under the influence of hallucinogenic drugs, especially LSD, seem to suggest an entering into the higher realms of consciousness. True, the visions described by those experiencing them under those conditions have the width and scope of extraordinary spiritual encounters, but the material thus obtained is artificial and due solely to the altered chemical state of the bloodstream in the subject. Mental imagery is largely controlled by the delicate chemical balance in the bodily system. When alien substances, such as hallucinogenic drugs, are injected into the system, they produce altered states of consciousness. While these altered states may mimic authentic states of bliss or even ecstasy, they are nevertheless due to interference from outside agents rather than genuine contact with another dimension.

D. H. is a resident of one of the eastern states, son of an attorney in a small town and educated in Catholic schools until the eighth grade. Later he attended a liberal college and studied for a master's degree in library science. Although raised a Catholic, he eventually turned agnostic. Scientifically oriented, the young man was given to inventions and hoped to make a living as an inventor. He kept searching for some evidence that his scientific mind could accept concerning an afterlife. Until that time he thought that psychic phenomena did not exist. Mr. H., in addition, is a man honest about himself. In a statement given to me about his ESP experiences, he said:

"I am a heavy drinker and used to stand first in drinking in a college of six hundred students. I still do pretty good, but I can't drink like I used to. During three semesters, I experimented with drugs, grass, Dexedrine and methadone, and LSD. I've only had acid three times, and that was the only one that I liked, and I would take it more often if I were certain that it did not produce mutations.

"When I took acid for the first time, I had the greatest time of my life, and the following day, in a period of about an hour, I underwent a change that caused me to throw away a dime's worth of grass and to stop living with a girl I had been living with because I considered our relationship to be too superficial. Life became very meaningful to me, I became very relaxed, and I looked upon my body as integrated, whereas before I considered it to be a mind attached to what is below my head. I started to study hard and I gave up excessive drinking. The effect lasted for about three months, and then mostly left me except for the fact that I have never gone back to excessive drinking.

"At a time when I had been dropping about thirty milligrams of Dexedrine a day, but not taking any other drugs, I sort of fell in love with a girl whom I had seen in the dining hall. She looked interested, but we did not meet. That night I went to bed and suddenly I started sending out brain waves, for lack of a better word. I thought I was imagining it, but I could send waves from my brain in a steady stream. They seemed to be circling around and gradually extending out farther and farther. After perhaps five minutes, they stopped circling, and wavered back and forth in the direction of a girls' dormitory, where the above-mentioned girl lived. Then the waves stopped wavering and were steady in one direction for perhaps half an hour, after which they went away and I was able to go to sleep. I thought that all this had been in my head, but the next day, when I went to lunch, a strange girl came over to my table, sat down, glared at me and said, 'My roommate wants you to stop sitting on her head.' The experience scared me, for I did not know what was happening. But the same thing happened again every day for the next week and a half. I had little control over what was happening except for one night when I was able to prevent these waves from establishing contact with another mind. On one occasion I was tuned into someone else in another dormitory. In this instance, there was no exchange of information, but it felt sort of like completely possessing a girl, more so than in sex."

I am frequently asked about ESP in children. I find that children up to the age of five are quite often psychic and can describe situations, scenes, or give the names of people they couldn't possibly know. There are cases of young children speaking in the voice of an adult, reporting in great and authentic detail experiences they could not possibly have had. Some of this may be due to reincarnation memories that later fade. There seems to be a period between the ages of five and eight when such occurrences recede, only to return after puberty. There is nothing frightening about ESP in children, provided it is handled sensibly by the parents. One should neither deny the fact that the child has an unusual experience nor particularly encourage his dwelling upon it. Rather, the parents should point out that ESP is a perfectly natural ability in man and gently encourage the child to talk about it with them.

PHYSICAL PHENOMENA

Occasionally, the psychic ability turns into something more tangible, more three-dimensional, often in violation of known physical law. The energy required for such manifestations is much greater than the mental phases of being psychic.

Physical phenomena are those requiring some bodily action or sensitive through whom the phenomenon takes place. They are also observable in the conventional way, and seem to rely upon energies drawn from living bodies, usually the body of the principal sitter or medium and others in the immediate vicinity. Physical phenomena include deep-trance mediumship, teleportation, or the movement of objects by mental powers, and materialization. In Joseph Rhine's view, there are two main aspects of psychic phenomena: ESP and psi. Rhine attributes the physical phenomena to the presence of the psi force and calls the movement of objects due to mental efforts "psychokinesis." In my own view, both ESP and the psi force are aspects of one and the same force: in the ESP phenomenon, mental results are obtained by mental efforts, whereas in psi phenomena, physical results are obtained by mental effort. If we consider the Einsteinian theory that mass and energy are but one and merely different aspects of the same force, the difference between the two phenomena narrows down even more.

In the case of deep-trance mediumship, the personality of the sensitive is temporarily displaced, voluntarily in and involuntarily on occasion, by the alleged personality of an outsider, usually a deceased person. There are also cases on record where incarnates may inhabit the physical body of a sensitive for the purpose of making a communication known, but the largest percentage of veridical cases of deep-trance mediumship involve communication between a discarnate or dead person and a living being, the medium. In these cases, the medium serves merely as a channel of communication, allowing the discarnate entity to take over the speech mechanism of the medium's body without being involved in the communication in any way. One of the hallmarks of genuine deep trance is the lack of memory on the part of the medium upon returning to full consciousness as to what has transpired during the trance and as to what has come through his entranced lips. Partial trance is very common; in that case, some memory remains.

Although full materialization depends primarily upon physical factors such as ectoplasm drawn from the physical medium as well as from the sitters to cover the mental projection from the other dimension, the heart of the matter is an ESP phenomenon. The materialized body of a discarnate is maintained only by the continuing ESP projection of its former self as remembered by the discarnate.

The power to make this phenomenon possible is the same power used in the projection of the living personality. In fact, there is no distinction to be made between psychic phenomena in the living person and in discarnate states; the techniques and underlying principles are alike. This is so because the incarnate personality within the physical body is identical with the latent etheric or spiritual body released to independence after physical death. In addition, some ESP invariably plays a role in materialization séances, in that the sitters and the medium, through their extrasensory powers, sense a presence of discarnates in the room. This is particularly so in the initial stages; once full visible materialization has been accomplished, the ESP phase is no longer necessary and generally ceases. In a marginal way, ESP has been quite useful to the researchers with a degree of sensitivity who went to a number of American spiritualist camps to investigate materialization phenomena. In nearly all cases, they found fraud. Their inner feelings, another term for intuitive processes, led them to suspect some of the principals in these fraudulent sittings. In that respect, ESP is not used to communicate or make contact with discarnates, but purely on a personal basis as an extension of the ordinary senses to gain additional knowledge.

The subject of *teleportation* has fascinated physical researchers for many years. Just as with materializations, fraud has certainly been practiced in this field, since teleportation represents a most difficult phase of physical phenomena. Teleportation means the rapid and seemingly instantaneous movement of a solid object (or even a person) from one location to another without the usual means of transport. A popular subdivision of teleportation phenomena is called "apport," a term used for the unexpected appearance or disappearance of solid objects from either a person or a location. There is no doubt in my mind that genuine apports exist and that the power making such movement possible is essentially psi power, the physical force within man; whether the force is directed by an external entity or by part of the unconscious of the principal remains a debatable issue. There are a number of verified cases of discarnate manipulation of apports. ESP enters the question of teleportation only in an indirect sense. The actual movement of the object is due to psi, but the awareness and the understanding of the meaning of the process are realized by the recipient on the usual ESP "beam."

There is no other mode of communication available, except for the phenomenon of the direct voice. This phenomenon, in which a human voice is heard independent of a medium and is an objective reality that can, among other things, be recorded on tape, requires the presence of a strong physical median. Although in essence related to the informative form of mediumship represented by mental mediumship and ESP, direct voice phenomena are nevertheless classed as physical phenomena since a voice box is said to be constructed from invisible ectoplasm to make the phenomena possible at all.

In spiritualist séance rooms, especially in the 1920s, trumpets were used allegedly to increase the volume of such spirit voices. Frequently, the trumpets would float in the air without visible support and voices would originate in them. Although a number of such séances have been unmasked as fraudulent, there is an equally impressive number of occurrences where trumpets have floated without trickery or means of wires. But the energies that are capable of maintaining a metal trumpet in the air for long periods of time and of producing human voices loud and obviously independent of the speech mechanism of an entranced medium are physical energies not properly of the ESP variety, at least not in the sense that Rhine would use the term. Psi and psychokinesis are definitely physical phenomena, utilizing other aspects of the human personality and body than merely the mind. But I doubt that psi forces could operate independently of ESP; ESP, on the other hand, can exist without the need for physical phenomena as expressed in psychokinesis.

Teleportation usually takes the form of inexplicable disappearances and reappearances of objects or sometimes disappearance without reappearance. In the majority of cases on record, there doesn't seem to be any reason for these phenomena except perhaps as attention-getters. If we attribute teleportation to a split-off part of the personality of the subject, we might explain it as an unconscious way of demanding attention or working out submerged frustrations. In German, the general range of noisy and physical phenomena is referred to as a *poltergeist*. Poltergeist phenomena represent only the physical phase of regular hauntings or attempts at spirit communication, and are not phenomena by themselves, that is, caused independently by living people alone. Conventionally, such phenomena are connected with young people before the age of puberty who are present in the household, but that, too, is incorrect: the majority of cases do not concern youngsters at all but apply equally to older people, retarded people, and, if there is a common denominator among those who experience poltergeist phenomena, it seems to be people whose sexual lives are not fully expressed, leaving a residue of unused life-force within their bodies.

Some of the witnesses to phenomena of this kind are beyond suspicion, keen observers whose testimony is of much value. Mrs. M. Ball is a practical nurse with special training in psychiatric work. She makes her home in the Midwest but has also spent much time in California. From childhood on she has experienced a full range of ESP phenomena. Here is part of her report to me:

"Teleportation has been a nuisance to me all my life. Recently something of this nature happened that almost flattened me in surprise. Upon awakening from an afternoon nap, I found a greeting card on my chest. It was small, with tulips and lilacs on the left side. It was printed in Swedish and contained a verse from Matthew 5:3. My house is always locked with double locks. No one could possibly have entered. The card could have entered the house in a book or newspaper, but it could not have located itself on my chest without help.

"When I was in Saint Louis in 1956, the keys to my bedroom and to the outside apartment door vanished almost while I was looking at them. I searched but found it impossible to locate them. I therefore could not get back into the apartment hotel in which I was staying and had to refit a room in a nearby rooming house. Three blocks away from my apartment hotel, in the rooming house, I placed my purse open on the bedside table and emptied it of all its contents. There was little in it to begin with. While it was sitting open on my bedside table, I had the sudden desire to check it once more. Just as I reached out to touch it, the keys fell with a clink, obviously out of the air. I did not see them fall, but I heard them.

"Four pages of a manuscript I had prepared at one time in the hope of selling an article to a romance-type magazine disappeared from the envelope on my dresser in Riverside, California. This was in a new, uncluttered room with no possibility of anyone entering. I had been home all day on a Sunday, and late that afternoon I went to make a final inspection of the manuscript in preparation for mailing it early the next day. I found the first four pages missing. They had been in place late Saturday evening. I looked through everything in that room, but the four pages were not to be found anywhere. Two hours later I was standing at a metal-topped card table, which was bare. Suddenly the pages, with an extra page from some carbon copies I had not seen for weeks, were lying on the table before my eyes. I had not seen them transported through the air, nor did I see any movement of any kind. They just materialized, face-down, on the clean card table. One moment it was empty, the next the five pages of typed script were there miraculously."

The power that moved the keys and the manuscript was psi; but the intuitive processes that made Ball look in certain places or be near a spot where the missing object would shortly be found is an ESP process, utilizing mental channels.

Phenomena of this kind cannot be induced at will; a state of expectancy can be produced if the subject is inclined toward physical phenomena. It would be wise to choose a quiet, not too bright, room for the experiment, and to empty one's conscious mind of all extraneous thoughts. Once a state of repose is reached, the subject might project simple and direct requests for some proof that would tend to reinforce his own faith in physical phenomena. A request for a demonstration from one's unseen friends is sometimes answered and sometimes not. It helps if the subject is well rested, in excellent physical health, and not troubled by any problem or extensive worry. Total darkness in this type of phenomenon is probably advisable since physical phenomena do require it. But apports have also occurred in plain daylight.

To be sure, not every mysterious disappearance of an object is due to psychic causes. People do forget or misplace things or allow themselves to be victimized by others without realizing it. But there are a sufficient number of cases, similar to the ones reported by Ball, to warrant the statement that physical objects can be made to disappear spontaneously and reappear equally spontaneously in different locations. Whatever pattern of purpose emerges from these phenomena seems to indicate a dual reason: to prove that such phenomena are possible to begin with; and to call attention to the subject of the presence of some discarnate entity who wishes to be noticed, and possibly desires to work with the subject.

foretelling the future

NOTHING FASCINATES PEOPLE MORE THAN the ability by some to foretell future events. The desire to know what lies ahead is a natural instinct, not just idle curiosity. Many serious people, even businessmen and other professionals, consult psychics regularly in the hopes of getting advance information, or warnings so that they can act accordingly.

Next to telepathic communication between living persons, incidents of foretelling the future are the most common ESP experiences. In biblical days, these were referred to as prophecies, and on the least desirable level they are called fortune-telling—though the fortune made is mainly that of the fortune-teller. Again, the basic characteristic of the phenomena is a seeming disregard for the conventional boundaries of time and space. Distance in either time or geographical location has no effect on the results of this faculty.

I am convinced that it is one faculty with three different forms of expression. It depends merely on the particular "phase" of the psychic person—that is, the area in which the psychic talent manifests itself. Just as some musicians are good on the piano while others are better with a violin and still others are singers, so we have people who foresee things, others who hear things before they happen, and still others, though least in number, who can get olfactory impressions, or peculiar smells associated with events seemingly ahead of actual occurrence.

Clairvoyants are by far the most numerous. Their visions can be subjective (in the mind's eye) or objective (before them). *Clairaudience* means the hearing of voices or messages in one's inner ear without seeing the person who speaks. Although *clairsentience* can also be useful at times, most of the scientifically reliable data stem from the first two categories of *precognition*. That is the word now used in parapsychology to describe all three faculties of obtaining information ahead of the actual occurrence of the events.

CLAIRVOYANCE

I consider these faculties a step more advanced than telepathy, since they involve insight into the future, or, at the very least, beyond great distance. First, let us take clairvoyance, which is sometimes called second sight. The word, of French origin, means "seeing clearly," that is, seeing clearly what most people cannot see at all. The practitioner of clairvoyance is called a *clairvoyant* or *clairvoyante*, depending on sex. Every honest fortune-teller, every capable spiritualist medium, and every person able to have strong hunches about future events, comes under this heading.

The scientific term "precognition" means to recognize in advance, and it covers the same ability. People have been able to foresee future events from time immemorial. The traditions of every religion speak of the seers and prophets of old. Some of these gifted people were held in high esteem, especially when their predictions proved true. Others were feared and persecuted as associates of the devil. It is human nature to desire the supernatural while at the same time to be afraid of it. In ancient Egypt, the seers were respected court officials who tried to harness the gift of prophecy for the benefit of their king.

Clairvoyance, even less than telepathy, cannot be produced at will, and the flashes of sudden insight, or meaningful dreams, were always considered important events. Among the Ancient Hebrews, prophets were held in similar regard, and in many instances they held power comparable with that of the popes of the Roman Church. Naturally, they came into conflict with both the temporal power of the ruler and the political or spiritual power of the high priest, but such was the reputation of a Jeremiah or an Elijah that no one dared touch him. Among the common people, their words were listened to with great awe, and frequently, though by no means always, their predictions came true. Though they couched their visions in poetic language or word pictures, the prophets of ancient Israel were nevertheless using clairvoyance to get their messages across.

That the warnings were rarely heeded is not surprising. To this day, the majority of those forewarned refuse to accept clairvoyant bids to change their courses. Was not President Kennedy told many times over what was in store for him? Caesar heard the soothsayer warn him of the Ides of March, but he did not stay in bed that day, either. There is a curious question here about fate and free will. If a clairvoyant can foresee the future and warns a person of impending disaster, will this event take place in any case or is the warning sufficient to ward off evil in time? Apparently, the clairvoyant can foresee the trend of events toward which one moves. The events themselves are stationary, or, shall we say, fixed, in time. People move toward them in the normal course of their daily lives. When their own time track crosses that of the event, the event "happens" to them. If they have been forewarned, they may react more immediately or more cautiously to what is thrown at them, and thus may be able to deflect the blow. If they refuse to heed the warning, the event will take place as foreseen. In other words, free will is really the reaction that one has to certain events in the future when they occur, and, depending upon one's own reaction, events will either be harmful or not.

The great patterns of events seem to me set in motion long before we reach their place in the time stream by what some call fate, some call God, and others, like myself, prefer to call The Law. Foreseeing events does not necessarily involve any form of spirit communication. It does not prove survival of the human personality, but it does prove the existence within man of an extrasensory faculty that enables him, under certain conditions, to pierce the barriers of time and space, or, as it were, to look around corners.

A few years ago, the British television star Michael Bentine told me of an incident of this nature. Both he and his late father, the Peruvian envoy to Britain, were aware of their psychic inclinations and talents. Bentine was planning a trip north to the English provinces. A few days before the journey, he had a vivid dream in which he saw himself driving his car at great speed: suddenly there was a sharp bend in the road, and another car's headlights appeared almost in front of him. A head-on collision followed.

Bentine took this warning soberly, and set out on his trip. It was nighttime and he was driving on a road on which he had never been. Suddenly there was a sharp bend in the road, and he at once recognized the stretch of road as being identical to the one in his vision. With this realization came the memory of the rest of his dream. He slowed down at once—just in time to see the oncoming headlights of another car that would have hit him head-on had he not been forewarned.

Sometimes people have premonitions of impending events without realizing it. They may say strange things to friends or relatives, which later, in retrospect, assume different meaning. Such was the case when the late U.S. ambassador to the United Nations, Adlai Stevenson, left for his final trip to London in July, 1965. Asked when he expected to return, Stevenson replied without a moment's hesitation, "If I survive this trip, I'll be back in three weeks." He didn't.

Asian philosophers will argue the question of *karma*—that is, credits or demerits from a previous incarnation—and say that karma determines whether a warning is successfully heeded or not. Perhaps this is true, but it seems to me largely a matter of personality. How much stock does the average person put into predictions? We all know that an overwhelming percentage of gypsy fortune-tellers are fakes and that about half of all predictions made by basically honest professional psychics and readers are at least off on their dates. I know the latter to be true from statistical charts I have kept of predictions made to me over a period of several years by about a dozen psychics. Certain names and events show up more frequently than others, and there is a respectable percentage of evidential material in all this, perhaps as much as 20 percent, far too much for chance to account for.

But there is also a large amount of rubbish, guess-work, and half truths. Events are correctly foretold, but the date is wrong. I don't condemn the art of predicting because of the many poor practitioners engaged in it. There is no question in my mind that predictions can be accurate and often are. But I am a trained parapsychologist and have access to large amounts of material. Unless he is an aficionado of ESP, the average person tends to disregard, or at least play down, any prediction or warning coming his way. However, to the minority of people who have taken precognitive warnings seriously, it has proved a boon. Here are some of the cases I have examined.

Through the courtesy of newsman Nick Kenny, a psychic, I heard of an incident in which clairvoyance was able to save a life. Mildred Liebowitz of East 45th Street, Brooklyn, New York, reported the incident: "I always wanted a radio in my own room when I was a teenager," writes Liebowitz. "Many years ago, not having a dresser or night table on which to set the radio, I had a shelf made above my bed and placed the radio there. Months passed. Then one night my mother could not sleep. She kept seeing my arm against the wall with the electric cord from the radio wrapped around it. Then she saw me turn, pulling the radio set down on my head and killing me. It was so real that she ran into my room, and sure enough, my arm was against the wall, the electric cord wrapped around it, and one more move on my part would have brought the radio crashing down on my head."

Not every premonition of impending disaster is as explicit, however. Sometimes it is merely an uneasy feeling of doom, but if the recipient heeds the warning, it will be just as helpful.

According to the Associated Press, dateline of Miami:

Royce Atwood Wight was taking a nap in the bedroom of his small cottage but suddenly awoke and dashed out of the room.

Seconds later, a thirty-six-foot, three-ton concrete piling, which workmen had been erecting near the place, crashed through the roof.

"I had a premonition of trouble," said Wight.

Sometimes the psychic warning is strong, but not detailed enough to allow one to take steps to prevent the event. *The New York Mirror* reported an automobile accident involving television personality Arlene Francis, who had a premonition about her auto accident:

At 12:45 P.M. Sunday, as she was leaving her agent Gloria Safier's home in Quogue, Long Island, Arlene said to Gloria, "This trip is doomed. I wish I didn't have to make it." Arlene, who is one of the most sensitive and kindest people in show business, was en route to New York for her weekly *What's My Line?* appearance when her car skidded out of control, hit another car, and killed a woman.

Francis did not know who would be the victim, only that something terrible would happen. Since events as a whole are usually foreseen by the clairvoyant person, rather than individual actions taken as a consequence of these events, it is rarely possible for a warning to be heeded unless one is to call off a contemplated step altogether.

But then again we have the ancient story *Death in Samara*, about the wealthy man who was told that Death was looking for him. So he left Baghdad and journeyed to distant Samara to escape his fate. Unfortunately, when he got to Samara, Death was already there, waiting for him.

One thing is certain: if thousands have correctly foreseen events before they occur, these events must have been planned ahead of that moment. There is no other logical explanation but that some sort of universal law operates this world, and also the neighboring one, which is invisible to all but the psychic. Fate is not all-powerful *kismet*, but an intelligent, just system in which the individual is neither pawn nor power, but partner: what he makes of his opportunities determines his progress.

It may sound cruel and unjust when apparently innocent people suffer or are killed in tragedies. Only reincarnation with its karmic laws of reward and punishment offers a logical explanation for these apparent inequities. But Carl Jung has pointed out that there is another law, beyond the law of cause and effect, called the "law of meaningful coincidence," which comes into play in our universe. Could it then not be that a variety of factors, stationary events caused by forces beyond human scope, individual efforts, reactions and developments following these events, and a little-understood link between past, present, and future, are all contributing to what eventually happens to us?

Take the case of the couple planning their Florida vacation, as reported by the *New York Journal-American*:

When Max Elsasser, 57, and his wife, Pauline, 59, decided to drive to Hollywood Beach, Florida, for their annual vacation instead of flying, as they had done for years, Mrs. Elsasser told her son Max, Jr., "I really don't feel like going this time. Something is going to happen." But the Florida vacation had also become part of their way of life, and Monday they left their home at 30 Hudson Pl., Weehawken. They picked up another couple, Mr. and Mrs. Herman Kruse of 184 Kimberly Rd., Union, N.J., then headed for Florida. Elsasser was driving.

On a strip of U.S. Highway 301, eight miles west of Marion, S.C., Mrs. Elsasser's premonition came true. The auto slammed into a bridge wall on the divided highway and the four occupants were killed instantly. There had been no other traffic on the road, and the weather was clear and dry. The only explanation given was that the setting sun may have blinded Elsasser.

What about the other couple? Had they been brought together with the Elsassers because their fates were to be united? Who was pulling strings upstairs? Would a change in plans have saved all of them or some of them, or merely postponed their final fate?

Probably the most publicized of all premonitions of impending doom was the assassination of President John F. Kennedy, which took place on November 22, 1963. I know of a dozen clairvoyants and mediums who claimed that they had foreseen the murder of the president and had written warning letters, but had gotten nowhere with their warnings. The trouble is that most of these testimonials from otherwise honest psychics came to me after the fact. They are therefore not so valuable as if they had been submitted prior to the event and could be later verified under what I consider test conditions.

Nevertheless, the great tragedy that befell the nation in 1963 had such force that a number of psychic people felt it approach. Probably the most famous of all predictions came from Washington real estate dealer and soothsayer Jeane Dixon, who has since gone on to national prominence for her unfailing predictions and as the subject of a book, *The Gift of Prophecy: Jeane Dixon*, by Ruth Montgomery.

I know Montgomery, one of the top *Hearst Headline* writers, who was present with me during a haunted-house investigation at Arlington not long ago. She is a good reporter whose own interest in the occult has made her open-minded concerning the unseen world around us. Her report of Jeane Dixon's phenomenal accomplishments is without overstatement. But long before Jeane Dixon came into the national limelight, she had already startled Washington friends with uncanny predictions that had, often unfortunately, come true.

On the morning after the assassination, the *New York Journal-American* carried a brief account of Dixon's role in the great tragedy:

> The tragic death of President John F. Kennedy was forecast in 1956 and reiterated twice in the past week by Jeane Dixon, a Washington, D.C., socialite and seer.
>
> For years, she has electrified Capitol Hill with a succession of eerie and accurate predictions of things to come.
>
> "As for the 1960 election, it will be dominated by labor and won by a Democrat. But he will be assassinated

or die in office, not necessarily in his first term....The assassination of the president was planned and finalized between 5:00 and 6:00 P.M. Sunday. In fact on last Sunday I told John Teeter, director of the Damon Runyon Cancer Fund, with whom I had dinner, that I felt a black veil closing over the White House. That I had seen this veil in the past many times—but it was drawing closer."

> Dixon said that on Tuesday, she had expressed fear for the president's safety, while lunching with Inspector Charles Benter, conductor of the U.S. Navy Band and with Mrs. Harley Cope, widow of admiral Harley Cope. "I told them, 'Dear God, something terrible is going to happen to the president, soon,' " Mrs. Dixon recalled. "Again I mentioned the black veil that seemed to be getting closer all the time."

The Sunday pictorial magazine *Parade* summed up Jeane Dixon's accomplishments and added some other details to this amazing woman's record as a highly talented psychic. Jack Anderson, a *Parade* reporter, had known Jeane Dixon for some time before the assassination. He first interviewed her in 1956, and it was then that she made the initial prediction about Kennedy's fate:

> Many in Washington, including *Parade*'s reporters, have been skeptical of the occult Dixon. Yet there's no denying she has foretold the future with uncanny accuracy. Those who swear by her include senators, congressmen, ambassadors, cabinet officers, and other public officials.

Going back to our 1956 interview, our notes recall one prediction that we considered so far-fetched we decided not to print it. Mrs. Dixon claimed she saw in her crystal "a great silver Russian ball circling the earth." It was a little less than two years later—1957—that Russia slammed her first sputnik into orbit.

She also said at the time that President Eisenhower would get a second term despite his heart attack and that the three Democrats then leading the presidential polls (Adlai Stevenson, Averell Harriman, and Sen. Estes Kefauver) would never call the White House home.

Born in Wisconsin of German parents, Mrs. Dixon grew up in California. As a child she had a German nurse who encouraged her to close her eyes and tell what she saw. She recalls: "Sometimes I saw things that had not happened yet. Once I asked Mother for the black-bordered letter. She said she didn't have such a letter. About two weeks later, a black-bordered letter came from Germany telling of the death of my grandfather."

There are many more predictions made by Jeane Dixon that have come true, and a few that haven't. She freely admits that she is fallible when she interprets her "induced" readings, which she does with the aid of a crystal ball, apparently a means of concentrating her "inner forces." However, her spontaneous "visions," those she does not seek nor expect, have *never* been wrong.

Speaking of induced predictions—readings, if you wish, culminating in definite predictions—some psychics use a crystal ball, while others get the same results with tea leaves, coffee grinds, or tarot cards. These are merely forms of concentration and have no supernormal powers as such.

Nick Kenny, a columnist for the *New York Mirror*, had a psychic mother who was given to predictions when the "spirit moved her":

She was French-Canadian, maiden name Duval, and possessed of a high degree of extrasensory perception.

But there were disbelievers. Men like a certain Irish police captain in the Astoria precinct. His wife was entertaining neighbors one afternoon. When he came home he found himself right in the midst of a tea party.

"I see a lumber yard near a river," Mother said, gazing intently into the captain's teacup.

"I also see a tall young policeman standing with his back against a pile of lumber. His gun is drawn. His hat has been knocked off and a gang of hoodlums are ringing him in!" The women laughed.

But the police captain's smile was suddenly wiped off his face. "Good heavens," he gasped. "That must be my son James. He's a rookie cop. I warned him to watch out for that Hell-gate gang at Tisdale's Lumber Yard."

The police captain found his policeman son, surrounded by hoodlums, just as Mother had told him she saw it in his teacup.

Many clairvoyants, especially in New York, are continually harassed by the police, who cannot understand the difference between a psychically gifted person making a harmless living by reading a person's future and the few gypsies who defraud the gullible. Thus we have the peculiar situation in parts of the United States that psychics, in order not to go to jail for being what they are, must become religious ministers. They may practice their art freely as long as they are "reverends" of a spiritualist church—honest or fraudulent—but woe be unto the little neighborhood lady who does not have a phony minister's "certificate" (by mail, mainly) and who engages in a little predicting for pocket money. The police can be very harsh in such matters.

For once, as UPI reported some years ago, a judge was fair to a psychic:

> Charges of fortune-telling against 71-year-old Jean Fraser were dismissed when three slightly embarrassed policewomen testified that her statements to them were accurate.
>
> Mrs. Fraser read tea leaves to tell about the past and cards to forecast the future.
>
> Policewoman Kay Burford said Fraser told her she came from a family of three, that she would be married in April and her marriage date would have the number two in it.
>
> When Crown Attorney Peter Rickaby asked how many were in her family, Burford replied, "Three."
>
> "Are you contemplating marriage?" Rickaby asked.
>
> "Yes," was the reply.
>
> Rickaby commented: "Oh, no. When?"
>
> Mrs. Burford replied she would be married April 28.

> Policewomen Dorothy Ellis and Shirley Read also testified Fraser had told their fortunes correctly.

The question arises of why the clairvoyant could not have foreseen her own difficulty with the police and avoided the issue altogether. It has been my experience with psychics in general that they are almost never able to read for themselves. This is perhaps because they are too close to their subject and unconsciously fear that their own personality and conscious knowledge might interfere with their psychic reading or because of some etheric law that we understand only in part. I am convinced that all matters dealing with the unseen world are subject to laws and not merely haphazard forays into a colorful world of mysticism. Then, too, the reincarnationists will argue that it was the woman's karma or predestined fate that she meet up with a difficulty to test her mettle. Perhaps.

CLAIRSENTIENCE

Another form of supernormal activity transcending the conventional barriers of time and space is *clairsentience,* the ability to smell scents that others who are not psychic cannot register. This form of psychic talent is probably the rarest of the three forms and the least capable of scientific verification, but it exists and we must reckon with it and try to explain how it works.

This is perhaps a little easier for me, for I do have a fair amount of it myself. Whether it is due to my prominent nose—Austrian, not Roman—or merely to my generally acute sensitivity in other areas, I have on occasion registered smells that others were unable to detect. This ability goes beyond the psychic realm in my case, for I can discern the slightest whiff of gas long before others become aware of it.

My first encounter with "supernormal smells" came back in 1955. I had followed the invitation of an amateur medium to visit her in her home in Brooklyn for a test sitting. There was no money involved, and she knew very little about me or my family, except that she had met me once at a lecture on psychic subjects and had talked to me without realizing who I was. I found her apartment to be a typical lower-middle-class flat, devoid of anything special in the way of style or beauty, but comfortable and convenient. Bertha was a widow living on a pension, and there was nothing remarkable about her somewhat plump person.

In the living room with the two of us were two other people, friends of hers, who were her sitters. We put out most of the lights and Bertha became clairvoyant. As she was "reading" that is, mentioning names, places, and situations that she felt coming into her consciousness—I was relaxing in a deep easy chair, not thinking of anything or anyone in particular. I am not at all keen on the spiritualistic idea of contacting the "loved ones" at will, and my presence in this apartment was strictly as an observer of genuine phenomena, should any occur.

Suddenly, I had the distinct impression, in the semidarkness, that a kind of smoke-pot or censer was being swung back and forth in front of me. I did not see this, merely thought it, and as I did

so, I experienced a strong smell of lilies-of-the-valley right in front of my face. I started to look around, best as I could in the darkened room, to see if any flowers were about, when Bertha announced that my mother had "come in" and wanted me to know she was present. She named my mother's initial, M, correctly. This was not so startling, since many psychics have done the same for me. What I found interesting was the fact that my mother's favorite perfume was lily-of-the-valley. I had smelled this scent several moments before Bertha had announced the presence of my mother in the circle. As soon as we turned on the lights, I carefully examined the room and Bertha's clothes, and I stepped near the two other sitters. No one had on any perfume or any scent remotely similar to lily-of-the-valley. Furthermore, only I had registered the scent of this flower.

Frequently, when physical phenomena take place in a séance room, or on location, some people report a pungent odor for which there is no rational explanation. There seems to be a connection between this odor and the formation of ectoplasm and its origin within the glandular apparatus of the medium. Just as the release into the air of certain chemicals may create an odor consisting of small, aerated particles of that substance, so a fine mist or spray of ectoplasm can often be felt in the form of this strong odor. It disappears as soon as the ectoplasm is returned to the body of the medium and sitters, it seems. These impressions are not subjective hallucinations, but wholly measurable, neutral occurrences with tangible substances involved.

The value of being clairvoyant or clairaudient is clear—to learn about impending dangers or conditions, and to be forewarned is to be helped, regardless of the final outcome. But it is not so clear with clairsentience, which is rarely capable of delivering a clearly understandable message. I think that clairsentience is an accompanying factor where clearer identification of a personality is desired or necessary. A person who is not fully recognized by a first name might conceivably be accepted as a certain individual if a peculiar scent is re-created, a scent that this person was closely associated with in his or her physical state.

PRECOGNITION

Precognition, the ability to have foreknowledge of future events, or events transpiring at a physical distance, flies directly into the face of established reality. Nothing matters more than knowledge of what lies ahead, since it covers conditions that have not yet come to pass so that there is the possibility of preparing for them in one way or another. Knowledge of contemporary events, even if they transpire at a distance in space, are less dramatic. True, Swedenborg told his audience of the great fire of Stockholm while hundreds of miles away and while the fire was actually going on. The effect was most dramatic, but his audience also realized that there was little if anything they could do about the event, and it would take some time before Swedenborg's statements could be confirmed. As it was, he had been entirely correct in his visionary experience.

There is still another aspect that makes the ability to foretell future events more controversial and tantalizing than any other aspect of ESP. An event that has not yet come into being is something that the ordinary person cannot perceive or even conceive, something that does not exist and has no reality. Yet thousands of people are able to describe in great detail situations and happenings that come to pass only at a later date. If this is true—and research has amply borne it out—our concept of time and the sequence of events are subject to revision.

Clearly, if people in significant numbers can foresee and foretell future events far beyond the law of chance and far beyond guesswork or generalities, either our sense of time is wrong or the events themselves are predestined by some superior law with which we are not yet fully familiar. It is very difficult to judge such matters from within the same dimension, and it is impossible for anyone to be totally outside it at any time. One must therefore construct a theory that would satisfy the existence of many such experiences pertaining to the so-called future, while at the same time satisfying our basic three-dimensional concepts of life on earth and the established view of the time-space continuum. I will examine the nature of time in a later chapter, but for purposes of this aspect of ESP, let it be stated that time is a human convenience, adopted to have a reference point; events are predestined to a large degree by a system that I prefer to call the Universal Law. About this also more anon.

Precognition is the ability to know beforehand, to have accurate information about events, situations, and people ahead of the time so that we become consciously aware of them. The majority of precognitive experiences occur spontaneously and unsought. Some people may have an inkling of a precognitive situation shortly before it occurs by feeling odd, experiencing a sensation of giddiness or tingling in various parts of the body, or a vague foreboding that a psychic experience is about to take place. To others, these things come entirely out of left field, surprisingly and unexpectedly.

Many find the ability to foretell future events more of a burden than a blessing because they begin to believe that foretelling bad events may in some way be connected with their causing them. This is not true. By tuning into the existing conditions and through ESP picking up that which lies ahead, the receiver is merely acting as a channel without responsibility to the event, the outcome, the timing, the result of the event, or the moral implications of it. He has no more control over what he foretells than a radio set has control over programming coming through it.

I have a number of letters from people who think that they are "evil witches" because they have foreseen an accident or the death of a friend or loved one and had it happen exactly as they had foreseen. They wonder whether their thoughts have caused the event to occur, especially in cases where there has been an unpleasant relationship between the psychic and the victim. There are cases on record where thought concentrations may cause people to be influenced at a distance, may even make them do certain things that are not consciously in their will, but this requires a conscious and deliberate effort, usually several people

working together, and lacks the spontaneity of ESP flashes generally associated with true precognitive experiences.

The ability to look into the future is in every one of us, starting with primitive instincts, when man senses danger or love or warmth and reacts accordingly, through intuition in which his inner voice warns him of danger or somehow vaguely makes him react with caution against dangerous people or situations, to the higher stage of the "hunch" where actual ESP begins.

A hunch is an illogical feeling about a person or situation that influences one's thinking and actions. Following a hunch means to go against purely logical reasoning. If the hunch turns out to be correct, one has had a mild ESP experience. If the hunch turns out to be false, it may not have been a hunch at all, but fear. The two are very much alike. Fear of failure or fear of a confrontation that is undesirable may frequently masquerade as a hunch. The only way to tell the two apart is the sense of immediacy, the sudden appearance and the short duration of the true hunch, whereas fear is a lingering and generally somewhat extended feeling. Beyond the simple hunch lies the ability to foresee or foretell actual events or situations—precognition, meaning "foreknowledge." Whether the foreknowledge is of events that occur one minute later or a year afterward is of no importance. The technique involved is exactly the same, since we are dealing here with a dimension in which time, as we define it, does not exist. The precognitive process goes through a variety of stages or degrees.

There is the situation where one foresees or foretells an encounter with either a situation or a person without "getting" any specifics as to time and place, mainly receiving only the basic message. When this simple precognitive experience occurs in the dream or sleep state it may be surrounded by, or couched in, symbolic language, in which case parallel situations may well masquerade as the message. For instance, you may have a precognitive dream about your brother having bought a new car that he wants to show you. The following day there is a phone call from him advising you that he is going to visit you in the near future. When he arrives, it turns out that he has just remarried and wants you to meet his bride. The car of the dream experience was the symbol for the new wife. In the waking condition descriptive material is much more precise, and even though not every precognitive experience contains the desired details of time, place, and description, the absence of the material from the unconscious mind allows the message to be much clearer and more precise.

Next comes the *precognitive impression* where a time or place element is concluded; this may be only partial, such as a numeral "flashed" above the face of someone who appears as a precognitive vision. Or it may be a key word spoken by an inner voice that relates to the circumstances under which the precognitive experience will take place. Depending upon the individual personality of the receiver and his state of relaxation at the time of the experience, the precognitive message will either be partial or more involved. If the material is merely routine although of some emotional significance to the receiver, it is less likely to contain dramatic descriptive material than if we are dealing with catastrophes, warnings

of dire events, or precognitive material of importance to more than one individual. Those who are able to foretell plane crashes, for instance, which is a specialty among some clairvoyants, do so with a great deal of detail; fires and earthquakes also seem to evoke graphic responses in the ESP consciousness of those able to foretell them.

Not all such occurrences take place as predicted. This is not due to the inaccuracy of the vision or precognitive experience, but to the total lack on the part of the visionary as to correct judgment of the time element, coming as it does from a timeless dimension. There remains the question whether the person with ESP ability foresees the future around a specific individual or independent of that individual. If a number of precognitive predictions are made about one individual by a number of seers independent of one another, the future event must cling to the aura or electromagnetic field of the individual about whom the predictions are made. If, on the other hand, people foretell such events in the future about a person without being in that person's presence, a channel into the future seems to have been opened in which the individual who is concerned with those events merely plays a part over which he has no control.

Anyone doubting the factuality of precognition need only consult the records of psychic research societies throughout the world for detailed descriptions of cases, carefully recorded by them over the years.

Premonitions are a milder form of precognitive experiences in the sense that they are usually feelings about events to come rather than sharply defined flashes of actual scenes. Premonitions are much more numerous than the more complex form of precognitive experience. Theodore Irwin, in an article entitled "Can Some People See into the Future?" published in *Family Weekly*, reports on the strong premonition by a London piano teacher named Lorna Middleton concerning the fate of Senator Robert Kennedy. Nine months before the assassination, Middleton felt a strong premonition that he would be murdered. On March 15 of the year in which Kennedy died she actually saw the assassination take place and felt it was while the senator was on tour in the West. This impression was followed by another one on April 5 and again on April 11, when she had a foreboding of death connected with the Kennedy family. The actual murder took place on June 5.

As a result of peoples' premonitions frequently reported in the press, a British psychiatrist named Dr. R. D. Barker set up the Central Premonitions Registry, where people could register their premonitory feelings toward the day when their impressions might become reality. The greatest impetus toward some sort of registration of the phenomena the project received was in October 1966, when a huge coal tip buried the Welsh village of Aberfan, killing 138 children and adults in the process. Many people in Britain reported premonitions concerning the event, some even giving exact data as to when and how the disaster would occur. Among those who had an inkling of the catastrophe was my good friend Michael Bentine, the writer and comedian, who had scheduled a TV sketch dealing with a

Welsh village on the fatal day. For reasons unknown to him, however, he canceled this sketch at the last minute.

Barker thought of the registry not only as an instrument to prove scientifically that people do foretell the future, but as a kind of clearinghouse to warn of impending catastrophes. To do so, it was necessary to prove that a significant percentage of the premonitions were coming true. A study of premonitions filed with the registry during 1967 disclosed 469 separate entries. Only eighteen of these proved to be accurate, and of those, twelve were made by only two people, the aforementioned Middleton and Allen P. Hencher, a telephone worker.

"They are absolutely genuine," Barker is quoted in *Family Weekly*. "Quite honestly they stagger me. Somehow these sensitive people can gate-crash the time barrier—see the wheels of disaster starting to turn before the rest of us. It is difficult to attribute their experiences to coincidence alone."

Taking a lead from the British doctor, several Americans have also attempted to set up premonition registries. Among them is Dr. Stanley Krippner, clinical psychologist and director of the Dream Laboratory at Maimonides Medical Center, Brooklyn. A young man named Richard Nelson, part of a twin team of sensitives, also has set up a registry of this kind. Unfortunately, the majority of people with premonitory experiences never bother to register them with anyone. I receive a fair number of such claims, but only a small fraction of the number that actually transpire. This is because most premonitions concern disaster or negative aspects of life. People are afraid to bring bad news and frequently prefer to dismiss the impressions or suppress them. As a result, much valuable psychic material is undoubtedly lost to science, and where there might have been warnings, and possibly prevention of disaster, there is only the *fait accompli.*

Allen Hencher, one of the two British sensitives, said, "Most of the premonitions come while I am working, maybe because there is a lot of electricity at the telephone switchboard, yet they also come at night, when the air is clear, or after a glass of wine. Usually my premonitions are accompanied by headaches, like a steel band around my forehead, but as I write them down, the headaches recede. When I feel that a premonition has been borne out, I feel utter relief. It is as if something had been bottled up in me."

Probably the most surprising premonition recorded by Hencher, which was quoted widely in the British press at the time, was a hunch relating to an airplane accident. He had been awake all night because of an ominous headache, and during that period clearly foresaw an airplane crash in which there would be 124 victims. He described the scene as reminding him of Greece and detailed some statuary around a church when he telephoned Barker with his report the following morning. Instinctively, Hencher felt that he was referring to Cyprus. Several weeks later, there was an airplane crash on Cyprus in which 124 people were killed.

Krippner said, "Our notion of the dividing line between present and future is probably incorrect. We interpret the present as being the exact moment when something is going on. In reality the pres-

ent for an event may come within a wider span of time. There are forces at work now that will probably not become obvious for a year or two. Then, when an event does take place, in retrospect we realize that it is part of the present."

Helen Ann Elsner of Iowa has worked as a nurse's aide in various hospitals and currently as a laboratory assistant in animal science. Her paranormal occurrences usually took the form of premonitory dreams. As a child she had a recurrent dream in which she saw a drugstore and a dime store in a town she was not familiar with. When she was staying in Grand Falls, Canada, in the summer of 1958, she suddenly recalled those dreams. She felt compelled to walk into the town and to her surprise found the two stores she had so often seen in her dreams. From that moment on, the dream ceased.

As a child she had dreamed also about a three-story mansion with a long curved stairway leading into the main living room. Years later she found herself in Lowell, Massachusetts, as a missionary student. The house she went to live in was that house, exactly as she had seen it years before in her dreams.

In the summer of 1961, Elsner was stationed at Fort Belvoir, Virginia, as a medical corpsman of the Women's Army Corps. In the cafeteria of the military hospital she met a young man named Jackson, a fellow corpsman. About two months later she had a dream about him that stayed vividly in her mind. In the dream she saw Jackson in patient's pajamas and felt that she was the hospital aide taking care of him. She saw herself straightening the covers of his bed as part of the evening care, when he reached up and tried to kiss her. At that moment a woman walked into the room. She heard Jackson remark, "There's my ex-wife. I did not know she knew where I was, let alone sick, because we are divorced." On that note the dream ended. Several weeks later when she came to the cafeteria, she saw Jackson in hospital pajamas and immediately recalled her dream. He asked her to come to his ward. As she was standing by his bed and talking about a book she had read, Jackson looked up and interrupted with the comment, "There is my ex-wife. I didn't know she knew where I was, let alone sick, because we are divorced." How could Elsner have guessed or in any way foretold the exact words spoken on that occasion, especially as she lacked the fundamental knowledge concerning Jackson?

Only by tapping the so-called future can we explain incidents of this kind, which are numerous. Sometimes the ESP apparatus projects events at a limited distance in both space and time. In November 1972, Elsner was driving home from work at about six in the evening. When she neared 24th Street in the town of Ames, she could not get it out of her mind that there would be an accident scene ahead. She took this as a warning and became very cautious for the next few blocks. When she got to 24th Street, there was the scene she had pictured in her mind: two wrecked cars, three police cars, and an ambulance.

Barbara Moeller worked as an office manager for a painting and decorating company in Omaha. She is psychic and has valid experiences with haunted houses as well as communications with the alleged dead. She said, "Once I had a dream in which I was driving either to or from work along a narrow street from my business place to the main artery. I saw very clearly how my car hit a small boy. I saw the boy's boot fly in the air and a profusion of blood stream down his face. I am a very careful driver so this dream bothered me greatly. I confided in my husband and also a cousin and revealed the dream to them several weeks prior to it becoming reality. For several weeks I watched very carefully as I drove along this street. One day when I was absolutely not thinking about the "accident" and was approaching the area of my dream, a young boy darted from between a car and a truck. Immediately I applied my brakes, but too late. I had struck the boy and just as in the dream, he lost his boot and his nose bled profusely. Even though I had been forewarned, I was greatly upset. Fortunately, the boy was not seriously injured."

Kaye Schoerning of Oklahoma has a long record of ESP experiences. When she still lived with her family in Hillsboro, Texas, where she was working as a nurse, her family owned a hotel that had a Western Union agency. One day she read in the local newspaper that three gunmen had robbed a Sears store to the southwest. That night she dreamed that the same men would come the following night at exactly 12:00 A.M. to rob their local Sears store. In the morning the agency received a telegram from the Sears district manager warning them of the three men and to be on the lookout for them. Since Schoerning's father was also mayor of the town, she took the telegram to him and asked him to do something about it. At the same time, she informed him of her premonitory dream. Her father shook his head. Why would three gunmen want to rob such a small store? But when she insisted, he called the police in. At exactly 12:00 A.M. the three men appeared at the store and tried to rob it. Because of the warning the police captured the thieves and Schoerning's dream proved to be entirely accurate.

Although it is impossible to channel one's ESP powers to guarantee the desired results, especially in dreams, sometimes dream material of a very mundane nature may come to the surface.

Mary Pugar of Oregon has had a series of premonitory experiences, mainly in the dream state. "The first such dream I had was in North Dakota when I was about eight years old," she told me. "One night I dreamed I was pulling the curtain of the window where my mother was sleeping. Suddenly the large curtain pole came down with a crash, almost killing her. Forty-two years later, when I was teaching in central Oregon, an incident occurred that brought that dream back to me. I was just about to leave for school when Mother said she was going to go to the woodshed to get some wood. I put my books down and said I would go get it for her. I had just started to pull the shed door open when a slight sound made me hesitate. The next thing I knew, a heavy two-by-four over the door fell down in front of me. In that instant I recalled that dream. If Mother had gone out she would not have hesitated but would have gone right in, since she was

hard of hearing and would not have heard the slight sound."

John Gaudry, who has worked with me on several occasions, dreamed that he "saw a large helicopter crash into cold waters, either a bay or a river. It was painted either orange or red and was a cabin-type helicopter. People were splashing around in the water but seemed to be able to make it. I fear this may happen within the next few days and within the New York area." According to the *New York Daily News,* four days later, a helicopter piloted by *Apollo 14* backup pilot Eugene Cernan crashed with terrific impact into a river and burst into flames while the astronaut was making simulated lunar landings. Cernan was picked up by one of several passing boats and was rushed to a nearby marina. Later he was examined by space-agency physician Dr. John Teegen and was pronounced unhurt.

TIME AND SPACE PHENOMENA

When science fiction speaks of "time warps" and "time travel," we know this is fiction, for our entertainment. But we do know of *out-of-body experiences*—astral projections—in which a person seemingly journeys from out of the body to other actual places to observe people and things at that distant location, and then returns to the body, usually to wake up with the feeling of falling from great heights, as the respective "vibrations" of travel (speeds) are adjusted and the subject "slows down" psychically to be earthbound once more. OOBs are not hearsay or fiction; they are a psychic experience that people have reported in large numbers.

There are several ways in which we can actually transport ourselves, or parts of ourselves, into the so-called past. In *psychometry*, we derive impressions from an object, person, or place about events that have taken place sometime before our experiment. These impressions are always emotionally tinged. Purely logical material does not seem to survive. The outburst of emotional energy whenever traumatic events occur furnishes the raw material with which objects, people, or places are coated and that contains the memory banks of the events themselves. In touching an object or person or being in the immediate vicinity of the event, we are merely replaying it the way a phonograph replays a prerecorded record. The events themselves do not possess any active life and the reproduction is faithful, subject only to the limitations of the transmission and the personality traits of the receiver. Therefore, the message may contain part or all of the original event, it may come through correctly or partially correctly, or it may be a combination of event and personal interpretation, since, after all, the receiver is human and not a machine. But the process is basically an impersonal one; it should work equally well, no matter what the occasion or where the location of the experiment is.

In psychometry, we read a kind of emotional photograph of past events. In reconstructing it through the psychometric impulses and with the help of our conscious mind, we are not actually re-creating the event but merely an imprint or copy of it. This is sufficient to derive information about an event and thus learn facts that may otherwise be lost in history. Some years ago, in a book entitled *Window to the Past,* I showed how a medium can be taken to historical "hot" spots, places where puzzles in history have not been fully resolved, and attempt psychometry to resolve pending issues. Sybil Leek was thus able to pinpoint the actual location of Camelot in England and of the first Viking landings on Cape Cod in Massachusetts. ESP in this application is a valid and valuable tool of historical exploration and can undoubtedly be used much more than it has been in the past, when all other means of historical research fail. To be sure, the information obtained in this manner is by no means used verbatim to correct missing parts of history but is used only as a departure point for research in conventional ways.

A second method of visiting the past is astral projection, also called out-of-body experiences, in which our inner self, the etheric body, leaves the physical abode temporarily and travels, usually at great speeds. Ordinarily, astral projection is in space rather than in time. It is possible to direct one's astral projection into a predetermined segment of history. It works better if done at the location one aims to investigate, but can also be done a distance away from it. The success will depend upon the power of visualization by the subject, and the absence of interference from conscious or unconscious sources. Induced astral projection should not be undertaken alone but only in the presence of a competent observer. The subject, who should have a history of past astral travel, will then suggest, or have suggested to him, that travel into a particular region of space and time is requested and that all the information obtained once one gets there should be recalled upon return and awakening.

Somewhere on the borderline between astral projection and psychometry lies what Eileen Garrett called *traveling clairvoyance*. In traveling clairvoyance, part of the medium is projected outward and is able to observe conditions as they existed in the past without actually leaving the physical body. This is a talent found primarily in professional mediums and those with a great deal of experience in controlling their phases of mediumship. It is not an easily acquired talent. Astral projection is accomplished by lying on a comfortable surface, preferably at a time of day when the body is reasonably tired and relaxed, and by gently suggesting an outward motion of the inner etheric body. Closing one's eyes while suggesting to oneself the loosening of the bonds between conscious and unconscious minds initiates an outward floating, which will eventually become a physical sensation. The inner self may leave the physical body through the upper solar plexus, at the top of the head or through the stomach area. Return is accompanied by a sensation of rapid deceleration, experienced as a kind of free fall, a spinning and occasionally an unpleasant feeling of having fallen from great heights. This is due only to the rapid change of speed between the etheric body and the physical body. The adjustment is undertaken in a comparatively short time and can therefore be momentarily unpleasant, but is in no way representative of danger to either body or mind.

Hypnotic regression, as it is used in connection with reincarnation research, also propels the individual into the past.

Such experiments, always undertaken under the supervision of a professional hypnotist trained in parapsychology, may result in the obtaining of information from past incarnations and can be verified independently afterward. With regression, it is always best to suggest to the subject that the past memory will not be retained upon awakening, in order to avoid any traumatic residue. Thus, the only information about the past available to the researcher is what the hypnotized subject brings while in the hypnotized state. Since hypnotic regression is more concerned with personal experiences in past lives than with historical exploration, the thrust of the investigation is somewhat different from that required for purely past-oriented research.

There are a number of instances on record where people have accidentally entered a time warp, that is, areas in which a different time stream was still extant. One such case concerns a young man who drove from northern Oregon to California and suddenly found himself in a mining town among people dressed in clothes of the early 1900s.

On June 1, 1967, I sat opposite Robert Cory, a thirty-year-old designer and an actor, living on Elmwood Street in Burbank, California. Premonitions and dreams were accepted phenomena in his family, which was of Near Eastern extraction.

In 1964 Cory made a trip by car to visit his future in-laws in Kenwick, Washington. His fiancée was with him, and he left her with her parents after a few days to drive back to Burbank by himself. His car was a '57 Corvette in excellent condition, and Cory was an experienced driver. The autumn weather was dry and pleasant when he left Washington State. It would be a twelve-hour trip down to the Los Angeles area.

Cory left Washington around 11:30 P.M. and started to climb up into the mountains on a long, winding road south. About four hours after he had left Washington, around 3:30 A.M., he was rounding a bend and with one fell swoop he found himself in a snowstorm. One moment it was a clear, dry autumn night—the next a raging snowstorm.

"I slowed down, I was frightened," he explained, still shuddering at the experience now, "the road was narrow, mountain on one side, a drop on the other."

Cory got out of the car, as he could drive no farther. Then he saw in the distance what appeared to be a bright light, so he got back into the car and drove on.

When he got to "the light," it turned out to be a road sign reflecting light "from somewhere." But he was now on top of a hill, so he coasted downhill until the car came to a full stop. Cory looked out and discovered he had rolled into some sort of village, for he saw houses and when he got out of the car, he found himself on a bumpy street.

"It looked like a Western town, the road went through it but the road now had bumps, as if it needed much work."

Cory found the car would not go any farther, but because it was late, he was glad to be in this strange place. One building had the word "hotel" on it, and he walked toward it on wooden sidewalks. When Cory arrived at the building, there were six to eight inches of snow outside. He noticed wagons parked out-side the hotel, wagons that hitch on to horses! He found this peculiar in this age.

He knocked at the door. Everything was dark. But the door was open and he found himself in the lobby of the hotel. Cory noticed animal heads on the walls, old furniture of another era, and a calendar on the wall dating back to the early 1900s! Also, some notices on a board on the wall with dates in the late 1800s. The telephone had a sign reading CRANK BOX FOR OPERATOR. There was a barbershop chair, and in the back, a desk and a big clock on the wall, ticking loudly. There were kittens in one of the chairs.

He yelled for someone to come, but no one came—yet there was a potbellied stove with a fire in it, so he placed himself in front of it to get warm.

"I went to the stove, ready to go to sleep and maybe in the morning there would be somebody there to talk to. After all, they've had a fire going, so there must have been some life in the place. So I lay down on a sofa, when I heard a rattling noise coming from what looked like a cardboard box in a corner. I figured it might be a snake and got real worried. The heat was putting me to sleep and I was exhausted, so I just fell asleep. I woke up because of some sound upstairs, and I saw a man coming down the steps, an old man of maybe seventy-five, wearing big boots, which made the noise.

"He wore old coveralls, like a farmer. Slowly he came down to where the stove was, he sat down in a rocking chair across from it. Then he went to the men's room, or something, and again sat down. He saw me, and we nodded to each other. Then he kept on rocking while I was trying to get up the courage to ask him some questions. Finally he said to me, "You couldn't fall asleep. Why don't you fall asleep?" I said, "Well, that's all right, I'm not really tired," but he replied, "No, you couldn't fall asleep, it's okay, it's okay.

"His voice sounded like an old man's voice, and as he kept saying over and over again, 'It's okay,' I fell asleep again. Once or twice I opened my eyes and saw him still sitting there. I slept till daybreak. When I woke up and opened my eyes, I saw eight or ten men walking around, talking, doing different things. I sat up but no one paid attention to me. *As if I were not there.* But I got up and said hello to one of them, and he said hello back to me; there were a couple men around the stove with their backs to me, talking, and then there was a man standing behind the barber chair *shaving somebody who wasn't even there.*

"He was shaving somebody, talking to him, moving his razor but there was no one in that chair. He held up the invisible chin and carefully wiped the razor into paper. It was frightening to watch this. The razor was real, all right.

"The people all seemed like normal people except I had the feeling they were in some way smaller. They all looked very old, like the first man I saw coming down the stairs. One of the men was walking back and forth in the hotel lobby, talking to no one, carrying on a conversation all by himself. Finally, I got up and looked outside. My car was still there, and the snow had stopped. There was no sign of life outside. I turned to the three men around the stove and asked, 'Is there a gas station around?' Now I could understand they were speaking to me but the words made no sense. One of the men grabbed

my waist as if to point out a direction. Then I heard someone yell out 'breakfast.' I noticed in the back of the lobby where the desk was that two doors were open now, leading into a dining room. Again the voice yelled, 'breakfast, come, breakfast,' and this time the old man whom I had seen first coming down the stairs came over and grabbed my arm, saying, 'come have breakfast.'

"I became so frightened I backed off and for the first time raised my voice, saying 'No, thank you.' Everyone turned around and started to walk slowly toward me. I said, 'Where am I? Where am I?' and the old man, who still had my arm, said, 'don't worry, don't worry,' but I turned and walked out and got into my car. I had forgotten about running out of gas.

"The car worked, and I drove down this bumpy road, and the faces of the men looking out of the windows of the hotel behind me."

"You say he actually touched you?" I asked. "Did you feel it?"

"Yes, I certainly did."

"The clothes these people wore— were they of our time?"

"No, no. When I drove off, I saw some more people in the street, one of them a woman. She wore a long dress like the Salvation Army women do.

"I drove past the people on the sidewalk and then there was something like a foggy cloud I went through for about thirty seconds. Next thing I knew, I came out into one of the brightest, shiniest days you could imagine. I drove another half mile or so until I saw a gas station, just in time. I was back in today's life."

"Here I was with a sweater, all buttoned up and the gas-station attendant in short sleeves, sweating, and he gave me a funny look. I just couldn't tell him what had just 'happened' to me."

"Was there anything different about the atmosphere in that place you left?"

"Yes. I was very tense and nervous. But I was not dreaming this, I touched the sofa, I was fully awake."

One must not classify such experiences as hallucinations, even though hallucinations are possible with certain people. With cases of this kind, the material obtained during the incident is the crux of the explanation: in the case of the young man, detailed descriptions of his encounter seem to indicate that he did enter a time warp of sorts. Whether this was due to his own mediumistic abilities or to the location at which he encountered the phenomenon is difficult to assess. But similar cases have been reported from time to time where people, and even vehicles, from the past have been observed amid contemporary scenes, only to vanish a few moments later or to return on other occasions or to other observers. Scenes from the past are not unlike ghosts except that ghosts are tied to specific locations and personal fates, whereas these scenes seem to exist independently and encompass a variety of individual people within them. Why some of these scenes from the past "hang around' while the majority have faded away, we do not as yet know.

In all cases known to me there have been emotional connotations involved, so I think that unresolved emotional problems may be at the base of keeping such scenes in existence. Perhaps someday we will devise an apparatus to replay historical occurrences at will.

On May 11, 1967, I was contacted by a reader of my books, Susan Hardwick of Philadelphia, who wanted to share an amazing experience with me in the hopes of getting some explanation: "In the summer of 1960 I took a ride with a friend, Sal Sassani, along my favorite road, Route 152 starting in Philadelphia as Limekiln Pike, a beautiful, winding country road that goes way up into the mountains. I have traveled it for years and knew every curve with my eyes closed. About an hour after darkness fell, I sat stiff with a start: I knew we had not made an improper turn, yet the road was unfamiliar to me suddenly. The trees were not the same. I became frightened and asked Sal to make a U-turn. As we did so, we both smelled what to us seemed like a combination of ether and alcohol. At the same time, the car radio fell silent! Suddenly we saw a shepherd puppy running alongside the car; his mouth was moving but no sound was heard. Then from our right, where there was no real road, came a ghostly shadow of a long, hearse-like car; it crossed directly in front of us and disappeared. The odor vanished and the radio came back on at the same time."

I responded with questions and on May 23, 1967, she contacted me again. To my question of whether she had ever had any other strange experience at that location, Hardwick went on to report an earlier incident, which had apparently not been as frightening to her as the one later on.

"In the summer of 1958 I was driving with a friend, Jerry, on this same road, Route 152, and we turned off it onto New Galena Road. Halfway toward 611, which is parallel to 152, we came upon a wooden building I had never seen there. We stopped and entered and sat at a table and Jerry noticed a man who resembled his late father. We each had a Coke. This man addressed both of us by our names, calling Jerry "son" and told him things only Jerry's father would have known. Jerry became convinced it was his father. We left and drove on a road I had never seen, yet I knew exactly what lay around every bend and curve! The incident took place about an hour from the city; I know exactly where this spot is but I have yet to see this structure or these roads again."

I decided to go to Philadelphia with medium Sybil Leek and investigate the case. On July 24, 1967, Sybil and I met up with Hardwick, and a friend of hers, Barbara Heckner. I had told Sybil nothing about the case but as we were driving toward the area, I asked her if she received any kind of psychic impression regarding it. "This is not a ghostly phenomenon," she began, "this is a space phenomenon....we're going to cross a river." We were approaching Lancaster, Pennsylvania, and no river was in sight. Five minutes later, there was the river.

Sybil conveyed the feeling of masses of people in an open place, gathered for some reason and she compared her feelings to those of an earlier visit to Runnymede, England, where people had once gathered to sign the Magna Carta.

Now we had reached the point forty miles from Philadelphia, where Hardwick had been twice before and experienced the inexplicable. What did Sybil feel about the location? "It's a happening...not a ghost...in the past...two hundred years ago...out of context with time...I feel detached...no man's land...we shouldn't be here...as if we were aliens in this country...I have to think what day it is, why we are here...it feels like falling off a cliff...I feel a large number of people in a large open space."

We began walking up an incline, and Sybil indicated the vibrations from the past were stronger there. "We are in their midst now, but these people are confused, too. Why are they here? Unity...that is, the word I get, Unity."

I then turned to Hardwick and asked her to point out exactly where her two experiences had taken place. This was the first time Sybil heard about them in detail.

"When I drove up here in 1958 with my friend, this road we're on was not there, the road across from us was, and there was a building here, a wooden frame building that had never been there. We felt compelled to enter somehow, and it seemed like a bar. We sat down and ordered Cokes. There were several men in the place, and my friend looked up and said, 'That man over there looks like my father.' The man then spoke to us and called us by our first names. He began predicting things about my friend's future and called him 'son.' "

"But didn't you think there was something peculiar about all this?" I asked.

"Yes, we did, because Jerry's father had died when he was a baby."

"Did everything look solid to you?"

"Yes, very much so."

"How were the people dressed?"

"Country people...work shirts and pants."

"Were the Cokes you ordered...real?"

"Yes, real, modern Cokes."

I looked around. There was nothing whatever in the area remotely looking like a wooden building. "You're sure this is the spot, Susan?"

"Definitely; we used to picnic across the road. That little bridge over there is a good landmark."

"What happened then?"

"We finished our Cokes, walked out of the place, got into the car and Jerry turned to me and said, 'That was my father.' He accepted this. So we drove off and came upon a road that I had never seen, and have yet to see again. I have tried, but never found that road again. Then I told Jerry to stop the car and told him that there would be a dilapidated farm building on the left, around the bend in the road. We proceeded to drive around it, and sure enough, there it was. Then I stated there would be a lake on the right-hand side. And there was."

"Did you ever find these places again?"

"Never. I am very familiar with the area; throughout my childhood I used to come here with friends."

"When you left the area, was there anything unusual in the atmosphere?"

"It felt humid...but it was an August afternoon."

"Did you go back later to try to find the place again?"

"Yes. We retraced our steps, but the building was gone. The road was still there, but no building."

"Was there anything in the atmosphere that was unusual when you wandered into that wooden bar?"

"Humidity...an electrifying feeling. Very cool inside."

"The people?"

"The man who seemed to be Jerry's father, the bartender, and several other men sitting at the bar."

"Any writing?"

"Just signs like 'sandwiches' and different beer signs."

I thought about this for a while. Was it all a hallucination? A dream? A psychic impression? Susan assured me that it was not: both she and Jerry had experienced the same things, and neither had been asleep. "What about the people you met inside this place? How did they look to you?"

"Solid...they walked...and...that was the funny thing...they all stared at us as if to say, who are you, and what are you doing here?"

"When you first drove up here and noticed that the area was unusual, did you notice any change from the normal road to this spot?"

"Only where the stop sign is now. That did not exist; instead, there was gravel and that wooden building. It started right in from the road, maybe fifty feet from the road. Farther back it was as normal as it is today. Suddenly it was there, and the next moment we were in it."

I decided to go on to the second location, not far away, where Susan's other "time warp" experience had taken place in the summer of 1960. Again, as we approached it, I asked Sybil for any impressions she might have about the area and incident.

Even though this was a different location, though not too far from the other place, Sybil felt that "the strength of the force is constant" between the two places. But she did not feel any of the odd excitement she had earlier picked up en route to and at the first location. Once again, Susan pointed out the clump of trees she remembered from the incident.

"We were riding on this road," Susan explained. "It must have been around midnight, in the middle of July 1960. Suddenly, this stretch of the road became extremely unfamiliar. The trees were not the same any more, they looked different, much older than they are now. There were no houses here; it was completely open on the right side of the road."

There were small houses in the area she pointed to.

"This clump of trees was very thick, and out of there where today there is no road, there was then a road. Suddenly, on this road came a ghost car, like a black limousine, except that you could see through it."

In her earlier letter to me, she had mentioned the peculiar smell of what to her seemed like ether and alcohol mixed, and the car radio had stopped abruptly. At the same instant, she and her friend Sal saw a shepherd puppy run alongside their car, with his mouth moving but without any sound, no barking heard!

"How did the dog disappear?"

"He just ran off the road. When the black limousine pulled out in front of us and—a hearse I'd say. There is a cemetery right in back of us, you know."

There still is.

But as Susan and Sal were driving in the opposite direction from the one they had come from, the hearse was going away from the cemetery, not toward it.

"What about the driver of the hearse?"

"Just a shadow. The hearse went alongside our car and suddenly vanished. The whole episode took maybe seven or eight minutes. We drove back toward Philadelphia, very shook up."

Rather than drive on through the strange area of the road, they had decided to turn around and go back the other way.

Now it was our turn to turn around and head back to the city. For a while we sat silent; then I asked Sybil to speak up if and when she felt she had something to contribute to the investigation.

"I think if you stayed in this area for a week, you wouldn't know what century you're in," she suddenly said. "I feel very confused...almost as if we had entered into another time, and then somebody pushes you back as if they did not want you. This is a very rare situation, probably a higher intensity of spiritual feeling."

I then turned to Susan's companion Barbara and asked her about her impressions, both now and before. "An apprehensive kind of feeling came over me," she replied. "We were here a week and a half ago again, when we came upon this side of the road, and it was...different...it felt as if it were not normal. All along this run as soon as we hit 152, through New Galena I feel as if I'm intruding...I don't belong, as if this whole stretch of country were not in existence in my time. I've been out here hundreds of times and always had this odd sensation."

While neither Hardwick nor her friends had ever attempted to research the history of the area of their incidents, I did. I contacted the town clerk at Trumbauersville, Pennsylvania, because that was the nearest town to the area. Specifically, I wanted to know whether there ever was a village or a drugstore/bar/restaurant of some sort at the junction of Highway 152 and New Galena Road, not far from the little bridge that is still there. Also, what was the history of the area?

The reply came on March 1, 1968, from the director of the Bucks County Historical-Tourist commission in Fallsington, Pennsylvania:

"It is rural farm area now and has been from the beginning. From what I know about this area, and from MacReynolds's *Place Names in Bucks County* and Davis's *History of Bucks County*, I know nothing of a drugstore in the area."

There was something else. Susan Hardwick reported finding some strange holes in the road in the area: "They seemed like left from the snow...filled with water...like a whirlpool. Many times we stopped the car and put our hands into those potholes and we could not feel the road underneath them. My friends and I stuck our arms into the holes and got wet. There was water in them. But when we came back another time, there were no holes. No water. Nothing."

This got me to search further in George MacReynolds's excellent work, *Place Names in Bucks County*, which also contains a detailed history of the area. And here is where I found at least a partial explanation for what these people had experienced along New Galena Road. It appears that back in the 1860, galena (and lead) ore was discovered in this area. Soon there was a mini-goldrush for lead and silver, and people in the farm area began driving shafts into the earth to see if there was valuable ore underneath. Those must have been the potholes, with water in them, but deep and bottomless—or at least their imprints from the past.

The town of New Galena became a mining center. Mining fever hit the rural population and turned farmers into speculators. By 1874, it was all over, though another attempt at exploiting the mines in the area was made in 1891, and as late as 1932, work was done to restore railroad tracks to the mines. But it all came to naught. "Today the place is deserted," writes MacReynolds, "a ghost of itself in the boom days of the 1860s and 1870s."

This explains the strange feeling of not wanting "outsiders" intruding into their own mining bonanza, and explains the water-filled shafts in the road. What it fails to explain is Jerry's father and the Coke bottles that Susan Hardwick and Jerry drank from. I can only suggest that so intense an emotional fervor as that of a small, backward rural community suddenly caught up in a mining fever and dreams of great riches might create a kind of psychic bubble in which it continues to exist in a time-space continuum of its own, separate from the outside world—except for an occasional, accidental intruder, like Susan and her friends.

While these kinds of experiences are rare, they are by no means unique. Somewhat similar is a case reported to me by Rebecca B., who lives in the Philadelphia area.

"My husband and I were traveling on River Road from Route 611 on our way to the Poconos. We should have been in the Easton area when we "hit the curve," but we were not! I knew the trip by heart since I had been traveling that route since infancy to visit my grandfather. Over the years, despite hurricanes and floods, much of the landscape and housing was the same.

"Yet on this trip suddenly we found ourselves in this very strange place. We stopped. Across the street was an old saloon made of wood, the doors wide open and darkness inside. The sidewalk was not of cement but rather a raised wooden sidewalk unlike anything we had ever seen outside of old movies. The people standing in front of the saloon were wearing work clothes, jeans, flannel shirts, Stetson-type hats, and there was a dog and a couple of men standing and one sitting on the 'porch,' his feet dangling down. One woman with a 'grapes of wrath'–type cotton dress was also there. Everything seemed covered with dust—building, shoes, earthy dust, not coal dust.

"There was no one on the road except my husband and me, and the 'townspeople' stood and stared at us with a haunting look, as if to say, 'what the hell are you doing here?'

"We felt unsafe and 'not in the right place' and decided to drive off. The road was like a dirt road, bumpy and rutted with a dust effect not seen anywhere else on our journey. The incident happened in broad daylight, there were no other vehicles around (which is strange). And there was *no sound at all!*"

Albert Einstein pointed out that energy cannot dissipate but must continue to exist even if it is transmuted or otherwise changed in form. Could it not be that the emotionally tinged scenes, which, after all, represent energy, exist in a dimension not ordinarily accessible to us for observation? On occasion some people are able to penetrate into this dimension where past events continue to move on a differ-

ent time track from the one we have created for our own convenience.

Thus, walking into the past is both a matter of choice and a matter of accident. Either way, the past is far from dead and continues to intermingle with our present. Probably the most common form of "reading" the past history of a person or a place is the kind of ESP that permits one to tell facts about such a person or place without having access to any information or any previous conscious knowledge of the person or place. Since this is a very common talent, it must be assumed that the past continues to exist all around us—that it, say, exudes tiny particles of itself so that those sufficiently sensitive to it may derive information from the emanations.

When I first wrote of "time travel" experiences in a magazine devoted to psychic research, I was contacted shortly after its publication by a woman in Australia, Anita Stapleton of Labrador, Queensland, who wanted me to investigate an incident in the life of a close friend. Rather than have her lucid account of what he told her, I asked to speak to the man directly, and so it was on May 5, 1991, that Kenneth B. Burnett of Southport, Queensland, got in touch with me.

Burnett is a man of keen observation. He has spent most of his adult life in a variety of jobs, including being a ceramic-tile salesman, a lumberjack, a steelwork painter, and a private detective. At age fifty-eight, he was forced to retire on a pension because of a physical condition brought on by his war service.

His strange adventure occurred in the northern part of New South Wales, on the eastern coast of Australia, when Burnett and his wife, Meg, decided to visit her brother, seventy miles from where they lived at that time. They knew the area like the back of their hands. Here is his initial report, as he had jotted it down previously:

"In 1968, Meg and I decided to drive from Katoomba to her brother's house in Armidale. We traveled via the Mitchell and the Oxley Highways. It was a cold, snowy winter. We spent the first night sleeping in the back of our Toyota station wagon on the outskirts of Dubbo. It was so cold that we set off at a very early hour, when it was still dark, to complete our journey to Armidale.

"We were driving along on a mountainous, twisting road, hills or cliffs on one side, and sheer drop on the passenger side, the edge clearly marked by a white painted railing all the way. On several occasions, when we approached bends, the lights failed completely and it was only my ability to retain a mental "picture" of where the fence had been that enabled me each time to stop safely and search for the fault. Each time the lights came on again we would set off until the next time. It became really hair-raising. When we stopped at Tamworth for fuel at an overnight petrol station, I made a real search for the lighting fault but could not find anything that I could definitely say had been the problem. As it was dawn, I did not worry any more.

"Shortly after leaving Tamworth, near Moonbi, we came to a point on the highway where detour signs directed us off into the bush on the right. After about two hundred yards, I noticed that there were no other tire marks on this track. That made me uneasy. After about another two hundred yards, the track narrowed to one cart's-width and the ground suddenly dropped away on each side, making me even more uneasy because if another vehicle came toward us, it would not have been possible for either vehicle to move forward and pass. We were traveling then on a sort of whitish chalk base, and each side of the road or track accommodated very spindly trees that appeared to be mainly ash or aspen. We were on this track a long time and must have driven about ten terrifying miles when we came to a tunnel. This was no wider than the track and convinced me that we were on some sort of old and disused railway track, although there was not the slightest sign that a track had ever been laid on it. The tunnel proved to be about half a mile in length but because of the extreme narrowness, it seemed much longer.

"When we came out of the tunnel, the track gradually became wider until after about a mile, when it was almost wide enough for two vehicles to pass each other. We must have driven another ten miles when we came to a bituminized highway. Opposite the outlet of our track was a very poor road sign showing Walcha to the right and Armidale to the left. We turned left and after a while reached Bendemeer, where a road sign indicated that Armidale was to our right. I turned right and eventually reached our relatives' house in Armidale. They were extremely worried about our being so late and it turned out that we had taken all of a very full day to drive from Tamworth to Armidale, a distance of seventy miles! Where had we been?

"My brother-in-law assured me that the highway from Tamworth to Armidale was an excellent one and there had been no roadwork, and certainly no detour sign there for years. The track I described, and particularly the tunnel, have never existed in the area. Because of the terrain, there is no ground suitable for such a track ever to have been built."

There were some unanswered questions I put to Burnett, especially with respect to his feelings, sensations, and anything out of the ordinary suggesting a strange phenomenon. For one thing, Burnett thought that the whole thing was due to some mysterious "evil force" or spirit trying to harm them, though I must confess I have not found this to be so from the evidence I have. However, Burnett (and his family) have had true psychic experiences for many years, and his gift of ESP may have some bearing on the case.

"I had put the problem of the car's lighting problems down to being 'just one of those things' until later events convinced me that it was otherwise. The lights only failed at highly dangerous parts of a mountain road, and on curves, where only an expert driver could hope to avoid an accident of some sort.

"When the detour signs showed up, I turned off the road onto an area about sixty feet wide and forty feet deep, which acted as a sort of foyer at the beginning of the chalk road. I first felt nervy here because as I left the bitumen of the highway I could see that no other vehicle had used this detour previously, and that the ground was covered with a thick carpeting of autumn leaves from aspen trees. Only Australian timbers grow in this area, and I was further disturbed and alerted when I found that the narrow chalk road was lined very neatly on each side by aspen trees, all in autumn leaf. We were driving in winter for one thing, and for another thing, there are no aspen trees in the area.

"My wife had felt extremely uneasy all along but could not explain why because she has always had complete confidence in my driving ability. My nerve ends tingled again as we approached the old road sign as we were leaving the chalk track. We had come to a crossroads, in very bad repair, and looking at us was an ancient and bleached road sign with barely legible printing on it, directing us to Armidale on the left. The wood of that sign was bleached gray with age and badly weathered and cracked. No council would have left it in that state.

"The country surrounding Armidale is very mountainous and there is nowhere where such a long track and tunnel could exist either then or in the past! I am convinced that such a road did not ever exist in that area. The only trees on the edge of that road were aspen. Not even one Aussie tree anywhere in sight! That made me feel queerer than anything else at the time, because while we drove on that road I had a strange feeling of unreality and timelessness. The tunnel was cut right through a mountain of sandstone, and the rocks of that area are all granite conglomerates.

"The biggest shock of all to an experienced long-distance driver was the taking of something like twelve hours to cover a distance of seventy miles! Simply not possible! On the return trip, my wife and I took particular care in looking for the spot where we had been detoured off the highway. Such a spot did not exist. Also, just as my brother-in-law had stated, the highway between Armidale and Tamworth was in superb condition!

"Two or three years after that incident, I was able to learn from someone who had worked on the railways in that area for over forty years that a track or tunnel could not have existed. Although some narrow tracks had existed in the Cobb & Co. coach days, none were chalk, and there were no known tunnels of any kind anywhere in the area!

"I still do not know how we could just 'disappear' for about twelve hours on a main highway in broad daylight, which it was when I left Tamworth for Armidale. Had we sat on the side of the road, someone would most certainly have stopped to offer help, and at least one police patrol would also have wanted to know why we were stopped. It remains the greatest mystery of my life, and I am no stranger to mysteries!

"What could be an important omission is the fact that while on the chalk road, I noticed that the trees along the sides of the road did not throw a shadow, as they should have done."

I asked Burnett for further data: did such a tunnel and road exist somewhere else, perhaps? There was also the tantalizing possibility of a UFO abduction to account for the lost time. Did he and his wife observe any UFOs in the area at the time?

Burnett was very cooperative. He contacted the Tamworth Historical Society on December 11, 1991, with respect to information about the road, the trees in

the area—elder or ash, or even poplar. To his surprise, the answer came back quickly, and Arthur Maunder, the research officer of the Society, confirmed both road and trees as really in existence. Which does not really solve the puzzle at all. How and why did Burnett drive so far off his goal? How was it that on a road he knew well, he suddenly "saw" a detour sign that did exist but at a distance—what made him lose twelve hours?

My guess is that the road and trees, though still in existence, appeared to the Burnetts in an earlier time. Witness the fact that Burnett did not see any road beyond the detour sign, only the "track" they were forced to take because of it. What caused him to leave the present and make a detour into what appears to be the past? My inclination is to involve his known psychic abilities—did he, for a time, become a vehicle for a spirit entity, or was he guided by one to go off the intended road for some reason?

If "time" as we know it can be penetrated by some with the psychic ability ahead of its becoming objective reality for us, would not the same apply to time elapsed, time that has receded into the past and cannot ever be lived again? Can we actually step into the past, as it were, and obtain information, even experiences, that we would not normally be familiar with? It seems that some people can.

There is one basic difference between the past and the future. The future is not yet, when seen from the present, and therefore has no realistic existence in terms of the ordinary five senses. The past, on the other hand, has existed already and therefore does have a track record of having been at one time. The difficulty in coming to terms with these expressions lies not so much in the limitations of our ordinary five senses as in the terminology we are forcing ourselves to use.

By dividing our consciousness into three distinct segments—past, present, and future—we are arbitrarily cutting a steady flow of consciousness into separate and distinct units. In actuality, the progression from past to present to future is continuous and uninterrupted. It is also relative to the observer, that is, the present of now becomes the past of now plus one. The past is nothing more than the present gone on. In essence, past, present, and future are made of the same stuff. The dividers are artificial and flexible. The only proof that something has become objective reality, that is, has already happened, comes from observation of the event. If we were not there to notice it, the event would transpire just the same, even though there would be no witness to record it. When we thus speak of the past, it is to be taken as subjective in the sense that it is the past as seen from our individual points of view. These individual points of view may be similar among most people, but they are nevertheless nothing more than the sum total of individual observations and reflect the past only because the observers are at a later juncture in time than the observed event. Perhaps it would be more accurate to speak of such events as accomplished events rather than as past events.

By contrast, future events could be characterized as unrealized events. The reality of the events would be identical; only their relationship to the observer would differ. From the point of view of the observer, past events have occurred and can no longer be altered. Future events, on the other hand, exist independently but have not yet occurred in relationship to the observer and may conceivably be altered, at least in some instances.

prophecy: fact, fallacy, or possibility?

WHEN IT COMES TO THE FUTURE OF our world, people tend to fall into three categories: those who really don't believe in any kind of prophecy or psychic predictions; those who are convinced that the dire predictions of the great prophets—from Saint John to Nostradamus, from Malachy to Edgar Cayce—will come to pass exactly as made and who live in a kind of undercurrent of fear of it all; and those who are impressed by the track record of prophecies fulfilled, and try to balance the likely with the unlikely by examining the track record of past prophecies. I belong to the last group, and thanks to my training and long experience as a parapsychologist, I can look at the prophecies dispassionately and rationally, more so as I consider it my task to sort it all out for the people who really aren't sure, and wish they were.

Over the years, I have learned from empiric evidence from many sources that there is no such thing as accuracy among those who would predict the future. On the one hand, one can blame that on the lack of human perfection, because, after all, psychics, mediums, and prophets are people, and the knowledge they give us must be filtered through their personalities and minds. On the other hand, could it not be the *intent* of the "system," whatever you wish to call that system, or law, or Divine Providence, to let us have just so much certainty and no more, and to give us foreknowledge only when it is proper for us to have it? I think so; it is a system that will at once help humanity along by hinting at what is yet to come, and still encourage our dealing with it, preparing for it, and choosing *the right path* based on what bits and pieces of advance knowledge we are given. We can call this "destiny" or "karma" or "free will." It is still a very orderly and fair system: we cannot possibly earn good karma if we are not making decisions, choices, taking actions—the system provides us with opportunities, with encounters carefully programmed ahead of our becoming aware of them in the time stream, but the system also expects us to be individuals and express our preferences.

There is a destiny up ahead and we are not immune to its powers. But destiny has its rules and laws, and within those we have a great deal of freedom of choice. How we choose will depend primarily on who we are, what our personality is like in this lifetime, and how we use our abilities, talents, our sense of judgment, our sense of fairness, our understanding of what is patently evil, and what is obviously good.

Thus, while prophets can and do predict catastrophes, they cannot always predict a person's behavior when the event strikes, and there is a certain margin for error in that we have the power to deflect the event once we understand its likelihood, and counteract its oncoming influence in ways that would balance its negative force with the power of the positive, individually, and as part of groups and movements.

This chapter presents my experience with prophecy between 1966 and the present, and it will deal with my perception of its impact upon our future and how we handle it. It will be clear that only a small minority of the prophecies made in 1970 as part of my survey have come

true and are not likely to come true in the future either, whenever firm dates are given. Could some of these prophecies, especially the ones dealing with war and natural disasters, still come true in our future, over twenty-five years later? There is that possibility in some instances, but it is remote.

I will present the prophecies of the great prophets—a few people who are professional prophets and mediums with a strong track record of accuracy. Keep in mind that even these stars of the prophetic gift can and have failed at times. I am grateful that they have, and can, and that tomorrow's world may yet turn out a lot better than some of us fear.

Prophecies can be of two kinds: events foretold that will surely occur, and events that may occur but are still subject to being changed if certain steps are taken by mankind. It is unfortunately not always clear which kind of prophecy we deal with, but sometimes it is, especially when determined people refuse to accept the inevitable and fight back in whatever way they know how, in order to alter the outcome of the dire prophecy. Then the prophecy becomes a warning prophecy, something parapsychology calls a *premonition*.

In 1970, I began a systematic project of surveying the field of prophecies and world predictions, which, in addition to spontaneous prophecies come to my attention, would allow me a scientific evaluation of the quality of prophecies and predictions. The idea was to formulate specific questions about the future of our world, and put these same questions before a selected group of people, then record the results, correlate them, and come to a composite conclusion as to what the future might hold for us. Naturally, this was all guesswork until the predicted event had either occurred or hadn't, and the time for it passed, although time is almost impossible to predict accurately, according to most professionals in the field.

As for the people selected at random from a pool of psychics, both professional and amateur, their track records of predictions made and come true (or not) was the determining factor of whether to include them in the survey. There is a great deal of difference between a prophecy—the result of a spontaneous vision, urge, dream, or other emotionally tinged event, unique and very personal to the individual to whom it happens—and a survey aiming for scientific data and statistics as to accuracy. But if the people who had agreed to take part in my project had "the gift of prophecy," tapping it at will should also yield results of one kind or another, even if the results would differ in accuracy or quality from those obtained spontaneously.

It is just as important to present here the pro and cons of a survey of this kind, as it contributes to a better understanding of what the odds are that some of the more momentous and dire predictions and prophecies may actually come to pass. Since the survey took place in 1970 and was first published in 1971, the reader has the chance to see what has actually taken place at the time it was supposed to have happened, and what clearly has not. The people surveyed are known psychic people and their responses do have a certain weight, if only to show that many predictions never come true as made.

I chose the following subjects for my survey: world peace and war; breakthroughs in medicine; racial problems in America; tomorrow's world leaders; natural catastrophes; and crime involving public figures. Keep in mind that modern prophets are rarely connected to organized religion, which was the base of ancient prophets. Even fundamentalist preachers, when they refer to dire things to come, do so on scriptural bases, rather than an evolving religious link to modern prophecy.

The purpose of republishing, with commentaries, prophecies made by a number of people in 1970 (and before) is twofold: since all the people who have gone on record with these predictions have an established track record of psychic ability, the likelihood of some of the unfulfilled prophecies also materializing must be considered. The other reason that giving this information now is one of common sense is this: since the majority of the predictions, especially those pertaining to war and disasters, have failed to come true either at the precise time predicted, or even years later, we need to assess our position toward such dire predictions with a more balanced attitude. Neither ignore prophecies of doom, nor swallow them whole.

There is no inherent difference between a prophecy uttered or registered by an amateur or minor prophet of our time, and the grand prophecies of biblical prophets right up to Nostradamus, Malachy, and Cayce, except one important respect: the quality of the gift of prophecy. A student playing the piano can make fairly good music, but no one will confuse it with the work of Paderewski.

In presenting these 1970 surveys, we gain a better handle on the nature of ordinary prophecy, the people who have been shown to possess the gift, and the low percentage of realization that these prophecies made in 1970 (or before) have ultimately revealed. A comforting thought to those who scare easily!

A certain number of prophetic dreams involving catastrophes yet to come can be perhaps explained as resulting from the dreamer's anxiety about the future of the land. This is less easy to accept when the dreamer, or the person having the vision, also has an established track record as a psychic able to foresee events. It would be easy to ascribe all such dreams and visions to widely read prophecy accounts from past prophecies made by great prophets of yesterday with a proven record of having made specific predictions already come true. But that would make the question of prophecy even more complex, just as the question of what comes true and what will not cannot be so easily answered.

GREAT PROPHETS OF THE PAST AND PRESENT

No documented prophet in relatively recent times has been as detailed, accurate, and upsetting to humanity because of the nature of some of his prophecies as Michel Nostradamus, a sixteenth-century French physician and astrologer. Dozens of books have been written about his prophecies, with all kinds of interpretations and translations, many of which are either false or misunderstood. There is also a book by Henry Roberts, a New York antiquarian book dealer, who had become so obsessed with his Nostradamus studies

that he became convinced that he was Nostradamus reincarnated.

Among the many books giving Nostradamus's prophecies, Roberts's is least likely to be reliable. The most accurate of Nostradamus scholars was Stuart Robb, a man whom I knew well and who was not only a leading scientific investigator of the paranormal, but also a great musicologist and authority on classical composers, such as Richard Wagner, whose works he translated.

I am confident with Robb's translations and interpretations of the "quatrains," or verses, which Nostradamus used to camouflage his prophecies. Those who are sophisticated enough to read between the lines or know what the hints mean that he gave in the verses had no great trouble understanding, though some of the hints are still controversial. The French seer did this because in his time, enlightened Renaissance though it was, it was still not healthy to prophesy the murder of a king of the country he lived in, or the destruction of the papacy in centuries to come. In Spain, particularly, but also elsewhere in Catholic Europe, the Inquisition was rampaging and burning anyone who dared have ideas about the future, since clairvoyance was considered witchcraft and witches had to be destroyed as being in league with the devil.

There is no rational explanation for Nostradamus, and no fakery involved. The manuscripts are genuine and readily available to scholars. His first book of prophecies contained some 354 four-line verses expressing his predictions, and several volumes followed. Nostradamus died in 1566, by which time he was held in high repute, or, as Robb put it, "a prophet with honor in his own country."

The prophecies extend from the sixteenth century until the middle of the fourth millennium, and Robb has painstakingly pointed out those that have already been realized. Among other things, Nostradamus foretold the periscope submarine, airplane, the Montgolfier balloon, atomic warfare, and the coming of many wars and events that have become part of history. It would take an entire volume to list them all. During World War II, for example: "An old man with the title of chief will arise, of doddering sense…the country divided, conceded to gendarmes." Marshal Pétain, chief of state, was an old man when the Nazis made him ruler of a portion of divided France—the portion to be ruled by Vichy *gendarmes*.

It is an axiom that if a large portion of a statement is correct, all of it may well be correct. Every prophecy made by Nostradamus between 1555 and 1566 pertaining to the period between then and today has come true. Not only are his prophecies specific; they use terminology completely unknown at the time he made them. Around the middle of the sixteenth century he spoke of communism, of aerial bombardments, of atom bombs, of submarines, and other ideas that came into being only centuries later. He gave the name and profession of the assassin of a French king, an event that transpired in the following century.

There is a total of 942 prophecies. Nostradamus scholar Dr. Alexander Centgraf, a German, has reassembled the deliberately mixed-up chronology of Nostradamus's verses. In 1968, Centgraf

published these verses in their correct sequence. In one of the verses Nostradamus referred to the year 1607, in which the priests would be threatening astronomers because of their discoveries. It was in 1607 that a Dutchman named Lippershey invented one of the first telescopes. Shortly thereafter, Galileo Galilei used this new instrument to discover that the earth circles the sun and not vice versa. When he proclaimed this exciting new discovery, he came into conflict with the Church and was eventually forced to recant. But he knew it was the truth. Almost three hundred years before the planet Neptune was discovered, Nostradamus predicted it and referred to the unknown planet by its present name, Neptune. As for our future, Nostradamus predicted a widespread eclipse of the sun in 1999, at which time the French monarchy will be restored following a disastrous war.

One of the most remarkable lines is in Stuart Robb's translation: "There will be a head of London from the government of America." It must be kept in mind that this was written at a time when no one had heard of a "government of America," when there was no connection between England and America—the first colonists had not yet come to America.

Nostradamus predicted in a number of verses that there would be a great war in 1973, that it would be caused by a leader of Arab background setting up headquarters at Constantinople, that the war would last twenty-seven years, on and off, and that in the course of it, parts of Europe would be occupied and such cities as Paris and Rome damaged or destroyed by atomic bombs.

This picture changes for the better in July 1999, when "a great king of terror will descend from the sides" and the forces of good will triumph over evil. Much of the final struggle would be fought in Palestine, and would include the battle of Armageddon. After that, we can expect a millennium of peace—that is, for those who survive.

Nostradamus prophesied that a great Tartarian warlord would descend on Europe and the Near East in 1999. But Erika Cheetham, in her interpretation of Nostradamus, connects this prophecy to the Christian millennium syndrome, the medieval belief that at the millennium, something terrible will happen to our world. An Arab is believed to be the leader who, backed by fanatic Muslims, unleashes a major war again.

The year 1999 cannot possibly be meaningful, being that Jesus was born seven years earlier than the year 1, as we all know. So if the great war were to break out, the year would have to be 1992, and we know it did not happen.

One of the most noteworthy statements by Robb concerns the validity of all predictions and prophecies, including those of Nostradamus. "Prophecies of disaster and doom that have not yet occurred need never occur," writes Robb. "Any predicted evil can be declared, circumvented, or prevented."

I am indebted to John Hogue, today's greatest Nostradamus scholar and author, for his help with a reference I consider of some importance with respect to recent world history. The terrible nuclear accident that occurred in Ukraine at the Chernobyl atomic energy plant in 1986 was one of the greatest disasters to befall Europe in decades. Did Nostradamus hint at this event?

In Nostradamus's epistle to King Henry II of France, there is reference to *fiel*, which means "bitter" in the French of Nostradamus's time. The line reading *le miel du fiel* likewise could be translated as "the passion or suffering of the bitter," and the term "bitter" could then be a mask hiding the terms *amoise amere*, or "bitter herb." "Bitter herb of Artemis" is the French term for what we call wormwood, or, by extension, absinthe. *Chernobyl* in Russian means "wormwood." Thus, the reference to a future "suffering by wormwood [Chernobyl]." Even more ominous is the mention of *wormwood* in the Apocalypse, the prophecies of Saint John: here there is no code, no disguise, and the term is plain. It only made sense after the Chernobyl catastrophe had taken place.

For those who wish to delve into the prophecies of the great Nostradamus themselves, I am listing the principal books dealing with his work. There are others, I am sure. No other prophet attracted as much attention among the broad masses as he did. One should study these books with caution, however. The original text is reliable, but the translations from sixteenth-century French are not always correct, as the French of his time and modern French often differ in meaning. Further, as Robb has pointed out, certain terms have specific meaning to Nostradamus, but may have a different meaning to anyone else of the same period. For instance, when Nostradamus speaks of "oriental," he does not mean "an Oriental, " but simply "a person from the East"—the east of France, that is.

The most accurate books on Nostradamus are Robb's; his *Nostradamus: And the End of Evils Began*, has been republished by Longmeadow Press. Here are the other books:

Stuart Robb, *Nostradamus and Napoleon*

Erika Cheetham, *The Prophecies of Nostradamus*

Erika Cheetham, *The Further Prophecies of Nostradamus: 1985 and Beyond*

Stuart Robb, *Prophecies on World Events by Nostradamus*

Charles A. Ward, *Oracles of Nostradamus*. This is a very old book.

Frank J. MacHovec, *Nostradamus— His Prophecies for the Future*

Henry Roberts, *The Complete Prophecies of Nostradamus*. Controversial.

John Hogue, *Nostradamus and the Millennium*. Excellent, visual.

Karl Drude, *Nostradamus*. German.

Rudolf Putzien, *Nostradamus—Weissagungen über den Atomkrieg*. German.

Hogue's new book, *The Millennium Book of Prophecy*, is even better than his first. Between Hogue's books and Robb's, you really don't need to look at any others on the subject of Nostradamus. It is all in there, and correctly.

H.G. Wells wrote a remarkable book that became an impressive film called *The Shape of Things to Come*. What he foresaw was total destruction of the England he knew and the emergence of a kind of latter-day caveman culture until the survivors of the atomic holocaust that had destroyed England emerged again from hidden centers and took over, thanks to an advanced technology they had meanwhile developed.

These events never took place, but they might have, if the course of human events had run differently. Even so astute a prognosticator as H.G. Wells, correct many times, could be wrong here. Nineteenth-century novelist Jules Verne predicted the submarine and many other later events: that was inspired intuition, if you wish, but not prophecy. But since our future is the only future we have, so to speak, we had better examine very closely and dispassionately the likelihood of certain destructive prophecies coming true as made.

There never was an age in the development of mankind and history where prophets did not speak. Today, they are free and safe to do so without fear of being accused of witchcraft or of being in league with the devil. Not so long ago, this would not have been possible, and prophecy was allowed and accepted only so long as it worked within the framework of the current state religion, whether Judaism or Christianity or any other mainstream faith. While this inevitably inhibited the prophets somewhat, they also found a way to tell the truth (as they saw it) in such a way as to not offend authorities, yet get the message across to the world.

Edgar Cayce of Virginia Beach, Virginia, well-known psychic and psychic healer, predicted that between 1968 and 1998, Los Angeles, San Fransisco and New York would be hit by major destruction. While this was likely for the California cities, it was not likely for New York, though Manhattan does rest on a deep fault in the earth.

The end of communism, along with the United States and Russia becoming allies and friends, was an unlikely situation when Cayce stated it, but it did occur. Christianization and democratization of Red China, also foreseen by Cayce, is yet to come, but the rising of Atlantis, the lost continent, while a reality to many of us, has not yet shown any sign of happening, especially by the date set by Cayce.

Between Nostradamus and Cayce and their dire prophecies of catastrophes and changes to come, many people, not just true believers, are scared. Did Cayce know of Nostradamus's prophecies, and did they influence his own? Possibly, but not likely. So when both prophets sound a similar alarm about the future, they might be drawing on the same source, but individually, thus reinforcing the validity and even probability of the events taking place.

Just as with Nostradamus, whose prophecies I take very seriously, I regard Cayce's with respect. I find troublesome the fatalistic position of people accepting these dire predictions as inevitable. The "higher level" of destiny places any one of us at a place and in a time where that person is meant to be. Time as we know it is only a convenience and not an absolute, certainly nonexistent in the dimension beyond this one. The power of prayer and spiritual renewal can and will influence the outcome of events, though we cannot really know which prophecy will be fulfilled as made, and which may yet be averted. That, too, is part of the karmic system, to encourage our efforts toward preventing evil and destruction in the world.

The power of the popes has always been shrouded in a kind of mystery, just as the "divine right of kings" has for many centuries kept rulers of sometimes doubtful qualifications in power. The pope is nothing more than the head of the Roman Catholic Church, a man, inspired perhaps, but not a miracle worker. Yet the enormous energies stemming from the religious faith of millions of people have endowed the papacy with almost supernatural status. No other head of a religious community shares that unique reputation, except perhaps the chief rabbis of some Hasidic sects believed by their followers to be the real Messiah.

Thus, it is not surprising that prophets have commented upon the fate of the papacy for centuries. In the Middle Ages the popes were also temporal rulers—contrary to Jesus' kind of Christianity—and only in modern times have the popes of Rome retreated to their spiritual sanctuaries, where their position is unchallenged. In the nineties, the fate of the papacy is of less impact than it might have been five hundred years ago, but its destiny, while no longer of geopolitical importance, has tremendous spiritual and moral implications for millions of people. In the following pages I am presenting precise prophecies regarding the Vatican and certain popes: there are amazing similarities between them, suggesting, at the very least, a common "source."

Saint Malachy was a medieval abbot whose prophecies of doom foretold the end of the Vatican some eight hundred years ago—giving a description of every pope elected since that time. The reign of John Paul I was characterized as "of the waxing moon" and indeed, his reign lasted just about that long—thirty-four days. According to the Malachy prophecy, the pope following John Paul I would come "from the eclipse of the sun"—an apt description of the Iron Curtain country Poland.

Malachy warns that only three more popes remain before the Holy See vanishes at the death of Peter II, and Michel Nostradamus, the sixteenth-century prophet, predicted the end of the Vatican in our time.

Apparently, the impact of what may well have be a fated event was so strong it penetrated the unconscious, psychic level of several other people.

Bohdan Zacharko is a tool and die maker of Ukrainian descent, now living in Connecticut. On August 27, 1978, during Mass, he suddenly had a vision. "I saw two coffins," he said, "one open and the other closed. I seemed to be standing in front of the Vatican. I knew that the open coffin held John Paul I, but I could not see anything more of the closed coffin, except that to the right, I saw the towers of Moscow. From this I received the feeling that John Paul I would live only for a short while, and that his successor would not be Italian but Polish. I shared my vision with my coworkers and my family, but everyone laughed at me."

Edith Filliette has had ESP experiences all her life but never thought too much of them. A few years ago she began to write them down as they occurred. Educated in Europe and Canada, Filliette worked as a writer for the *Readers Digest* and as a direct-mail promotion consultant, making her home in Massachusetts.

She had a vivid dream that left her very puzzled at the time.

"I was walking down a busy street somewhere in Europe, looking for transportation to the other side of town. I asked a woman passerby for directions. 'I know of a shortcut but you must pass through the Polish embassy,' she replied. At the Polish embassy I noticed a grand marble stairway winding up to another floor. I glanced upward and saw three Catholic cardinals in full regalia coming down the stairway. I thought it strange and at the same time I felt they were cardinals from Poland and had come to the embassy for some official papers. Two of the cardinals passed me without a look in my direction. But the third one stopped, looked straight at me as if he were trying to convey a message. He was very close, and I could see his face very distinctly.

"He was an attractive man of between fifty and sixty, clean-shaven, with light or gray hair slightly protruding beneath the biretta, with a dignified and strong appearance. After some seconds of staring at me, he turned away and continued his walk downstairs, and I continued through the Polish embassy, walking up the marble stairs, then through a long corridor, until I reached the other side of town. There the dream ended."

As soon as news of the death of Pope Paul VI reached the world, Filliette told two friends that the next pope might be Polish and she described him. However, when John Paul I, an Italian, was elected she had the feeling that a mistake had been made. Soon she was to learn how right she had been. "The day John Paul I died," she explained, "I was hospitalized at Massachusetts General in Boston. I did not know the pope had died during the night, and I was sitting up that particular morning around 6:45 A.M. Suddenly I heard an inner voice urging me: 'Turn on your TV. Something important has happened.' I rejected the idea, as I have an aversion to watching TV. But the voice returned more insistently. 'Turn to number 5 and see what happened.'

"I did, and there on the screen was Pope John Paul I and the announcement of his sudden death. At that moment I felt my dream had taken on meaning and that the next pope would be Polish. I said so to a friend and that he would be elected on October 16." Filliette's strange encounter with the unknown was not over by any means. Since she has no interest in Poland, or any Polish relatives, she knew nothing of any Polish cardinals as seen in her dream. When the new pope was elected on October 16, as she had predicted, she was shocked to recognize his face: it was the face she had seen so vividly in her dream months before. Filliette's witnesses are her husband, a seminarian priest, and a business executive. Their names are known to me.

There is no doubt about the truth and dates of Filliette's amazing prophecies. Edith Filliette saw three cardinals in her dream: Poland does have three cardinals. But more ominous seems the connection with Saint Malachy's prophecy: three more popes, the present one and two more, then the Church will come to an end.

A Dutch seer, a Connecticut tool and die maker, a Massachusetts copywriter, and who knows who else: do they have a pipeline to the future?

Jan Cornelius van der Heide lives in a small town in the Netherlands. He is about forty-five, married, and makes his living as an artist and sometime poet. The Dutchman claims that a long-dead monk inspires his many religious paintings, which have a strange etheric quality to them.

From time to time, van der Heide has had visions about future events, many of which have already come true—such as the time he woke up and saw his father "with hands and face covered with blood, his head had gone through a pane of glass, his car wrecked." Two months later the accident occurred, but the elder van der Heide somehow survived.

Perhaps because of his religious orientation, van der Heide was chosen to warn the world on September 13, 1978, that the newly elected pope, John Paul I, "would not live long, but would die within four months." In addition to this entry in his diary, van der Heide told a number of witnesses of the impending death of the newly elected pope. All have signed affidavits to that effect. Stated R. la Grouw of Noordwijk, Netherlands: "On Saturday, September 16, 1978, I visited van der Heide's family. That evening, after Jan had read to us one of his poems about religion, he suddenly said, 'Pope John Paul will die suddenly within four months.' "

As the weeks passed, van der Heide felt more and more that the tragic event was not far off. On September 28, he decided to write to me to reiterate his concern about John Paul I. That letter, sent off the following day, reached me several days later. But on September 29, Pope John Paul I suddenly died. No sooner had a new pope been elected than Jan van der Heide's second sight tuned in on him. "John Paul II will be involved in an airplane accident in a southern country, perhaps South America. It will be near dry, arid land with rock soil and coast. The figures 1 and 8 suggest the year 1981."

According to van der Heide, the new pope would show himself very orthodox and unyielding in matters of doctrine. Van der Heide wrote this on October 19, 1978. By now it is clear he was correct: the new pope's unyielding stand on celibacy has already been made known. Van der Heide predicts that because of John Paul II's stand, more splinters will occur in the Church. Polarization will become more pronounced.

I first heard about Jan Cornelius van der Heide in the fall of 1978, and got to meet him the following year, when he offered to put me up in his little house in Oegstgeest, a town halfway between Amsterdam and Leyden. Then, as now, the bearded, jovial, kindhearted man was known locally as a "paragnost," a psychic.

With his wife, Ans, he lived a pleasant life trying to advance the cause of genuine parapsychology, helped publish a magazine about it, and gradually became well known in the Netherlands as a prophet. Van Heide's prophecy about Pope John Paul I is so uncanny, and so well documented, that one expects the majority of his visions also to come true. When they do happen, they are startlingly similar to what Jan had predicted, but there are also many prophecies that have not occurred, and though some may yet happen at a later time, the majority cannot, because of time elements and facts on the ground.

Could it be that such detailed and ominous prophecies as van der Heide's description of World War III and Russian attacks on the West were actually in the minds, even the planning stages of some people in the East? Obviously, this prediction never came to pass and could not come to pass unless a new, belligerent Soviet Union were to rise in what could only be a distant future, practically speaking. But that is unlikely, so I must conclude that the prophet saw what may have been a thought pattern or a warning manufactured by spiritual forces to induce humanity to work together, possibly also triggered to some extent by the pervasive fear of Soviet intentions in the 1970s that many Europeans harbored.

Jan van der Heide has registered prophecies with me from time to time with the postmark guaranteeing the proper time reference. A great deal of this material refers mainly to Holland and to people and situations of little impact for the world at large. But a good deal is also relative to international conditions, and a great deal of it never came to pass, at least not in our time.

Still, there are some interesting predictions:

November 23, 1980. "Someone will shoot at Reagan."

September 2, 1989. "The Berlin Wall will come down." Witnessed by radio journalist Marion Dietrich, originally from East Germany.

November 18, 1989. "People will try to kill Gorbachev."

November 18, 1990. "There will be a short and heavy war in the Middle East. I see American bombers above Baghdad."

November 18, 1990. "Limited use of nerve gas by Iraq."

November 18, 1990. "Gorbachev will disappear from the scene in 1991. We will soon be able to read his memoirs."

January 18, 1991. "Arafat will speak about peace with Israel in a short time."

Some of these predictions were broadcast by Radio Veronica in the Netherlands:

February 19, 1993. "Unsuccessful attack by shooting on President Clinton."

February 19, 1993. "British and United States aircraft over Yugoslavia in March and April of 1993."

October 11, 1993. "Civil war in Russia."

It is reassuring that even an excellent prophet like van der Heide can equally often be wrong as not. There is a great deal of difference between a talented psychic predicting future events to individual clients who seek him out precisely for that purpose, and a gifted individual making world predictions and prophecies spontaneously and to no one in particular. Those who are witness to such prophecies will vouch for them, but the true prophecy comes unsought and usually as a surprise to the practitioner of the psychic arts. It is a moot question where the source for such material is, whether it is the deeper level of the prophet's own consciousness, or a spirit communicator or guide inspiring the prophet with this material. What counts is the quality of the prophecy, the track record of the prophet with respect to past prophecies having actually come true, and the likelihood of the prophecy being fulfilled at some point in time.

There are millions of people driving cars. Some are truly brilliant at it, and many are terrible and cause accidents, and the majority of people lie between those extremes. So it is with prophets: there are very few truly great ones, and even they are far from completely right all the time. It appears that this is the will of the powers that be, to give us a little leeway to doubt the terrible events prophesied, and yet warn us about them sufficiently so that we may take heed and action to change the outcome. No doubt there are outstanding prophets alive and active today, of whom I know nothing. The ones I will touch upon here are people with whose work I have been familiar for a long time; I am therefore able to judge the likelihood of their being correct as to the outcome.

MODERN PROPHETS

Apart from the Dutch seer Jan Cornelius van der Heide, there are three people I respect as modern prophets, whose prophecies were never sought out by tabloid reporters at will, which would make them far from spontaneous. They are all women and they called me to confide their prophecies in the hopes, perhaps, that I could warn the world in some fashion, and thus help prevent the outcome, if the prophecy was of a dire nature.

No one can be sure as to which prophecies are warnings, and subject to alteration by human will or action, and which are only previews of certain things to come. It is unwise to allow oneself to panic at an outcome that, although prophesied by a serious prophet, may nevertheless never come to pass. Or if it does occur, the person worried about it may find himself far from the disaster when it happens, perhaps because destiny so wanted it in his case.

Here are some of the prophecies communicated to me, and in some instances to other witnesses, regarding situations and events affecting a great many people.

Rosanna Rogers, of Cleveland and New York, is a remarkably gifted professional psychic reader, whose knowledge of the tarot cards far exceeds that of any other tarot specialist, living or dead. Rosanna uses some 220 cards of her own inimitable design, whereas everyone else uses the traditional 78 cards. Now and again, Rosanna has a flash of prophecy, which she communicates to me, and other witnesses, and when the event predicted occurs, she reminds all of her prophetic statements.

Rosanna Rogers was born in Austria and brought up in Germany, where she attended high school at the Convent of the Sisters of Saint Francis in Pirmasens, and college at the Convent of San Lioba, in Freiburg. She lives in a house on Švec Avenue in Cleveland, and has her own local cable television program. But people from many parts of the world reach out to her for predictions.

Over the years, Rosanna has sent me predictions, or made them in my presence or to reputable witnesses who have testified accordingly.

Here are some of the outstanding ones relating to world affairs:

January 10, 1990: "I see a 707 airplane, approaching the Atlantic coast, crashing. I perceive digits... 5?" January 26, 1990. Colombian airliner, Flight 52, a 707, crashes near New York City.

September 23, 1983: "The United States and the Soviet Union will recognize the need to work together in unison as the danger comes from nations with nothing to lose, such as Iran, Iraq, and Libya." June–July 1990: The U.S. and Soviet Union chummy as never before and worries about Iraq and Iran greater than ever.

July 19, 1973: "Nixon may get out of the Watergate affair elegantly by resigning." August 7, 1974: Nixon resigns.

During the summer of 1989, Rosanna, whom I had been monitoring carefully as to her accuracy for thirteen years, insisted that all was not well with the president and his family. She insisted there were health problems and we would hear about them soon and other problems even more worrisome concerning his immediate family! On January 10, 1990, she put her concerns in writing to me. How accurate was all this?

On February 15, 1990, Barbara Bush went through surgery on her lip and dealt with an eye problem; on January 29, 1990, Neil Bush, the president's son, started having serious business problems which mounted in ominous proportions, and on April 12, 1990, the president discovered signs of an early glaucoma problem.

For a European-born woman with horrible memories of the Hitler era, predicting the innocence of a man accused of being a concentration-camp guard and war criminal placed her professional integrity above her deep feelings. But Rosanna Rogers did just that. While all the world knew that a man named Demjanjuk, deported by the United States, was being tried in Israel for his life because he had been identified by witnesses as "Ivan the Terrible," a particularly vicious and murderous concentration camp guard, no one much doubted the outcome. But Demjanjuk and his lawyer insisted all along that he was not the man.

Was it really a case of mistaken identity?

On January 10, 1990, Rosanna Rogers stated to me that "the Demjanjuk case will get a new twist, they've got the wrong man." Personally, I doubted it but events proved me wrong and the Cleveland psychic right.

February 26, 1990: Polish villagers who live near the former Treblinka concentration camp tell reporters for the television program *60 Minutes* that the man dubbed "Ivan the Terrible" was really named Marczenco, not Demjanjuk, and nicknamed at the time "Ivan Grozny" or "Ivan the Terrible" because of what he did to the camp inmates.

February 28, 1990: Ohio congressman J. Trafficant, in whose district the accused man lived for so many years, takes up his case in Congress.

May 14, 1990: The Israeli court hears an appeal of the man's death sentence imposed by a lower court. Result: the Demjanjuk case is reopened and a new investigation by the court sets the man free. He now lives quietly back in Cleveland.

From the very serious to the very superficial, Rosanna stated to me throughout 1988 and 1989 that million-aire builder Donald Trump was heading for a fall. On January 10, 1990, she put it this way: "He will learn the raw fear of losses, both emotionally and in business, but he will bounce back... On the same day, Rosanna assured me that former president Reagan would be the first president in American history to testify in court. He did in February and March.

Rosanna foresaw more trouble in the world, emphasizing that it is the small nations "with nothing to lose" that present nuclear threats—Iran, Iraq, and Libya in particular. Not a word about North Korea, though. In the Middle East, she prophesized a major conflict involving several countries, sometime before 1999. In the United States, she predicted "open warfare in the streets" and "tax revolt" by the citizens.

Yolana Lassaw, usually only called by her first name (which is actually her mother's name, adopted years ago for good luck), is today the leading deep-trance medium in America. In the tradition of Eileen Garrett, Ethel Johnson Meyers, and Trixie Allingham, to name but a few of those I have worked with over the years, Yolana makes her living as a psychic reader available to clients for consultations about their private lives and future.

She has also become a busy adjunct to the police, giving freely of her time in the investigations of murder cases and missing persons, in particular. I have taken part in some of these journeys, and she is truly on target. Now and again she has prophetic visions and communicates them to me, as we are close friends and have been close associates in this work for twenty years.

Here are some of the prophecies by Yolana and the outcomes:

On November 12, 1978, Yolana told me of an impending railroad catastrophe of a silver and blue train that would derail, resulting in many injuries. She saw this for late November or early December of that year. On December 3, the crack Southern Crescent, en route to Washington from the South, derailed on a curve near Charlottesville, Virginia, killing six people and injuring forty.

On December 17, 1978, Yolana told me she foresaw a bombing at a busy New York terminal right after the New Year, that people would be hurt, and that it would be the work of a crazy person. On February 19, 1979, three teenagers set fire to a subway token booth, as a result of which three people died. The motive was personal revenge.

On December 19, 1978, Yolana spoke to me of an airplane crash over hills or mountains in a suburban area; there would be trouble with the left wing, and there would be casualties. The figure "7" was also part of her vision. The following day a light plane crashed in a suburban area on the West Coast, the left wing hit a tree, and of the seven people involved, only one survived.

On January 11, 1979, Yolana stated that "one oriental country would invade another very shortly." On February 17, China surprised the world by invading Vietnam.

On January 16, 1979, Yolana spoke of a "terror ride" on a train going to Coney Island. On February 26, 1979, a holdup man terrorized and victimized people on just such a train.

On November 15, 1980, Yolana confided to her secretary, Rose Pannini, a vision in which she saw someone in terrible danger near black gates; a man gets out of a car, someone is going "to be killed, it is very big—I hear many shots." She thought someone named David was involved. Three days before John Lennon was shot in front of the black gates of the Dakota apartment building in New York, by a man named Mark David Chapman, Yolana reported that a name like "Lemon" kept running through her mind.

On October 15, 1985, Yolana predicted to me an earthquake near Bernardino, California, that would be felt in New York. That is exactly what happened on February 18, 1986.

At the same time, she spoke of a "bombing by the PLO at a military base in Germany," but was not sure about the place name, which she thought sounded like "Bogen." A nightclub frequented by US personnel was bombed by Arab terrorists on October 24 in Berlin.

In June 1994, Yolana gave me the following predictions, prophecies that had "come to her" unsought during the last year:

An earthquake would hit New York City during the next four years;
a major earthquake would occur in the Bay Area (San Francisco) during the next two and a half years;
she foresaw trouble in the Far East involving China and North Korea— and a war in five years;
a nuclear explosion at an upstate New York atomic plant, if not corrected in time;

the collapse of a bridge (George Washington Bridge) and trouble with the 59th Street Bridge in New York; finally, a market crash.

None of these prophecies are particularly new or unique, but coming from Yolana, whose track record is very good, even unrealized predictions need to be noted here.

While not exactly in the same league with Yolana and Rosanna Rogers, a woman from Brooklyn named Lucy Rivera has over the years proven to me her remarkable psychic gift. She primarily does private readings, so it was startling that she came up unexpectedly with spontaneous prophecies.

Lucy visited me on December 27, 1990, very concerned about a vision she had first had in 1989. In it, she saw four airplanes over Manhattan, which she felt were threatening, and she connected this to the then-ongoing struggle with Saddam Hussein of Iraq. But she also "saw" a bomb going off in the Wall Street area of Manhattan and smoke rising. She described the people involved as dark-skinned, wearing a kind of blue uniform like overalls, and she saw people running all over and great turmoil. She felt that the people who had caused this came from the Newark, New Jersey, area. The same basic vision occurred to her on January 15, 1991, and again she decided to see me about it so I could warn the authorities, which I did.

When the events failed to materialize during the Persian Gulf crisis, I thought no more about it, until the World Trade Center bombing took place two years later. The perpetrators, now imprisoned for life, did include some that came from New Jersey, and the overalls were work clothes worn by them, as they were posing as a kind of repair crew when entering the building; they were dark-skinned Arabs.

Jeane Dixon of Washington, D.C., became a prophetess of world renown. Ruth Montgomery, a Hearst reporter, has recorded Jeane Dixon's predictions in *A Gift of Prophecy*, which has been a bestseller from the start. The most famous of Dixon's prophecies was President Kennedy's assassination, but the coming of Russia's sputnik and the change in Russia's leadership also rank among her remarkably accurate prophecies, all well documented as to time and circumstances. Dixon predicted the fall of Malenkov, the election of President Truman, the death of President Roosevelt and many other events of lesser political significance. Not all her predictions have come true, but enough have materialized to secure her a place among the great prophets.

Prophecy is neither to be ignored nor feared. As prophets are humans, subject to failure in even the very best of cases, one should consider prophecies as possibilities rather than accomplished fact in our future. Only by acknowledging a higher order governing our destinies can we come to terms with prophecy. But it would be prudent to act as if dire prophecies were to take place as predicted in the sense that we can and must abort them by sheer will power, spiritual or moral renewal of our lives, and the actions we take in this, our mundane world, for catastrophes involving human beings are the result not only of divine will (to test us, perhaps) but very much of human action—for, or against, as the case may be. And each prophecy must be dealt with individually, and on its own merits, ultimately not because other prophecies by the same prophet have already been fulfilled.

Ours is a less than perfect world, and evil is rampant—evil expressed by us, the humans. But we also have the power given us by God, or the forces divine, if you prefer, to alter the outcome.

psychic dreams

BEFORE WE CAN DISCUSS DREAMS, WE MUST fully understand the nature of their companion, *sleep*, without which dreaming would have no objective reality. If man were only a living organism, consisting of certain chemical combinations, without a nonphysical component called spirit or soul, he would rest for periods of time to recharge his batteries of energy. In that case, sleep would be simply the absence of consciousness and would result in a disconnection of all ongoing activities within the body. That is not the case: we know that certain vital functions continue during sleep, even if at reduced levels, and that sleep is by no means a total disconnection from activities, as is shutting off a machine. So the materialistic concept of man, as it was popular in the nineteenth century, is without validity, and his position in the universe is by no means similar to that of a manmade machine, but something far more complex.

The need for sleep arises from the expenditure of physical or mental energy. Either of these expenditures may induce fatigue, not an unnatural state but rather, the result of activity cycles and "built in" in the vehicle, that is, man. When the energy potential runs down, the human machine stops, and sleep results. After sleep has been completed, the human machine continues to function. During sleep the conscious mind rests temporarily, while the unconscious part of the mind continues to function. Vital activities of the bodily machine are carried on automatically to preserve the organism.

The temporary exclusion of the conscious mind allows the body and the unconscious mind to regain spent energies from the reservoir represented by the human energy field that is located within the confines of the physical body.

Human personality consists of an electromagnetic field containing a certain power potential that is encased in an outer layer of denser matter called the physical body. This field, which is unique with every human being and contains varying amounts of energy, reaches slightly beyond the physical skin. Its outer limits can frequently be observed by those who are sensitive enough to see it and is called the *aura*; the inner body is the astral or etheric body referred to by psychic researchers, and it is this inner body that is the seat of personality, memory, emotions, and all that makes up a human being, while the outer layer, or physical body, does not possess powers of its own without directions from the inner body. This is at variance with nineteenth-century materialism, but more researchers are becoming aware of the existence of this secondary body, even in Russia. The latest Russian publications speak of a "bioplasmic" body that is responsible for the occurrence of psychic phenomena, including psychokinesis, or the movement of objects by thought power.

This arrangement seems logical: when we disconnect the user of energy from the reservoir, we allow the "backup crew" to stock up on fresh energy so that the user can have it when he returns to consciousness. Perhaps the following simile will be easier to understand: you had a certain amount of money in the bank, and you have spent it. But you know that a payment is due regularly every other week. You lay low as to spending for a few days, until the next payment comes in. As soon as the new payment is in the bank, you are notified that you have money in your account, and you can spend once again. This is how sleep restores the power reservoir of the human body.

Since the amount of sleep required by people varies greatly according to personalities, conditions, health factors, age, and even social and economic situations, it is difficult to say just how much sleep a human being needs. I think that the amount of sleep depends on the state of the power reservoir, the need to restore spent energies, which may differ not only with various people but with one and the same individual, depending upon circumstances.

Sleep is that amount of time required for a particular individual to restore his power reservoir to maximum efficiency, to that level that his power reservoir had when he came into this life. I am convinced that the newborn baby already contains the seed of his eventual power reservoir even if the full extent of that reservoir is not reached until some years later. The amount of this life force within all of us differs from person to person, and sleep restores the power reservoir only to that extent. Even if a person were to sleep enormous amounts of time to strengthen his power reservoir, he would not be able to accumulate more than he had to begin with. This is so because his power-reservoir capacity was set at birth and, once filled, excess energies restored through long hours of sleep would simply drop off and find no storage capabilities within his system.

Many people suffer from insomnia or irregular sleeping habits. The desired sleeping period, whether it is six, seven, eight, nine, or even ten hours, should be consummated in one stretch. Occasionally, this is not possible, because of health problems, unresolved emotional problems, environmental discomforts, noise, lack of air, lack of proper sleeping surfaces, or other external factors. Regardless of what causes the irregular sleeping patterns, the approach in dealing with them should take into account the need to establish uninterrupted sleeping habits, if possible. The less the restorative cycle is interrupted or weakened, the better for the organism. Short sleeping periods never equal the total of one long period spent asleep. The continuity of sleep is of paramount importance.

In dealing with insomnia, it is important to establish what factors cause interrupted sleep. Once the reasons have been isolated, they should be written down. Then a list of potential remedies should be written next to the causative factors. Reading this "prescription" to oneself, preferably aloud, and determining what one will do the following day to remedy the problem, is the first step toward resumption of uninterrupted sleep. While the removal of the unresolved problems is of great importance, the second step is equally as vital in restoring or preserving uninterrupted sleep. This is the "light suggestion" that sleep should come at such and such a time, without the pressure of concentration or any kind of forceful order. The stronger the command, the less it is likely to be obeyed by the unconscious, which controls the sleep pattern.

Once the suggestion has been made to go to sleep at a certain time, the clock should be visualized with the hands pointing at the particular time desired for the dropping off to sleep. Then the subject must be changed immediately, and not dwelled upon. At the appointed moment, the unconscious will nudge the mind to give the proper command to the sleep center in the brain, and sleep should ensue. Reliance upon chemical agents is not advised: they may work faster at first, but eventually they lose their effectiveness, resulting in a backlash of anxiety. I have frequently heard people say that the body will fall asleep when it is tired enough; that is not entirely true, because unresolved emotional factors can prevent the body from exercising its natural functions.

Another element of importance in the restoration of uninterrupted sleep is the realization that a person's sleeping period is in tune with his natural pattern. A diurnal person should not attempt to do night work, and a nocturnal person should not force himself to rise early in the morning. Going against one's own nature is never warranted, despite such poetic dicta as "The early bird gets the worm."

Even some well-educated people frequently do not know the difference between sleep and dream, that is, they are not cognizant that certain processes occur during the sleep stage while others occur only while a person is dreaming. This is understandable since sleep and dream come together, occupying the same period in the time continuum. But they are not identical—to sleep does not necessarily mean to dream, and there are states of dreaming that are not truly part of the sleep state, in which a person can come close to being awake though not fully conscious. The majority of dreams certainly occur while a person is asleep. I would prefer to say one is either asleep or awake, and one can be asleep and "adream" at the same time. Not remembering a dream does not mean that a dream has not occurred. Individual observation of the dream state, while it is the primary source of content, is not reliable in an objective way. The dream memory fades quickly upon awakening and the sleeper may not remember.

Although some materialistically inclined people tend to dismiss dreaming as the equivalent of fantasizing, this was not always so. Prior to nineteenth-century materialism, dreaming was considered serious business. Shakespeare frequently refers to the dream state as a state of great significance. "To sleep, perchance to dream" *(Hamlet),* and "This is the stuff that dreams are made of" *(Midsummer Night's Dream),* are two of the better-known quotations that indicate how important Shakespeare and his contemporaries found dream material to be to the creative and intellectual processes in man.

What exactly happens to body, mind, and spirit when man is asleep? How do dreams come into being? According to Sandra Shulman, English writer on comparative religion, oneirology, the study and interpretation of dreams, was originally associated and inseparably tied in with the mystic roots of civilization, religion, and magic, to which medicine was also closely tied. She says, "Dreams might have remained in the nebulous atmosphere of poetry, superstition, and fairground quack-ery, but at the end of the last century a Viennese doctor, Sigmund Freud, saw them as the keys with which to unlock the doors of man's unconscious."

But what hath Freud wrought? Nothing less than the total rejection by establishment scientists and those following them of the ancient wisdoms contained in pre-Freudian dream interpretation, nothing less than the rejection of the psychic elements contained in the dream material and all the other manifestations of, an external derivation that did not fit in with Freud's notion of dreams representing man's suppressed libido. One of the best-known authorities on dreams is Calvin S. Hall, director of the Institute of Dream Research in Santa Cruz, California, and the author of a number of books on dream psychology. "A dream is a succession of images, predominantly visual in quality, which are experienced during sleep," Dr. Hall writes in *The Meaning of Dreams.* He views dreams much like stage plays. "A dream commonly has one or more scenes, several characters in addition to the dreamer, and a sequence of actions and interactions usually involving the dreamer. It resembles a motion picture or dramatic production in which the dreamer is both a participant and observer. Although a dream is a hallucination, since the events of a dream do not actually take place, the dreamer experiences it as though he were seeing something real."

This is a statement from what appears to be a specialist in dream research, and it is solidly based on Freudian concepts. Is a dream not real at times? Hall dismisses or, rather, avoids any discussion of psychic dreams or projection, both of which contain elements of reality and are not hallucinations. Nor does he acknowledge the amazing cases of inspiration contained in dreams, in which seemingly unqualified or uninstructive persons obtain specific information that leads them to invent things, to perform tasks for which they have not been schooled, and otherwise show evidence of external inspiration through the dream state. I am not referring here to the vaguely worded statements of poets and writers and musicians, that they are "inspired" by external sources, but to specific cases where entire projects have been completely designed through the channel of dreams.

"From our study of thousands of dreams, we know that they are relatively silent about certain kinds of conceptions and relatively vocal about others. Dreams contain few ideas of a political or economic nature. They have little or nothing to say about current events in the world of affairs. I was collecting dreams daily from students during the last days of the war with Japan, when the first atomic bomb was exploded, yet this dramatic event did not register in a single dream," writes Hall.

His statement as to the absence of political or economic ideas in dreams is false. As will be shown in some of the material presented in these pages, it is exactly such material that pervades the dreams of those capable of prophetic expression. As for the absence of registering a specific event even though the experimenter expects it to be registered, that is like saying, "Why doesn't the medium get my Uncle Joe?" when I want her to get him. Surely we must judge results on scores, not try to explain why

they don't score when we want them to. Hall considers dreams primarily authentic records of a mind made anxious by conflict, that they are due to our inability to solve our problems in the waking state.

A somewhat different approach is taken by Erich Fromm, internationally recognized authority on psychology and author of a number of works, among which I consider *The Art of Loving* perhaps the most monumental contribution to human understanding. In a recent book entitled *The Forgotten Language*, Fromm says that it is more important to deal with the understanding of dreams than with their interpretation. He considers dreams to contain symbolic language, which he calls a language in its own right, "the only universal language the human race ever developed," and he sees the problem of dealing with dream material one of understanding this symbolism rather than looking for some artificially created code. "I believe that such understanding is important for every person who wants to be in touch with himself, and not only for the psychotherapist who wants to cure mental disturbances." Fromm quotes the Talmud, the sacred Hebrew book of learning: "A dream that is not understood is like a letter that is not opened."

Where Hall flatly refuses to recognize dream material as anything but hallucinatory, Fromm says, "The dream is present," real experience, so much so that it suggests two questions: what is reality? how do we know that what we dream is unreal and what we experience in our waking life is real?" The Italian playwright Luigi Pirandello has fashioned several dramas on this theme. Where

Freud and his disciples tended to look to dreams as expressions of unresolved libido conflicts, Fromm sees in them symbolic material, which, incidentally, is identical no matter what background the dreamer may have, no matter what kind of people are concerned. Fromm thinks that the symbolic language of dreams is "a language in which inner experiences, feelings and thoughts are expressed as if they were sensory experiences, events in the outer world. It is a language which has a different logic from the conventional one we speak in the daytime, a logic in which not time and space are the ruling categories, but intensity and association."

But dreams are all those things, and more. To begin with, the dream state covers such a large segment of human experience that it nearly rivals the waking state, although it may occupy only a small fraction of the conventional time spent by man while awake. I consider the dream state a state of heightened receptiveness, necessary to convey to man certain information that he would normally not accept because of the nature of his psyche. To perform effectively in the waking state, the unconscious part of the mind is generally shut off or subdued. Were it not so, man would not be able to function as efficiently as he frequently does. On the other hand, concentrating man's energies on purely mechanistic actions results in the suppression and shutting out of the more gentle vibrations of a creative-perceptive nature. Thus it is necessary to have two sets of circumstances if man is to function properly on all levels.

We already know what happens to man's body when he is asleep: the uncon-scious part of the mind is allowed free range of expression, while the physical body continues to function on a reduced scale, maintaining vital functions by an ingenious system, allowing just enough activity to maintain life, but not enough to intrude into the sleep state—at least, not in a fully balanced, healthy individual. The two other components of human personality, mind and spirit, or psyche, are not necessarily dormant. Freed from the necessity of operating the body vehicle, they can turn their energies toward goals that they are incapable of pursuing when they must look after the body. As far as the mind is concerned, as the "guardian of the vehicle," the natural task seems to be the filtering of information from outside, allowing it to come through and reach the unconscious level of mind in order to be understood by the dreamer. A degree of filtering is involved to make the material acceptable to the individual. The *psyche,* or spirit, is now free to send symbolic material upward toward the conscious level so it can be understood when the dreamer awakes.

We thus have two-way traffic, external material being received and sorted out, and internal material being sent out to the dreamer's conscious, to call his attention to certain conditions of which he is not normally aware. Both processes use imagery to express themselves, supplemented by seemingly auditory material; that is, the dreamer not only sees scenes but also hears sounds, or feels that he does. Since no one else outside the dreamer either sees the same scenes or hears the same sounds, they are evidently produced internally, stimulating the brain centers directly without the need to go through auditory or visual organs of the body. In a way, this is similar to transferring recordings from one machine to another without the use of an external microphone. The transfer is better since unwanted external noises are eliminated. The dream circuit is also direct and therefore more powerful than if the material were to go through external picture or sound sources.

I have divided the dream material into four major categories: dreams due to physical problems resulting in nightmares or distorted imagery; dreams due to suppressed material and useful for psychoanalytical processes; dreams of a psychic nature; and out-of-body experiences, also referred to as *astral projections.*

As far as physically induced dreams are concerned, there is little quarrel among psychiatrists as to their reality and frequent occurrence. When the body is loaded down with poisonous substances, through overeating or other malfunctions of the system, these processes can "press upon" the nerve center and cause nightmares or other forms of biochemically induced traumas, albeit of short duration, ending with the restoration of balance in the physical system, or the awakening of the dreamer. Even ordinary states of discomfort, such as the need to void, can cause this kind of dream. Only gypsy dream books would attach importance to expressions of this kind. But it is interesting to note that Dr. Hall sees a connection between such physical dreams and possible paranormal material. In discussing the ancient belief that dreams are produced "by the distemper of the inward parts," he speaks of dreams indicating future illnesses as *prodromic* dreams. The word comes from the Greek for "forerunner," and is interpreted by Hall as "a premonitory sign of disease." In this ancient belief, dreams of being suffocated or crushed, or of flying, were supposed to indicate the beginning of a lung disease. Hall puts emphasis on environmental factors affecting the sleeper as being responsible for certain types of physical dreams, such as a room that is too cold or too warm, or that does not contain enough air, and so on.

Dreams caused by physical pressures in no way relieve these pressures, nor do they contribute anything to the sleeper's well-being except perhaps to notify him of the existence of some disturbance in his body or environment. This is not surprising since I consider them due to a purely mechanical chain of reactions in the biochemical system of the body, not under the sleeper's control at all, or due to any kind of external forces. The physical system is out of balance because of one or the other cause, and the apparatus reacts to call attention to its plight. The moment the system is in balance again, the need for this action no longer exists and the physically induced dreams cease.

Dreams of the second category, those due to suppressed material, are grist for the mills of psychoanalysts. If the analyst follows the Freudian line of thinking, he will see suppressed libido and sexual symbols in every dream, and will explain the dreams on the basis of sexual maladjustments, needs, and symbolisms. If he is a Jungian he may do so in a number of cases that are sexual in content, but may explain other dreams as wish-fulfillment dreams or symbolic expressions along the lines of Erich Fromm. There is no gainsaying that dream material is a valuable tool for psychoanalytical interpretation, that psychoanalysis is very useful in many cases. But it is most useful when we are dealing with psychoneurotic persons, because a psychoneurotic can at times be cured through discussion of his suppressed problem. Not so with the psychotic individual, who is much less accessible to discussion of this kind. In that case the dream material becomes merely an informative tool to the doctor, but the two-way dialogue is either nonexistent or very much restricted, and practical results are therefore harder to obtain.

It is not the purpose of this book to go into the question of psychoanalytical dream interpretation, except to say that a certain percentage of all dreams belong in the category of such material, while an equally large and impressive number of dreams do not. Unfortunately, very few trained psychoanalysts understand the difference between symbolic dream material and true psychic dreams. They deal with psychic material as if it were simply symbolic material and, as a result, distort the interpretation. This is because the majority of clinical analysts and psychiatrists do not as yet recognize parapsychology as a sister science, or, if they do, they are not properly trained to apply its principles to their own work. Individual psychiatrists and analysts who know parapsychological methods are few, and there is a great need for more training of specialists in this field.

I went through psychoanalysis myself in the late 1940s, at a time when I was under great external pressure, and

thought that analysis would help me understand myself better. My therapist was Dr. E., who had been an assistant to Carl Jung. We spent a great deal of time looking over my dream material, and the doctor's method consisted in my first interpreting my own dreams, after which he would interpret them as he saw the material. There were a number of psychic dreams in the lot, and invariably, we came to different conclusions as to their meanings and derivations. After six or seven months I discontinued the sessions, and did not meet Dr. E. until many years later, when Eileen Garrett sponsored a psychotherapy forum in New York. "I am happy to see you here," Dr. E. said when he recognized me. I shook my head and replied, "No, Doctor, I am happy to see you here." Indeed, Dr. E. had become interested in the work of psychotherapy as practiced by leading parapsychologists of our day.

Before we turn our attention to the remaining two categories of dreams, that is, psychic dreams and out-of-body experiences, I will state what the differences are between these and conventional dreams. Dreams due to physical discomfort or environmental pressures and dreams of a psychoanalytical connotation are not nearly as vivid as psychic dreams or out-of-body experiences. The first two categories of dreams are more easily forgotten upon awakening unless they are immediately written down. Not so with psychic dreams or out-of-body experiences: one is rarely able to shake them, even if one does not write them down immediately. Some psychic dreams are so strong that they awaken the dreamer, and in most cases the dream remains clearly etched into the memory for long periods after the dream has occurred.

With dreams of categories one and two, impossibilities occur with great frequency. Perhaps Dr. Hall's statement that dreams are hallucinatory and not real is understandable in the light of the nature of such dreams. Clearly, dreams in which impossible events take place, mostly out of ordinary time-and-space sequence, must be hallucinations; but psychic dreams and out-of-body experiences are nearly always logical sequences of events, entirely possible in terms of ordinary logic, and are received by the dreamer with a sharpness and clarity of which the first two types of dreams are not.

Although all four categories have a common denominator, that is, the dream state, the first two categories are jumbled, sometimes very confusing bits and pieces of information, while the latter two categories are nearly always complete messages or events, devoid of the fantasy trips and sleight of hand so common with the first two categories of dreams. Of course, there are cases in which the categories of dreams are intermingled, and purely symbolic material may become superimposed on true psychic material. This happens when a dreamer is not fully relaxed, or is not a very good recipient of external material. But a skilled parapsychologist can differentiate between the portion of the material properly belonging to category one or two and that representing authentic psychic material.

A *psychic dream* is a dream in which material from an external source or from an internal source not ordinarily active in the conscious state is received. In the vernacular, this means that psychic dreams contain information from messages, warnings, or other communications from individual entities outside the dreamer's consciousness, or they may contain material obtained through psychic abilities of the dreamer, abilities that he does not normally use in the waking state. This is the main body of the present work, a much neglected aspect of dreaming. Although the evidential material in this field is nearly overwhelming both in scope and amount, comparatively little of it has found its way into the works on dreams and dreaming used as textbooks.

Norman MacKenzie in *Dreams and Dreaming*, published in 1965, devotes a few scant pages to paranormal dreams as such, unearthing the old chestnut about Abraham Lincoln's premonitory dream of his death, and Bishop Joseph Lanyi's dream of the assassination of Archduke Franz Ferdinand in 1914. MacKenzie writes, "The difficulty is that no aspect of dreams is more intriguing and less amenable to systematic inquiry. It may not be impossible to set up significant experiments to test the extent and character of such dreams, but it is very hard and such experiments are still in the earliest stages." MacKenzie is not a doctor, but essentially a journalist, although he has taught sociology in England and in the United States. For a knowledgeable writer to say in 1965 that "experiments are still in the earliest stages" shows a monumental lack of knowledge and understanding of parapsychology.

By the mid-1960s tremendous amounts of material had been gathered at Duke University and other centers of learning,

Professor Hornell Hart had already published his famous dream experiments, and material was freely available to those seeking it. As for Hart's dream experiments, they consisted in a methodical survey of the dreaming habits of three hundred students under his control. The participants were required to allow themselves to be awakened at regular intervals, and to record their dream experiences. Hart later concluded that many of the dreams involving the apparitions of the so-called dead were veridical, and that these apparitions were what they claimed to be, i.e., the spirits of the dead.

George Nobbe, in the New York *News* of November 2, 1969, undertook a popular survey of dream research then going on. At that time the Central Premonitions Bureau in New York, headed by R. B. Nelson, served as a channeling organization for premonitory dreams. My own organization, the New York Committee for the Investigation of Paranormal Occurrences, founded in 1962, also had already accumulated a significant number of such dreams. Nelson breaks down his material into eleven categories, from death and disaster, news, prominent personalities, natural disasters, war, space, politics, and so forth, to a special category for the Kennedy family. This is not a scientific approach but simply a convenient arrangement. Nevertheless, some impressive cases are quoted, such as the dream of a California woman that the United States would be attacked by a foreign country somewhere in southern California. Incredible and as unlikely as the dream was, a few days later a Mexican vessel fired on a tuna boat in the Pacific Ocean near San Diego.

Another contributor to Nelson's office reported a dream concerning illness on the spacecraft *Apollo 7* and difficulty while landing. It turned out later that the spacecraft came down upside-down in the Pacific, and that the crew were suffering from colds. Far from making light of recent investigation into paranormal dreams, the article quotes Maimonides Hospital experimenter Dr. Stanley Krippner from an article he published in *Psychoanalytic Review*, "Paranormal dream data collected at the Maimonides Medical Center include several incidents of precognition."

Katharine Cover Sabin, in a work entitled *ESP and Dream Analysis*, brings some common sense to the vast field of psychic dream material. "The psychological dream factors discovered by Freud do not rule out precognition in dreams; instead the dream psychology often forwards the parapsychological content. Dreams can be *realistically* true or *symbolically* true. Gifted psychics are more prone to receiving understandable predictive material than non-psychics, who usually receive dream guidance through symbols. However, both the gifted and the ungifted should make a study of dream symbols, for parapsychological material is most often presented symbolically."

This is only partially correct. An impressive number of dreams are devoid of all symbolic material and present events in the dreamer's life or in someone else's life that have not yet transpired, but eventually do, precisely in the same manner and in all detail as foreseen in the dream state. In fact, to accept symbolical dream material as indicative of precognition presents a somewhat dangerous attitude: when it becomes necessary to interpret symbolic material to arrive at some clear-cut meaning concerning future events, the conservative or orthodox psychiatrist may justifiably reply that his interpretation is just as valid, or more so. Fortunately, there is an overwhelming body of "clear dreams" free of symbolic embellishments, and capable of immediate understanding by experts and laymen alike.

"The future is not irrevocably fated. When we know the trend of the future, we can often avoid pitfalls or be led to opportunities," Sabin continues. She holds that there are four keys to the parapsychological content of dreams, namely, fixed symbols, association, the play upon words, and arbitrary coding. This is a vastly superior method to pure psychoanalysis, especially as Sabin is a professional psychic and accepts the existence of discarnate entities, i.e., *spirit*. But it still uses the methodology of psychiatry with material that often seems hard to categorize, because so many dreams are applicable only to the individual involved and to no other. Sabin has developed special cards, which she uses with the help of computers to give dream interpretations. As the title of her book implies, she is primarily concerned with ESP content in dreams, but the ESP-type dream is merely one of several kinds of paranormal dream occurrences.

The evidential material obtained through the mediumship of Edgar Cayce is so impressive that his views concerning psychic dreams should also be taken into account when evaluating a proper approach to psychic dreams. Dr. Harmon H. Bro, in his book *Edgar Cayce on Dreams*, states that "in Cayce's view it was not only business details that would present themselves in advance to the dreamer and that any condition ever becoming reality is first dreamed. He meant major developments that were the outgrowth of the directions and habits of a life or lifetimes."

Cayce also taught others how to dream constructively, as it were, and to recall their dreams upon awaking. Bro, in another work, entitled *Dream in the Life of Prayer*, says, "It was the contention of Cayce in his hypnotic state that every normal person could and should learn to recall his dreams so that he might study them for clues for better functioning in his daily life." Bro remarks that later studies of dreams in the laboratory uncovered a remarkable ability shown by some subjects to interpret their own dreams while under hypnosis. "Had Cayce done his work several decades later he might well have been studied for his hypnotic interpretations of his own if not the dreams of others."

Cayce died in 1945, at a time when research hypnosis was not yet as widespread or as fully recognized as a tool as it is today. Like Jungian analysts, Cayce believed that dreams should be studied in series, not just as individual dreams. Since Cayce never claimed credit for his own pronouncements, this approach must be credited to the "source" working through the entranced Cayce. "Using sets of dream in this way, one could proceed as a cryptographer: using gains of interpretation made in one dream to illuminate others similar to it," writes Bro. Of course, since Cayce or his source used a unique system of looking at life, the

Cayce view concerning dreams must of necessity also be specific and in line with his general thinking.

Although Cayce held that the great majority of dreams could be interpreted and were best interpreted by the dreamer, once he knows how to do this, Cayce also contributed a great deal to the interpretation of dreams of others.

"As the entranced Cayce interpreted dreams," Bro states, "he began with their *function*. They could be found to operate in one of two ways—a combination of these two ways. Some dreams are primarily concerned with advancing the dreamer's practical effectiveness in the concerns of his daily life; these problem-solving dreams were the province of the 'subconscious' that held the dreamer's habits, functions, style of life and immediate practical problems. Other dreams were clearly concerned with changing the dreamer, with improving his commitments, and enlarging his self-image, enhancing his understanding of life, or even relating him better to God. Such dreams were primarily the province of the 'superconscious' though mediated through the subconscious for the actual dream production on the stream of consciousness. Still other dreams contained elements of both kinds of dreaming: problem-solving and transformative. Such mixed contents might appear in successive portions of one dream, or more often in layers of meaning of the same dream symbols (as Freud so well demonstrated). In any case, dreams were 'answers' to the life of the dreamer."

I have subdivided psychic dreams, or paranormal dreams, into three categories: *prophetic dreams*, in which future events are foreseen or foretold; *warning dreams*, in which future events are depicted in such a way that one can alter the results; *ESP dreams*, containing telepathic material frequently of simultaneous events or retrocognitive material, such as psychometric dreams in which events from the past unknown to the dreamer are experienced.

From the dawn of civilization, attention was paid to what a man dreamed, but the evaluation differed from culture to culture. Unfortunately, there was no distinction made between purely symbolic dreams and true psychic dreams, and astral projection was lumped in with the other dream material as well. Consequently, great significance was attached to dreams containing symbolic material pertaining solely to the individual dreamer, and having no relation to the future. This went to extreme lengths: the Bible and other ancient documents are full of interpretations, in which differentiation has to be made between the dream image and its meaning in the world of ordinary reality.

There were such clear-cut psychic dreams as that of Calpurnia, the wife of Julius Caesar, who told her husband on the day of his murder that she had dreamed of his assassination that night, that she had seen his statue in the Senate bleeding from many wounds. Caesar, however, rejected his wife's warnings as hysteria and went to the Senate, where he was assassinated by the daggers of many politicians. Even less inclined to accept the generally prevailing attitude toward dreams was the philosopher Cicero, who expressed his doubts that dreams had any meaning whatsoever, and opined that the gods had better things to do than to warn people through such unreliable means as dreams.

Philosophers of antiquity were like the conventional scientists of today: Aristotle could not accept the possibility that supernatural beings were in contact with men through dreams, or that the soul could detach itself from the body during sleep, as in astral projection. If anything, he was a skeptic. On the other hand, there was hardly a ruler of importance in ancient Greece or the Roman Empire who did not consult with an interpreter of dreams. The Bible is full of such incidents, beginning with the amazing rise of Joseph in Egypt and going all the way to the angel who appeared to Joseph, the father of Jesus, in a dream advising him that it was now safe to return to Israel since Herod was dead.

The second-century philosopher Artemidorus stated that "dreams and visions are infused into men for their advantage and instruction," and it is on his work that most of the subsequent dream books are based. However, Artemidorus went to great pains to explain that the interpretation of a dream depended largely on the interpreter, and not so much on the dreamer. Contemporary psychiatry and analysis put the emphasis on the dreamer, not the practitioner. Sandra Shulman, in her book *Dreams*, makes an interesting point here. "Artemidorus preceded Freudian thought by nearly two thousand years when he wrote that dreams of excrement and mud signify wealth and treasure, an interpretation also to be found in the Assyrian Book of Dreams."

Artemidorus considered dreams from two points of view: ordinary dreams caused by mental or physical conditions of the dreamer and his environment; and dreams pertaining to the future, that is, containing material and symbols that could be interpreted to foretell events.

The ancients put great stock in omens, portents of events in the future that were not by themselves clear-cut or definitive, but that could be interpreted as having significance for either the person observing the omen, or sometimes entire groups of people. Omens are more in the nature of disguised warnings of things to come, a sort of bonus for those who can read the signs and benefit from that ability. To this day many Asians put great stock in omens, even to the point of stretching connections. The interpreter's point of view plays a significant role in the interpretation of such omens, if not his suggestions, which may in some instances help make the omen become a reality. I find the majority of omens far-fetched and the links between them and actual events in the future extremely tenuous. On the other hand, there are numerous instances of clear-cut visions obtained in the dream state that give details of future events that should render the dreamer capable of doing something about the impact of such an event.

Why should it be necessary to disguise so many warnings in obtuse terms, poetic language, hints, and other indirect forms of communication? I therefore regard the majority of such symbolic material as not objective per se but derived largely from the mind of the beholder. Examples include dreams of flying, which once were interpreted as signifying happiness, wealth, and fame, if the dreamer landed easily, but if he fell and hurt himself, the dream signified the opposite. In the Far East it was believed that it was important to know the cause of bad dreams because that way one could get rid of fear or worry. Frequently, opposites were seen in dream actions: if one dreamed of taking something, it really meant giving or if one dreamed of being hungry, it really meant that one was more than satisfied. All over the ancient world, people were encouraged to sleep inside the sacred precincts of temples, in the expectation that healing gods would descend and heal them in their sleep. Many of the results were due to autosuggestion but there are instances in which psychic healing took place during sleep very much as it does in modern healing practices.

As the ancient world gave way to Christianity, much of the advanced knowledge concerning human nature accumulated by pagan civilizations was either lost or destroyed by the emerging Christian church. Although the early Christians accepted dreams and sleeping in specially constructed churches as part of seeking divine guidance, gradually dreams became suspect because so many of them seemed to be psychic in nature and thus were linked with witchcraft and the occult. As the Church became less tolerant of other religions, dream interpretation became dangerous for those practicing it publicly. It did not stop people from interpreting their own dreams or seeking the help of "wise men" or "wise women."

PROPHETIC DREAMS

All those dreams in which some information is received pertaining to the future are *prophetic dreams,* in essence something

that could not occur by orthodox standards, but that nevertheless does. Prophetic dreams may range all the way from giant prophecies involving entire peoples or the world, to minor concerns of persons pertaining to their own future or that of friends and relatives. What all prophetic dreams have in common is the element of future events that have not yet transpired, that have not yet begun to shape up in any form whatever, and that therefore could not be foretold by the use of the ordinary five senses.

A frequently heard criticism of prophetic material alludes to the probability factor, or informed guessing on the part of the psychically gifted person. Such arguments are easily disposed of. No serious researcher in parapsychology takes a dream at face value unless it contains detailed material of a nature that makes it capable of being verified later. For example, a psychic announcing that a certain well-known statesman will be deposed or that some great luminary of the screen will remarry or that an aged politician will die is of no evidential value, because all these situations have a high degree of likelihood. If they come to pass it does not disprove the psychic's ability, but it leaves a great margin of doubt as to whether the psychic was drawing upon his inner resources or simply using his external reasoning faculties coupled with shrewd phrasing to make these "astonishing" predictions.

In some of my earlier works I made a distinction between prophecy and predictions in that I described prophecy as pertaining to major issues, worldwide situations, and prominent persons, whereas predictions might apply to anyone. A better term for foretelling events is *precognition*, implying foreknowledge, whereas predicting means foretelling. Often the prophecy is visual or perhaps only intuitive, and actual words are not used. The common denominator of this material is the future element, something that has not yet come to pass. It is essentially of little significance whether the information comes to the dreamer through visual stimulation, verbal expressions, intuitive feelings, or some other form of communication. The essence of it is that the message be clear, precise, and sufficiently detailed to warrant the term "prophecy."

Prophetic dreams are dreams in which some event or situation pertaining to someone's future is contained and remembered upon awakening. Prophetic material can be obtained in the waking state, too. I have already mentioned that a great percentage of psychic material comes unsought to persons in the dream state because it allows for a deeper and easier penetration of the conscious-mind shield that man possesses. Because of upbringing or our modern approach to phenomena of this kind, most people apply logical values to psychic material coming to them, and in the dream state, logic is absent. From the point of view of external persons wishing to convey messages to human beings, it is easier to get through to them while they are asleep and ready for dreams, than while they are busily engaged in their daily activities. In the dream state, they have man's full attention, even though he must wake up and remember in the end.

Some people go through psychically active periods and at other times they are unable to have any ESP experiences or they sleep many nights without recalling any unusual dreams. Undoubtedly, the ability to have psychic dreams is connected with the receptiveness of the individual, which in turn has a relationship to physical states, mental condition, and environment, if only concerning the "instrument" through which the material is received. Mrs. S.J.G. of Long Island, New York, explained, "I find that I go into psychic periods when almost every dream will be prophetic or I become more sensitive or even telepathic. I have also learned that if a dream of mine is prophetic, the time frame in which it will come true is from a few hours to around six years from the time of the dream."

Frequently, psychic people have to have company: when a prophetic dream is particularly upsetting, they take some consolation from similar dreams by other psychics, especially by well-known ones. Mrs. G. dreamed that the United States would be attacked by an atomic power, and she was shown the areas in which the attack would occur. The dream occurred to her in 1970, and she took great comfort from a similar prediction published by me in 1968, according to which we would be attacked on December 29, 1970. Happily, this prediction turned out to be out of date, if not false. Equally unreliable is the date of a similar prediction made by celebrated Chicago psychic Irene Hughes, who foresaw such an event around 1973. But mediums frequently foresee events without getting exact dates, or they may be off by considerable spans of time.

It would be foolish to dismiss some prophetic dreams just because the date for the predicted event has come and gone without the event transpiring. Mrs. G.

says, "Although I have many prophetic dreams I can never be sure when one is a prophetic dream and when not. There is one clue: my prophetic dreams are definite in their message. There is no symbolism, such as with most dreams. I see the events and actions as they will happen. The message is clear and not surrounded with symbols."

It is easy to see why "true dreamers," people gifted with the ability to foresee events in dreams, were considered in league with the devil in olden times. Mrs. G. had a rather unusual dream one night about a fire in the living room, and the strange thing about that fire was that it ran up the wall. The following day she happened to be talking to her neighbor, Jean, and Jean's mother, and she mentioned the unusual dream she had had the previous evening. The mother gave Mrs. G. a terrified look and ran away. The neighbor explained that earlier that morning her little boy had started a fire in the living room that caught on the curtains and did run up the wall. Fortunately, they were able to put it out in time. There was no way in which Mrs. G. could have had prior knowledge of this event.

Dr. Calvin Hall states, "Dreams are purely and simply hallucinations." He goes on to explain that a hallucination is an event that isn't really taking place, and that "dreams are creative expressions of the human mind," again intimating that for some reason we manufacture our own dreams, that dreams are the product of man. Hall has made no allowances for psychic dreams. He goes to great lengths to explain seemingly psychic dreams as expressions of human longings, needs, and problems. But he doesn't explain

how it is possible for dreamers to obtain exact knowledge of future events, details of which are not even in existence at the time of the dream.

German actress Christine Mylius has dreamed true since age twelve. At that time she had a dream in which she saw her elder sister on the water but somehow in the Alps as well. Three weeks later her sister drowned in a mountain lake in Bavaria. Since that time Mylius has registered over 2,500 dreams with Professor Hans Bender of the Freiburg Institute of Parapsychology. Her dream journal, containing two hundred pages of prophetic dreams, has just been published in Germany. These dreams contain correctly predicted traffic accidents involving her mother and her son, various suicides of friends and relatives, and material pertaining to total strangers that nevertheless turned out to be true. Mylius also was very good with newspaper headlines long before the events took shape and long before the printer actually set type for the headlines she dreamed of. On January 4, 1967, she correctly foretold and registered with Bender the headline pertaining to the *Apollo* catastrophe of January 27, 1967. Mylius notes that her most evidential dreams occurred to her when she was under emotional stress or pressure. With the realization of the dream material and her registration of it, the tension left her.

All kinds of people have "true dreams," that is, dreams that later come true. The ability spans every conceivable class of people, and there is absolutely no way of narrowing it down to any specific group of people. If anything, one might say that people who have no strong prejudices against ESP and who live fairly harmonious lives are more likely to have psychic dreams then others not so inclined. An example of a well-balanced individual who has shown an increasing amount of ESP is the artist Ingrid B., with whom I have worked on many occasions, investigating cases or experimenting with various forms of psychometry.

On March 8, 1972, Ingrid reported to me a dream she had on February 29, 1972. "I had a dream concerning a man at work. I dreamed he came into my office, was wearing a plaid sport jacket and turtleneck sweater and said, 'How are you?' and 'We must get together for a drink sometime.' The next morning the same friend did come into my office wearing the exact clothes I had seen him wear and he said, 'How are you?' followed by, 'We haven't talked in a while so we have to get together sometime.' Except for the slight variation in the last line, the dream was completely exact."

Since Ingrid's dream occurred only a day before the actual happening, one might conceivably assume that the thoughts of the event were already embedded in the unconscious mind of her friend. But there are difficulties with that explanation. While it might hold water for the clothes seen in the dream and actually worn by the man in real life, the choice of words could not have been preplanned, even if the man had intended to visit with the artist.

Ingrid reported another dream, which occurred on January 29, 1973. In the dream she saw a girlfriend she had not seen for almost a year. Ingrid was returning from Manhattan to her home on Staten Island, and as she was walking along Battery Park, she saw her friend coming the other way. It was springtime, and the friend looked thinner and better than she had ever seen her look. Ingrid noticed that her friend was wearing an antique white dress with embroidery on the front. Behind her lagged a tall, thin young man with sandy hair. He was wearing dark slacks and a white shirt with rolled-up sleeves and an open collar. He looked bored. As Ingrid passed her friend, she called out to her but her friend stuck up her nose and said, "Who needs you anyway?"

The dream seemed so unusual to Ingrid that she decided to call her girlfriend to check on its content. Her friend confirmed that she had been thinking of Ingrid the night before, and that she had recently lost twelve pounds and had stopped seeing a steady boyfriend. She described the boyfriend as tall, with sandy hair and wearing the clothes Ingrid saw him wear in her dream. As for the white dress that to Ingrid looked like an antique nightgown, her friend confirmed that she owned such a gown but that it had been in storage with her mother. At the time Ingrid was having her dream, she was thinking of getting it back. From this it would appear that Ingrid, in the dream state, was able to tune in on her friend's thoughts and permit her own unconscious mind to report them to her conscious mind to be sorted out, and eventually take some sort of action, which she did by meeting her friend.

A third dream reported by Ingrid: in September 1974, Ingrid and her fiancé had been thinking of buying an antique sofa, but could not find the right one. On September 10, 1974, Ingrid dreamed that she and her fiancé went into the country and stopped the car in front of a house where they saw a woman wearing a simple housedress. The house had a door in the center, a very peaked roof. As the woman in the dream stepped onto the lawn, she said, "I have something for you." The dream was so vivid that Ingrid decided it had significance for the future. On a hunch, she decided to follow up on an ad she had previously seen in *Antiques Magazine*, telephoned the advertiser and discovered that this dealer did have a sofa that looked like the one they were looking for. Under the circumstances, they decided to drive up that same weekend. "As we drove up to the house it appeared just as I had seen it in the dream. It was an eighteenth-century farmhouse with a door in the center of the eaves and the reason for the peaked roof was that it was actually a side entrance from the road. The woman was a simple lady wearing a flowered sort of housedress and I did buy the sofa."

Susannah D. of New Jersey is a housewife who has had evidential dreams since the age of twenty. After her marriage she lived for a time in Lake Worth, Florida, but three months later the family decided to come back to New Jersey. The night before they were ready to leave, Mrs. D. had a dream. She saw a woman dressed all in black standing beside a car turned upside-down, dabbing at her eyes with a white handkerchief. In the dream, the woman said to Mrs. D., "Please find my daughter, tell my daughter." Mrs. D. remembered clearly thinking in the dream that she forgot to ask the stranger for the name of that daughter, so how

could she tell her? The following morning Mrs. D. told her husband of the dream and begged him not to leave that morning. She felt it was a sure sign from fate that they would have an accident. But her husband became irritated at the thought of delay and insisted that they leave as planned. They weren't out of the state of Florida yet when upon rounding a curve they noticed a long line of cars and police cars rushing by. They stopped, and looked to see what was the matter. Down in a gully was a car upside-down, and a woman dressed all in black standing alongside, crying. Mrs. D. got out of her car and inquired what had happened. She was informed that the woman's daughter had been killed and was still trapped in the car.

Again, the dream content nearly fits the actual event, except that the information about the dead daughter was obtained from witnesses rather than from the woman in black. Nevertheless, this type of dream clearly shows that some people can tune in on future events before these events have become objective reality.

Sandra M. and her husband were on active military duty with the air force, stationed at Travis Air Force Base in California, when one of her many veridical dreams occurred to her in July 1970. Their best friends at the base were named Darlene and Reuben, the latter stationed in Vietnam and at the time not due back for another six months. In this dream Mrs. M. had the impression that Reuben was coming home soon but that when he got to the base he could not find Darlene. He looked and looked for her but then left because he could not wait. Mrs. M. reported this dream to her husband upon awakening and later in the day also to her friend Darlene. It seemed an unlikely dream since Darlene hardly ever went anywhere, so the likelihood of her husband returning and not being able to find her was remote. A month later Reuben came home on an emergency leave and when he got to Travis Air Force Base he couldn't find Darlene. So he left a note and went on to Santa Monica, where his grandmother was dying. Even though Darlene normally stayed around the house, that particular time she had gone square-dancing and did not return home until after midnight.

Another interesting dream concerned a future assignment. In May 1971, Mrs. M. dreamed that she and her husband would be assigned to Robins Air Force Base in Georgia. At the time there were thousands of possible bases for them to be sent to, so it was not a question of informed guessing. In October of the same year, her husband's orders came through that they were going to Robins. At the time when she had had the dream, even the air force did not know where to send them.

These two dreams and others of Sergeant Sandra M. are attested to by her friends and her service supervisor, so there is no doubt as to the authenticity of the reported material and the timing of it.

Frequently, events that come true at a later date cast a shadow ahead of them, and become known to people who have nothing whatsoever to do with the events themselves. Why this is so, and why certain people can thus tune in on future events that do not concern them personally is hard to figure out. But there is an overwhelming body of evidence that it occurs, sometimes frightening the dreamer, sometimes merely puzzling him.

Elaine F. of Chambersburg, Pennsylvania, had a dream in 1969 in which she saw a group of people at a party. They seemed like Girl Scouts to her. She was off in the trees looking on while the group was celebrating. Suddenly some people came out of nowhere and began killing the "Girl Scouts." The killers were dressed in black and had bushy hair. In the dream she was particularly frightened by the eyes of the leader, whom she saw clearly. When she awoke the following morning, she described the scene and how she had seen blood running from the wounds of the victims. Ten days later the Sharon Tate murders broke into the headlines. As soon as Mrs. F. saw a picture of Charles Manson in the newspapers, she recognized him as the man she had seen in her dream.

It is interesting to note that dreams, like other psychic impressions, sometimes reverse left and right or up and down, though not always. There is an old tradition that one can enter the world of magic by stepping through a mirror, and that a mirror is the borderline between the world of reality and imagination. Our retinas see things upside-down and straighten them up before forwarding the impression to the brain centers dealing with sight. In other words, we see the world upside-down, but perceive it as right-side up.

I am indebted to Dixie B. of Winston-Salem, North Carolina, for the account of a friend, choreographer Peter Van Muyden. The two belonged to an experimental group that had been practicing meditation and various forms of consciousness expansion under the direction of Pastor George Colgin of their local Baptist church. The dream that Van Muyden reported was this: when he was a young man in Holland, he had the same dream several times. He saw a castle with a "freeway" in front of it and a river flowing beside it. In the dream, he went through the gates, through a rose garden and into the castle. On the right he observed a stairway and in the middle of the stairs he saw an old woman. He went past her and saw two doors. He opened the door on the right and saw a room papered with Bordeaux red wallpaper, and a man hanging.

The dream made no sense to him at the time, but many years later he visited a castle and recognized it as the one in his dreams. There was the freeway in front, the river at the side, and the gates were the same, except that the position of the rose garden was reversed, as if seen through a mirror. When he entered the front door, the stairway was on the left. An old woman, the owner's aunt, did live there. He went up the stairs and since the garden stairway had been reversed from what he had seen in his dream, he decided to try the doorway on the left instead of on the right, and found it locked, but when he asked if he could see the room, he was told that the owner's aunt preferred to have it locked. It seems that the contractor who had renovated the castle had hanged himself in that

room. When the room was finally opened to Van Muyden, he saw that it was covered by the Bordeaux red wallpaper he had seen in his dream.

The dreamer not only foresaw a future event before he had knowledge of it or before he had any contact with those who would eventually lead him to the place where the event would take place, but his dream even includes a tragedy, the contractor's suicide, which is subject to a number of imponderables. Nevertheless, the contractor hanged himself, and the dream became reality many years after the dreamer had perceived it. Dreams of this kind seem to indicate an almost fatalistic sequence of events, even covering the seemingly free will and actions of other people unconnected with the dreamer.

Probably the least likely group of professionals to accept psychic material as true are magicians and other illusionists. There are a few notable exceptions where magicians have had experiences themselves that they cannot explain away. Such was the case of Barrie Schlenker, who worked under the professional name of Vincent Barrett, and who made his home in Lehighton, Pennsylvania. Billed as the man with the X-ray eyes, Barrett presented a program of mentalism feats, which are termed "stunts" and do not involve any kind of psychic ability. Nevertheless, on the morning of March 10, 1964, while he was living at home with his mother and grandmother, he had a dream that he recorded upon awakening:

"The dream was one of those vivid ones that seemed so real at the time. I was dreaming that for a reason unknown to me I was driving my car in my bathrobe and pajamas. I didn't know where I was going. Perhaps if I would have been allowed to finish the dream I would have found out, but I was suddenly awakened by the sound of a bell ringing with urgency. I knew immediately what I was hearing: my grandmother had been ill for several years, she had had several strokes and many bad heart spells during that time, and I had built a bell-pull system in our house so that if she needed help at any time she could pull a cord in any room of the house and a bell would ring in the stairwell loud enough for anyone else in the house to hear. This was the bell I heard on the morning of March 10, 1964. I got up as quickly as I could out of a sound sleep and went downstairs to see what was the matter. My mother and grandmother had gotten up about an hour earlier, had breakfast and had been washing their breakfast dishes when my grandmother had suffered another heart spell. She sat down on a chair in the kitchen, never to get up again. Mother ran to the bell rope and rang it to wake me. As I ran downstairs I could see my grandmother propped up on the kitchen chair and I knew what had happened. My mother said I should quickly call the doctor and then go out in the country to get my aunt, mother's sister. I made the phone call and without taking time to dress, just putting a coat over my shoulders on top of my bathrobe and pajamas, I got into my car and drove away, just then remembering my dream of only a few moments earlier."

Dreams are by no means always harbingers of important events, nor do they necessarily contain messages of vital sig-

nificance. The majority of dreams seem unimportant in the long view, since they pertain to relatively unimportant matters. One wonders why the powers that be bother to allow people a glance into the future in such trifling matters. The answer is obvious: paranormal dreams are subject to laws, just like everything else in nature. They are not the whim of people, even those on the Other Side of life. If a person has the gift of psychic dreams, whatever material impresses itself on his unconscious mind at the time will be received and remembered upon awakening, whether it is important or not. There is no such thing as selective dreaming in this category of dream material, i.e., material pertaining to the so-called future.

Sometimes paranormal dreams occur in spurts, and a person may have one, then none at all for several years thereafter, when the ability resumes again. Whether this has to do with the need for paranormal dreams to be received, or whether this reflects changes in environment or physical and mental dates of the dreamer, is hard to tell. After all, even the most renowned mediums have "off" days when they do not function at all in terms of psychic receptiveness. When it comes to dreams with messages of some urgency, certainly the need to be received plays an important part in their frequency. In this chapter I am dealing primarily with general psychic dreams, mainly the tuning in on future events without selective evaluation on the part of the dreamer and apparently spanning the entire width from very unimportant detail to material of considerable significance to either the dreamer, someone known to the dreamer, or someone not known to the dreamer who might be notified.

Thus it is by no means unique that Judith White should not have had any psychic dreams between 1955 and 1964, the year that the next event took place. In 1964 her mother-in-law was in the hospital, having been in poor health for a number of years, in and out of the hospital. This time White had a feeling her mother-in-law would not come home. Such feelings could be explained on the basis of her knowledge and her concern for her relative. Unless such feelings of impending doom are of a specific and detailed nature, containing dates and circumstances and such that could be compared with actual happenings, it seems unreasonable to call them psychic, premonitory material although they may be. Alternate explanations are also possible and should attempt to explain events of this kind first by ordinary means, before turning to psychic avenues.

One morning while her mother-in-law was still in the hospital, White was at the stage where sleep was about to end, yet she was not fully awake. At this moment she saw the entire family together, including her husband's brother who lived in California and whom she had never met. She had seen pictures of him, however. She had the feeling that they were all together because her mother-in law had died. This was in the first week of March 1964. On March 22 her mother-in-law died and the family was all together, including the brother from California. It was exactly as she had seen in her vision shortly before awakening, several weeks earlier.

To illustrate how seemingly unimportant dreams of this nature can be, another of White's experiences serves as an example. In her dream she saw herself sitting at a round table. With her were an unidentified woman and a man in uniform whom she did not know. They were drinking coffee when White asked the man for his name. He pointed to a name tag on his uniform that read "D. J. Brook." White felt there was another letter at the end of the last name and thought that the name should be spelled Brooke. She asked him what the D. J. stood for and he said that he was a disc jockey in the service. With that she awoke, wondering who the man was and why she remembered the dream so clearly. She immediately called a friend, Heather MacDonald, of Indian Orchard, Massachusetts, and told her of this dream in case she should meet someone by that name.

Three days later White stopped at the local library to pick up a few books. After she returned home she opened one of the books and started to read, and the first sentence jumped out: "The nameplate on the door read Dr. John Brooke." It is easy for the conscious or logical part of the mind to interpret, even in the dream, the initials D. J. as disc jockey, because of the popular term DJ used for disc jockey. But why would so insignificant an event as reading a line in a library book selected at random for entertainment purposes be foreshadowed in a psychic dream? Again, the answer can only be that this category of psychic dream is an almost mechanical tuning in, at random, as it were, by the sleeper into the so-called future, not necessarily for any particular purpose. It may be compared to a searchlight mounted high on a tower scanning the beach below as a matter of routine; once in a while an object may be picked out by the searchlight and come to the knowledge of the man operating the light. More often, the light just scans the beach and nothing particular is observed.

Barbara Heath has had a number of veridical dreams—psychic dreams that do come true—throughout the years. One of her most interesting premonitory dreams occurred on July 3, 1969. She dreamed she was back in her hometown of Richmond, Virginia, driving down Brookland Park Boulevard, the section of town in which she had grown up. But it didn't look the same in her dream: buildings that used to be standing at the time she lived there were now torn down; new buildings had been erected in their place. Even the old house in which she used to live was torn down. Heath felt lost, as if she were in a strange town where nothing was the same as she knew it. The streets were more crowded with people than she remembered, and as the dream proceeded, she noticed that she was looking out of the window of a house. There was a terrible storm outside, the wind was blowing furiously and trees were bending in the wind. She noticed that water was reaching up to the window that she thought was a second-story window, and waves were breaking all around the house. Then she noticed a boat bobbing nearby, and for some reason she wanted to go out and cross the street to get some aspirins, but a woman whom she did not recognize wouldn't let her go, telling her that she would drown. As the boat passed

by a building, the back part of it, which was some sort of recreation hall or banquet room, caved in. There seemed to be no one in it, however. Suddenly Heath saw herself in front of a large department store, either Miller and Rhodes or Talheimers', downtown, near the James River. By now it had stopped raining and people were taking down their umbrellas. She noticed that two women were selling flowers in front of the store, a common practice in Richmond. At this point she awoke from her dream.

Nine days later, Heath and her family took a vacation to Richmond to visit her mother and relatives. While there they were riding down the same street she had seen in her dream, in the same section, and she found buildings torn down and new ones put up and everything exactly the way it had occurred to her nine days earlier in her dream. Although her old house was still standing, which it had not been in her dream, it had changed a great deal. Still, Heath could not understand the second part of her dream involving a possible flood. Upon returning home, Heath confided her dream to a friend, Nancy Ernest, of Lafayette, Louisiana. Two weeks went by and then the newspapers brought accounts of a flood in Virginia and of the James River overflowing. The area around Talheimers' department store was particularly affected by the flood.

Here we have two separate paranormal dreams joined together by the common denominator, i.e., the location. Even though the dreamer was not present during the second part of the dream, it occurred to her because she happened to have been tuned in on the future of a place she was going to visit, and because she had paid a visit to Richmond, a future event in the "life" of the city of Richmond also intruded into her original dream. It is almost as if one were to take photographs at random of a specific area; depending upon the position of the camera, one will get a section into the picture, and part of an adjoining section perhaps. If one were to move to the left or to the right one would get a different section of the panorama into the photograph. The panorama is indivisible, stretching from left horizon to right horizon, and up and down; but the field of view is limited to the eyes of the beholder or the lens of the camera and accordingly one will obtain a picture of a certain section of the whole.

Heath wondered whether dreams of this kind are always exact duplications of events to follow. "In some of my dreams that have come true the details are a little different and sometimes instead of the person I dreamed about it is his friend or kin it happens to. And at times I play the part of the person the incident happens to and my family are the actors for someone else's family."

Many dreams of this nature foretell death or tragedy, but such subjects should not be confused with so-called warning dreams. In the case of *warning dreams* action may be taken to avert the outcome of the dream, whereas in the dream discussed here, the events take place as foreseen, perhaps with minor changes in detail, but not in outcome.

Grace Middleton, a retired nurse living in Kentucky, had a number of psychic experiences, ranging all the way from experiences with apparitions to premoni-

tory dreams. Middleton and her husband were on vacation in Florida when she dreamed that her husband and she were walking down the aisle of their church in a funeral procession. She saw a casket at the front and when she tried to see who was in it, she was pulled back by a hand on her shoulder. Their church has a platform for the pulpit and flowers had always been arranged to each side of the casket when there was a funeral. In this dream funeral the flowers were on the platform on each side of the pulpit. That had never been done, so on awakening, Middleton told her husband about the dream and said that when they got home she would inquire of the florist, who happened to be a friend. The dream came to her twice more on the trip home, each time exactly the same. By that time they had reached their house and as she entered her front door the phone was ringing. When she answered, she heard a strange voice telling her, "Thank goodness, you all got back. They are trying to hold the funeral for you and can wait no longer."

It turned out that the dead man was her husband's cousin Irvin, who had been raised by her husband's mother, with the result that the two men had been like brothers. They rushed to the church, and as they went down the aisle, Middleton grabbed her husband's arm and pointed to the pulpit. The flowers were arranged just as she had seen them arranged in her dream in Florida two weeks earlier.

Here we have a need to be informed, although the message did not quite accomplish what it evidently had meant to: bringing them home faster so they could attend the funeral without it having to be held up for them. However, since Middleton had the dream three times in a row there is the possibility of spirit intervention, that the dead man had been trying to get through to them to be sure they would attend his funeral. Nevertheless, in the absence of an identifying name to allow the Middletons to hurry home, we cannot be sure of this interpretation.

Another example of a warning dream that was not recognized as such, but that could not have been acted upon anyway, occurred to Middleton some years later, when she was vacationing during the summer in Denver. Again, she dreamed the same dream twice. In the dream she saw a casket in their local funeral home and noticed that the furniture, which had never been changed, was somewhat different from what she knew it to be. In the dream a davenport that had always faced the casket was now to the right of it. She saw her Sunday school teacher come in, and saw herself seated in the middle of the davenport. The teacher passed the vacant space to the left and in front of her and sat to her right. She put her arm around her and said, "I feel so sorry for you. I don't know what to do." Middleton saw flowers with a large white lily cross in the middle. When the same dream occurred to her a second time, she told her husband about it, remarking that she feared something might have happened to her Sunday school teacher's grandson, who had been seriously ill when they had left town. She decided to write the Sunday school teacher a letter, telling her how much she meant to her and the church and town.

When she arrived home she found that her teacher's grandson was well, and

under the circumstances, she dismissed the dream. Then her premonitory dream became reality: she found herself at the funeral parlor of her hometown, the furniture had been moved just as she had seen it in the dream, and the flowers were exactly like the large white lily cross she had seen in her dream; but her husband was in the casket, having died suddenly from a heart attack, and her old Sunday school teacher was consoling her, uttering exactly the same words she had heard her speak in her dream two months prior to the event.

Here we have more than a premonition of an actual event that took place later; we have words selected by a person that could not have been thought of before there was need for them to be spoken. The teacher could have chosen different words to express the same sentiment, yet she did not. What compelling force makes us use ideas and words in just such a way, and no other, and how is it possible that someone may have foreknowledge of our choice of specific words on specific occasions long before the occasions have arisen that would allow us to formulate our sentences in just that manner? Are we controlled by some powerful force of destiny without realizing it, or do our independent, willful actions and thoughts cast a shadow ahead of what we call objective reality in such a manner that some people can become aware of them ahead of time? Such considerations seem to involve a reevaluation of our concepts of time and space.

There is another consideration to be taken into account: to what extent are we permitted to obtain advance information on events that will later occur in our lives? I have no doubt that an orderly system exists, beyond the law of cause and effect as we know it, and that this system rules the nature and amount of information we may obtain concerning future events. From the material I have investigated over the years it seems to me that at times we are given exact advance information, while at other times we are given nothing whatsoever. In between lie the "veiled information" type dreams, not symbolic, but significant only in retrospect or to a very astute person, exhausting every conceivable avenue of interpretation.

In the case of Middleton one should include a dream that she had shortly before her husband's death. In that dream she saw her dead mother standing in the doorway of her bedroom, looking at her as if she felt sorry for her. She had this dream three times in a row, and the day after the last occurrence of it her husband died. Obviously, her discarnate mother was aware of the impending death of Middleton's husband, thus providing that the dead frequently have advance knowledge of events that we, in the physical state, do not possess except when we have psychic experiences. This does not mean that the dead are necessarily smarter than the living, but it does mean that there must be a reservoir of information upon which the dead can readily draw. It also proves that the system involving our departure from the physical world is a well-supervised setup, regulated by laws of which we know as yet very little. In other words, people do not die accidentally, nor does death occur unexpectedly, as far as "the system" is concerned. It only appears that way to us

because we do not see the entire picture from our vantage point.

But the more we familiarize ourselves with psychic dream material and the possibility of it, the more likely we are to intrude into the area of foreknowledge and the more we will understand larger portions of the whole picture, both from the physical side and from the spiritual side of life. By being incarnate we are in effect cut off from knowledge of the entire picture, and only when we leave the physical body do we partake of the complete information concerning ourselves. Only the spirit entity is complete, while in the body it conforms to the limitations of a three-dimensional world that ordinarily excludes foreknowledge of events to come. During psychic dreams we are temporarily and partially able to pierce the "iron curtain" between the three-dimensional world and the fun world of spirit, thereby obtaining bits and pieces of information that in the spiritual world are clearly visible to one and all.

Paranormal dreams are comparatively frequent in young children. This is not surprising since ESP seems to be prevalent between the ages of four and eight, after which it frequently disappears, only to resurface around age seventeen or eighteen. A case in point is Sandra Staylor of Chesapeake, Virginia. Staylor is a housewife with two sons, and lives just outside Portsmouth, Virginia. Her husband works for an electric power company, and prior to her marriage, Staylor worked as a cashier and bookkeeper. She clearly recalls her first paranormal dream, when she was six years old. The dream was as follows:

Her father was building a house on a lot between their house and that of a neighbor whose daughter was a year younger than Sandra. There was a pile of dirt from the digging of the foundation and it was near the property line close to the kitchen door of their house. The neighbor's girl and Sandra were playing on the dirt mound when the girl said, "My aunt had a baby girl last night and she named her Nancy." The dream ended there.

A little more than a year later, Staylor's father purchased the lot between their home and that of the neighbor. As he was a contractor, he planned to build a house on the lot and sell it. From the foundation digging there was a pile of dirt in exactly the place Sandra had dreamed. One day, the neighbor's daughter and Sandra were playing on the mound of dirt. While playing, the girl suddenly said, "My aunt had a baby girl last night." And before she could finish the sentence, Sandra said, "Yes, I know, and she named her Nancy!" This proved to be entirely correct. It should be noted here that the intent to buy the empty lot had not yet come into the consciousness of Sandra's father, nor had the name Nancy been selected for the baby girl inasmuch as at the time of Sandra's dream the girl's aunt was not yet pregnant!

Sometimes paranormal dreams of this kind tune in on events in the distant future, sometimes into events only a few hours away. When Staylor was in high school, she happened to be out of school for two weeks because of the flu, and was not in touch with the goings-on at school, including coming events. The

night before she was to return to her class, she had a dream in which she saw herself giving an animal show in the school auditorium. She had snakes, an armadillo, a lion, and many other animals to show. When she took the lion from his cage, a boy in the audience started roaring at him and the lion broke loose and went into the audience after the boy. In the dream all the children had to leave the auditorium and the lion was caught before he could hurt anyone.

The following day Staylor returned to school and that same morning her home room and several others were taken to the auditorium for an animal show. A woman was giving it and she had all the animals Sandra had seen in her dream. When she took the lion from his cage, the boy sitting next to Sandra began roaring at him, the lion broke loose, and school authorities told the children to leave the auditorium. Fortunately, the lion was caught before anyone was hurt, precisely as Sandra had seen in her dream.

Here we have no element of warning, no particular gain from foreknowledge of the event, except in the nature of seeing a preview of a movie before the rest of the population has a chance to see it.

"I believe very strongly in God and feel that this is his way of warning us of things to come," Sandra explains. "I do not believe in predestination. I believe we create today what will happen in the future and God is warning us of the consequences of our actions. I believe that some predictions do not come true because the people involved see or are told what is coming and change their ways, thus changing their destiny."

That is Staylor's personal conviction, and based only upon her own experiences. Possibly, if she had access to other psychic dreams where the warning element was absent or where nothing could be done to avert a foreseen event, she might feel differently about the nature and reality of predestination.

The so-called future is not a set condition, inflexible and inalterable. Certain events are programmed for us to encounter, because our reaction to these events seems to be of great importance in determining our progress. This is of particular importance in determination of karmic accomplishments or indebtedness. But there is some indication that the future keeps forming as we go along, and that perhaps a dreamer might be able to tune in only on part of it at a given moment, while at a later time he might see more of the future.

I have on record an interesting dream reported by Sara McA., who at the time of the report made her home in Magnolia, Arkansas. When she was ten years old, Sara had a recurrent dream in which she saw a certain house that she had never seen in her present life. There was nothing outstanding about the house, but she noticed that a gravel road ran directly in front of it. Seven years later she took a trip to a town she had never visited. There, to her amazement, was the house she had seen in her dream, except for one detail: there was no gravel road in front of it. It so happened that the following year Sara took another trip to the same town, and again found herself in front of the house of her dream. Imagine her surprise, when she noticed that the

gravel road of her dream had now been completed.

It almost seems as if events are moving at a set speed along a time track and we, the actors, are moving on another band. At times we seem able to jump from our slower-moving track to the faster-moving time track and glimpse part of what lies ahead in our future, but that is in the present as seen from the point of view of the faster-moving time track itself. The relationship between the psychic dreamer and events in the future is strictly relative and if we were capable of viewing both our progress and that of the events depicted in our dreams from an outside vantage point, perhaps we would be able to understand better the nature of what we now call, for want of a better term, the future. Unless we gain new understanding of the nature of time we will never be able to reconcile certain prophetic dreams with our natural view of a well-ordered, logically impelled universe.

Take a dream reported to me by a psychic friend, artist Ingrid B.: "The week of January 6, 1975, I had a vivid dream, in which I went to an antique show and some dealer friends I knew were there. I had not seen these people for at least nine months and before I moved away from my previous apartment, we had not been on good terms. In the dream this man had some nice folk-art birds that I had been wanting for a long time. I saw myself purchase one and heard him say, 'This is very good, you know, we've had it in our own collection for a long time.' That was the end of my dream. The following week, January 14, we did go to the show and the people I had seen in my dream were there and the folk-art birds were there also just as I had seen them in my dream. As I was about to leave, the man said, 'I think you will enjoy these. You know they have been in our own collection for a long time.' "

It would be preposterous to suggest that the exact wording of the antique dealer's parting message could have been made up in his mind a week earlier, before he even knew that a woman whom be had not seen in nine months would drop by his booth at an antique fair. Obviously, Ingrid was not reading the man's mind through some form of psychic divination, since the man's mind did not contain these thoughts or even any thoughts pertaining to her purchase of the folk art. On the other hand it seems equally preposterous to suppose that some superpower in the beyond had directed her to go to the antique fair and at the same time ordained the dealer to speak the exact words that Ingrid heard in her dream a week earlier. There doesn't seem to be any particular significance to the entire incident, as it is, so we cannot see in it any deeper moral or other meaning, except perhaps to convince Ingrid that she could foresee future events in her psychic dreams.

What then is the method by which many people can do this? Why are they able to do so? It appears from dream material of this kind that there must be some form of impersonal system in operation that does not distinguish between important and trifling dream material, which is put into operation almost mechanically if certain conditions prevail. What these conditions are we do not as yet know fully, but as we examine more and more verified dream material we may yet stumble upon a relatively simple setup explaining these extraordinary occurrences.

But it does imply a system in which a "pattern of destiny" is at work: as I said in more detail in my book of that name, nothing in the universe happens by accident or without good cause; surely, there is strong supportive evidence that the events in our lives are predestined to test our reactions to them, and if some of these events seem unimportant to us, it may just be that they are of a different order of importance than the one we are used to in our evaluations of them.

The overwhelming majority of dreams I have placed in this category of psychic dreams do not require extensive interpretation on the part of the dreamer. They are more like the relaying of a message from the unconscious state to the conscious state, in the expectation that it will eventually materialize precisely as it has been dreamed, or as close to it as possible. But there are occasional dreams that call for some sort of judgment, even symbolic interpretation, on the part of the dreamer.

On March 12, 1964, Helen J. had a dream in which she saw herself awake to the ringing of the doorbell. She hurried downstairs, wondering who it could be, as she knew her husband and three sons were at home at the time, sound asleep. When she drew back the curtain on the door to see who was outside, she froze with terror. "Although I couldn't see anyone, in one moment I became aware of the 'Spirit of Death' on my porch. I knew I could never keep him out and at the same moment I could actually feel a great sense of compassion flowing from the Spirit of Death into me. In panic I ran upstairs to the bedroom and felt compelled to open the window." As she did so, still in her dream, she saw the scene of an accident, with a crowd of people, police, and ambulance. She began to scream and woke up in her bed, still crying. She turned on the lamp and looked at the clock: it was exactly 11:30 P.M.

She then fell back into a troubled sleep. The following morning she told her husband that they would hear of a death, and all day long she felt uneasy. That night, Friday the thirteenth, her son David, age sixteen, was killed in a highway accident at approximately 11:30 P.M.

After her son's death, Mrs. J. had his portrait painted from school pictures and hung it on the wall in her bedroom. The painting of her late son became a focal point of further dreams, it seems. On December 27, 1967, she had a dream in which she saw herself enter her bedroom and walk over to look at her son's portrait. His hair had been a beautiful golden blond, and so it was in the portrait, but as she stood there looking up at it, the color of the hair in the painting gradually changed to a light brown shade. At this instant she "knew" that one of his friends with light brown hair would soon be dead. Again, she told this dream to her husband and a friend of hers, Mrs. B.K. Four days later, on December 31, 1967, Specialist Fourth Class G.W. was killed in Vietnam. He had been her late son's closest friend, having gone to high school with him, and his hair was the same light brown shade Mrs. J. had seen in her dream.

The portrait continued to be a focal point of further psychic dreams. In April 1968, she dreamed she was before it. She seemed to be speaking to someone, saying, "This is my son David." Suddenly his face became alive in the portrait and he bowed his head with eyes closed. The next instant real tears flowed out of the portrait and formed a large pool at her feet.

She felt herself fainting and fell to the floor unconscious. Upon opening her eyes, she saw her family doctor bending over her, holding a hypodermic needle. At this point she awoke. Again, she related the dream to her husband and two friends. A week later she awoke with a lump on her leg and had to be admitted to the hospital because of a large blood clot. She spent nine days in the hospital, taking many hypodermic needles as part of the treatment.

At times, a psychic dream may not concern the dreamer at all, but pertain to other people. Sometimes the principals of the dream are not even known to the dreamer, and occasionally there is a connection. A case in point occurred to Charles S., supervisor for the telephone company, who makes his home in Florida. On the morning of February 13, 1974, he had a three-part dream. In it, he saw himself standing in the street looking for his car. A person whose face he could not see told him that people thought he had been killed in an accident and that his car had been taken away to the funeral home. In part two of the dream he saw himself standing in front of the funeral home, looking at his car. It was the 1959 Dodge that he then actually owned, except that in the dream the car was white, when it was actually blue. The 1959 Dodge has rather high rear fenders. There were some people standing around in the dream, saying it resembled the tail section of an airplane. In part three of the same dream, Mr. S. was standing in the funeral home explaining to a man that he had not been killed in an accident. At that point he could see four coffins: in one he could see a man and in another a woman. They were neither very young nor very old. However, he could not see their faces clearly.

At this moment the alarm went off and Mr. S. awoke. At work, he thought about the dream, trying to figure out what it meant, but he was unable to come to any conclusions. He also discussed it with his wife that evening. The following morning, February 14, 1974, he learned that on the previous afternoon, four people had taken off in a white airplane from a nearby airport. Two minutes after takeoff the plane had plunged to the ground, killing all four instantly. Although Mr. S. did not know the four people intimately, one of the women killed was the daughter of a very good friend who also worked for the telephone company. He had met the young woman and her husband once before, but had never met the older couple, their in-laws. In the dream he could not make out the faces of the older couple. Evidently this message, if that it was, had somehow come to him in the dream state because of his relationship with two of the people involved, although there doesn't seem to be any clear-cut purpose to it.

There is a category of psychic dreams that may more properly fit in with my category of warning dreams, because they contain an element of forewarning, usually of disaster or tragedy, which *might* be averted—that is, if the proper person to whom the warning applied could be identified. Unfortunately, in this category of psychic dreams *the identity is not clearly given,* so the connection cannot be made by the dreamer. As a result, the dream comes true as foreseen, leaving the dreamer feeling helpless and convinced that fate has been cruel in giving him this advance knowledge without allowing him to do something about it.

Some of these dreams seem to be prophetic concerning events taking place in more or less the immediate neighborhood of the dreamer's house. That is, there are a number of such dreams that depict events in the future, with which the dreamer has no connection, but that nevertheless occur within an area with which the dreamer is familiar.

A case in point is a dream that occurred to Margaret R. of Boston. Mrs. R. had a dream in which she saw a little yellow-haired girl, about three years old and wearing a white dress with small pink flowers on it. In her dream the little girl was standing at the curb, waiting to cross the street. As she started across, a black car came speeding toward her, hitting her with such force that her tiny body was tossed into the air and landed many feet away in a small huddled mass. She lay there without moving and Mrs. R. knew that the girl was dead. No one moved to touch her. Finally, after what seemed an eternity, a cobbler came out of his shop, lifted the lifeless body gently, and carried her onto the sidewalk. The dream ended there. However, it was so vivid that Mrs. R. told her mother about it the next morning. All day long, she thought about it at work. When she arrived back home that evening, her younger brothers and sisters ran to tell her of an accident that had occurred just a short time before her return home. It was exactly like her dream, even to the pink and white dress, and it occurred in exactly the same spot she had seen in her dream.

Possibly dreams of impending disasters are more powerful, if not more frequent, just shortly before the event takes place. There are thousands of veridical dreams that come true months or even years later, but there is a sizable number of such dreams that occur within twenty-four hours prior to the event.

Strong emotional events cast a sort of shadow ahead of themselves, in some as yet not fully understood manner. Could it be that those who are responsible for such unfortunate happenings are setting them into motion prior to their occurring in our consciousness? And are the dreamers perhaps tuning in on the thoughts of those originating these disasters in the next dimension, rather than on the disasters in the near future themselves? This presupposes that there is an orderly "board of directors" in the next dimension, planning our destruction or that of certain people whose "numbers" are up.

There are psychic dreams that encompass more than one dream message, more than one incident. At times, one part of the dream comes true, and is duly registered as such, while the other part lies in the future.

An interesting case of this kind happened to Marguerite P. of Saint Petersburg, Florida. On December 12, 1971, she reported the following dream to me. She saw herself entering the White House, although she never had the slightest interest in politics or in the White House. She found herself in a large room in which she noticed a portrait of John F. Kennedy on the wall. There was a long table in the room with chairs all around it. She sat down in one of them and immediately all the other chairs were occupied.

There was a man at the head of the table, with gray hair and a distinguished appearance, but who was very angry. Mrs. P. heard him say, "There will be changes in the balance of power in Congress, due to elections and deaths of leaders. We must try to whitewash the scandal about the president, but I fear it will mean his leaving office." In the dream, these words were followed by absolute silence. Then the men all disappeared and Mrs. P. found herself again alone in the room. As she left the White House, a young man passed, bearing a placard that read, "Mississippi New Negro State." Mrs. P. was mystified by the dream when it occurred to her, but since that time, the first part of her dream has become reality.

It seems that momentous historical events may show themselves to individual dreamers even if the dreamer has no interest in politics or in the public figure involved. This supports Jay's view that this type of precognitive dream is not selective or individually directed but merely represents a random tuning in to the so-called future dimension.

Since childhood, Carolyn C. of Indiana has had a number of ESP experiences. But the experience she remembers stronger than any other occurred to her at the time when Senator Robert Kennedy was to visit her hometown in Indiana. It was during his political campaign, and he was to speak at a meeting to be held in a restaurant. Four nights prior to Kennedy's visit, she was awakened by a vivid dream in which she saw the senator walk through a kitchen and someone shooting at him. The following morning she communicated her dream to her parents.

When Kennedy arrived in Indiana, he did enter the restaurant, through the kitchen and Mrs. C. thought, with some relief, that this was the subject of her dream. However, on the night of the California primary, she was getting ready to turn off her television set, when she suddenly felt she should watch the report from California. To her horror, she saw the shooting exactly as she had seen it in her dream two months before. This scene, as we all know now, took place near the kitchen of the Hotel Ambassador in Los Angeles.

With the overwhelming number of veridical dreams, it is inevitable that there is a fair percentage that do not. This does not mean that the dreamer is making up his dreams, or distorting them in any way, but an ordinary dream based on impressions left in the unconscious may be mistaken for a psychic dream, or, if we are dealing with a genuine psychic dream, a date may be incorrect and the dream may yet come true in the future. However, to be considered evidential such a dream must contain a fair amount of specific, detailed information, not merely generalized statements.

Betty B. described herself as a professional medium, living in Brooklyn. She has a good reputation and a fair-sized clientele. On October 16, 1972, she communicated to me a statement that she had seen, in three identical dreams, three days in a row, a newspaper headline reading, "Frank Sinatra Dead." Another strange dream Mrs. B. reported concerned New York City, which she thought would be under water and disappear. She set the singer's death in 1972, the disappearance of New York in May 1973. As I write these lines, Sinatra died in 1998 and hadn't been well for years and New York City is definitely still above water. To dismiss Mrs. B.'s dreams as publicity-seeking attempts would be unfair and incorrect since she has a good record of psychic accomplishment. But perhaps her conscious self has an interest in Frank Sinatra, or she had read of him at the time of the dreams, and very likely she is familiar with the much publicized Edgar Cayce predictions concerning the inundation of New York City sometime this century. This material, stored in the subconscious, then surfaces again and masquerades as psychic dream material, when it is nothing more than impressions from external sources retold—not genuine psychic communications.

In summing up this category of prophetic dreams, it appears to me that they cannot be forced to occur at will, that they are not directional in the sense other categories of dreams are, but much more haphazard, as if the precognitive contact were made at random, regardless of importance, regardless of the dreamer's own needs or connections. We must therefore seek an explanation for this ability to dream true in the mechanics of dreaming itself. Something occurs in the makeup of the dreamer's personality during sleep that allows his unconscious mind to tune in on the future events recorded in his dream. It may be that the area covered by the dreamer is linked to geographical concepts, or to intensity concepts, or to some other form of attraction. For the present let us state that prophetic dreams are fairly common, cannot be regulated in any way, but can be verified and should always be told upon arising to competent witnesses.

WARNING DREAMS

Warning dreams portray scenes precisely the way psychic dreams do, but with the difference that they are portrayed merely as possibilities that may be averted under certain conditions. The tantalizing thing about these warning dreams is that you are never sure whether you can avert the outcome of the dream. As I look at the material accumulated in my files or that I have studied through the years, I find certain characteristics in these warning dreams. For one thing, the overwhelming majority of warning dreams present a scene in which the dreamer is an onlooker rather than a participant. Even where the dreamer appears in the picture, it is with a clear understanding that this does not actually happen, and is without the sense of foreboding so common to psychic dreams pertaining to future happenings.

There is a purpose in warning dreams, and that is to forewarn the principal or someone known to the principal, of a potential danger, or some other impending event, usually with a degree of sever-

ity. It is clear that whoever sends these warning dreams intends them to be regarded as just that. Of course, if the dreamer is unaware of the nature of such dream material and chooses to ignore it, the "authority" who has supplied the warning dream is off the book, so to speak. There seems to be some kind of delicate law of balance here, by which certain people are given warnings of disaster, while others are not so favored. This may relate to accumulated or earned karma, possibly to other factors unknown to us. It isn't always necessary for a dreamer to realize the warning nature of his paranormal dream, so long as he is aware of the possibility of receiving such information through the dream state. In that case, when the dangerous situation begins to come into his consciousness, his memory will be jogged and the dream warning will trigger some sort of preventive action.

A case in point is a dream that occurred to my good friend Michael Bentine several years ago. At that time he was traveling to various parts of England as a cabaret performer, frequently going to smaller places in the provinces for the first time. During one season he had a particularly vivid dream, while in London, in which he saw himself in his car driving along a country road that he did not recognize. He saw himself round a curve, when suddenly there appeared ahead of him the headlights of an oncoming car, traveling at great speed. Michael did not actually see the crash, but he felt that a crash was imminent as the dream ended. Nevertheless, the dream slipped his memory as the weeks went by. Toward the end of the season he happened to be in the North Country of England, when one night he found himself driving along unfamiliar roads. As he was about to round a bend in the road, he noticed in the distance the headlights of an oncoming car. At that moment, the road seemed suddenly familiar to him, even though he had never traveled on it. In an instant he recognized it as the strange road of his dream, and the oncoming car as the headlights of his dream car. The recognition of this situation allowed him to take evasive action, just in time to avoid a head-on collision.

Whenever the dreamer finds himself in the dream suffering some tragic fate, and feels that the tragedy befalling him is real, I don't think we are dealing with a warning dream but rather with a premonitory experience that will eventually happen to the dreamer. On the other hand, much of the warning dream material is not precise but vague, in that one dreams one should not do certain things, or undertake certain journeys, or see a certain person on some particular day. The line between premonitions occurring in the state bordering on sleep and actual warning dreams is sometimes very thin, and there is a connection between the two phenomena.

Warning material may also be contained in a different category of dreams that I have termed *survival dreams*, with which I will deal in later pages. In this type of dream, a discarnate entity, a spirit, as it were, appears or speaks to the dreamer and warns him of certain dangers in the future. I have not included such dreams here because they are primarily communication dreams, not images or impressions in which the dreamer is the primary recipient. The degree to which such dreams are accepted will depend on the dreamer's attitude toward the possibility of spirits communicating with him in the dream state. Unfortunately, many psychiatrists have explained dreams of dead relatives as suppressed emotional hang-ups of one kind or another, not as the actual intercession by those deceased relatives. Such dreams are not warning dreams in the true sense because they do not permit the dreamer a choice, they either spell it out for him or actually protect him from the coming hurt.

Actress Gloria DeHaven was driving on a road she was not too familiar with, when her deceased mother "appeared" to her in the windshield of her car, holding up a hand. Immediately DeHaven stopped her car, and the image disappeared. On getting out of the car she found that she was but a few yards away from an abyss. Unknown to her, the road had been washed out. Here we have an incident that does not permit the percipient to consider the matter: the dead take action, and the action is successful. The incident reported by DeHaven occurred while she was fully awake, but similar occurrences have been happening to people while asleep, because it is easier for discarnates to make contact with people in this dimension when they are in the sleep state.

As with all psychic material, we must be aware of externalized personal pressures, or material originating in one's own unconscious. It is entirely possible for people with psychoneurotic problems to create false dream material, which is the proper province of psychoanalysts. But such dreams are heavily interlarded with symbolism, are usually extremely confused in content, and contain entire series of images. True warning dreams are nearly always precise and to the point, almost like a Western Union message.

Mrs. Howard Hitt, a housewife and mother living in northern California had the dream in question during the last week of June 1970, when she and her husband were planning a trip to Reno. In the dream she became aware of an accident involving two people; however, the two people were not clear enough, though Mrs. Hitt had a strong feeling that an infant was involved. On awakening, she remembered the dream, without being able to give exact details concerning the nature of the accident. But the feeling was so strong that she wanted to cancel the trip. On the other hand, she knew that her husband had been looking forward to it, so she did not at first tell him about the dream. However, she decided to leave their six-month-old baby at home with her mother.

All week long she felt uneasy about undertaking the trip. "Finally at about 11 P.M. on the night before our Fourth of July trip, as we were resting for it, the feeling was so strong that I decided to mention it to my husband. To my surprise he confessed he also had had some apprehension all week," Mrs. Hitt said. They decided to go anyway, but to be extremely cautious because of the dream. To their relief they arrived safely in Reno. But on their return trip they had a lot of trouble with their car, and what should have been an easy four-and-a-half-hour trip turned into ten hours. Under the cir-

cumstances Mrs. Hitt thought that the dream had been a warning that there would be difficulties with their car. But when they reached home, her mother informed her that someone had been trying to reach her by telephone. It turned out that the Hitts' best friends, Mr. and Mrs. Richard B., had been returning from a drive-in movie on July 4, when they were struck by an oncoming car about a block from their home. The car was completely demolished and both friends were hospitalized. Mrs. Hitt now felt that the dream had pertained to her best friends, rather than to herself. On the other hand, how was she to explain the feeling about an infant being involved? Mrs. B. then admitted that they had been thinking of taking the Hitts and the Hitts' children with them to the movie, but on learning later that they were about to leave on a trip to Reno had abandoned this idea.

It is interesting that Mrs. Hitt's dream "tuned in on" the situation as it existed prior to the final arrangements being made just before the trip. But because the dreamer was unable to identify the couple in the dream, she was not in a position to relate it to the proper people, and thus take preventive action.

There is no satisfactory explanation as to why some ordinary people dream about celebrities with whom they have absolutely no connection, not even as fans. The fate of famous people is no different from that of the unknown among us, yet there are instances where average people dream of well-known actors or other people in the limelight, without being in a position of doing anything about their prophetic dreams.

Frequently, pregnant women are unusually sensitive to psychic communication and intuition. Marjorie F. lived in Illinois at the time she registered this dream material with me in May 1974. She has a bachelor's degree in elementary education, and is married to an officer in the United States Air Force. In May 1969, she was pregnant with her third child. At that time she had a dream that a boy would be born to her but that he would not live. On May 31, 1969, she became the mother of a son, born three months prematurely. Despite an early negative prognosis, the child picked up in health and gained weight. Three weeks after birth, all seemed well for the premature baby, so much so that a photographer was called in to take pictures. But on the thirtieth day of his life, the baby died suddenly, just as she had foreseen in her dream.

Jean M., a widow with four children, living in Nova Scotia, had worked as a bank clerk until her marriage to an air force officer. All her life she remembered having had veridical dreams, but feared to mention some of them because of prevailing prejudices. In March 1959 her husband was sent on a course at Saskatoon, while stationed in Chatham, New Brunswick. A few nights after he left Mrs. M. had a terrible nightmare: she saw herself and her children standing around a casket, crying. Next she saw herself in a car with a hearse ahead of her and the air force guard of honor marching. The dream was so vivid that she was sure something had happened to her husband and she was on edge until he returned home safely. Then the memory of her dream gradually faded, and eventually she decided that it

had been nothing more than a bad dream. But in November of the same year, he suddenly died from a heart attack. As a result of this tragedy, she found herself in a car behind a hearse, and the honor guard marched precisely as it had in her dream, eight months before.

Not all warning dreams are as tragic in their consequences as that Canadian woman's. Denise Shamlian of San Francisco, an artist by profession, with an IQ of 155, moved to Paris in January 1972. There she had occasion to see a dentist named Dr. Jean-Claude W., one of the most prominent dentists in Paris at the time. He gave her a gold inlay. Three nights before she left Paris, she had a vivid dream in which she saw the inlay halfway out of her tooth, and causing her a lot of pain. The following day she mentioned this to a friend, who laughed at her because the inlay seemed in fine shape and the dentist had a brilliant reputation. Dismissing her dream fears, Shamlian returned to San Francisco. The night before Easter 1972 she woke up with a toothache due to the inlay being halfway out. It was exactly as it had come to her in the dream in Paris.

Robert B. was a captain in the United States Air Force when he registered one of his wife's dreams with me on July 26, 1971. He holds a bachelor's degree in microbiology. His wife, Nina, studied at the University of Southern California extension in Munich, Germany, while they were stationed there. It was in Munich that Mrs. B. had the following vivid dream. On July 11, 1968, she saw herself with a black eye; furthermore, she received the impression that a good friend of hers named Jeannie also would have a blackened eye received in connection with the terrace of her third-floor dormitory room. The following morning, Mrs. B. related the dream to Jeannie and advised her to stay away from her terrace. But her warning was ignored, and the following Saturday night, July 13, Jeannie went to a dance at one of the servicemen's clubs in Munich. She returned to the dormitory by curfew time, about 10:30 P.M. During the course of the evening she had had a disagreement with her boyfriend, and about midnight she decided to sneak out of the dormitory to try to make up with him. She did this by tying a rope to the terrace of her room and trying to slide down to the ground, but she slipped and fell three stories. She received various injuries, including two blackened eyes. She then remembered the warning given her by Mrs. B. and blamed her, in some strange fashion, for the incident, thus giving Nina a "spiritual" black eye as well.

Sue T. still wants to develop her innate ESP ability, despite some harrowing experiences with psychic dreams. The attractive young woman is a model, thirty years old, and lives with her husband and children in Pennsylvania. The first dream she ever had seemed silly to her. She was in her bathroom trying to remove a splinter from her finger. Suddenly she remembered a dream she had had that afternoon, in which she saw herself pricking her finger just as her mother-in-law and father-in-law came to the door of the bathroom. She had barely thought about this when her in-laws

appeared at the door just as she had dreamed.

But her next dream was not as silly to her, and turned out to be a nightmare in the end. She and her husband had moved into a new house, and had had their second and third child. At that time she had a strange dream, from which she awoke crying. In her dream she had had an apartment of her own and several children, when there was a knock at her door and outside stood her husband saying, "I want you to meet my wife." There was a strange woman with him but Mrs. T. could not remember what she looked like. She reported the dream to her husband, remarking how silly it all seemed to her.

A short time later her husband was transferred to a small town in Pennsylvania. Somehow this began to destroy their marriage, and the difficult times she went through made her forget the strange dream she had had before they moved. Then she had another unusual dream. In this one she saw herself walking from their living room into the bedroom and when she opened the door she could see the kitchen table from the door. There sat her husband with a man she had never seen. At this instant in the dream, a thought flashed through her mind that the man was someone who was supposed to kill her, on her husband's instigation. With this she awoke screaming.

About that time her marriage came to an end and she left her husband. Late the next year, her ex-husband was supposed to have brought a car down to show her and she was therefore expecting him. When he arrived at her house, a young woman was with him whom Mrs.

T. recognized as the woman in her first dream. However, he did not introduce her as his wife, even though the implication as to her relationship with him was clear. After this, relations between Mrs. T. and her ex-husband became worse, and there were arguments over some property. She realized that her ex-husband had a key to her apartment, and remembering her second dream, she lived in constant fear of him. Eventually, she moved away to be safe.

Mrs. S.G., a grandmother with eight grandchildren, worked as a law secretary in the eastern United States. During World War II she and her husband had bought a number of United States bonds but had difficulty finding a safe-deposit box for their safekeeping. Her husband mentioned that his employer would keep the bonds in the company safe for them. A few years went by and then one night she dreamed that two thieves broke the skylight in the building, blew up the safe and took out all the contents. She told her husband about the dream and insisted that he take out the bonds, but he only laughed at her. The following night she had the identical dream, and this time she made such fuss over it that on the Friday of the same week he asked his employer for the bonds. The following Monday, her husband returned from work and informed his wife that her dream had come true over the weekend. When he asked for his bonds back, Mr. O.'s employer had asked why, but instead of telling him about his wife's premonitory dream (thus possibly preventing the burglary), he made some vague excuse, and let the matter pass.

Miss T.L. of Long Island, New York, is an artist by profession. When her ex-husband was in the army, he frequently stayed away from home for weeks on temporary duty assignments. One night she had a dream in which she saw her ex-husband driving in the mountains. There was heavy snow everywhere. Suddenly she saw an avalanche come down and the car was buried in it. The dream woke her up. At the time her husband was in Utah, so she decided to wait until he would telephone her Sunday night. At that time she mentioned the dream to him. There was a pause on the telephone, then he replied that he had gone up to a ski area, when an avalanche came down the mountainside. It just missed his car but buried the one behind him.

"When I dream of future events that later come true, the dream is always accompanied by a strange feeling of knowing it is not just another, ordinary dream," Margaret B. stated, even though her husband ridicules her psychic dreams and considers her superstitious. Mrs. B. has been active on behalf of certain American Indian groups, taking up their cause against injustice. She and her husband and their small girl live in upstate New York. At the time of the following dream, they were, however, living in Arizona.

Mrs. B. dreamed she was lying on her bed and it was dusk. She heard a shot from the general area of the guesthouse, sprang from her bed and raced downhill to the guesthouse, where she saw two men. One seemed to be her husband lying face down alongside the building; the other was standing on the hill above, watching over the scene. The little light left in the sky allowed her to see only that he was tall and thin, definitely not built like a Yaqui Indian, the people whose cause she and her husband were then furthering. The stranger, in the dream, held a long gun in his hand, with the stock on the ground. She looked hard, but could not make out his face. Then she continued to run to where her husband was. When she reached him, she felt that he was dead, but when she pulled at his shoulders, to turn him over, she realized that he was still alive. Immediately she thought that if the man on the hill realized this, he would shoot again and it was better to pretend that her husband was dead. She told her husband, and looked again at the man on the hill, wondering whether he would shoot at her also. At that moment she woke up. Despite her husband's negative reaction to the dream, she was terrified and insisted that he not go near the guesthouse at any time.

About that time pressure against her husband, herself, and the members of the committee favoring the cause of the Indians mounted. Attempts at arson and attempted murder came with increasing frequency, and, convinced that the dream had been a warning for what was in store for her husband, she insisted that they leave the house and area. In the end, her husband gave in and they left. Here we have a warning dream heeded, with the likelihood of it coming true great indeed.

Mary C., a native of Arkansas, worked as a waitress until she settled down as a housewife with two children. When her son was seventeen, he owned a 1963 Austin Healy car. On March 14, 1973, Mrs. C. had a dream in which she could see the car going from one side of the road to the other. Suddenly, it was smashed up. There was a girl in her dream whom she did not know. Immediately on awakening, she informed her son of her dream, but he would not accept it as meaning anything. Several days later, the boy decided to pay a call on a girlfriend. He promised to telephone Mrs. C. as soon as he got to his girlfriend's house. A short time later a telephone call came, but it was to advise her that there had been an accident. When Mrs. C. reached the scene of the accident, it looked exactly the way it had looked to her in her dream of several days before. The girl, whom she did not recognize in her dream, was a nurse who had been passing in her car, stopped by and looked after her son. Here we have a warning dream that could have been heeded but was not.

Jeani Magee of Louisiana has had remarkable incidents of ESP almost all her life. But the warning dream she will never forget occurred to her at five in the morning of July 16, 1973. She woke up her husband to tell him of the dream, in which she saw a man being shot. Since she did not know who he was, she went back to sleep, remarking, "I don't know what is going to happen to me." She awoke again at eight-thirty, and asked her husband not to go to work that day, which would have been easy since his secretary was on vacation. Her husband promised that he would go to the office only to open his mail and would return at noon. It was 10:15 when he left the house. The only people left in the house were Jeani Magee, the housemaid, the

Magees' nine-year-old daughter, Cathy, and their ten-month-old daughter, Ashley. What transpired fifteen minutes after her husband left the house was reported by the Associated Press:

"A kidnapper who held off Sheriff's deputies by pointing a gun at a ten-month-old baby's head was shot in the back and killed at a roadblock on Monday when he turned to shoot at officers. About 10:45 A.M. two men broke into the Magees' home, tied Mrs. Magee with rope, robbed the house and fled with about $400 in cash, Magee's car and the girl. A neighbor called the police and officers quickly spotted the big white Cadillac in which the men fled."

After the chase, the child was recovered without injury and returned to her parents, but no description can sufficiently reflect the horror Mrs. Magee went through when her baby was taken by bandits. Had her husband heeded his wife's warning and not gone to the office to look after his mail, perhaps things would have come out differently; perhaps not.

The next dream may be a plain warning dream, or it may be due to the indirect action by a discarnate friend, trying to make what was to come easier to bear. At any rate, Sue P. of California dreamed that her son and she were in a large gathering. Her husband was with them, but suddenly he disappeared, and Mrs. P. told her son, in the dream, to look for his father. Shortly afterward the son returned crying, saying his father was dead. The following morning she related this dream to her husband, Dr. C. P. The doctor laughed, and dismissed it as "only a dream." He was in perfect health, and

there was no reason for alarm. Several weeks later, Mrs. P. had another dream. In this one she saw herself scanning a local newspaper, when she turned to the obituaries. There she saw her husband's name among those who had died, plain as day. The dream frightened her, especially as it recurred another time a week later. The following week, Doctor C. P. died suddenly from a heart attack.

Could the doctor's acceptance of the dream have prevented his demise at that point? Assuming that he took his wife's dream seriously, he might have undergone special testing, and perhaps discovered some indication of a pending heart attack. Was the dream "sent" to Mrs. P. by "the authorities" beyond this world to give the doctor an even chance to do something about his intended death? Is this a case where free will enters the picture, that is, the action undertaken by the individual having drastic bearing on the outcome? Or was the doctor on "the list," regardless of his reaction to his wife's premonitory dream. Clearly, we cannot be sure in this case, since the event took place as foreseen.

Last, there are seemingly valid warning dreams resembling those that actually come true later, except they haven't come true as dreamed. That is, not as of the time I write these lines. Such material may either be "false" dream material caused by personal fears of the dreamer, or it may be dream material still pertaining to the future. We do not know, therefore, whether the dream was a warning dream or not.

An interesting and typical case of this kind is a warning dream reported to me by Carol C. of Huntington Beach, California. She is a housewife with two children, in her early thirties, and living in a lovely house on the beach. She doesn't consider herself psychic, although she has had a few things happen to her that "surprised her." She admits having a vivid imagination, and a lively interest in the predictions of others, is well read in ESP material, and aware of the many predictions made about earthquakes and tidal waves in California. Nevertheless, she reported a dream in which she saw a tidal wave come onto a beach where she found herself with her children. There were other people there also, when the huge wave came in, and she could feel rock walls around her buckle and crumble, but somehow she and her children were not hurt.

To my knowledge, the dream has not yet become objective reality, as no large tidal wave has been reported hitting Huntington Beach as of this date. Was the dream the result of general, deep-seated fears concerning natural catastrophes involving the California coastline, or was it a specific, individual dream pertaining to a situation that may yet come true?

ESP DREAMS

The term *ESP dreams* may surprise some who are used to other terms, but I have chosen the term because I am covering here three types of dream material with one thing in common—they in no way pertain to the future. ESP dreams are *telepathic dreams* in which the dreamer perceives or receives messages or information from another person, either living or dead, but pertaining to the present, even if at a distance. In telepathic dreams, the transmission need not be conscious, or exact. The dreamer picks up thought energies. Both contemplated events and actual events may be the subject for such dreams.

Somewhat different is the second type of ESP dream, *simultaneous dreams*, in which the dreamer tunes in on an event going on at a distance. In simultaneous dreams, the dreamer is present without being seen, seemingly extending part of his consciousness beyond the barriers of space and without regard to distance or solid objects between. Those dreams where the dreamer is also noticed at a distant location from his physical whereabouts are not dreams at all, but are part of the phenomenon called out-of-body experience, with which I will deal in a subsequent chapter.

Finally, there is the dream category called *retrocognitive dreams*, in which the dreamer relives an event that has already taken place in the past, but with which he is not familiar in his conscious state. Retrocognitive dreams somewhat resemble psychometry experiments, in which a psychic person touches an object and reconstructs the object's past merely from this contact. With retrocognitive dreams, the dreamer does not have a choice of direction. Usually, the dream is unexpected and does not necessarily require the physical presence of the dreamer in a location to which the dream material refers. ESP dreams are tensions of ordinary consciousness, and they afford the dreamer insight into events or situations that he would not normally be familiar with at the time of their occurrences.

We should be careful not to label as ESP dreams, dreams that are clearly symbolic or of psychoanalytical value. What I've said pertaining to the difference between psychic dreams in general and those more suitable for psychoanalytical interpretation, is particularly important here, where we do not have an element of prophecy but are dealing with contemporary or past matters, the latter having already occurred and therefore at least theoretically capable of being picked up consciously by the dreamer. But the clarity of the ESP dream and its strong remembrance upon awakening sets it apart from the dream material suitable for psychoanalytical interpretation. A trained observer will know the difference.

Mrs. A.W., mother of two sons and a daughter, was working as a statistical typist in a bank when she contacted me. Mrs. W. has had many psychic experiences throughout her career. One of the first ones is of interest here since it belongs in the category I am discussing.

At the time she was eight years old she had great difficulty understanding long division. She thought she was the only one in her class who couldn't grasp it; her teacher was exasperated because of her lack of comprehension. When she tried to get help from her classmates, she couldn't understand their explanations either. She then turned to her sister to learn the intricacies of the subject, but received little solace there. One night, worried over her incomprehension, she prayed for help, and went to bed. That night she had a most enlightening dream. She saw herself back in the schoolroom. Her teacher summoned her to the blackboard, where she was confronted with three problems in long division. In the dream, Mrs. W. picked up the chalk and solved the problems effortlessly and correctly.

The following morning Mrs. W. went to school as usual. In class, the teacher summoned her to the blackboard. Three problems in long division confronted her, exactly as they had in her dream, and just as she had dreamed it, she proceeded to solve them correctly and effortlessly.

This dream pertains to the future and should therefore be listed among the examples in my chapter on prophetic dreams. But this is not so: the ability to solve long division was buried in Mrs. W.'s unconscious, present but unrealized. Surely, her teacher had selected the next day's assignment when going to bed that night. What the girl dreamed then was of a dual nature: on the one hand, she was tuning in on her teachers thoughts, obtaining a simultaneous view of the problems she would be confronted with the following day, and on the other hand, she was unlocking her own unconscious as a reassuring step to help her with the next day's work.

Catherine H. is a housewife who lives in Pennsylvania. Her entire family, consisting of her husband and three daughters, is extremely telepathic, so she has no problems being recognized in this area. She has had precognitive dreams for many years, too numerous to list. "I have precognitive dreams that are sifted from the rest by the presence of the color green somewhere in the dream," she says. One particularly impressive dream she reported to me under the postmark of

February 8, 1971: she saw green mountains, and several trucks sinking into black slime that was covering the mountain. She saw the trucks and suddenly found herself trapped deeply under the trucks and some wood. She heard herself scream until she almost lost her voice. At that moment someone called out to her, warning her that she would lose her voice. That was the end of the dream.

Two weeks later, the great tragedy at Aberfan, Great Britain, shook the world: a coal slag slide burying a schoolhouse and killing many children. The newspaper story, which reached Mrs. H. two weeks after her dream, stated that a worker heard a child screaming, because she was trapped under the rubble. The worker called out to the child to stop screaming and asked for her name, to which she replied, "Catherine." "Most experiences become a reality about two weeks after I dream them and most of them pertain to world disasters," Mrs. H. said. "I also feel the pain of a stricken person for the tragedy." Because of this unwanted talent, she consulted a medical doctor, hoping that he would rid her of it. But her psychic ability has remained with her.

Mrs. H. is by no means the only one who has tuned in on the Aberfan disaster. A London newspaper investigated the prophetic dreams of many who foresaw it and described it in accurate detail. What makes this dream different from all the others—and the reason that I am reporting it here in my chapter on ESP dreams and not with other prophetic dreams—is Mrs. H.'s personal identification with another individual. Mrs. H. does not merely dream of an event in the future,

seeing people at a distance of whom she knows nothing. In this at least, she became the child trapped under the truck. There is no easy way of explaining how this was possible. If the event was already slated at the time Mrs. H. had the dream, the reaction of the trapped girl could not have been. Mrs. H. makes much of the identity of the names, she and the stricken girl both being named Catherine.

But the dream, more than anything else, seems to me to contain the key to a better understanding of the time-space continuum in which we live, and permits me to offer the tantalizing suggestion—far from making it a theory—how such dreams are possible: what if our realistic experiencing of events was somehow a *delayed* realization of the events, while the events themselves take place *earlier*, without our being aware of them until later? Those who have psychically foreseen such events are not looking into the future but are able to pick up the *present* when it happens, while the majority of us are not. This is merely idle speculation.

Mrs. C. is a third-grade schoolteacher who lives in Indiana and has five daughters and one son. One of these daughters, Laverne, is a housewife and works as a part-time practical nurse at a hospital. She never believed in the reality of psychic phenomena until her mother had a certain dream in 1967, when the daughter was five months pregnant. Laverne went into labor and had to be taken to the hospital at one in the morning. Medical authorities said she would lose the baby, and at 2:00 A.M. her husband was sent home. At 3:00 A.M. Laverne woke up and began to cry, "Dear God, please help me, I want my mother." She repeated it several times until she drifted back to sleep. Although she had been married for five years, she had never felt so much in need of her mother, but she also knew that her mother couldn't come to her aid since her mother was then living in Indiana.

When next she saw her mother, four months later, her mother informed her of a strange dream she had had at the same time Laverne had been in the hospital. At 3:00 A.M. her mother had dreamed that she was in a bedroom downstairs in the house belonging to another daughter. In the dream she had turned the bedroom light off and started upstairs when she heard her daughter call for her. She turned back into the bedroom. There was a bright light coming from a corner where her daughter lay on a flat board or stretcher. She was wearing a pale blue gown. Since Mrs. C. had five daughters she was not sure which daughter this was, but assumed it was Laverne's elder sister, since the dream occurred in that sister's house. She went upstairs, where she found her son sitting on the sofa, and begged him to come downstairs to see what was wrong with his sister. He refused to go and kept saying not to worry because everything would be all right. Finally, the mother became angry and turned to go downstairs alone, but the light had faded and the daughter on the stretcher was now gone.

Mrs. C.'s dream was so vivid that it woke her up, and she began to pray for Laverne's elder sister. At the time, that sister was in Africa as a missionary and the mother assumed that she was in some sort of danger, since the dream had taken

place in her home. The following morning the mother was informed that Laverne had lost her baby and it was then that she thought about her dream. It occurred to her that the sister in Africa always wore pajamas, while Laverne usually preferred gowns. Also, she remembered that the last time Laverne had visited with her sister and mother, who were then living together, she had slept in the downstairs bedroom and worn a pale blue gown.

What we have here is a *simultaneous dream* in which the mother was able to tune in on her daughter's condition, hearing her cries for help but somehow intermingling this direct telepathic material with unconscious knowledge of her daughter's appearance the last time she had actually been at the house of the dream. In this case, the dreamer unconsciously draws upon earlier accumulated dream knowledge and uses it to "flesh out" the new dream in which telepathic material is received.

Simultaneous psychic dreams generally relate to events taking place at exactly the same moment, although at a distance, which can range anywhere from the house next door to some location across the country. Occasionally simultaneous dreams allow for time differences so that the dreamer gets the impression at the time the event occurs in its own time zone, but at a different time where the dreamer lives.

I also consider simultaneous ESP dreams those where events occur within a few hours before the dream takes place but without the dreamer's knowledge of the event. For instance, an event may take place in the dead of night, but it comes to the dreamer's attention only when he wakes the next morning. At that time the dreamer is able to confirm his dream of the night before, even though, technically speaking, he dreamed of it afterward. I also consider dreams becoming objective reality slightly later than dreamed as part of this category, pointing out the need to reappraise our concepts of time. Perhaps time is not as absolute as we think, but is capable of flexibility. All this remains to be worked out by future observation and experiments.

Dorothy T. lives in northern California. She is a housewife and has several children. Brought up a strict Roman Catholic, her psychic gift was suppressed in boarding school, but was allowed to develop freely later on in life. Although she lived hundreds of miles away, she saw, in a dream, her son being brushed by a car in San Francisco. In her dream she saw not only a car, but also her mother-in-law being hurt, although not badly. Immediately upon awakening from the dream, she went next door to tell her neighbor. Two days later there was a telephone call informing her that the accident had taken place as she had seen it, but that neither victim was seriously hurt.

Perhaps the most astonishing psychic dream Mrs. T. recorded with me concerned the assassination of President Kennedy. Oswald had been arrested and the day's events had been most upsetting when Mrs. T. went to bed that night. She had dreamed of a conversation between two people, someone saying, "We will get him in the stomach, it is a painful death," and this woke her up. She immediately

told her husband that Oswald was dead by shooting and before her husband could reply, she went into the living room and turned on the television set: the scene was *just then* happening before her eyes!

Not every true dreamer is happy at having the power. "My problem is that I get feelings or dream about things before they happen. Unfortunately they are not always good," Jan S. of Maryland complained to me. When Jan was a junior in high school, a boy she knew would always pick her up at school. One day another boy, Ronnie, came with him. Jan had not seen Ronnie for at least three months and the conversation was an ordinary one. That night she had a dream about a boy who shot himself but she could not make out a face; however, she knew it was a friend. The next day when she came to school she found out that Ronnie had shot himself during the night.

Jane Duke is a tremendously gifted psychic woman living in Bakersfield, California. She was able to foresee her first husband's death and prepare for it, as well as many other events in her life, to the point where she can program herself to dream of a certain problem and frequently gets answers to her questions. At present she works as a professional palmist, using this method as an induction agent for her wider psychic talents.

Not long ago a young woman whom she did not know came to her for a palm reading. Shortly before the arrival of her client, Duke took a nap and dreamed of the problem her client would have on her mind. While she dreamed it, she did not realize that the dream was about her next client, but realized it only when she saw her. In the dream, she saw a man who strongly resembled a well-known film actor. The man put his hand out to her and she looked at it. From it she judged that he was not a good person. Next, in the dream, she saw a dark-haired girl being taken by the hand by this man and led into an elevator, which went down. In her dream, Duke interpreted this as being a negative situation for the girl. Shortly after she woke up, her client arrived and turned out to be the girl she had seen in the dream. Duke went on to describe the man she had seen in the dream and it turned out that he was the reason for the girl's visit to her. Duke warned her about him, describing the dream. But the girl would not listen and married the man. Two weeks after marrying him, he beat her up badly and she left him.

An interesting incident of *retrocognitive dreaming* occurred to artist Claudia Cunningham of Pennsylvania. A friend, Emma Black, owned a farmhouse in eastern Pennsylvania, which she had made available as a guesthouse to visiting artists. Not long ago, Cunningham stayed there for a few days. That particular week there were six women staying at the guesthouse, two to a room. Cunningham's roommate had gone into the big bedroom across the hall to play cards with the others, who were not yet ready to go to sleep. They were talking and laughing as Cunningham undressed and opened the window by her bed. She set the alarm clock and lay down.

As she started to relax, ready to drift into sleep, she still heard the voices across the hall. At the threshold of sleep she saw superimposed on the room in which she lay an older, shabbier room with stained wallpaper, poorly furnished and drab. A woman was sitting on a straight chair and leaning her arms against the window sill. She had long, dark hair hanging over her shoulders and was weeping. Cunningham could hear her sobs over the fainter sounds of the chatter from the other room. There was the sound of feet running down the stairs and the back door slamming. Gradually the woman in the room faded and only Cunningham's room remained. The sound of the other guests' voices across the hall increased to the usual level. At this point Cunningham fell into deep sleep, still wondering about her experience.

The next morning at breakfast, she discussed her experience with the others. Black confirmed the fact that the room in which Cunningham had slept had belonged to the dark-haired woman she had described, and that the woman had had a great deal of grief because of a retarded child. However, the woman in question was still very much alive and living in a nearby town. What Cunningham had experienced was a dreamlike state or perhaps a light dream in which she went back into a previous period of the house, and relived a scene from the past. It does not seem to make any difference whether the scene concerns living people or dead people, the psychic essence being of one and the same kind.

psychic photography: evidence for the other side

Not everyone who is psychic (and has ESP) has contact with someone who is dead. But a fair number of people with psychic ability do have such experiences, because to communicate with the Other Side, you must have the psychic gift. Many scientifically minded people will readily accept the reality of ESP while objecting to the possibility of survival of human personality beyond physical death. Whereas ESP, to them at least, indicates an extraordinary faculty between people, the idea of an existence beyond death involves a religious concept, to some people enough of a deterrent to look the other way, even in the face of considerable evidence.

Many of the phenomena attributed to ESP in its various forms, from telepathy to psychometry, and even clairvoyance and the ability to look into the future, can be explained without the need to assume a world beyond. Most of these ESP phenomena happen between living people, and although they may be in contravention of accepted laws of cause and effect, they do not imply the existence of another order of things, one that necessitates a radical rethinking of one's philosophy. But when we come to the question of ESP communication with the realm of the dead, we are opening a Pandora's box. If there is such a thing as communication with the so-called dead, our biological concept of life and man needs to be greatly modified. Nearly all "establishment" scientists, especially in medicine, postulate that the physical body of man is nearly all there is, with mind taking the role of a personality complex rather than an invisible unit. Until the discovery of psychiatry and, later, psychoanalysis, the concept of a mind separate from the body was as unacceptable to those scientists as the concept of another dimension beyond death is to them today.

Perhaps the strongest reason that the existence of a world of the dead is so difficult to accept by the scientific mind lies in the seeming invisibility of that realm. Trained to accept only what we can see, hear, touch, or otherwise come in direct contact with by our five senses, we find it difficult to give credence to a set of conditions that we cannot measure with those same senses. We are forced to go by assumptions, deduced by the testimony of others, and to work with indirect material rather than with the direct approach so useful in dealing with physical matters. But this is merely prejudice on our part. Many areas of human knowledge are based upon invisible values: we know that electricity and electric current can accomplish certain things and we can measure the results, but we cannot actually see the electric current flowing through a wire. Even if we touch the wire and receive a shock, we are merely experiencing the result rather than the causative element. To be able to photograph electricity, we have to conduct it through certain substances, such as gases, before we are able to trace, and thus, photograph it, but the current remains invisible without help. Magnetic waves cannot be seen by the naked eye nor can they be touched. They can be measured by sensitive instruments, and the result of magnetism is capable of verification. Perhaps an even better parallel lies in the causative factors of disease. Until man invented microscopes sensitive enough to see microbes, he did not know about them. He assumed that illnesses were caused by a variety of factors,

ranging from ill will of the gods to human accidents.

Once we have perfected sensitive instruments to measure the etheric body in man, we will be able to understand its workings much better. Now we can only assume that it exists because we see it at work in psychic phenomena. It seems, as Bishop James Pike might have put it, "the best of several possible alternatives." We have photographed the human aura—the electromagnetic field that reaches out beyond the human skin and indicates the state of health of the individual—among other things. We have measured and studied the tiny electrical currents going through the nerve fibers from the brain, and we know that the electroencephalogram does not lie; electricity does go through the nerves. We can look at the heavens and see only a tiny portion of the bodies in space because our instruments are not refined enough to see it all. This does not mean that there are not additional worlds beyond those that we can currently register. It merely means that we have not yet been able to reach out that far.

It is the same with "inner space": our inability to record objectively the fine elements making up the etheric body within should not be confused with the absence of that body. Everything in the study of paranormal phenomena indicates the existence of such a body within man; taken as a whole, the phenomena generally associated with ESP cannot be explained better than by assuming that man has within himself at all times an inner layer or dimension that is capable of breaking through the time-space barrier and accomplishing seemingly paranormal phenomena. I say "seemingly," because they are perfectly normal phenomena that become extraordinary only because of our lack of comprehension. In Procrustean fashion, we make the observed facts fit the established theory instead of building a theory upon existing facts. This cannot go on forever; the scientific establishment is bound to reform itself when the pressure to do so becomes unbearable.

The haphazard and surprising way in which communications from the so-called dead occur to the living, the suddenness of apparitions, the voice in an empty room identified with a known dead individual, visits from long-dead relatives and friends, farewell greetings at the time of death —all these phenomena, which are common, would not be so numerous if we the living were not continuously bombarded with a philosophy of living based upon false values and false information. Whether we are materialistically inclined or pay lip service to an established religion, even if we are devout religionists, our attitude toward the possibility of spirit communication is inevitably one of doubt, if not of fear. Only a small minority of people are prepared to consider such occurrences as natural and desirable. Perhaps in a world where the question of channels between the physical world and the next dimension is no longer one of doubt but one of certainty, the need for the dead to manifest to the living as much as they do now will be no longer compelling.

The majority of communications between the dead and the living is for the purpose of acquainting the living with the continuous existence of the dead in another dimension. Whether the dead person has lacked this understanding in his lifetime in the physical world and now wants to make amends for it, or whether the living person to whom the communication is directed is in that sore state of ignorance and therefore needs to be educated by the dead individual for the living person's own benefit, there is a compelling desire on the part of many "dead" people to let those they have left behind in the physical world know about their own world, about the fact that they continue to live a useful and seemingly complete life. A comparatively small number of such cases is due to unfinished business during the earth life of the deceased.

Scientists unfamiliar with the material on this subject tend to shrug off the apparitions of the dead or vocal phenomena along those lines as hallucinations, putting the blame on the observer and suggesting that either the phenomenon did not take place at all or was due to emotional and psychological malfunction in the observer. While this may hold true in a small number of cases and may be, on the surface at least, an explanation in a number of other cases where there exists an element of mourning, it does not hold true in cases of "surprise visits" by dead people to people who did not know they had died, or who did not know them at all and who had to ascertain afterward from independent sources the identity of the apparition they had seen. Such cases are in the majority among those observed by sane, sound people and told to reliable witnesses or registered in the records of reputable research societies.

People stay at houses and are surprised by the apparition of a dead individual about whom they know nothing. Later, on checking their experience, they find that they have seen a dead person formerly associated with the house.

People are visited by strangers who represent themselves to them as long-dead relatives; on checking with family members, the identity is later established. People report the appearance of a dear one at the same time as the family member is dying or has died, without the knowledge of the time or place of death.

All this is well established and documented in the files of such research societies as the American Society for Psychic Research and the British College of Psychic Sciences, and in my own extensive files. That there is another dimension close to this one in which we live I do not doubt. The nature of that dimension seems essentially to be a thought world; everything consists of specific electromagnetic fields, containing memories and emotional stimuli identifiable with people formerly alive in physical bodies. For all practical purposes, the dead are nothing more than the inner selves of living people, looking like them, thinking like them, feeling like them, being able to move rapidly since they no longer have to carry the weight of a physical outer layer called a body.

The people who have had experiences of this kind with the "dead" run the gamut of professions, ages, national and educational backgrounds.

Sally C. is a registered nurse in Georgia. "In the past I have worked with the National Institute of Health in Bethesda, Maryland," she explains. "I mention this because it was there in the Institute of Neurology that I was taught to note and describe full details. I am thirty-five years old and at the time of this incident I was living in the same town with my mother but my two children and I lived in a house that was several blocks away from my mother's house. My husband, Captain M.G., was at that time serving another tour in Vietnam. My brother, Captain Joseph D., was in army intelligence in Vietnam when on February 28, 1967, his plane crashed and burned. The pilot and my brother died instantly.

"Several months after my brother's death my mother fell and broke her hip and dislocated her shoulder. Naturally she had to be hospitalized, and when she returned home about a month later, she had to have around-the-clock help. When this incident I am about to relate occurred, she was not in the house alone but had a practical duty night nurse who was then in the living room. My mother's apartment was on the downstairs floor. At the time she had her bedroom door closed and her room was definitely darkened as she had always been a light sleeper and was sensitive to noise and lights. She was lying in bed and was beginning to feel relaxed, although she was not yet asleep, when the room suddenly seemed to be illuminated and sort of 'pressurized.' Then she saw her son, Joseph, standing near the foot of her bed, smiling at her. She could see him as clearly as if it were daylight."

There followed a brief conversation between mother and son, in the course of which she asked him how his father was and he replied that his father, who had died four years before, was fine. The vision then disappeared, but Mrs. D. could still sense him in the room with her. She began to tremble and started to cry. She called out to her night nurse, but since the door was closed the nurse couldn't hear her, so Mrs. D. picked up a small object from her night table and threw it against the door. The nurse, Mrs. F.S., came into the room, where Mrs. D. was now crying uncontrollably. When the nurse entered the room, Mrs. D. cried out, "Oh, Mrs. S., Joseph was here." To her surprise, the nurse replied, "Yes, I know. I saw a brown shadow go past the dining-room table."

The following morning Mrs. D. became somewhat calmer after she had informed her daughter of the event of the previous night. Another nurse was on duty then, and shortly after she had had her nursing care Mrs. D. went back to bed with the intention of taking a nap, since she had been awake so much of the previous night. As soon as she was alone in her room with the door shut, her dead son reappeared suddenly and said to her, "Mother, I am sorry that I frightened you last night." Then he disappeared again. This time Mrs. D. was not upset. For one thing it convinced her that she had not been dreaming the incident the night before. There was no doubt about it; the apparition had been that of her late son, Joseph. He had appeared solid, not transparent, as legendary ghosts usually are. Mrs. D., under questioning by her daughter, Mrs. G., stated that Joseph had been dressed in civilian clothing, a shirt and pants. Mrs. G. thought that that was significant because her brother, Joseph, although an army career man, had been

bitter toward the service at the end and would have wanted to appear in civilian clothing on his last journey.

William Hull of Brooklyn, New York, is a member of an amateur theatrical group called the Promenade Players. "During our last show, our director, Joan Bray, became ill, and nearly died," he told me. "Joan loves to entertain especially us in the group, but because of her illness had not been able to most of the summer. On July 31 of this year she felt good enough to have us over for dinner. She invited half of the group on Friday and the rest for Monday, August 3. Because he had moved and not left a phone number, she had not been able to contact Chuck Taylor, our lead in the last show.

"While she was preparing dinner on Friday afternoon, the thirty-first, Chuck called and in a characteristic manner asked when he would be invited over for dinner. Joan told him he could come either that evening or the following Monday. He replied that he would much rather come when he could eat alone with Joan and her teenage daughter. Joan didn't think this request out of the ordinary as Chuck was a person who was always 'on stage' with a group but liked to relax and was a different person when he was alone with someone. So no definite date was set, but Chuck did give Joan a phone number to reach him at so that she could invite him when she felt like it. Then, in closing the telephone conversation, Chuck made an unusual request: 'Take care of yourself, Joan,' he said in a sober voice. Joan replied that she would. 'No, I really mean it. Take care of yourself,' he repeated. Again Joan replied that she always took care of herself. To placate him, Joan promised and this ended the conversation. Joan didn't think about the conversation except to mention to those of us that asked that she had heard from Chuck and he had left a number to reach him.

"About the twelfth of August a photographer friend of mine, also a member of our group, tried to contact Chuck to tell him that some long-ago ordered prints were finally ready. He discovered that Chuck had collapsed and died on the seventeenth of July. Of course, we thought that there must be some mistake, but by careful check we found that he had died and had been buried on the twentieth. Now the only other explanation was that it was not Chuck that called that afternoon, but Joan Bray knew Chuck better than anyone else. Her long and close relationship with him seemed to rule out any possibility of an imposter calling."

Romer Troxell, father of twenty-four-year-old Charles Troxell, whose body had been found punctured with bullets and stripped of identification by a roadside in Portage, Pennsylvania, can attest to the reality of communication from the dead. According to the *Los Angeles Times* of May 30, 1970, the father kept hearing the son's voice directing him to the accused killer. It all started when he looked at the face of his dead son in the Portage morgue. "My son just spoke to me," the father is quoted as saying, "He said, 'Hi, pop. I knew you would come. He's got my car.'"

After the body had been positively identified, the father was notified. Since the police were tight-lipped about the

investigation, Troxell and his family went to stay with his brother in Gary, Indiana. But he became restless and found himself in his car with his wife and sister-in-law as if he were searching for something. His dead son, Charles, was guiding him. He drove along a road he had not been on when he suddenly heard his dead son's voice telling him, "Here he comes, Pop." But there was just a hill ahead and no sign of any car. Then he saw the yellow Corvette coming over the crest and Charlie told him, "Here he comes, Pop. Take it easy. He is armed. Don't get excited. He's going to park soon." The father followed the car, and as soon as it had parked outside a high school he went up to the young driver later identified as the murderer. "The boy knew who I was," the father continued his story. "He said he had seen my car at my brother's home." But he claimed that Charles had sold him the car, adding that he had not seen Charles for two days. When the father asked, "Are you sure?" the boy said, "No, but isn't he dead?" Then Troxell knew he had the killer before him because his son's identity had not been published in the newspapers and only the police and the family knew about it. As the father continued his conversation with the young man, he again heard his son's voice saying, "Be careful, Pop. He's got a gun." Under the circumstances, Troxell decided to play it lightly. He knew that the police, summoned by his sister-in-law, were en route. As soon as the boy had been arrested and charged with the murder, the son's spirit voice faded and has not been back since.

Examples like these can be found by the thousands, all fully documented.

Communications between the living and the dead, whether initiated by the dead or by the living, use the faculty of ESP to make themselves felt. Only if the recipient of such communication has sufficient ESP to convert the fine emanations sent out from the nonphysical world can the conscious mind register the information. An emergency, an emotional necessity, or any kind of urgency will make the impact much stronger. In the cases just discussed, the need to communicate was present. Ordinary communication was impossible. The majority of such ESP communications from the dimension beyond the physical are initiated by the dead themselves. All the recipient can hope for is to be a good channel. The way to accomplish this is to achieve a relaxed attitude of body, mind, and spirit; by relaxing the body, the nervous system is likely to exclude external interference and disturbances; the mind, by clearing itself of cross-current thoughts and becoming as blank as possible, permits itself to serve as receiver; and the spiritual self, by accepting as reality such communications and the higher guidance that it implies, ties it all up in a neat package of possible breakthroughs.

To initiate communication with the dead via the ESP route is another matter. If there were a compelling reason for such communication, putting oneself in a state of receptiveness would be the first step. Visualizing the desired contact on the Other Side of life may help if a specific contact is desired. But you cannot summon the dead; you cannot reach out to them at will and command them to appear or to get in touch with you. At best you can hope to set up conditions favorable to their wanting to communicate with you. If your need is genuine and your state is one of relaxed receptiveness, the communication may occur. Patience and a disregard of time is also valuable, since conditions may appear favorable to us but are not so when seen from the point of view of the Other Side. At any rate, there is no other way of communicating with the Other Side except by ESP. Only thought forms can break through the barrier separating the two worlds. The stronger your ESP, the more disciplined your application of it, the more likely it is that you will be able to have contact with those who have gone on to the nonphysical world.

Communications and experiences involving loved ones or friends who have died are but one kind of contact due to the psychic ability. Entering a haunted house or area, a psychic person may easily have one of two types of experiences. The person "relives" a scene from the past, usually emotionally tinged, but without actual spirit entities present—"ghosts," in common terms. The less frequent experience is an actual encounter with a spirit unable to leave the area where his tragic death has taken place: a true ghost, not always seen or heard the same way, but always tied to the place where the unfinished transition to the next world began through physical death. Being psychic, the person seeing or hearing such a spirit person can communicate with that person and perhaps try to convince the ghost that passing over is desirable.

But as newspaper editor William Allen White stated, "A picture is worth ten thousand words," and so it is that genuine psychic photography is a scientific instrument to explore and prove the existence of a hereafter, the Other Side.

THE DEVELOPMENT OF PSYCHIC PHOTOGRAPHY

Ever since man first wondered about a life after death, he has tried to find some convincing proof, or at least evidence, that there is something within us all that survives the death of the physical body. For the past hundred years, psychic research has painstakingly assembled proof for the continuance of life and has gradually emerged from a metaphysical mantle into the full glare of scientific inquiry. Although various researchers interpret the results of these investigations according to their own attitudes toward survival of human personality, it is no longer possible to bury the evidence itself, as some materialistically-inclined scientists in other fields have attempted to do over the years. The challenge is always present: does man have a soul, scientifically speaking, and if so, how can we prove it?

Material on communications with the so-called dead is very large and often convincing, though not necessarily all of it in the way it is sometimes presented by partisans of the spiritualist religion. But additional proof that man does continue an existence in what Dr. Joseph Rhine of Duke University has called "the world of the mind" was always wanted, especially the kind of proof that could be viewed objectively without the need for subjective observation through psychic experiences, either spontaneous or induced in the laboratory. One of the greatest potential tools was given man when photogra-

phy was invented: for if we could photograph the dead under conditions that carefully exclude trickery, we would surely be so much the wiser—and the argument for survival would be stronger.

Photography goes back to the 1840s, when the technique evolved gradually from crude light-and-shadow pictures, through daguerreotypes and tintypes to photography as we now know it. Major Tom Patterson, a British psychic researcher, in a booklet entitled *Spirit Photography*, has dealt with the beginnings of photographic mediumship in Britain, where it has produced the largest amount of experimental material in the century since.

But the initial experiment took place in 1862, in Boston, not Britain, twenty-three years after photography came into being. William H. Mumler, an engraver who was neither interested in nor a believer in spiritualism or any other form of psychic research, had been busy in his off-hours experimenting with a camera. At that time the photographic camera was still a novelty. The engraver liked to take snapshots of his family and friends to learn more about his camera. Imagine Mumler's surprise and dismay when some of his negatives showed faces that were not supposed to be on them. In addition to the living people he had so carefully posed and photographed, Mumler discovered the portraits of dead relatives alongside the "normal" portraits.

This was the beginning of psychic photography. It happened accidentally—if there is such a thing as an accident in our well-organized universe—and the news of Mumler's unsought achievements spread across the world. Other photographers, professionals and amateurs, discovered talents similar to Mumler's, and the psychic research societies in Britain and America began to take notice of this amazing development.

Since then a great many changes have taken place in our technology and we have greater knowledge of its pitfalls. But the basic principle of photography is still the same. A film covered with silver salts is exposed to the radiation called light and reacts to it. This reaction results in certain areas of the emulsion being eaten away, leaving an exact replica of the image seen by the camera lens on the photographic film. Depending on the intensity with which light hits the various portions of the film, the eating away of silver salts will vary, thus rendering the tones and shadings of the resulting negative upon light-sensitive photographic paper and hence the positive print, which is a mechanical reproduction of the negative's light and shadow areas, but in reverse.

To make a print, the operator inserts his finished negative into a printer, places the light-sensitive paper underneath the negative, and exposes it through the negative with an electric light. Nothing new can be added in this exact manner, nor can anything already on the negative be taken away, but the skill of the craftsman operating the printer will determine how well balanced the resulting positive print will be, depending on the duration and intensity of the printing lamp.

The obtaining of any sort of images on photographic paper, especially recognizable pictures such as faces or figures, without having first made a negative in the usual manner is a scientific impossibility—except in psychic photography.

Until the arrival of Polaroid cameras and Polaroid film, this was true. The Polaroid method, with its instant result and development of film within a matter of a few seconds after exposure, adds the valuable element of close supervision to an experiment. It also allows an even more direct contact between psychic radiation and sensitive surface. The disadvantage of Polaroid photography is its ephemeral character. Even the improved film does not promise to stay unspoiled forever, and it is wise to protect unusual Polaroid photographs by obtaining slide copies. Actually, Polaroid photography uses a combination of both film and sensitive paper simultaneously, one being peeled off the other after the instant development process inside the camera.

Fakery with the ordinary type of photography would depend on double exposure or double printing by unscrupulous operators, in which case no authentic negative could be produced that would stand up to experienced scrutiny. Fakery with Polaroid equipment is impossible if camera, film, and operator are closely watched. Because of the great light sensitivity of Polaroid film, double exposure, if intended, is not a simple matter, as one exposure would severely cancel out the other and leave traces of double exposure. And the film would have to be switched in the presence of the observer, something not even a trained conjurer is likely to do to an experienced psychic investigator. A psychic researcher must also be familiar with magic and sleight-of-hand tricks to qualify for that title.

The bulk of psychic photography occurred unexpectedly and often embarrassingly to amateur photographers not the least bit interested in parapsychology or any form of occultism. The extras on the negatives were not placed there by these people to confuse themselves. They were the portraits of dead relatives or friends that could be recognized. The literature on this phase of psychic photography, notably in Britain, is impressive; I particularly recommend the scholarly work by F. W. Warrick, the celebrated British parapsychologist, called *Experiments in Psychics,* in which hundreds of experimental photographs are reproduced. Warrick's work concerns itself primarily with the photographic mediumship of Emma Deane, although other examples are included. It was published in 1939 by E.P. Dutton. Warrick points out that he and his colleagues, having spent some thirty years working with and closely supervising their subjects, knew their personal habits and quirks. Any kind of trickery was therefore out of the question, unless one wanted to call a researcher who propounded unusual ideas self-deluded or incompetent, as some latter-day critics have done to Harry Price and Sir William Crookes, respected British psychic researchers, now dead.

Anyone who is not present when the original experiments or investigations take place and who does not possess first-hand knowledge of the conditions and processes of that investigation is no more qualified to judge its results than an armchair strategist trying to rewrite history. Although Major Patterson's booklet uses the scientific evidence at hand to support the spiritualistic view, it also serves as a useful source of factual information.

Mumler's record as the "first" spirit photographer is upheld by U.S. Court of Appeals judge John Edmond, who investigated Mumler and obtained photographs under test conditions of people known only to him who were dead. Originally, Judge Edmond had gone into the investigation thinking it was all a deception. In a letter published by the *New York Herald* on August 6, 1853, however, the judge spoke not only of Mumler's experiments but also of his subsequent sittings with well-known mediums of his day. These investigations had convinced him that spiritualism had a valid base, and he became a confirmed believer from then on, displaying psychic abilities of his own as time went by.

In England, the craft of psychic photography developed slowly from the 1870s onward. The first in Britain to show successful results in this field was Frederick Hudson, who in 1872 produced a number of authentic likenesses of the dead under conditions excluding fraud. Several experiments were undertaken under the careful scrutiny of Dr. Alfred Russel Wallace, a famed naturalist in his day. Wallace attested to the genuineness of the observed phenomena. Since then several dozen talented psychic photographers have appeared on the scene, producing for a few pennies genuine likenesses of persons known to have died previously in the presence of "sitters" (or portrait subjects) they had never before met in their lives.

As the craft became better known and men of science wondered about it, researchers devised more rigid test conditions for this type of experimental psychic photography. Film, paper, cameras, and developing fluid—all implements necessary to produce photographs of any kind—were furnished, controlled, and held by uncommitted researchers; the medium was not allowed to touch anything and was kept at a distance from the camera and film. In many cases he was not even present in the room. Nevertheless psychic "extras" kept appearing on the properly exposed film and were duly recognized as the portraits of dead persons, often of obscure identity, but traceable as relatives or friends of someone present. Occasionally, as with John Myers, once America's leading psychic photographer, early portraits obtained by the photographic medium were strangers to all concerned until the pictures were published in *Psychic News*, a leading spiritualist newspaper of the day, and the "owners" of the psychic "extras" had written in to the editor to claim their dead relatives!

Despite the overwhelming evidence that these photographs were genuine—in almost all cases even the motive for fraud was totally absent—some researchers kept rejecting then and now the possibility that the results were anything but fraudulently manufactured double exposures. Even so brilliant a person as Eileen Garrett, president of the Parapsychology Foundation, insisted for many years that all psychic photographs had to be fraudulent, having been so informed by a pair of self-styled experts. It was only when I produced the photographs of ghosts herein published, and acquainted Garrett with the camera, film, and other details of how the pictures were obtained, that she reluctantly agreed with me that we had made a breakthrough in the field of psychic photography. Prejudice against

anything involving a major shift in one's thinking, philosophy of life, and general training is much stronger than we dare admit to ourselves sometimes.

Often psychic photography occurs at so-called home circles, where neither money nor notoriety is involved and where no need exists for self-delusion by those taking the pictures. They are, presumably, already convinced of the survival of personality after death, otherwise they would not be members of the circle.

Photographs of ghosts or haunted areas are much rarer because of the great element of chance in obtaining any results at all. Whereas psychic photography in the experimental sense is subject to schedules and human plans, the taking of ghost pictures is not. Even I had neither advance knowledge nor control over the ones I managed to obtain, and I could not do it again that way if I tried. We still don't know all the conditions that make these extraordinary photographs possible and, until we do, obtaining them will be a hit-and-miss affair at best. But the fact that genuine photographs of what are commonly called ghosts have been taken by a number of people, under conditions excluding fraud or faulty equipment is food for serious thought.

An example is the photograph of a Danish sailor fighting for his life at Ballyheigue Castle, Ireland, taken by a vacationing army officer named Captain P. D. O'Donnell, on June 4, 1962. Unbeknownst to Captain O'Donnell, that was the anniversary of the sailor's death during the "silver raid," in which the silver stored at the castle was stolen by local bandits and fighting ensued. Captain O'Donnell took this snapshot without thought or knowledge of ghosts, while inspecting the ruins of the once proud castle. The picture was later lost in transit and could not be located by the post office. The captain, a professional officer and a practical man, did not pay too much attention to what to him was a puzzling fact and nothing more.

Many newspapers the world over, including *The People* of July 3, 1966, which published a ghost photograph taken by eighteen-year-old Gordon Carroll, a clerk, of Northhampton, England, in Saint Mary the Virgin Church, Woodford, Northhamptonshire. The picture clearly shows a monk kneeling before the altar, but at the time he took it Gordon was the only person inside the church. Fortunately, he found an understanding ear in the person of Canon John Pearce-Higgins, provost of Southwark Cathedral and a member of the Church's Fellowship of Psychic and Physical Research. Pearce-Higgins, after inspecting the camera and film and questioning the young man, was satisfied that the phenomenon was authentic.

Gordon had used a tripod and a brand-new Ilford Sportsman Rangefinder camera. He loaded it with Agfa C.T. 18 film, which he often uses to photograph stained-glass windows in churches, a hobby of his. The Agfa Company, upon examining the film, confirmed that trick photography had not been used and that neither film nor developing showed any faults. As for the ghost, no one seems to have bothered to find out who he was. The church is an ancient place, mentioned in the *Domesday Book*, a list of important properties compiled under William the Conqueror. A church stood

on that spot even before the Norman conquest of Britain, so it is possible that at one time a monk died there, tragically becoming the ghost that Gordon's camera accidentally saw and recorded.

Joe Hyams, writer and husband of actress Elke Sommer, had shared a haunted house with her for some time in Hollywood, only to give up to the ghost in the end. During the last stages of their occupancy, a photographer named Allan Grant, strictly a nonbeliever, took some pictures in the aftermath of a fire of mysterious origin. The pictures, published in *The Saturday Evening Post* of June 3, 1967, clearly show manifestations not compatible with ordinary photographic results.

The latest development in the area of psychic photography, although not concerned with images of ghosts, is still germane to the entire question. *Thought forms* registering on photographic film or other light-sensitive surfaces are the result of years of work by Colorado University's Professor Jule Eisenbud, a well-known psychiatrist interested in parapsychology, with Chicago photographic medium Ted Serios. These amazing pictures have been published by Eisenbud in an impressive volume called *The World of Ted Serios*. In addition, more material has become available as the experiments continued and are continuing today, thanks to the efforts of a number of universities and study groups that have belatedly recognized the importance of this type of experiment.

Serios has the ability of projecting images onto film or a TV tube of objects and scenes, often at great distances in space, or even *time*. This includes places he has never visited or seen. Dr. Eisenbud does not suggest that there are spirit forces at work here. He points out, quite rightly, that we do not as yet realize some of the areas in which the human mind can operate. Without having been present at the many sessions in which Eisenbud and a host of other scientists subjected Serios to every conceivable test, I cannot judge the results. But it appears to me from what I have read in the book, and from other Serios photographs shown to me privately, that Serios is capable of what we call astral projection. In these out-of-body states he visits distant places in a flash, then almost instantly returns to his physical body and records the impressions received by his etheric eyes onto Polaroid film. I think that Ted Serios is one of an impressive line of photography mediums.

There may be differences of opinion concerning the implications of psychic photography, with some taking the attitude that it represents a record of past events that somehow got left behind in the atmosphere during the event. This is possible in a number of cases. But there are also an impressive number of other instances where this view does not fit and where only the unpopular theory (scientifically speaking) of survival of human personality in another world will satisfy as an explanation.

THE PSYCHIC PHOTOGRAPHERS

The *possibility* of fraud is always present when planned experiments take place. But the possibility of an explosion is also always present when munitions are being manufactured, and no one stops making them. One proceeds with great care in both cases. Magicians and other conjur-

ers have, almost to a man, assaulted psychic photography as patently fake, since *they* could fake it. This is a neat trick. By suggesting the possibility as the probability, these limited people (spiritually speaking) miss the point of scientifically controlled experiments in psychic photography: it is not what *could* be that matters, but what actually *does* happen.

I have no reason to doubt the majority of the older psychic photographs I have examined but, since I was not present when they were taken and have no way of knowing how rigid the controls were at the time, I will not vouch for them. Anything I vouch for has occurred in my presence or under my controls and with persons known to me under conditions considered appropriate by professional parapsychologists.

When I studied the literature on this subject, notably Warrick's work *Experiments in Psychics*, I was impressed by the sincerity of Warrick's approach and by his sensible controls, through which he made sure that his subjects could not obtain their amazing results by trickery. Warrick's work deals to a large extent with the mediumship of Mrs. Deane, a British psychic famed for her ability to produce photographs of the dead under conditions excluding fraud.

It was the same Mrs. Deane who was once visited by John Myers, then a novice in the field. He came to have a "sitting," like everyone else who sought out the elderly woman, and, for a few pennies, was photographed in her presence. He was to discover afterward the portrait of a dead loved one near him on the plate! To Myers's surprise, Deane told him that some day soon he would be taking her place. Myers smiled incredulously and walked out. But when Deane's health failed some time later, Myers, who had since discovered his own psychic and photographic powers, did take over her studio.

I met John Myers in New York in 1959 because I had heard of his special psychic talents and was anxious to test him. Myers, at that point, and more so later, was a man of independent means, a successful industrialist and well-known philanthropist who could not possibly gain anything from exposing himself to psychic research. But he also felt he owed something to his benefactors on the Other Side, as the spiritualists call it, and for that reason he agreed to meet me. This indebtedness went back many years to when he was a dental surgeon in London, already aware of his psychic abilities and practicing two of his special crafts as sidelines: psychic photography—later a full-time occupation—and psychic healing. As a healer, he managed to help a wealthy American regain his eyesight when orthodox doctors had failed. In gratitude this man offered him a position in his company in New York. At the time Myers was not making too much money, since he charged only a few pennies for each psychic photograph he took, and nothing for his healing work. He felt that the opportunity to go to America was being sent his way so that he might be useful in his new career as a psychic, so he accepted.

In New York, Myers proved himself an asset to the company and eventually he rose to become its vice president. Because of his new duties Myers now pursued his psychic work on only a sporadic basis, but behind the scenes he often backed other psychics or sponsored spiritualistic meetings that could not have found a hall were it not for Myers's financial support. He continued his activities as a psychic healer. Occasionally Myers agreed to tests, but only when important scientists or newspapermen were to be present. What Myers could no longer do in amount of work he made up for by the sheer power of observers' rosters.

I was able to test Myers's abilities as a psychic photographer on several occasions, under conditions I will presently describe. At no time did he try to influence me in any way, or suggest anything, except that he was a sensitive man who resents being insulted. On one occasion I managed to persuade him to give a second public demonstration of his psychic photography on television. Since the first TV test in 1961 was, to my mind, very impressive, I felt another such test might prove valuable. The program that had requested this test was ABC's late-night show emceed by Les Crane. This brash young man had, on a previous occasion, proved himself to me to be a man without sympathy toward psychic research, but I was there to protect Myers from any unpleasant remarks. We had brought the usual chemicals, all open to examination, and the program's producer had provided the photographic paper to be exposed; that is, they had it ready. But the moment never came. They had booked too many acts on this occasion, so that time ran out before Myers and I could undertake the test. For over two hours Myers sat waiting quietly in the wings. But the people who were in charge failed to understand the significance of Myers's willingness to do this experiment, so he went home angry, quite rightly, and I hadn't been able to coax him onto television again. Here, then, are the exact circumstances of my experiments with John Myers.

My first meeting with Myers in 1959 was followed by a sitting, which was arranged for the purpose of demonstrating his abilities as a psychic photographer. This was in late July, and I set up the following test conditions: Myers was to accompany me on the afternoon of the planned sitting to a photographic supply store of my choice and selection, where I would purchase the light-sensitive paper he required. Myers asked the clerk for ordinary developing paper. There are many types, of varying light-sensitivity, and Myers selected a medium-fast paper. The clerk brought the package of paper and I satisfied myself that it was from a fresh batch of materials, properly sealed and in no way damaged or tampered with. I then placed my signature across all corners of the outer envelope, and Myers did the same. The reason for Myers's insistence that he too should be allowed to place his own safeguards on the package goes back many years. When still a young man in England, gaining a reputation as a psychic photographer, Myers was challenged to a test by a brash young journalist named Lord Donegal. Not content to look for possible fraud by Myers, Donegal wanted to make sure he *would* be able to find some. Rather than take his chance that Myers might be honest, Donegal switched plates on him and thus produced a foolproof "fraud"— marked plates he had supplied. Myers was accused publicly, and it took years of work to undo the damage. In the end, tiring of the joke, Donegal admitted his deeds. But the whole sorry business had turned Myers from a friendly, open-hearted man into a cautious, suspicious person who never quite trusted any experimenter fully.

For this reason, Myers wanted his signature on the package next to mine, so that he too could be sure I had not been tampering with the package to his detriment. As soon as the bill for the paper was paid, I took the package and put it into my pocket. At no time did Myers hold it in his hands. We parted company and I went home, the package still in my possession. After dinner I went to Myers's apartment on Sutton Place, where he and five other witnesses were already present. One of these was a photographer named Hagedorn, a skeptic, and one was Myers's legal adviser, Jacob Gerstein, an attorney well known in business circles for his integrity and keen observation. Also present was Danton Walker, Broadway columnist of the *Daily News*, himself psychic and keenly interested in the subject, but by no means sure of its implications. None of the observers was a "believer" as the term is usually used, but all were enlightened witnesses who were willing to accept unusual facts if they could be proven.

1. a. Posthumous portrait of Holzer's mother obtained on television through mediumship of John Myers. Photograph taken during her lifetime is at left.

b. Portrait of Holzer's aunt, killed during World War II, and her psychic picture.

c. Psychic picture of Holzer's friend Myers never saw.

HOW THIS PICTURE WAS OBTAINED

TIME: September 1961, 8:00 P.M.

PLACE: On the air, during a television pro-gram entitled *PM East* for Channel 5, New York, Mike Wallace, moderator.

LIGHT CONDITIONS: Total darkness in the studio except for one overhead 60-watt yellow bulb, at a distance of about 20 inches.

CAMERA: No camera used.

FILM: No film, but ordinary photographic printing paper (gaslight paper), purchased independently by Mike Wallace at a shop of his own selection and kept sealed until air time.

EXPOSURE: Immediately upon opening pack-

Psychic photographs obtained on Channel 5 through the mediumship of John Myers, under absolute test conditions, with Mike Wallace as monitor, showing Holzer's late mother in upper right and her matching life-time portrait in upper left; psychic photograph recognized as Holzer's late aunt lower center, and her lifetime picture, lower left; and psychic photograph of a close friend of Holzer's on lower right—obtained under absolute scientific test conditions during a New York experiment.

a.

b.

c.

age of unexposed photographic paper, each sheet was immersed in developer individually by Wallace, then transferred by him to hypo for fixation of obtained images. At no time did medium John Myers or I touch photographic papers until after they had been covered by various impressions, which could not be accounted for by ordinary means of exposure. Each sheet was exposed to yellow light for the short time it took the hands of Mike Wallace to move the sheet from the package to the liquid.

OPERATOR: Mike Wallace, in the presence of myself and to my left, photographic medium John Myers, a dental surgeon and industrialist from London.

We repaired to a medium-sized room in which there was a table surrounded by four chairs, with additional chairs in the four corners. The only illumination came from a yellow overhead bulb, but the light was strong enough to read by without difficulty. The corners of the room were somewhat darker. Myers sat down on a chair in the left-hand corner, placed his hands over his eyes, and went into a trance. I took the photographic paper out of my pocket, where it had been all this time, and placed it on the table in view of everyone present. At no time had Myers or anyone else among the guests brushed past me or jostled me—a typical means of switching packages. Whenever I have the misfortune of sharing a microphone with a professional conjurer, this is one of his explanations of how the psychic phenomena must have been accomplished. I am familiar with many tricks of magic and always look out for them, but nothing of the sort was attempted. The package was

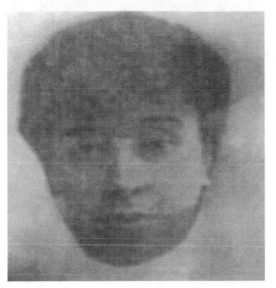

Enlargement of photos on facing page.

still sealed, exactly as it had been all afternoon. After about five minutes Myers breathed deeply and opened his eyes, saying with a somewhat tired voice, "The paper is now exposed. You can open the package." With that, Walker and I proceeded to tear open the outer envelope, then the package of light-sensitive paper, and quickly threw the twenty sheets contained in it into the developing liquid we had also brought along. As soon as the sheets hit the liquid, various things happened to them that really shouldn't have, if this had not been a psychic experiment.

2. Holzer supervising experiment of John Myers's psychic photography.

a. Pans for developer and fixative.

b. Holzer opening bag of chemicals.

c. Mr. and Mrs. Hans Holzer, fascinated by results in pans.

Unexposed photographic paper should show uniform results when exposed to a 60-watt yellow light and then developed.

But here we had different things happen with each sheet: some were blank; others had forms on them; some showed human faces; a few showed symbols, such as a tombstone, a tablet, a cross. As rapidly as we could, we worked over the whole pack. Walker pulled out the sheets and threw them into the developer. I pulled them from the latter and into the fixative solution and out into clear water. Myers was still on his chair in the corner. We then put all the papers on a big towel to dry, and turned on all the lights in the room. Without touching any of the

John Myers preparing himself for the experiment, with Holzer watching every step.

a.

b.

c.

prints, we started to examine the results of John Myers's psychic mediumship.

Clearly, if faces or figures appeared on these papers, fraud could not be the cause. One of the intriguing aspects of such an experiment is to hope for a likeness of someone one knew in physical life. Of course you never know who might turn up. Those who experiment or investigate psychic channels of various kinds and anxiously hope for a specific loved one to make an entrance are almost invariably disappointed. The result of these experiments is unpredictable, as well it should be. So it was with considerable glee that I discovered among the faces a familiar one. As soon as the paper was completely dry I took it over to a strong light to make sure I was not guilty of wishful thinking. There was no mistake about it. Before me was a portrait of an aunt of mine, not particularly close, but someone I once knew well.

Her name was Irma D. She had lived in Czechoslovakia and had fallen victim to the war. Exactly where or when she died we still don't know, for she, along with thousands of others, just disappeared under the Nazi occupation of her homeland. I found out about her sad end in 1945, when communications were restored with Europe. But this was 1959, and I really had not thought of her for many years. So it was with surprise that I found this sign of life, if you will, from a relative. I went to my family album on returning home, to make sure it was she. I did not have the identical picture, but I had a group photograph taken around the same period of her life. In this group shot, Irma is the girl on the right. The one on the left is my late mother, and the

one in the middle a school friend of both girls. This was taken when both sisters were single; the psychic face, however, dates to her early years of marriage, a period one might think she would have considered her best and happiest years.

I took the psychic likeness and presented it to my father, a total skeptic at that time, without telling him anything about it. Instantly he recognized his late sister-in-law. I tested various other relatives of Irma's, and the results were the same. I was so intrigued with all this that I implored Myers to give us another sitting immediately. He acceded to my request and on August 6, 1959, we met again at Myers's apartment. This time photographic film rather than paper was to be used, and a camera was brought into the room. The camera was a bellows-type using 120 film, and there was nothing unusual about its appearance. Myers uses cut film rather than roll film, and the bellows seemed to be in perfect condition when I examined the camera. But there is romance connected with the history of this old camera. It used to belong to the celebrated British psychic photographers William Hope and, later, Mrs. Deane, and passed into Myers's hands in 1930, coming with him to America five years later.

Again present were the photographer Charles Hagedorn and attorney Jacob Gerstein, along with two women, Gail Benedict, a publicist, and Mrs. Riccardi, an astrologer and artist. Hagedorn and Gerstein had bought the film at Kodak in New York, and the materials were in Hagedorn's possession until the moment when he and Gerstein loaded the camera in full view of the two women and myself. Farther back in the apartment, a group of about ten other people watched the entire experiment, without taking part in it. It took somewhat longer to develop the exposed film than the paper of the first experiment, but again strange "extras" appeared on the film. The paper experiment was repeated and several faces appeared on the sheets, none of them known to me or identified. This is not surprising, as psychic photography mediums are rare and the number of persons wishing to communicate from "over there" presumably very great. For what is more vital than to let those left behind know that life does go on? I kept in touch with John Myers after this experiment, but we did not try our hands again at it for the moment.

One day in 1960 I visited his office and he told me of some pictures he had recently taken by himself. I realized that these were not as valid as those taken under my eyes, but it seemed to me ludicrous to assume that Myers would spend an evening trying to defraud himself! So I asked to be shown the pictures. Strangely, Myers felt compelled to show me but one of the pictures. I blanched when I looked at it. Though not as sharp as an ordinary photograph, the portrait was clearly that of a dear friend of mine who had died unhappily and very young not long before. At no time had I discussed her with Myers, nor had Myers ever met her in life. To be sure I showed the picture to the young woman's mother and found her agreeing with me. At various séances and sittings this girl had made her presence known to me, often through strange mediums who didn't even know my name or who had never met me until then. So it did not exactly

come as a shock to see this further proof of a continued desire to communicate. But it was not until the summer of 1961 that Myers and I again discussed a major experiment. For one thing, he travels a great deal; and for another, I did not wish to subject him to repetitive experiments when his time was valuable. I wanted to try to add new areas of exploration each time.

But when a major television program came to me with the request to put together a package of psychic experiments, I decided to include John Myers and his psychic photography prominently. It was not easy to persuade him to step into this kind of limelight, with all its limitations and pressures, but in the end he agreed to come. We made our conditions known, and Mike Wallace accepted them on behalf of the show, called *PM East*, produced then by Channel 5, New York. Wallace, a total skeptic, was to purchase ordinary photographic paper in a shop of his own choice and keep it upon his person until air time. This he did, and the sealed, untampered-with paper was produced by him when the three of us went on camera. The developing and fixation liquids as well as the bowls were also supplied by the studio. Myers waited patiently in the wings while other segments of the program were telecast. All this time Wallace had the paper and liquids under his control. Finally we proceeded to take our seats on stage, with Myers on my left and Wallace on my right, perched on wooden stools without backs. The sole source of light now was an overhead yellow 60-watt bulb, and all the studio lights were turned off.

Immediately upon being on camera, the experiment began. When Wallace opened the package of sealed papers, and threw them one by one into the first liquid, immediately forms started to appear where no forms should appear, as we were dealing with virgin photographic paper. If by some freak condition these papers could have been exposed they should have appeared identical. This was not the case; several were blank, while others showed amorphous shapes and figures, one a human arm, one a head, and one an as yet indistinct face. At this point a commercially made continuation of the experiment was impossible, and the results were less than conclusive as far as the television audience was concerned. Something had appeared on the unexposed papers, but what? After the show I examined the dried prints carefully. One of them clearly showed a fine portrait of my late mother, who had died exactly four years before the experiment took place. I had not thought of having my late mother put in an appearance, so to speak, to convince the skeptics of survival, nor had John Myers any access to my family album. Myers did not even know that my mother had died.

Mike Wallace did not manufacture this picture, for he was and probably still is a nonbeliever in the possibility of personal survival. And I, as the researcher, would know better than to produce a fake picture of my own mother if I intended to put over a trick. If anyone's mother, then Wallace's or Myers's, not my own, when I would be the one person who had access to a likeness of my mother! The fact that the portrait that appeared is that of my late mother is less important than the fact that any face appeared, for even that is paranormal. Even if Myers had wanted to forge this psychic photograph, he would not have been able to do so. The picture of my mother in the family album is not accessible and had to be dug out from storage by me to match it up with the psychic image. I also had the negative stored away. The similarity is striking, notably the form of the nose and the parting of the hair; but there is a glow about the psychic photograph that is not present in the portrait made during her lifetime. The white cottonlike substance surrounding the face is what I call a "matrix," made up from substance drawn from Myers's body in some fashion and, in my opinion, superimposed upon the light-sensitive paper, thus making it psychically sensitive. Upon this "film upon a film," then, a thought form of my late mother was embedded, very much like a wire photo, except that the machine that made this possible was Myers's body. Controlled experiments of this kind have established that communications from the so-called dead can be received under conditions excluding any form of fraud, delusion, or self-delusion. No financial rewards whatever were involved for Myers in this experiment.

My next session with John Myers came about as a result of the interest taken by a United Press reporter named Pat Davis in the subject. I requested of John Myers that we try another experiment, and he agreed to do so on April 25, 1964. On this occasion the photographic paper was purchased by a trio of outsiders: Dr. S.A. Bell, a dentist; a woman associate of the doctor's; and Lee Perkins of New York. They accompanied Myers to a store of their own selection, where the paper was bought and initialed by them in the usual manner. Myers never touched the package. Three packages had been bought from a batch of photographic paper, presumed to be identical in all respects. The initialed three packages were then placed in a large envelope and the envelope sealed and stapled in the presence of attorney Jacob Gerstein, whose affidavit I have. Gerstein took charge of the paper and kept it with him until that evening, when he brought it along to Myers's apartment for the experiment.

In view of all those present—about a dozen observers unfamiliar with the subject matter, plus Davis and myself—Gerstein placed the three packages on the table and brought out three basins filled with developing and fixation liquids and water. Davis, who had never met John Myers until then, stepped forward and, on Myers's suggestion, picked one of the three packages, which again was examined by myself and Gerstein carefully as to possible violations. There were none. Davis opened the package and, one by one, placed the photographic paper sheets contained in it into the first pan. All this was in full electric light, with the observers standing close by around the table.

As soon as the sheets touched the first liquid, forms and faces began to appear on them, varying from sheet to sheet. Among them was a clear likeness of Frank Navroth, immediately identified by Jacob Gerstein, who knew this man before his death. Another photograph was that of a young girl who had died five or six years previously and was identified by one of

the observers present, Dan Kriger, an oil executive. Several people recognized the likeness of Congressman Adolph Sabath. Davis then requested that Myers leave the room so that we could determine whether his bodily nearness had any influence on the outcome of the experiment. Myers agreed and went to another part of the apartment. Davis then took the second of the packages and opened it and again submerged the sheets in it exactly as she had done with the first package. Nothing happened. All sheets were blank and exactly alike, a little fogged from the exposure to the strong room light, but without any distinguishing marks. She then opened the third and last package and did the same. Nothing appeared on the sheets. Finally we used a few sheets still remaining in the first package, and the results were negative as long as Myers was not at least in the same room.

John Myers is not the only reputable psychic photography medium. For many years I have known and worked with New Yorker Betty Ritter in cases involving her major talents as a clairvoyant.

3. Betty Ritter photograph showing ectoplastic concentrations.

HOW THIS PICTURE WAS OBTAINED

TIME: 1955. Evening.

PLACE: Reverend Boyd's spiritualist church in New York, during a quasi-public demonstration of Reverend M. Heaney.

LIGHT CONDITIONS: Normal room light (artificial). No strong reflectors of any kind.

CAMERA: Old-type bellows camera (Kodak), size 116.

FILM: Kodak, medium-fast film.
EXPOSURE: $\frac{1}{25}$ second.
OPERATOR: Betty Ritter.
DEVELOPING AND PRINTING: Local photography shop.

Since about 1955, Betty Ritter has obtained unusual photographs with her old-fashioned bellows camera, results that came as much as a surprise to her as to the people she photographed. She is guided by an intuitive feeling that she should photograph the audiences where psychic energies might be present, perhaps as a result of large-scale production of thought forms, prayers, and other man-made force fields. She has since taken her camera with her whenever going to a spiritualist church or meeting, or when sitting privately with people whom she knows well enough to be relaxed with. I have often examined her camera and found it in perfect working

order. She used standard film and average developing laboratories; later she finally learned to print from her negatives.

Pictures of this type are not too rare, and there seems to be a connection between the number of persons present in the room and the intensity of the phenomena. If ectoplasm is a substance drawn from the bodies of emotionally stimulated sitters, and I think it is, then this substance must assemble in some form or shape before it can be utilized via thought direction to perform some intelligent task. I suggest that these streaks, known as "rods," are the raw materials that are used in materializations of the dead, when these are genuine phenomena, and in poltergeist cases, when objects seemingly move of their own volition. The material, isolated some years ago in London and found to be a moist, smelly whitish substance related to albumen, undoubtedly comes from the body glands of the medium and

Rev. M. Heaney, spiritualist minister, demonstrating psychic photography in New York. Betty Ritter, medium, is the photographer.

her sitters or helpers. It is later returned to the sources, or that portion of it not used up at the end of the séance. It can be molded like wax into any form or shape. Strange as this may sound, it is thought direction that does the molding.

In the case of the spiritualist séance picture, no such molding has taken place and what we see on the picture is the free ectoplasm as it is manufactured and assembled. The naked eye does not normally see this. But the human eye does not register much of the spectrum, either. The combination of sensitive camera and sensitive photographer or operator seems

definite message or thought form.

One of those present at this small gathering in Reverend Boyd's church was Helen M., whose father had died seven years before. He had lost a leg in his physical life. The communicator, through the medium, wanted to prove his identity in some form and proposed to show his severed leg as a kind of signature, while making a point of his having two good legs once more in *his* world.

On the print (which matches the negative that I have seen), the white substance of the "new" leg is superimposed on the leg of the sitter. There appear to be two extra

Rev. M. Heaney demonstrating spirit whose leg was lost in life. Betty Ritter was the photographer.

to be the catalyst to put this material onto photographic film. Just how this works we don't know fully, but it happens frequently under similar conditions and in all such cases faulty materials or cameras have been ruled out.

In the second picture we see how the ectoplasm can be used to bring home a

hands in the picture, while the rest of the photograph is sharp, pointing to supernormal origin of the extras rather than conventional double exposure—the rest of the picture is sharply defined. It is my opinion that ectoplasm was molded via thought into the desired shapes and the latter then made capable of being photographed.

John Myers has passed on, but there are other psychic photographers doing this kind of work and research.

Gerri Warner has been able to do psychic photographs for many years; I met her through the medium Ethel Johnson Meyers in 1976 and tested her under rigorous scientific test conditions. She produced some remarkable psychic photographs, two of which are herewith presented. All her pictures are taken with a Polaroid camera and developed on the spot, from film I had carefully examined beforehand.

The first picture was taken in what was then my office and clearly shows me seated in front of filing cabinets but surrounded by ectoplastic formations. The picture may have been taken before these formations had fully materialized to represent either a person or some other rec-

ognizable image. The second example consists of two psychic photographs taken together and clearly showing the materialization of a woman—her arm and upper body. None of this was visible to the naked eye.

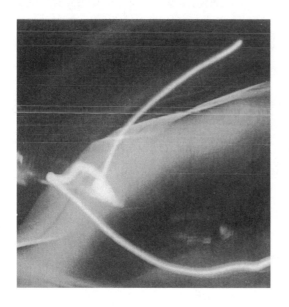

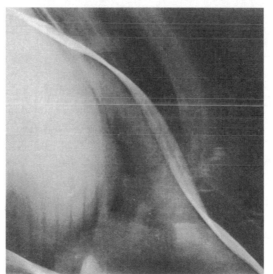

Above: Psychic photographer Gerri Warner took this unusual picture in Holzer's New York office, showing ectoplastic rods.

Left: In this experimental psychic photograph by Gerri Warner (Polaroid and developed on the spot), a female figure seems to begin to materialize.

Dr. Andrew von Salza, a West Coast physician originally without any interest in psychic matters, began to realize that he had a strange gift for psychic photography. He is a jolly and successful man and holds medical degrees from universities in Berlin and Tartu (Estonia). A leading rejuvenation specialist in California, he was nothing more than an amateur shutterbug without the slightest interest in anything supernormal or psychic.

Unexpected and unwarranted "extras" have appeared on his photographs, both those taken with regular cameras and with the speedy Polaroid type. He had known of my interest in psychic research through a mutual friend, Gail Benedict, the public-relations director of the Savoy-Hilton, where he usually stayed. Although I had heard about his strange encounters with this subject, my only previous meeting with the doctor was on a social occasion a year before, where others were present and when the chance to discuss the matter deeply did not present itself. At that time, too, Dr. von Salza met my then wife, Catherine, and was told that she was of Russian descent, to which he remarked that he was a Balt himself. But neither the doctor nor my wife went into any detailed history of her background.

In the second week of March 1966, von Salza arrived in New York on business and unexpectedly telephoned me, offering to experiment in my presence, as I had so long desired him to do. We arranged for a get-together at our house on Sunday, March 13, and I asked Gail Benedict to bring the doctor over. In addition, a friend of Benedict's, Marsha Slansky, a designer who was not particu-larly experienced in matters of psychic research, joined us as an observer. Shortly after the arrival of the guests, the doctor suddenly requested that my wife seat herself in an armchair at the far end of the living room, because he felt the urge to take a picture of her. It was at this point that I examined the camera and film and satisfied myself that no fraud could have taken place.

The first picture taken showed a clear superimposition, next to my wife, of a female figure, made up of a white, semi-transparent substance. As a historian I immediately recognized this as an attempted portrait of Catherine the Great. The sash of her order, which she liked to wear in many of her official portraits, stood out clearly on this print. We continued to expose the rest of the pack, and still another pack that I purchased at a corner drugstore a little later that evening, but the results were negative except for some strange light streaks that could not be accounted for. The doctor handed me the original picture, and the following day I had a laboratory try to make me a duplicate, which I was to send him for the record. Unfortunately the results were poor, the sash did not show at all in the reproduction, and I was told that this was the best they could do because the original was a Polaroid picture and not as easily copied as an ordinary print. At any rate I mailed this poor copy to Andrew von Salza in San Francisco with my explanation and regrets. To my surprise we received a letter from him, dated March 25, 1966, in which he enclosed two pictures of the same subject. Only this time the figure of Catherine the Great was sharp and detailed, much more so than in the original picture and superimposed upon the whitish outline of the first photograph. The whole thing looked so patently fraudulent at first glance that I requested exact data on how this second "round" was taken. Not that I suspected the doctor of malpractice, but I am a researcher and cannot afford to be noble.

Von Salza obliged. When he had received my poor copy of his fine psychic picture, he had tacked it to a blank wall in a corner of his San Francisco apartment to rephotograph it. Why he did this he cannot explain, except that he felt an urge to do so. I have his signed statement to the effect that he used a Crown Graphic camera with Polaroid back, size 4 x 5, an enlarging lens, opening of F/32, with the camera mounted on a tripod about a yard or less away from the subject. His exposure for the rephotographing experiment was one second by daylight plus one 150-watt lamp.

Von Salza offered to repeat the experiment in my presence whenever I came to San Francisco. What struck me as remarkable about the whole business was the fact, unknown to the doctor, that my former wife Catherine is a sixth-generation descendant of Catherine the Great. This was not discussed with him until after the first picture was obtained. Nevertheless Gail Benedict reports that on the way over to our apartment, von Salza suddenly asked, "Why do I keep thinking of Catherine the Great?" Now had he wanted to defraud us, surely he would not have tipped his hand in this manner. The two rephotographed pictures sent to me by the doctor are not identical; on one of them a crown appears over my

former wife's head! I should like to mention here that several psychics with whom my former wife and I have "sat," who knew nothing whatever about her or her background, have remarked that they "saw" a royal personality protecting her. New York medium Betty Ritter even described her by name as Catherine. My former wife has for years had a strong interest in the historical Catherine, and finds herself drawn frequently to books dealing with the life of the empress. Although her sisters and brothers are equally close in descent to the Russian ruler, they do not show any particular affinity toward her.

The whole matter of these pictures was so outlandish that I felt either they were clever frauds and that I was being duped (although I did not see how this was possible under my stringent conditions) or that the material had to be factual, appearances to the contrary. Circumstantial evidence can be misleading in so controversial a subject as psychic photography and I was determined not to allow opinions, pro or con, to influence my findings in this case.

Consequently, I went to San Francisco in the middle of May 1966 to test the good doctor. In my presence he took the original picture and mounted it on the wall, then placed film into his Crown Graphic camera with a Polaroid back. I inspected camera and film, and nothing had been tampered with. The first two pictures yielded results; again a clear imprint of Catherine the Great was superimposed upon the whitish outline of the original. But this time Catherine extended an arm toward her descendant! In her extended right hand the empress tendered a crown to my wife, but the two pictures are otherwise different in detail and intensity, although taken one after the other under identical light and exposure conditions in my presence. At this point I became impatient and said, "I wish Catherine would give us a message. What is she trying to tell us?" As if I had committed *lèse-majesté*, the psychic camera fell silent; the next picture showed nothing more than the whitish outline. We discontinued the experiment at this point. I inspected the camera once more and then left the doctor.

Before we parted, I once more inspected the camera. It looked just like any ordinary Crown Graphic does, except for the Polaroid back, but even that is now being used by better photographers everywhere. The enlarging lens was still set at F/32; the exposure, I knew, had been just one second, using ordinary daylight reinforced by one 150-watt lamp.

4a. Catherine the Great

Von Salza later sent me a cheerful note in which he said, "Seeing is believing, but even seeing, so many cannot believe, including myself." He found the whole situation amusing and made no serious effort to do much about it scientifically, except that he did cooperate with me whenever I asked him to.

4. a. Contemporary print of Catherine the Great showing similar sash of order; note also outstretched arm, contour of hair.

b. Dr. Andrew von Salza took this remarkable picture of Catherine Holzer in her home; white extra of Mrs. Holzer's direct ancestor Catherine of Russia on right.

c. Second impression of Catherine shows it similar to contemporary prints. This picture was produced under Holzer's control.

HOW THESE PICTURES WERE OBTAINED

TIME: March 13, 1966, 9:00 P.M.

PLACE: The living room of Holzer's apartment, New York.

LIGHT CONDITIONS: Ordinary room light, shielded from reflection and glare, occasional lamps, but no overhead ceiling lights.

CAMERA: Polaroid 103, the better model of the line.

FILM: Polaroid film pack, obtained from photographic dealer and examined by myself prior to insertion in camera, and found untouched.

EXPOSURE: 1/100 second.

OPERATOR: Dr. Andrew von Salza of San Francisco.

His first encounter with the uncanny was in 1963, when the widow of a colleague of his, Dr. Benjamin Sweetland, asked him to do a photo portrait of her. Von Salza obliged, but imagine their surprise when the face of her late husband appeared superimposed on a lampshade in the room. No double exposure, no fraud, no rational explanation for this phenomenon could be found. To test this situation, he decided to photograph the widow Sweetland again, but with another camera and outdoors. Using a Leica and color film, and making sure that all was in order, he found to his amazement that one of the twenty exposures showed the late doctor's face against the sky.

Dismissing the whole incident for want of an explanation and trying his best to forget it, he was again surprised when another incident took place. This time he was using up the last picture in his roll, shooting at random against the wall of his own room. When the roll was developed, there appeared on the wall the face of a young girl who had not been there when he took the picture. He was upset by this and found himself discussing the matter with a friend and patient of his named Mrs. Pierson. She asked to be shown the pic-

ture. On inspection, she blanched. Andrew von Salza had somehow photographed the face of her "dead" young daughter. Although the doctor knew of the girl's untimely death, he had never seen her in life.

Several more incidents of this nature convinced the doctor that he had somehow stumbled onto a special talent, like it or not. He began to investigate the subject to find out if others also had his kind of "problems." Among the people interested in psychic phenomena in the San

4b. Picture taken by Dr. Andrew von Salza, physician, at the home of Holzer and his then-wife, Catherine, in 1966. The ectoplastic bust of the Russian empress Catherine the Great appeared on previously sealed Polaroid film. Von Salza had no knowledge of Catherine's relationship with the empress, her ancestor five times removed.

4c. Immediately following, von Salza rephotographed the ectoplastic bust and a more detailed image of the great Catherine emerged, also under test conditions excluding fraud or delusion.

Francisco area was a woman named Evelyn Nielsen, with whom von Salza later shared a number of experiments. He soon discovered that her presence increased the incidence rate of psychic "extras" on his exposures, although Nielsen herself never took a psychic photograph without von Salza's presence, proving that it was he who was the mainspring of the phenomena.

In early May 1965, I went to San Francisco to observe the doctor at work—psychic photography work, that is, not his regular occupation, which is never open to anyone but the subjects! I fortified myself with the company of two "outsiders," my sister-in-law, Countess Marie Rose Buxhoeveden, and a friend, social worker Lori Wynn, who came with me to von Salza's apartment. There we met the doctor, Evelyn Nielsen, and Mrs. Sweetland, as well as two other women, friends of the doctor who had been sympathetic to the subject at hand. It was late afternoon, and we all had dinner engagements, so we decided to get started right away.

With a sweeping gesture the doctor invited me to inspect the camera, already on its tripod facing the wall, or, as he called it, his "ghost corner," for he had always had best results by shooting away from the bright windows toward the darker portion of his big living room. The walls were bare except for an Indian wall decoration and a portrait of the doctor. In a way, they reminded me of motion-picture screens in their smoothness and blue-gray texture. But there was absolutely nothing on those walls that could be blamed for what eventually appeared "on" them.

I stepped up to the camera and looked inside, satisfying myself that nothing had been pasted in the bellows or gizmo, or on the lens. Then I looked at the film, which was an ordinary Polaroid film pack, black-and-white, and there was no evidence of its having been tampered with. The only way to do this, by the way, would have been to slit open the pack and insert extraneous matter into the individual pieces of film, something requiring great skill, total darkness, and time. Even then traces of the cuttings would have to appear. The pack von Salza used was fresh and untouched.

The room was bright enough, as light streamed in from the windows opposite the L-shaped couch that lined the walls. The seven of us now sat down on this couch. Von Salza set the camera and exposed the first piece of film. Within sight of all of us, he developed the film in the usual fast Polaroid manner and then showed it to me. Over our heads there appear clearly four extra portraits, and the wall can be seen through them. I did not recognize any of the four in this instance. The doctor continued, this time including himself in the picture by presetting the camera and then taking his place next to Evelyn Nielsen on the couch.

The second picture, when developed, evoked some gasps of recognition from the audience. Four faces of various size appeared and a light shaft (of psychic energy?) was now evident on the left side of the photograph. But the gasp of recognition was due to the likeness of the late John D. Rockefeller, Sr. I might add that this man must have an avid interest in communicating with the world he left at age ninety, some years ago. His face has appeared in other instances of psychic photography, especially in Britain with John Myers.

Again von Salza cocked the shutter and prepared for an exposure. This time the results were puzzling, for all that showed were some smoky outlines, possibly an attempt at writing letters. I asked that another picture be taken immediately to see if we could improve on this. We could, and the result was picture number four. This time the letters clearly spell the word *WAR*, and above the letter *A* appears a portrait of John F. Kennedy. Immediately, speculation arose as to whether the late president wanted to warn us of impending war or lament the present conflict. My first reaction on

was over, inspected the camera, the film, and the room once more.

This picture could have been faked or imitated by a clever person, but not under the circumstances under which it was obtained in my presence. This is the whole point: not the question of whether a psychic photo could be forged but whether it was or wasn't under the watchful eyes of the experienced observer. Unless a miracle even greater than that of genuine psychic photography took place, of which none of us are as yet aware, this Kennedy photo was not a forgery or the result of willful manipulation of any kind.

5: Prior to von Salza's demonstrating his gift for Holzer in New York, Holzer came to San Francisco and had the doctor do some psychic photographs with Polaroid film purchased and controlled by Holzer. Some famous people, such as John D. Rockefeller, Sr., appeared on the Polaroid pictures, developed on the spot after the camera had been carefully inspected. The people next to Holzer were there as witnesses.

seeing the Kennedy image was one of doubt and worry. It had to be faked. But how? I went over every detail of the experiment again and, after the meeting

Andrew von Salza never showed the pictures publicly, never made any claims whatever about them, and he is as puzzled about them as any outsider might be.

This curiosity made him continue the experiments privately, usually with Evelyn Nielsen as his only associate. In the same manner as in my presence, they obtained a number of interesting photographs, which I am also showing here. Although I was not physically in the room when they were taken, they were produced under identical circumstances and with identical materials and tools as those that were taken earlier in my presence.

I am satisfied that they are not fraudulent because of the absence of a motive, because similar pictures obtained by the same methods in my presence were genuine, and because of my close relationship with, and knowledge of, the two people involved.

6a. One of the following exposures with the same Polaroid pack showed the doctor himself in the picture, using a remote tripper. The word *war* appears on the wall overhead. This was during the Vietnam War, in 1965.

6b. The next exposure added JFK's portrait to the word *war*.

5. *During San Francisco experiment with Dr. Andrew von Salza, several portrait "extras" appeared on Polaroid film. Others on couch are Evelyn Nielsen, associate, and Dr. von Salza and friends.*

6. *a. Partially completed exposure of Polaroid film appears to be writing on wall; operator von Salza seated on right. Camera was tripped automatically.*

b. *Next exposure clarifies smoky writing as the word "WAR" with late President Kennedy's portrait above it. Also taken under Hans Holzer's complete control and supervision.*

7. *Psychic photo taken in Holzer's presence by Dr. von Salza shows portrait of the elder Rockefeller in center.*

7. In the next exposure, Al Smith, late New York governor, joins John D. Rockefeller.

Probably the most controversial (but nevertheless authentic) psychic photograph shows the portraits of JFK and Lincoln, obviously "thought forms" reproducing existing actual photographs, which is the easiest way for those on the Other Side to transmit an image of themselves.

HOW PICTURES 5-7 WERE OBTAINED

TIME: May 1965, late afternoon, bright sun.

PLACE: Apartment of Dr. Andrew von Salza, San Francisco.

LIGHT CONDITIONS: Daylight coming into the room.

CAMERA: Crown Graphic with Polaroid film back, 4 x 5.

FILM: Polaroid black-and-white film, fast.

EXPOSURE: F/16, 1/250 second.

OPERATOR: Dr. Andrew von Salza.

DEVELOPING: Instantaneous by von Salza in full view of witnesses.

WITNESSES: Evelyn Nielsen, Marie Rose Buxhoeveden, Lori Wynn, Mrs. Sweetland, two other women, and myself.

The first of these four pictures is more likely to bring doubts than any other photograph of this kind. This is because of the cut-out quality of Lincoln's portrait in the upper-right corner next to Kennedy's. Now this fact is not exactly new; all psychic photographers have at one time been accused of fraud because of appearances. The majority of—but not all—psychic "extras" (portraits) are not "new" faces of the dead but faithful reproductions of photographs or paintings of them while in the flesh. This is so universally true that one would have to condemn almost all psychic photos taken over the past hundred years, including some highly evidential tests, if one were to consider the reproduction of "cut-out"-type photographs as fraudulent per se. The obvious is not necessarily true, as circumstantial evidence tends to be misleading at times.

Communicators have frequently explained the need for a discarnate person to visualize first a photograph of himself before being able to transmit a thought image of that portrait to the medium and thence to photographic paper or film. Certainly, one can cut out a photograph and paste it up on another and rephotograph the whole thing with results not so different from what we have here. The point is that it does not necessarily follow. Bear in mind that the conditions under which psychic extras are obtained are the most important part of the evidence.

On a Friday morning in July 1967, Sybil telephoned me in great agitation. She had just had a vivid dream, or at any rate fallen into a state similar to the dream state. Someone named Vivien had communicated with her and remarked that she was now going on a holiday. Did I know any Vivien? Why me, I asked. Because this communicator wanted Sybil to call and tell me. Was there anything more? No, just that much. I pondered the matter. The only Vivien I ever knew was a young girl not likely to be on the Other Side as yet. But one never knows. I was still pondering the matter when the Saturday newspaper headlines proclaimed the death of Vivien Leigh. It appeared that she had just been discovered dead in her London apartment, but death might have come to her any time before Saturday, most likely on Friday. Suddenly I saw the connection and called Sybil. Did she know Vivien Leigh at all? She did, although she had not seen her for some time. Years ago Vivien Leigh consulted Sybil in personal matters, for Sybil is good at sorting things out for her friends.

There was definitely a relationship. No one in the world knew that Vivien Leigh had died on Friday. The discovery was made on Saturday. Yet Sybil had her communication during Thursday night. The date? June 30, 1967. I felt it was the actress's way of saying good-bye and at the same time letting the world know that life continued. That was on Saturday. On Monday Sybil had a visitor at the Stewart Studios, where she usually stayed when in New York. Her visitor, Edmond Hanrahan, was so impressed with the unusual decor of the studio that he decided to take some color pictures with his camera, which he happened to have with him at the time. The date was July 3, 1967. Several pictures were of Sybil Leek. There was nothing remarkable about any of them, except one. Partially obstructing Sybil is the face of a dark-haired woman with an unmistakable profile—that of Vivien Leigh.

8. British psychic Sybil Leek partially eclipsed by psychic photograph of erstwhile friend Vivian Leigh. Picture was taken about a week after star's death by semiprofessional photographer-yachtsman Edmond Hanrahan.

HOW THIS PICTURE WAS OBTAINED

TIME: July 3, 1967. Afternoon.
PLACE: Stewart Studios, New York.
LIGHT CONDITIONS: Room light, electric. No flash.
CAMERA: Honeywell Pentax, 35mm.
FILM: Ektachrome, artificial light (twenty exposures).
EXPOSURE: ¹⁄₅₀ second, open lens.
OPERATOR: Edmond Hanrahan.

DEVELOPING AND PRINTING: Local photography shop (via Kodak).

Both Sybil and the photographer remember clearly that there was no one else with them at the time, nor was there anything wrong with either film or camera. The psychic extra seems soft and out of focus, as if the figure had stepped between the camera and Sybil, but too close to be fully in focus.

I questioned Hanrahan about the incident. He admitted that this was not the first time something or someone other than the person he was photographing showed up on a negative. On one chilling occasion he'd been photographing the widow of a man who had

8. In early July 1967, the medium Sybil Leek sat for a routine portrait with a London photographer. Picture her surprise when actress Vivian Leigh, a friend of Sybil's, appeared in the same picture! But it was only a day later that her body was discovered and the world realized she had died.

been murdered. On the negative, the murdered man appeared next to his widow! Hanrahan lists his occupation as yachtsman; clearly he is not too worried about income, although he does do commercial photography when the spirit moves him.

He owns a yacht named *Parthenia* and lives on it most of the time. An American, he is somewhat of a mystery man. But there is no mystery about the method he used when the present photograph resulted. Using a Honeywell Pentax 35mm camera and Ektachrome film, he did not employ a flashgun but used all the available room light. He was relieved to hear that there was nothing wrong with his ability as a photographer or his camera, and that he could not be held accountable for unseen models.

Evelyn England is a photographer who has worked for most of the big movie studios in Hollywood, where she now lives. Presently she operates her own photography studio as a commercial photographer. Ever since she was young she had ESP experiences, especially of the gift of finding lost objects under strange circumstances, as if driven by some inner voice. But despite these leanings she had no particular interest in the subject and took it for granted that others also had ESP. One of her jobs is photographing high school graduations.

So it was a routine assignment when she was called upon to take the picture of a mathematics teacher we will call Mr. G. The date was Saturday, April 3, 1965. He was the last one of the faculty to come in for his portrait. Sunday her studio was closed. On Monday she developed and retouched the print, and Tuesday morning she mailed it to the school. A few hours later she received a phone call from the school principal. Had Mr. G. come in yet for his sitting? Yes, England answered, and informed the principal that the print was already in the mail. There was a slight pause. Then the principal informed her that Mr. G. had died unexpectedly on Sunday.

In May of the same year a man came into her studio who remarked that he felt she had a good deal of ESP, being himself interested in such matters. England took his portrait. He then came in to pick his choice from the proofs. She placed the print into the developer, but to her amazement, it was not Mr. H.'s face that came up: it was Mr. G.'s, the dead mathematics teacher's, face. A moment later, while she was still staring in disbelief, the portrait of her client Mr. H. came up on the same print, stronger than the first portrait and facing the opposite way from it.

England is a meticulous photographer. It is her habit never to leave an undeveloped print around. She will always develop each print fully when she does it, never leaving half-finished prints behind. No one but she uses the studio. There just wasn't any explanation for what had happened. The smiling face of the late mathematics teacher was there to remind her that life was not over for him or—perhaps a token of gratitude for having been the last person to have seen him alive. Hastily, England printed another picture of Mr. H., and it was a normal photograph.

Since then, other "dead" persons have used her skills to manifest themselves, but this incident has been the most remarkable one in her psychic life.

9. Commercial photographer Evelyn England accidentally produced psychic photo of dead client while developing another man's portrait.

HOW THIS PICTURE WAS OBTAINED

TIME: May 1965.
PLACE: Evelyn England's photography studio, Los Angeles.
LIGHT CONDITIONS: Studio printing lights.
CAMERA: A standard printer.
PAPER: Standard printing paper.
OPERATOR: Evelyn England, commercial photographer.

One of my longest and most difficult investigations concerned a pleasant bungalow in Los Angeles, built around 1929, and owned by the same owners since the beginning. After a couple of years in the house, the owners were forced to sublease because of financial reverses, and for nine years strangers lived in the house, not all of whom can still be recalled by the owners. It was during that period of estrangement from their house that something evidently took place to leave an indelible imprint on its atmosphere. When they repossessed their home, the L.'s soon discovered that they were being plagued by a variety of psychic phenomena that frightened them. At the same time they started to make inquiries into the events that had taken place at the house in their absence.

The disturbances ranged from measured footsteps where no one was seen to walk, to raps at their door, and from the feelings of presences—there were actually two, one male and one female—to such specific and detailed occurrences as a fight to the finish taking place audibly, but not visually, in the living room over and over again, only to stop abruptly

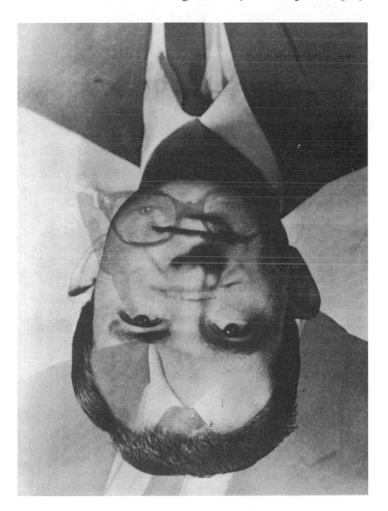

when a member of the family opened the door from one of the bedrooms. The

9. Los Angeles photographer Evelyn England took a routine photograph of a graduating class at a nearby school on April 3, 1965. A popular math teacher died the following day. That night, England cleaned out her printer and went home. Picture her surprise when she opened up the shop the next morning and started the printer for another portrait she had done, and the late math teacher's portrait appeared superimposed on it.

center of ghostly manifestations seemed to have been the bedroom where Helen L., the owner's eldest daughter, slept, and the patio in the back of the house. On one occasion the noise of a struggle on the furniture-filled patio awoke all members of the family, which consisted of Helen L., her aged mother, and another sister. But upon checking this out they found the furniture completely untouched.

It was then that they remembered a call from their erstwhile neighbors, while the L.s were living elsewhere, advising them that a terrible fight had taken place in their house. The neighbors had heard

10. At a wild party on Hollywood's Ardmore Boulevard, a young girl died and was apparently buried on the grounds to cover up the matter. On April 18, 1964, Holzer came to the house because of continued complaints of disturbances by the owner, and took a number of photographs, with Maxine Bell being the medium. One of them clearly shows a young woman at the window.

In the garden of the same house where the party took place, psychic "mass" has also been captured on film.

the noise of furniture being broken. When the L.s repossessed their house they found that the report had not been exaggerated. Broken furniture filled their house. Several witnesses confirmed hearing footsteps of someone they did not see, and Helen L. heard the sounds of someone trying to break into her bedroom through the French doors from the patio. That someone was a young girl, judging from the sound of the footsteps. The other footsteps, heard also by a number of witnesses, were heavy footfalls of a man in pursuit. In addition, the sounds of a wild party resounded in the darkness around Helen, and on one occasion she heard a voice telling her to get out of her own house.

Naturally, Helen was upset at all this and asked for my help. On my first visit I made sure that she was a reasonably rational individual. I later returned in the company of the head of the Los Angeles chapter of the American Society for Psychic Research as witness. I was also accompanied by Maxine Bell, a local psychic. Without any foreknowledge of where she was being taken by me, or an opportunity to talk to the owners of the house, Bell clairvoyantly described the sudden violence that had erupted in this house in 1948, involving two men and a girl.

With the head of the Los Angeles chapter of the American Society for Psychical Research had come an associate, an engineer who also had psychic leanings. Separately from Bell, he described his impressions of an older man and a young girl, a teenager, who had died at the same time here. I took routine location pictures all over the house with black-and-white fast film and without artificial light sources. I was alone in the haunted bedroom when I took six or seven exposures.

When these were later developed by the laboratory employed by Fotoshop of New York, one of them also showed a young girl in what appears to be a negligee standing at the window, looking toward the bed. The figure is solid enough, although the left flank is somewhat illuminated by the infiltrating sunshine from the patio. But on close inspection it is clear that the figure is not actu-

ally standing on the floor near the French doors, but rather above the floor near the bed. I examined the room again later to make sure no curtains could have been mistaken for this apparition; there were no curtains. Since the picture was taken, I made several trips back to Los Angeles to help send the two ghosts away, and much additional evidence has piled up. But essentially it was the story of a young girl with men fighting over her. Someone seemed to have been hurt in the process. There were indications that a body might still be hidden in the garden, but to this date the owner of the house has refused to dig for it. After the L.s had moved back into their house, they had found blood spots on the floor.

I was very much shaken up by the picture of the girl, especially as it came unexpectedly. None of the other exposures on the same roll showed anything significant. I felt that the presence of both Bell and Helen L. in the immediate vicinity was responsible for the picture, as I never considered myself psychic. I should add that I have since gone back to that same house several times, and never been able to duplicate the ghost picture. This is not surprising, since I believe that such apparitions are two-dimensional, and there are countless planes possible within the same 360-degree area. It is perhaps a moot question whether we are dealing here with ghosts in the strict sense of the term, meaning a human personality "hung up" in time and outside space, or with a mere impression, an imprint of violence left behind by an event in the past. Either way, it is a paranormal occurrence, but I am inclined to consider this case one of a genuine ghost, inasmuch as the personality did react in various ways at various times and showed traits of a disturbed human personality, something a "dead" imprint would not do.

10. "Girl in negligee," Holzer dubbed this time exposure taken by him in Hollywood house where murder took place.

HOW THIS PICTURE WAS OBTAINED

TIME: April 18, 1964, 3:00 P.M.

PLACE: Ardmore Boulevard, Los Angeles (exact location withheld), the house of Helen L., an executive secretary going to work in Los Angeles.

LIGHT CONDITIONS: Sunny afternoon. Inside the house, windows open. The bedroom windows, actually French doors, are covered by a pair of blinds, but no other curtains of any kind. Sunlight from the garden and patio coming through French doors. No reflecting surfaces inside room, except a mirror completely outside field of vision. Bedspread opaque, carpet opaque, no artificial light.

CAMERA: Super Ikonta B. Zeiss, in excellent working condition.

FILM: Agfa Record Isopan 120, fast black-and-while film, rated 1200 ASA.

EXPOSURE: Two seconds front a firm support camera resting on linen chest in back of bedroom. Normally, at this exposure, film should be burned completely and no image should show.

OPERATOR: Hans Holzer, alone in bedroom; medium Maxine Bell and owner of house, Helen L., seated outside bedroom in adjacent living room.

When large numbers of people gather within close confine, such as churches, they generate body heat, which is a form of energy. But religious fervor, prayer, incantations, and strong desires are all forms of thought projections—that is, the actual sending out of small particles of energy from the individual mind, each particle "charged," as it were, with a mission. Many, if not all, the thought projections of a community within a church or temple have parallel thought directions, i.e., desire for divine intercession on their behalf of one kind or another. This "calling forth" of intercession may create an electromagnetic field within the church, aided in its continuing consistency by thick walls, the high degree of moisture usually present in churches (especially in Britain and Ireland), and the darkness prevailing in the edifice.

A number of persons disinterested in psychic research and completely unknown to one another or to me, until they contacted me, have had strange experiences in churches when they took random snapshots, both in color and black-and-white. I have examined the results carefully and found a similarity between the pictures that is beyond the "coincidence rate." One of the cathedrals singled out for this kind of attention is Salisbury Cathedral, England. A number of people have had psychic experiences in the majestic church. Barry Bingham, editor and publisher of the *Louisville Courier-Journal,* a distinguished journalist, had an experience bordering on reincarnation and *déjà vu* when he first visited the cathedral. He had previously had a dream experience in which he had seen the church in great detail, but at an earlier age, or so it seemed to him. As a matter of record, he had never been to Salisbury, but one of his ancestors was a bishop there, and Bingham discovered the other Bingham's tomb on his first visit to the ancient church.

Mrs. Karl F. Wihtol is the wife of the president of Wihtol Industries, manufacturers of industrial and laboratory equipment, in New Jersey. She is an avid amateur photographer and travels quite a bit. On Saturday, July 28, 1962, she found herself at Salisbury Cathedral. The Bournemouth Symphony Orchestra was rehearsing for a concert of religious music. The musicians were grouped near the altar and there were a few spectators seated in the nave. The time was four in the afternoon and the light was not too bright. Wihtol used a stereo Realist camera, with 3-D effects, then popular with photography buffs. Unfortunately, she had to use time exposure without putting the camera down on a firm surface, so the result is not sharp. What is a mystery is the additional material that appears in sharp focus on the two negatives, while the rest of the picture is completely out of focus. In a maze of whitish substance—not as dense as the "cotton" of the séance photographs earlier discussed—there appears to be what Marjorie Wihtol calls "spaghetti"—curved, twisting rods of ectoplasm. Wihtol saw nothing special in the church at the time. She also took black-and-white pictures with her Rolleiflex camera, but they showed nothing special, either.

The 3-D slide, especially when viewed in stereo, shows the ectoplasmic formation spectacularly. At first, Wihtol suspected something was wrong with her camera or film. She took the slide to a meeting of her camera club, where one of the members, an instructor in photography at nearby Fort Monmouth, wondered if a light leak had occurred. Although both stereo negatives had the same "extra," they were three inches apart in the camera. Also, none of the neighboring negatives in the roll showed any signs of leakage. Wihtol sent the slide on to Eastman Kodak in Rochester, New York, and again stumped the experts. She then submitted the curious pictures to the photography experts at *Life* magazine, where no one could come up with a satisfactory explanation of the strange phenomenon. Finally she sent them to me, and I made sure that there had been no double exposure. Her camera does not permit accidental slip-ups of that kind. That's where matters stood in June 1965, when I first examined the slide.

11. Marjorie Wihtol's stereo picture of Salisbury Cathedral, England, reveals ectoplastic formations, possibly letters W.R.

HOW THIS PICTURE WAS OBTAINED

TIME: Saturday, July 28, 1962, 4:00 P.M.
PLACE: Salisbury Cathedral, England.
LIGHT CONDITIONS: Available daylight only.
CAMERA: Stereo Realist.
FILM: Kodak slides, 3-D.
EXPOSURE: Time exposure, hand-held camera.
OPERATOR: Marjorie Wihtol, Middletown, New Jersey.
DEVELOPING: Local, via Kodak.

My suggestion as to the meaning of the curious "extra" may sound far-fetched, but it is based on observation of this type of extra obtained elsewhere, such as with Betty Ritter in New York. To my mind the crudely drawn extra represents an attempt at a monogram, with the letter

W on the left and, more faintly, an *R* on the right. Using the available ectoplasm raised from the combination of spectators, musicians, and sound energies released by the music, the intelligent entity "writing" with this raw material wanted to record his name for some unknown reason. Evidently aware of the presence of a modem recording device—and this is speculation on my part—the unknown "writer" painted the letters *W R* into the soft ectoplastic mass, very much like a fingerpainting done in sand or clay.

The *W* is an early medieval form of this initial, not the customary printed *W* but the much less known "cursive" form of it. Most people do not realize that even the ancient Greeks and Romans used a flowing hand, that is, a cursive writing, for everyday use. Monuments and official documents show us the block or printed form of the alphabet by contrast, and it is that form of the alphabet we customarily refer to. During the Middle Ages, sharp, unyielding pens were used to write on parchment. Consequently, the letters had to adapt themselves to the medium on which they were placed, and a flowing hand developed naturally.

There remains only one more speculation guesswork until such time as I can establish through trance that there is a psychic presence at Salisbury Cathedral—speculation as to who W.R. is or was. The cathedral goes back to the eleventh century or earlier. William the Conqueror was one of the rulers of England closely connected with the cathedral. William usually styled himself WILLIELMUS REX rather than the expected GUGLIELMUS, a later development. On the coins of the period he is usually styled with a *W* or sometimes even a *P*, but never a *G*. Of course we may be dealing here with a different person whose initials are also W.R. But the *W* does belong to William the Conqueror's period, and the thought is tempting.

11. Salisbury Cathedral in southern England is where King William II, called Rufus, is buried. A visitor who happened to be a photography expert, Marjorie Wihtol, took this picture of the altar. The medieval-style letters *W.R.* appear plainly, signature-like. What is compelling here is the fact that William II Rufus never used the Latin form of his name—Gullielmus—but instead used a local English form, namely, William. The English language was then just beginning to emerge.

Not so spectacular, but equally interesting, is a photograph obtained by Jesse Joseph of New York at Westminster Abbey, London, on April 23, 1966. Joseph took two pictures with an Airespenta camera, which is a single reflex model, using 35mm Kodachrome, and no flash. It was noon and raining outside. Joseph saw nothing special at the moment, nor did he harbor any interest in the psychic or expect that his camera might turn up some unusual "extras." In fact the entire subject was alien to him, and his pictures were brought to my attention by his brother Reuben Joseph, who saw me on television.

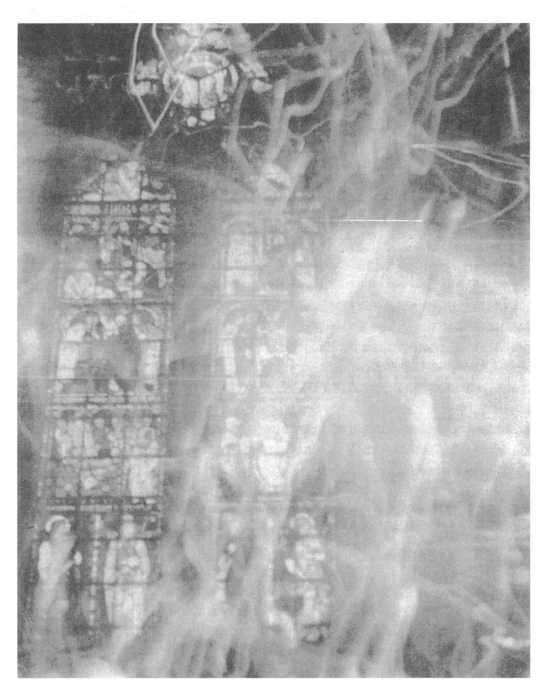

12. On April 23, 1966, a tourist named Jesse Joseph took a picture of the colorful big window over the altar at London's Westminster Cathedral. The ensuing psychic materials—ectoplastic rods that we call "spaghetti effect"—contain attempts at writing, and the script is early medieval.

The slide taken of one of the stained-glass windows (which looked normal to Joseph) shows a large amount of what Wihtol had called "spaghetti" between window and camera lens. The similarity is evident between this type of ectoplastic rod in the Wihtol picture and some of Betty Ritter's work. Several letters seem to be contained in the jumble of material. In the left margin area the letter *Y* appears clearly, and below it a medieval *A* and farther down an *O*, with the characteristic Gothic formation due to the inability of monks' pens to do perfect circles. In the lower right area I seemed to read a Gothic *B*. On turning the picture upside-down, an *F* becomes evident, superimposed in the area of the stained-glass window's cross. There is a great deal of writing here, most of it undecipherable. Looking at the picture right-side up again, I was struck by the outline of a bishop's miter in the lower-right area.

12. Jesse Joseph's color picture taken of Westminster Cathedral stained-glass window also revealed ectoplastic material including some jumbled letters.

HOW THIS PICTURE WAS OBTAINED

TIME: April 23, 1966. Noon.
PLACE: Westminster Cathedral, London.
LIGHT CONDITIONS: Available daylight. Rainy day.
CAMERA: Airespenta single-lens reflex.
FILM: Kodachrome, 35 mm.
EXPOSURE: ½ second, F/3.5.
OPERATOR: Jesse Joseph of New York.
DEVELOPING: Local shop, via Kodak.

While this may not be a clear-cut message in the sense a trance investigation

often is, it does point the way toward a new and exciting area of scientific inquiry with the color camera as tool.

There is no doubt in my mind that qualified observation is as scientific as re-creation under artificial conditions, if not more so. This is particularly true in this field, where emotional factors are at the bottom of the phenomena, and where environmental influences are also significant. A psychic person fully relaxed in my living room will perform a lot better after some low-pressure chatting than a medium placed in a sterile cubicle in a laboratory, with the cold, uncommitted eyes of the researcher demanding results. I am a researcher and I am not uncommitted. I have had significant evidence that psychic phenomena exist; my job now is to study them *further* and to learn more about them. The subject feels this and performs accordingly.

The use of subjective material, no matter how carefully screened and how well documented, still requires a basis of acceptance that the people involved—researcher and subject—are not fraudulently involved in reporting the results. Not likely, I admit, but some scientists, disturbed by the implications of a survival view in science, will go to great extremes to discredit what they cannot swallow, even if it is true.

I have found the camera a faithful servant, demanding neither emotional attachment nor loyalty on my part. The lens, often more sensitive than the human eye, will perform if its mechanical components are intact, and it does not manufacture anything of its own volition. Cameras and film are objective proof that what they deliver is true, provided the mechanical components are in proper shape.

Dr. Jule Eisenbud and Ted Serios have shown that men's thoughts can be put down on sensitive film at will, in what are close to controlled laboratory experiments. My own work leads the way into spontaneous fieldwork along the same lines, while it pierces the barriers of time and space as we know them. The implications of such photography, when one realizes that fraud is impossible, are that man possesses something more than a flesh-and-blood machine called the body. It follows that there must be some other place or state of existence where that part of man continues his being.

Man's personality, or soul, is also an electromagnetic energy field, and as such is capable of registering on certain instruments, some already in existence, some as yet to be built. Photographic film and paper are among the tools by which man can prove his nonphysical component. It is perhaps a pity that we find it so difficult to supply the funds to establish, equip, and staff an institute where psychic research is the only subject studied, where no theory is considered too far off the mark to be worthy of examination, and where scientists of every conceivable kind, persuasion, and background can work together toward the greatest of all remaining "last frontiers:" inner space, man himself.

near-death experiences

SOME PEOPLE, ORDINARY, AVERAGE PEOPLE without the slightest interest in, or knowledge of psychic matters, have been able to encounter the next world, without, however, remaining there. The cases are many, and while the medical profession is still divided about the causes, an increasing number of physicians are convinced that the experiences are not hallucinatory but real, a journey to the dimension next door, so to speak, but with a return ticket.

Evidently being psychic has nothing to do with these occurrences, but on their return the travelers seem to have undergone profound changes. For one thing, their attitude toward life and death has totally changed and allows them to lead more peaceful lives. In many cases, their psychic abilities have been fully awakened and to their amazement, they have become psychic. As the psychic ability is not really *external* to us, but is quasi built-in with all of us from the start (in widely varying degrees), it must be the *exposure* to the next dimension, the Other Side, that triggers these increases in psychic ability.

Cases involve people who were temporarily separated from their physical reality, without being cut off from it permanently into the state we call death. These are mainly victims of accidents who recovered, people who underwent surgery and during the state of anesthesia had become separated from their physical bodies and were able to observe from a new vantage point what was being done to them, and people who had traveled to the next world in a kind of dream state and observed conditions there that they remembered upon returning to the full state of wakefulness.

But the dream state covers a multitude of conditions, some of which are not actual dreams, but states of limited consciousness, and receptivity to external inputs. Out-of-body experiences are frequently classed with dreams although they are a form of conscious projection in which the individual travels outside the physical body.

I have always shied away from accepting material from people undergoing psychiatric care, not because I necessarily discount such testimony but because some of my readers might. As Dr. Raymond Moody noted, there is a definite pattern in these near-misses, or experiences of people who have gone over and then returned. What they relate about conditions is frequently similar to what other people have said about these conditions, yet the witnesses have no way of knowing of one another's experiences, have never met, and have not read a common source from which they could draw such material if they were in a mood to deceive the investigator.

Much of this testimony is reluctantly given, out of fear of ridicule, or perhaps because the individual is not sure what to make of it. Far from the fanatical fervor of a religious purveyor, the people whose cases have been brought to my attention do not wish to convince anyone of anything, but to report to me what has occurred in their lives. In publishing these reports I am making the information available to those who might have had similar experiences and wondered about them.

We should keep in mind that the percipient of the experience would perceive entities and conditions in a three-dimensional way because he himself is three-dimensional in relation to the experience once he leaves his physical body. It is entirely possible that an actual person would appear to the observer exactly the same way as a projection of a person would appear. If we accept the notion that the world beyond this one, in which so-called spirit life continues, is capable of creating actual images as desired by mind alone, even build houses by thought alone, yet is able to make them appear solid and three-dimensional, then the question of contradictions to physical law as we know it is no longer such a puzzling one. Obviously, an entity controlled by thought can pass through solid walls, or move at instantaneous speed from one place to another; during the temporary states between physical life and death, people partake of this ability and undergo experiences that might otherwise be termed hallucinations.

I cannot emphasize strongly enough that the cases I am reporting in the following pages do not fall into the category of what many doctors like to call hallucinations, mental aberrations, or fantasies. The clarity of the experiences, the full remembrance of it afterward, the many parallels between individual experiences reported by people in widely scattered areas, and the physical conditions of the percipient at the time of the experience all weigh heavily against the dismissal of such experiences as being of hallucinatory origin.

Virginia S. is a housewife in one of the western states but has held various responsible jobs in management and business. She underwent surgery for, as she put it, "repair to her muscles." During the operation, she lost so much blood she was clinically dead. Nevertheless, the surgeons managed to bring her back and she recovered. This is what Mrs. S. experienced during the period when the medical team was unable to detect any sign of life in her:

"I was climbing a rock wall and was standing straight in the air; nothing else was around it, it seemed flat, at the top of this wall was another stone railing about two feet high. I grabbed for the edge to pull myself over the wall and my father, who is deceased, appeared and looked down at me. He said, 'You cannot come up yet, go back, you have something left to do.' I looked down and started to go down, and the next thing I heard were the words, 'She's coming back.' "

Mrs. J.L.H., a housewife living in British Columbia, had an amazing experience on her way back from the funeral of her stepfather, George H. She had been given a ride by a friend, Clarence G., and on the way there was a serious accident. Clarence was killed instantly, and Mrs. H. was seriously hurt. "I don't remember anything except seeing car lights coming at me, for I had been sleeping," Mrs. H. explained. "I first remember seeing my stepdad step forward out of a cloudy mist and touch me on my left shoulder. He said, 'Go back, June, it's not yet time.' I woke up with the weight of his hand still on my shoulder."

The curious thing about this case is that both people were in the same accident, yet one of them was evidently marked for death while the other was not. After Mrs. H. had recovered from her injuries and returned home, she woke up one night to see a figure at the end of her bed holding out his hand toward her as if wanting her to come with him. When she turned her light on, the figure disappeared, but it always returned when she turned the lights off again. During subsequent appearances, the entity tried to lift Mrs. H. out of her bed, ripping all the covers off her, and forcing her to sleep with the lights on. It would appear that Clarence could not understand why he was on the other side of life while his friend had been spared.

Phyllis G., who is from Canada, had a most remarkable experience. She had just given birth to twin boys at her own home, and the confinement seemed normal and natural. By late evening she began to suffer from a severe headache, however. By morning she was unconscious and was rushed to the hospital with a cerebral hemorrhage. She was unconscious for three days while the doctors were doing their best to save her life. She later recounted:

"My husband's grandmother had died the previous August but she came to me during my unconscious state, dressed in the whitest white robe and there was light shining around her. She seemed to me to be in a lovely quiet meadow, her arms were held out to me, and she called my name, 'Phyllis, come with me.' I told her this was not possible as I had my children to take care of. Again she said, 'Phyllis, come with me, you will love it here.' Once again, I told her it wasn't possible. I said, 'Gran I can't, I must look after my children.' With this she said, 'I must take someone. I will take Jeffrey.' I didn't object to this and Gran just faded away. Jeffrey is the first twin that was born." Mrs. G. recovered, and her son Jeffrey wasn't taken either, and is now doing fine. However, his mother still has this nagging feeling in the back of her mind that perhaps his life may not be as long as it ought to be. During the time when Mrs. G. saw her grandmother, she had been thought clinically dead.

There are many cases on record where a person begins to partake of another dimension even while there is still hope for recovery, but when the ties between consciousness and body are already beginning to loosen.

An interesting case was reported to me by Mrs. J.P. of California. While still a teenager, Mrs. P. had been ill with influenza, but was just beginning to recover when she had a most unusual experience. One morning her father and mother came into her bedroom to see how she was feeling. "After a few minutes I asked them if they could hear the beautiful music. I still remember that my father looked at my mother and said, 'She's delirious.' I vehemently denied that. Soon they left but as I glanced out my second-floor bedroom window toward the wooded hills I love, I saw a sight that took my breath away. There, superimposed on the trees, was a beautiful cathedral type structure from which that beautiful music was emanating. Then I seemed to be looking down on the people. Everyone was singing, but it was the background music that thrilled my soul. A leader dressed in white was leading the singing. The interior of the church seemed strange to me. It was only in later years, after I had attended services in an Episcopal church and also in a Catholic church that I realized the front of the church I saw was more in their style, with the beautiful altar The vision faded. Two years later, when I was ill again, the scene and music returned."

R.J.I. of Pittsburgh was rushed to the hospital with a bleeding ulcer. He received a shot and became unconscious. Attempts were immediately made to stop the bleeding and he was operated on. During the operation, Mr. I. lost fifteen pints of blood, suffered convulsions and a fever of 106 degrees. He was as close to death as one could come and was given the last rites of his church. However, during his unconsciousness he had a remarkable experience: "On the day my doctor told my wife I had only an hour to live, I saw, while unconscious, a man with black hair and a white robe with a gold belt come from behind an altar, look at me, and shake his head. I was taken to a long hall and purple robes were laid out for me. There were many candles lit in this hall."

Many cases of this kind occur when the subject is being prepared for surgery or while undergoing surgery; sometimes the anesthetic allows dissociation to occur more easily. This is not to say that people hallucinate under the influence of anesthetic drugs, or because of the lack of blood, or from any other physical cause. If death is the dissolution of the link between physical body and etheric body, any loosening of this link is likely to allow the etheric body to move away from its physical shell, although still tied to it either by a visible silver cord, or by some form of invisible tie that we do not fully understand. Otherwise, those who have returned from the great beyond would not have done so.

Mrs. J.M. of Canada was expecting her fourth child. "Something went wrong and when I had a contraction, I went unconscious. My doctor was called and I remember his telling me that he might have to operate. Then I passed out, but I could still hear him talking and myself talking back to him. Then I couldn't hear him any longer and I found myself on the banks of a river with green grass and white buildings on the other side. I knew if I could get across I'd never be tired again, but there was no bridge and it was rough. I looked back and I saw myself lying there with nurses and doctors around me, and Dr. M. had his hand on the back of my neck and he was calling me and he looked so worried that I knew I had to go back. I had the baby and then I was back in the room and the doctor explained to my husband what happened. I asked him why he had his hand on my neck and he replied that it was the only place on my body where he could find a pulse, and for over a minute he couldn't even feel one there. Was this the time when I was standing on the riverbank?"

Deborah B. is a young woman living in California with a long record of psychic experiences. At times, when she's intensely involved in an emotional situation, she undergoes what we call a dissociation of personality. For a moment, she is able to look into another dimension, partake of visionary experiences not seen or felt by others in her vicinity. One such incident occurred to Deborah during a theater arts class at school. She looked up from her script and saw "a man standing there in a flowing white robe, staring at me, with golden or blond hair, down to his shoulders; a misty fog surrounded him. I couldn't make out his face, but I knew he was staring at me. During this time I had a peaceful and secure feeling. He then faded away." Later that year, after an emotional dispute between Deborah and her mother, another visionary experience took place:

"I saw a woman dressed in a long blue flowing robe with a white shawl or veil over her head, beckoning to a group of three or four women dressed in rose-color robes and white veils. The woman in blue was on the steps of a church or temple with large pillars. Then it faded out."

One might argue that Deborah's imagination was creating visionary scenes, if it weren't that what she describes has been described by others, especially people who have found themselves on the threshold of death and returned. The beckoning figure in the flowing robe has been reported by many, sometimes identified as Jesus, sometimes simply as a master. The identification of the figure depends on the religious or metaphysical attitude of the subject, but the feeling caused by his appearance seems to be universally the same, a sense of peace and complete contentment.

Mrs. L.L. of Michigan dreamed that she and her husband had been killed in an automobile accident. In November of that year, the feeling that death was all around her became stronger. Around the middle of the month, the feeling was so overwhelming that she telephoned her husband, who was on a hunting trip, and informed him of her death fears. She discussed her apprehensions with a neighbor, but nothing helped allay her fears. Later that year, Mrs. L. had another dream about imminent death. In this dream she knew that her husband would die and that she could not save him, no matter what. Two days later, Mrs. L. and her husband were in an automobile accident. He was killed and Mrs. L. nearly died. According to the attending physician, she should have been a dead woman, considering her injuries.

But during her stay in the hospital, when she had been given up, and was visited by her sister, she spoke freely about a place she was seeing, and the dead relatives she was in contact with at the time. She knew that her husband was dead, but she also knew that her time had not come, that she had a purpose to achieve in life and therefore could not stay on the "plane" on which she was temporarily.

The sister, who did not understand any of this, asked whether Mrs. L. had seen God, and whether she had visited heaven. The unconscious subject replied that she had not seen God nor was she in heaven, but on a certain plane of existence. The sister thought that all this was nonsense and that perhaps her dying sister was delirious. Mrs. L. remembers clearly how life returned to her after her visit to the other plane. "I felt life coming to my body, from the tip of my toes to the tip of my head. I knew I couldn't die. Something came back into my body, I think it was my soul. I was at complete peace about everything and could not grieve about the death of my husband. I had complete forgiveness for the man who hit us. I felt no bitterness toward him at all."

Do some people get an advance glimpse at their own demise? It would be easy to dismiss some of the precognitive or seemingly precognitive dreams as anxiety-caused, perhaps due to fantasies. However, many of these dreams resemble each other and differ from ordinary anxiety dreams in their intensity and the fact that they are remembered so clearly upon awakening. A case in point is a vivid dream reported to me recently by Peggy C., who lives in a New York suburb. The reason for her contacting me was that she had developed a heart condition recently and was wondering whether a dream she had had twenty years before was an indication that her life was nearing its end.

The dream that so unnerved her through the years featured her walking past a theater, where she met a dead brother-in-law. "I said to him, 'Hi Charlie, what are you doing here?' He just smiled and in my dream it dawned on me that the dead come for the living. I said to him, 'Did you come for me?' He said, 'Yes.' I said to him, 'Did I die?' He said, 'Yes.' I said, 'I wasn't sick. Was it my heart?' He nodded, and I said, 'I'm scared.' He said, 'There is nothing to be scared of, just hold on to me.' I put my arms around him and we sailed through the air in darkness. It was not a frightening feeling but a pleasant sensation. I could see the buildings beneath us.

Then we came to a room where a woman was at a desk. In the room was my brother-in-law, an old woman, and a mailman. She called me to her desk. I said, 'Do we have to work here too?' She said, 'We are all assigned to duties. What is your name?' I had been christened Bernadine but my mother never used the name. I told her 'Peggy.' She said, 'No. Your name is Bernadine.' After taking the details, my brother-in-law took me by the arm, and was taking me upstairs, when I awakened. I saw my husband standing over me with his eyes wide open, but I could not move. I was thinking, 'Please shake me, I'm alive,' but I could not move or talk. After a few minutes, my body jerked in bed and I opened my eyes and began to cry." The question is, did Mrs. C. have a near-death experience and return from it, or was her dream truly precognitive, indicative perhaps of things yet to come?

Dr. Karlis Osis has published his findings concerning many deathbed experiences, wherein the dying recognize dead relatives in the room, seemingly come to help them across the threshold into the next world. A woman in South Carolina, Mrs. M. C., reported an interesting case to me recently. She has a fair degree of mediumship, which is a factor in the present case.

"I stood behind my mother as she lay dying at the age of some seventy years. She had suffered a cerebral stroke and at this time of her life she was unable to speak. Her attendants claimed they had had no communication with her for over a week previously. As I let my mind go into her, she spoke clearly and flawlessly: 'If only you could see how beautiful and perfect it all is,' she said, then called out to her dead father, saying 'Pappa, Pappa.' I then spoke directly to her and asked her, did she see Pappa? She answered as if she had come home. 'Yes, I see Pappa.' She passed over onto the Other Side shortly, in a matter of days. It was as if her father had come after her as I had spoken with her when she saw him and spoke clearly with paralyzed mouth and throat muscles."

Sometimes, the dead want the living to know how wonderful is their newfound world. Whether this is out of a desire to make up for ignorance in one's earth life, when such knowledge was either outside one's ken or ignored, or whether this is to acquaint the surviving relative with what lies ahead, cases involving such excursions into the next world tend to confirm the near-death experiences of those who have gone into it on their own, propelled by accidents or unusual states of consciousness. One of the most remarkable reports of this kind comes to me through the kindness of two sisters living in England.

Doreen B. is a senior nursing administrator who has witnessed death on numerous occasions. Here is her report:

"In May 1968, my mother died. I had nursed her at home, during which time we had become extremely close. My mother was a shy woman who always wished to remain in the background. Her last weeks were ones of agony; she had terminal cancer with growths in many parts of her body. Toward the end of her life I had to sedate her heavily to alleviate the pain. After saying good-bye to my daughter on the morning of May 7, she lapsed into semiconsciousness and died at about 2:15 A.M. on May 8, 1968.

"A few nights after her death, I was gently awakened. I opened my eyes and saw Mother. Before I relate what happened I should like to say that I dream vividly every night and this fact made me more aware that I was not dreaming. I had not taken any drink or drugs. My mind and emotions revolved around my mother. After Mother woke me, I arose from my bed, my hand instinctively reached out for my dressing gown but I do not remember putting it on. Mother said that she would take me to where she was. I reacted by saying that I would get the car out, but she said that I would not need it. We traveled quickly, I do not know how, but I was aware that we were in the Durking Leatherhead area and entering another dimension. The first thing I saw was a large archway. I knew I had seen it before although it means nothing to me now. Inside the entrance a beautiful sight met my eyes. There was glorious parkland, with shrubbery and flowers of many colors.

"We traveled across the parkland and came to a low white building. It appeared to have the appearance of a convalescence home. There was a veranda, but no windows or doors as we know them. Inside everything was white and Mother showed me a bed that she said was hers. I was aware of other people but they were only shadowy white figures. Mother was worried about some of them and told me that they did not know that they were dead. I was aware that one of a group of three was a man. Mother had always been frugal in dress, possibly because of her hardships in earlier years. Therefore her wardrobe was small but neat and she spent very little on clothing if she could alter and mend. Because of this I was surprised when she wished that she had more clothes. In life Mother was the kindest of women, never saying or thinking ill of anyone, so I found it hard to understand her resentment toward a woman in a long flowing robe who appeared on a bridge in the grounds. The bridge looked beautiful but Mother never took me near it. I now have to return but to my question, 'Are you happy?' I was extremely distressed to know that she did not want to leave her family. Before Mother left me she said a gentle 'Goodbye dear.' It was said with a quiet finality and I knew that I would never see her again.

"It was only afterward when I related it to my sister that I realized that Mother had been much more youthful than when she died and that her back, which in life had rounded, was straight. I realized that we had not spoken through our lips but as if by thought, except when she said, 'Goodbye dear.' It is now three and a half years since this happening and I have had no further experience. I now realize that I must have seen Mother during her transition period when she was still earthbound, possibly from the effect of the drugs I administered under medical supervision, and when her tie to her family, particularly her grandchild, was still very strong."

There are many reports indicating that the dead revert to their best years, which are around the age of thirty in most cases, because they are able to project a thought-form of themselves as they wish. On the other hand, where apparitions of the dead are intended to prove survival of a person, they usually appear as they looked prior to death, frequently wearing the clothes they wore at the time of their death.

Not all temporary separations of body and etheric self include a visit to the next world. Sometimes the liberated self hangs around to observe what is being done with the body. Elaine L. of Washington State recently reported an experience that happened to her at the age of sixteen: "I had suffered several days from an infected back tooth and since my face was badly swollen, our dentist refused to remove the tooth until the swelling subsided. Shortly after Novocain was administered, I found myself floating close to an open window. I saw my body in the dental chair and the dentist working feverishly. Our landlady, Mrs. E., who had brought me to the dentist, stood close by, shaking me and looking flabbergasted and unbelieving. My feeling at the time was of complete peace and freedom. There was no pain, no anxiety, not even an interest in what was happening close to that chair. Soon I was back to the pain and I remember as I left the office that I felt a little resentful. The dentist phoned frequently during the next few days for assurance that I was all right."

The number of cases involving near-death experiences, reports from people who were clinically dead for varying lengths of time and who then recovered and remembered what they experienced while unconscious, is considerable. If we assume that universal law covers all contingencies, there should be no exceptions to it. Why then are some people allowed to glimpse that which lies ahead for them in the next dimension, without actually entering that dimension at the time of the experience? After investigating large numbers of such cases I can only surmise that there are two reasons. First of all, there must be a degree of self-determination involved, allowing the subject to go forward to the next dimension or return to the body. As a matter of fact, in many cases, though not in all, the person is being given that choice and elects to return to earth. Secondly, by disseminating these witnesses' reports among those in the physical world, knowledge is put at our disposal, or rather at the disposal of those who wish to listen.

EIGHT

out-of-body experiences

ORIGINALLY REFERRED TO AS *ASTRAL projection,* which is probably as good a term, it is now usually called *out-of-body experience.* Either way, it proves that we *can,* and *do,* function fully without the physical body, because there is within us all a secondary body, variously called etheric body, aura, or soul. This is the true vehicle of our "selves." The movement of this inner body, and all communications by and with it, are part of the dimension we call psychic or *etheric.*

This dimension is made up of fine particles and is not intangible. The inner body, which I think represents the true personality in man, is made up of the same type of substance; consequently, it is able to exist freely in the astral or etheric dimension upon dissolution of the physical body at physical death. According to theosophy and, to a lesser degree, ancient Egyptian religion, man has five bodies, of which the astral body is but one, the astral world being the second lowest of seven worlds, characterized by emotions, desires, and passions. This is a philosophical concept and is as valid or invalid as one chooses it to be. By relating to the astral world as merely the "other side of life," I may be simplifying things and perhaps run counter to certain philosophical assumptions, but it appears to me that to prove one nonphysical sphere is enough at this state of the game in parapsychology. If there be other, finer layers—and I do not doubt that there are—let that be the task at a time when the existence of the nonphysical world is no longer being doubted by the majority of scientists.

In speaking of astral projection, we are speaking of projection into the astral world; what is projected seems to be the inner layer of the body, referred to as the astral or etheric body. By projecting it outward into the world outside the physical body, it is capable of a degree of freedom that it does not enjoy while encased in the physical body. As long as the person is alive in the physical world the astral body remains attached to the physical counterpart by a thin connecting link called the "silver cord."

If the cord is severed, death results. At the time of physical death, the cord is severed and the astral body freely floats upward into the next dimension. We tend to call such projections *out-of-body experiences.* Robert Monroe, a communications engineer by profession and a medium by accident, has written a knowledgeable book about his own experiences with out-of-body sensations, and a few years before him, Dr. Herewood Carrington, together with Sylvan Muldoon, wrote a book considered a classic now, on the subject of astral projection.

The reason that out-of-body experience is a more accurate term to describe the phenomena is because projection, that is, a willful outward movement out of the physical body, is rarely the method by which the phenomena occur. Rather, it is a sensation of dissociation between physical and etheric body, a floating sensation during which the inner self seems to be leaving its physical counterpart and traveling away from it. The movement toward the outside is by no means rapid or projectionlike; it is a slow gradual disengagement most of the time and with most witnesses. Occasionally there are dramatic instances where astral projection occurs spontaneously and suddenly. But in such cases some form of shock or artificial trauma is usually present, such as during surgery and the use of an anesthetizing agent or in cases of sudden grief, sudden joy, or states of great fatigue.

Out-of-body experiences can be classified into two main categories: the *spontaneous* cases, where it occurs without being induced in any way and is usually as a surprise; and *experimental* cases, where the state of dissociation is deliberately induced by various means. In the latter category controlled experiments are possible, and I will go into this toward the end of this chapter.

The crux of all astral projection, whether involuntary or voluntary, is the question of whether the traveler makes an impact on the other end of the line, so to speak. If the travel is observed, preferably in some detail, by the recipient of the projection, and if that information is obtained after the event, it constitutes a valuable piece of evidence for the reality of this particular ESP phenomenon.

A Japanese-American woman, Mrs. Y., lived in New York and had a sister in California. One day she found herself projected through space from her New York home to her sister's place on the West Coast. She had not been there for many years and had no idea what it looked like inasmuch as her sister had informed her that considerable alterations had taken place about the house. As she swooped down onto her sister's home, Mrs. Y. noticed the changes in the house and saw her sister wearing a green dress, standing on the front lawn. She tried to attract her sister's attention but was unable to do so. Worried about her unusual state of being, that is, floating above the ground and seemingly unable to be observed, Mrs. Y. became anxious. That moment she found herself yanked back to her New York home and bed.

As she returned to her own body, she experienced a sensation of falling from great heights. This sensation accompanies most, if not all, incidents of astral travel. The feeling of spinning down from great heights is a reverse reaction to the slowing down in speed of the etheric body as it reaches the physical body and prepares to return into it. Many people complain of dreams in which they fall from great heights only to awaken to a sensation of a dizzying fall and resulting anxiety. The majority of such experiences are due to astral travel, with most of it not remembered. In the case of Mrs. Y., all of it was remembered. The following day she wrote her sister a letter, setting down what she had seen and asking her to confirm or deny the details of the house and of herself. To Mrs. Y.'s surprise, a letter arrived from her sister a few days later, confirming everything she had seen during her astral flight.

Ruth E. Knuths, a former schoolteacher who currently works as a legal secretary in California, has had many ESP experiences, and like many others, she filed a report in conformity with a suggestion made by me in an earlier book concerning any ESP experiences people wished to register with me.

"In the spring of 1941 when I lived in San Diego, where I had moved from Del Rio, Texas, I was riding to work on a streetcar. I had nothing on my mind in particular; I was not thinking of my friends in Texas and the time was 8:00 A.M. Suddenly I found myself standing on the front porch of Jo Comstock's house in Dell Rio. Jo and I have been friends for many years. The same dusty green mesquite and cat claw covered the vacant lot across the road, which we called Caliche Flat. People were driving up and parking their cars at the edge of the unfenced yard. They were coming to express sympathy to Jo because of the

death of her mother. Jo was inside the house. I knew this although I did not see her. I was greeting the friends for her. The funeral was to be that afternoon. Then as suddenly as I had gone to Del Rio, I was back in the streetcar still two or three blocks away from my stop.

"Two weeks later Jo wrote, telling me that on a certain date, which was the same date I had this vision on, her mother had been found by neighbors unconscious from a stroke, which they estimated had occurred about ten in the morning. Jo was notified at 10:30. She said that she badly wished me to be there with her. Allowing for the difference in time, two hours, I had had this experience at the time of the stroke, but the vision was projected ahead of that two days to the day of the funeral."

On May 28, 1955, she had another experience of astral projection, which she was able to note in detail and report to me:

"My husband and I had dinner with Velva and Jess McDougle and I had seen Jess one time downtown, afterward, and we spoke and passed. I had not seen Velva. Then on June 11, a Saturday, I was cleaning house, monotonously pushing the vacuum sweeper brush under the dresser in the bedroom, when suddenly I was standing at the door of a hospital room, looking in. To the left, white curtains blew gently from a breeze coming from a window. The room was bright with sunlight; directly opposite the door and in front of me was a bed with a man propped up on pillows; on the left side of the bed stood Velva. The man was Jess. No word was spoken, but I knew that Jess was dead, although as I saw him he was alive though ill. I 'came back' and was still cleaning under the dresser. I didn't contact Velva, nor did I hear from her. However, about a week later my sister, Mary Hatfield, told me that she was shocked to hear of McDougle's death. That was the first confirmation I had. I immediately went to see Velva, and she told me that he had suffered a heart attack on Thursday before the Saturday of my vision, and had died the following Sunday, the day after the vision occurred."

Richard Smith is a self-employed landscape service contractor, married and living in Georgia. He has had many ESP experiences involving living people and the dead. Sometimes he is not sure whether he has visions of events at a distance or is actually traveling to them. In his report to me he states:

"On one unusual occasion, just before sleep came, I found myself floating through the air across the country to my wife's parents' home in Michigan, where I moved about the house. I saw Karen's father as he read the newspaper, his movements through the rooms, and drinking a cup of coffee. I could not find her mother in the house. She was apparently working at the hospital. I was floating at a point near the ceiling and looking down. Voelker, her father, happened to look up from his coffee and seemed to be frightened. He looked all around the room in a state of great uneasiness as if he could sense me in the room. He would look up toward me but his eyes would pass by as though I were invisible. I left him, as I did not wish to frighten him by my presence.

"This experience I seem almost able to do at will when the conditions are right, and travel anywhere. Sometimes, involuntarily, I find myself looking upon a scene that is taking place miles away and of which I have no personal knowledge. These experiences have taken place since my childhood, although I have kept them to myself, with the exception of telling my wife."

ASTRAL PROJECTION

Astral travel is so common an experience that the files of the American Society for Psychical Research are bulging with this type of report. The loosening of the bonds between conscious and unconscious mind can be due to a number of factors, chiefly a state of relaxation just before the onset of sleep or just before awakening. It would appear that the physical body and the inner, etheric body are not as solidly intertwined in everyone as one might be led to believe. When thoughts wander and a person's attention drifts, the inner body containing the true personality may slip out involuntarily and wander about, leading a life of its own, unencumbered by the controlling influence of the conscious mind. It may be attracted to strange scenes or it might find itself compelled to well-known places or persons. The material on hand in research institutions seems to indicate a wide variety of goals.

Induced astral projection has been a subject that has fascinated physical researchers almost from the beginning of modern parapsychology. Because such experiments are repeatable and offer satisfactory control conditions, they are frequently used to demonstrate the presence of ESP capabilities in people. Certainly astral projection is more capable of being artificially induced than any other form of ESP. It is the one form of ESP that does not require true emotional motivation to succeed. The adventure and excitement of leaving one's body, even if temporarily, seems to be sufficient to stimulate the apparatus capable of producing the phenomenon.

Some years ago, when I was working with a group of interested students headquartered at the New York offices of the Association for Research and Enlightenment, better known as the Cayce Foundation, we had at our disposal a young man named Stanley C., who was capable of deliberate astral projection. One experiment consisted of setting up controlled conditions in an apartment on East 82nd Street, while another team met at the A.R.E. headquarters on West 16th Street. The team on 82nd Street was free to choose certain control conditions and decided to use as their earmarks an open book, marked at a certain page and at a certain line on that page, plus a flower in a vase. Stanley was placed into a light hypnotic trance in the office on 16th Street and was directed to visit the 82nd Street place, to report back after awakening everything he had observed, and, if possible, to make his presence known to the observers on the other end. The entire experiment took no more than half an hour.

When it was completed, Stanley woke up, rubbed his eyes, and started to report what he had experienced. Apparently, shortly after he had projected himself outward from his physical body, he had found himself floating through the apartment on 82nd Street. He remarked that he went to the kitchen of the apart-

ment, which he found bathed in blue-white light. At all times he had the sensation of being slightly above the floor, floating rather than actually walking upon it. He clearly saw the observers and, upon awakening, described them to the team on 16th Street. He also described the flower in the vase and the book that had been opened to a certain page. However, he could not arouse the observers to acknowledge his presence, even though he tried to touch them. His hand seemed to go right through them, and he was unable to make his presence known to them.

Controlled astral projection should not be undertaken by anyone without a helper standing by to arouse him if necessary—for instance, if there be any difficulties in his coming back to his own body. This is not to say that such projection may be dangerous, despite the dire warnings sounded by certain occultists. I know of no incident where evil entities have taken advantage of the situation and "slipped into" the body of an astral traveler while the owner was out. The danger, if any, of unobserved and uncontrolled astral travels lies in the lack of control of the time element, and the inability of the traveler to report immediately upon awakening what he may have encountered. It is therefore best to have another person standing by throughout the experiment.

People with somnambulistic tendencies are most likely to succeed in exteriorizing the astral body. These are people with mediumistic tendencies, imaginative and easily influenced. Hardheaded, businesslike, or basically suspicious people make poor astral travelers. This is not to say that imagination is necessary for out-of-body experiences to succeed. Nor should one assume that imaginary experiences are at the base of astral travel; the experiences are quite real. But the tendency toward imagery, a tendency toward dreaming, perhaps, is helpful to permit the purely mechanical disengagement of the astral body from its physical counterpart.

Whether the subject is particularly suitable to astral travel by his or her nature, or desirous of succeeding even though not particularly suited for it, the technique remains the same. It is best at an hour of the day when one is reasonably relaxed, possibly physically tired. The room in which the experiment is to take place must be quiet, not too brightly lit, and not too warm or too cold. Above all, there should be little noise or other distraction. The subject stretches out on a couch or bed, closes his eyes, and pictures himself floating up from his body toward the ceiling.

Inevitably, this self-suggestion leads to a sense of giddiness or lightheadedness. Eventually, the limbs will become lighter and may not be felt after a while. As the experiment continues, the person will feel himself rise, or rather have a sensation of weightlessness. At this point it is possible that the disengagement from the physical body begins, and some experimenters have described the sensation of slowly rising straight up to the ceiling of the room where they would stop and look down upon their sleeping bodies. Others have found themselves in the corner of the room, somewhat frightened, looking back upon their sleeping counterparts. At all times, the personality and the seat of the ego remain in the astral body. The sleeping physical body continues to breathe regularly and maintain its functions as if the personality of the astral traveler were still inside it. This is made possible by the connecting silver cord, which serves as a link between the two bodies, a kind of cable through which impulses go back and forth.

The moment of disengagement is by no means a moment of panic or confusion: the astral traveler thinks clearly, perhaps more clearly than when he is in the physical body. He is capable of directing himself toward whatever goal he has chosen. He may, at his discretion, choose to wander about or float out the window without any particular aim in mind, but he will be able to observe clearly the world around him. In this state the astral traveler is able to partake of two worlds: the physical world, which he has just left temporarily; and the nonphysical world, in which the so-called dead lead their continued existence. Thus it may well be that the astral traveler will find himself face to face with friends or relatives who have died or with people who are strangers yet seem clearly no longer in the physical life.

From the astral traveler's point of view, there is no difference between the so-called dead people he encounters in flight and the living people he sees. Both seem three-dimensional to him and there is no feeling of transparency or two-dimensional appearance. There is also an absence of the sense of time. Consequently, the traveler may not realize how long he has been out of the body. He is capable of ending his excursion at will. If this happens with a sense of panic, the return trip will be a rough one and the awakening in the body may be accompanied by headaches and nausea. Consequently, out-of-body travelers who experiment with this state of consciousness should not allow themselves to be drawn back too quickly; they should slowly direct themselves back toward their homes, meaning that they descend slowly and without undue haste until they find themselves once again in familiar surroundings.

When they arrive above their physical bodies, hovering above them for a moment, as it were, they will then direct themselves to descend the rest of the way until they "click" into place inside their physical bodies. This clicking into place is an important part of the return and has been described by nearly all astral travelers. If it does not occur, there may be delayed reactions upon awakening, such as a sense of displacement, confusion, or a dual presence. If this has happened, the subject must be hypnotized, and during hypnosis full reintegration of the astral and physical bodies is suggested; then the subject is brought out of hypnosis and the integration will have taken place. This is rarely necessary. Since astral travel requires a fair degree of energy, and since this energy comes from the physical body of the subject, the traveler should rest immediately following his return and partake of liquids to replenish his supply, which will definitely have been reduced during the out-of-body experience.

The majority of out-of-body experiences take place during sleep, and form one of four types of dream states described by people upon awakening. The other three are dreams due to physical discomfort, dreams due to suppressed material that is of significance to psychoanalysts and psychotherapists, and pre-

cognitive dreams, in which future events are foreseen. The difference between an out-of-body experience during sleep and ordinary dreams is marked. Ordinary dreams are frequently remembered only in part, if at all, and arc quickly forgotten even if they are remembered upon awakening; astral projections are remembered clearly and in every detail, and seemingly last several days in one's memory. They compare with other dreams the way a color photograph compares to a black-and-white print.

It stands to reason that the majority of out-of-body experiences occur during sleep, when the bonds between conscious and unconscious minds are relaxed. Occasionally, people have out-of-body experiences while fully awake, not only when resting or sitting down, but even while driving cars or walking. Some of these experiences are of short duration, and I know of no instance where accidents have occurred because of this momentary displacement. There seems to be a superior law watching over people with this gift, making sure that they do not suffer because of it. In the case of motorists driving on a highway at great speed and having momentary displacements, this seems particularly likely, since any purely logical explanation would not account for the amazing fact that accidents do not occur under such circumstances.

I know of no other field of scientific inquiry where so little progress is apparent on the surface than in parapsychology. I do not mean to say that progress is not being made—far from it—but in terms of public knowledge, little is being disclosed that hasn't already been disclosed ten or fifteen years ago. Perhaps this is because the climate for disclosures of this kind was more favorable in the 1950s and early 1960s than it seems to be today. Funds were available then that are not now at hand, but beyond this I notice a timidity on the part of responsible scientists in the field of parapsychology for which there is neither need nor explanation; the material obtained through the proper observation of spontaneous phenomena in ESP is tremendous and deserves a wider circulation, even in the popular sense of the term. On the other hand, material published ten or fifteen years ago is as valid today as it was when it was first disclosed to the public. Repeated experiments confirmed earlier findings and have continued to confirm them. Some of these repeated experiments are no longer necessary since the point has long been made, and can be found in reputable published sources. The energies and funds used to prove those points over and over again could be better employed for research in areas where we do not yet have full confirmation of assumed facts.

What recent works on out-of-body experiences have said has already been said ably, if perhaps not as entertainingly, by the late Professor Hornell Hart, chairman of the Committee on Spontaneous Cases, American Society for Psychic Research, associate professor at Duke University, and a close collaborator of Professor Rhine. Hart, whom I recall as an amiable, open-minded man, is best remembered, to my mind at least, as the scientist who said, after investigating numerous cases of so-called apparitions of the dead, "These apparitions seem to be what they claim to be, namely, the apparitions of the dead."

On November 4, 1953, Hart submitted a summation of his intensive research into out-of-body experiences. Entitled "ESP Projection: Spontaneous Cases and Repeatable Experiments," the report covered 288 cases of purported ESP projections and found that only ninety-nine of the 288 cases investigated were evidential in terms of the project. These ninety-nine cases were then classified into five types. Three of these types involved purported *ESP projections* produced experimentally: (a) the hypnotically induced projections, which totaled twenty cases; (b) the projection of one's own apparition, by concentration, reported in fifteen cases; and (c) self-projections by more elaborate methods in twelve cases. Professional mediums, preliterate medicine men, and amateur experimenters have each had their own methods. The two types of spontaneous ESP projections consisted of: (a) spontaneous apparitions of the living, corresponding with dreams or other concentrations of attention by the appearers reported in thirty cases; and (b) other spontaneous cases listed. Hart states, "The fifteen reported successes in projecting one's own apparition plus the thirty spontaneous cases of apparitions of living persons coinciding with dreams or other directions of attention by the appearer suggest that such experiments are at least occasionally repeatable."

One of the arguments sometimes put forth by both parapsychologists and outsiders against the reality of astral travel involves the explanation of the phenomena as simple telepathy, clairvoyance, or precognition. In this respect, Hart makes the following observations: "ESP projection does involve telepathy, clairvoyance, and precognition, but simple telepathy and clairvoyance do not require projection of viewpoint; ESP projection does involve perceiving from and being perceived in positions outside of the excursionist's physical body; shared dreams involve ESP projection; the ESP projection hypothesis provides a framework into which each of the ninety-nine evidential cases fits."

Hart concludes that the method likely to produce full and verifiable ESP projections experimentally is hypnosis: "The suggestions given the hypnotized subject should make use of knowledge that has been accumulated relative to the basic characteristics of ESP projection as most fully experienced in the best cases reported to date. The induction of catalepsy, and suggestions that the astral body in being detached from the physical body, is floating upward, is being lifted by unseen hands, and the like, should be promising in this connection. Responses should be elicited from the entranced individual to determine how far these subjected experiences are being realized. Subsequent stages in typical ESP projection should then be suggested, such as the movement of the projected body into the vertical position, its movement to a position standing on the floor, its release from catalepsy, its projection through an open door into an adjoining room, going through a closed door or solid wall projection to distant locations, with observations of people, objects and events at those locations, and the like, should follow."

Hart acknowledges the possibility that astral travelers might encounter the spirits of the dead en route. "In view of the frequency with which contact with what appeared to be projected personalities of deceased persons has been reported in past cases, it is of major importance that this phase of ESP projection shall be explored open-mindedly." He goes on to suggest that "if and when successful hypnotic projections have been established, experiments should be carried out with a view to transferring to the hypnotized subject the initiative in such projections and the capacity to induce them at will or under specified conditions."

Hart's one-line summaries of cases he has investigated contained such startling statements as, "announced experiment first to SPR; then succeeded" or "wrote plan to appear to mother, independent confirmation"; "worried about father, deliberately projected to him"; and among cases involving self-projection by other methods than mere concentration, "during séance, projected to mine explosion eight miles away"; "projected medium located body of missing man." Among the one-line summaries of spontaneous apparitions of the living, Hart lists, "apparition of worried mother of dying woman seen by nurse"; "wife projected to husband at sea, seen by cabin mate also."

In his summation of the investigation, Hart lists the following findings as due to the research undertaken: out-of-body experiences are frequent; such experiences may be veridical; ESP projections are reported evidentially to have been produced experimentally at least forty-seven times. Pilot studies at Duke University showed that, in representative samples of students, shared dreams were reported by 24 percent, precognitive dreams by 36 percent, perception of apparitions by about 10 percent, and out-of-body experiences by 33 percent.

Hart sums up the findings presented by the chairman at the International Conference of Parapsychological Studies at the University of Utrecht, the Netherlands, on August 3, 1953. These findings parallel his own findings based largely upon experiments at Duke University and the careful reevaluation of reported spontaneous cases.

TWO PLACES AT ONCE

Bilocation is a phenomenon closely allied with astral travel, but it is a manifestation of its own with certain features that set it apart from astral travel or out-of-body experiences per se. In bilocation, a living person is projected to another site and observed there by one or more witnesses while continuing to function fully and normally in the physical body at the original place. In this respect it differs greatly from astral projection, since the astral traveler cannot be seen in two places at once, especially as the physical body of the astral traveler usually rests in bed, or, if it concerns a daytime projection, is continuing to do whatever the person is doing automatically and without consciousness. With bilocation, there is full consciousness and unawareness that one is being seen at a distance as well.

Bilocation occurs mostly in mentally active people, people whose minds are filled with a variety of ideas, perhaps to the point of distraction. They may be doing one thing while thinking of another. That is not to say that people

without imagination cannot be seen in two places at once, but the majority of cases known to me fall into the first category. A case in point is Mina Lauterer of California, who has pronounced ESP talents. In addition she is a well-balanced and keen observer. She has had several experiences of being seen in a distant place while not actually being there in the flesh.

In one such case she was walking down the street in Greenwich Village, New York, when she saw a man whom she knew from Chicago. Surprised to find this person out of his usual element, she crossed the street to greet him. She tried to reach out toward him and he evaporated before her eyes. The incident so disturbed her that she wrote to the man in Chicago and found out that he had been in Chicago at the time she had observed him in New York. However, he had just then been thinking of her. Whether his thought projection was seen by Mina Lauterer or whether a part of himself was actually projected to appear is a moot question. He, too, saw Lauterer at the same time he was thinking about her in Chicago. This is a case of *double bilocation,* something that does not happen often.

In another instance, Lauterer reported a case to me that had overtones of precognition in addition to bilocation. "One night not long ago, in New York, as I was in bed, halfway between sleep and being fully awake," she said, "I saw a face as clearly as one sees a picture projected on a screen. I saw it with the mind's eye, for my eyes were closed. This was the first experience that I can recall, where I saw, in my mind, a face I had never seen.

About six weeks later, I received an invitation to go to Colombia, South America. I stayed on a banana plantation in Turbo, which is a primitive little town on the Gulf of Urabá. Most of the people who live there are the descendants of runaway slaves and Indian tribes. Transportation is by launch or canoe from the mainland to the tiny cluster of nearby islands. The plantation was located near the airport on the mainland, as was the customs office. The village of Turbo is on a peninsula.

"One Sunday afternoon I went into town with my host, a North American, and my Colombian friend. As we walked through the dirty streets bordered with sewage drains and looked around at the tin-roofed hovels and the populace of the place, I thought, 'this is the edge of the world.' Sunday seemed to be the market day; the streets were crowded with people mostly of two hues, black and red-skinned. As we passed a drugstore, walking single-file, a tall, handsome, well-dressed young man caught my attention. He seemed as out of place as I and my companions did. He did not look at me even as I passed directly in front of him. It struck me as strange. South American men always look at women in the most frank manner. Also, he looked familiar, and I realized that this was the face that I had seen in my mind, weeks before in New York.

"The following day we were invited to cocktails by our neighbor, the captain of customs. He told us that a young flyer arrived every month around the same time, stopped in Turbo overnight, and continued on his regular route to other villages. He always bunked in with his soldiers, instead of staying at the filthy hotel in the village. He mentioned that the young man was the son of the governor of one of the Colombian states, and that he had just arrived from Cartagena, the main office of his small airline. He brought the young man out and introduced him to us. It was the young man that I had seen in the village! I asked him if he had really arrived Monday morning and he later proved beyond all doubt that he had not been in Turbo on Sunday afternoon when I saw him. He was dressed in the same clothes on Monday as those that I had seen him wearing on Sunday in my vision. I do not know why I saw him when he wasn't there. Later he asked me to marry him, but I did not. When I and my companions went to Cartagena later on we checked and again confirmed the facts—he was miles away when I had seen him!"

I am indebted to Herbert Schaefer of Savannah, Georgia, for the account of a case of bilocation that occurred some time ago to two elderly friends of his: Carl Pfau was awakened one night by the feeling that he was not alone. Turning over in bed, he saw his good friend Morton Deutsch standing by his bedside. "How did you get in here?" he asked, since the door had been locked. Deutsch made no reply but merely smiled, then walked to the door, where he disappeared. On checking the matter, it was discovered that Deutsch had been sitting in a large comfortable chair at the time of his appearance at this friend's bedside and had just wondered how his friend Carl was doing. Suddenly he had felt himself lifted from the chair to Carl's bedside. There was a distance of about two miles between their houses.

Bilocation cannot be artificially induced the way astral projection can, but if you are bent on being seen in two places at once, you may encourage the condition through certain steps. Being in a relaxed and comfortable position in a quiet place, indoors or outdoors, and allowing your thoughts to drift might induce the condition. The more you concentrate, the less likely it is to happen. It is difficult to produce that certain state of dissociation that is conducive to bilocation experiences. The only thing I can suggest is that such a condition may occur if you set up the favorable conditions often enough. It should be remembered that the majority of bilocation incidents are not known to the projected individual until after they have occurred and been confirmed on the other end.

possession

THOSE WHO TRAFFIC IN THE FEAR OF "THE Devil" like to warn of the dangers of being possessed by "The Evil One" or one of his minions. To this day, many forms of organized religion rely on the potential danger of possession to keep the faithful in line. But their devil, and demons, exist only in their fertile imaginations.

Very few ideas in the field of psychic phenomena have aroused the interest of fiction writers as strongly as the twin intrusions of *possession* and *obsession.* This interest is only natural, for if we are to accept as proven the possibility that a discarnate human being can take over a living one, we may soon find ourselves face-to-face with the much larger questions of responsibility and culpability for actions apparently undertaken by one person but in effect the work and scheme of another. We must therefore proceed cautiously in this area, for the line between authentic intrusion and natural schizophrenia is often difficult to find.

Possession describes the abnormal state in which an otherwise well-adjusted person will suddenly show signs of an alien personality, temporarily or permanently, and will commit certain acts while under the influence of another will. This must not be confused with vague or minor changes in personality that occur normally in older persons as they grow senile. Possession is a sharply defined state; there is no doubt in the observer that a personality other than that of the person himself is in command. While under the influence of possession, a person may frequently do or speak exactly the opposite of what he would normally do. Before assuming that possession by an outsider has taken place and rushing to the nearest medium or parapsychologist, one must first rule out all alternative possibilities. No matter how emotionally close one may be to the subject, the possibility of mental illness, caused by psychological pressures or by biochemical changes in the body, is always present. It is therefore important to know the exact time and circumstances when the alleged possession took place. Very rarely does genuine possession show itself over long periods, gradually increasing in strength and implication. True possession comes on suddenly, or within a matter of weeks at the most.

There must be a causative factor, just as one may pick up a disease by partaking of spoiled food or water, or touching unclean objects, or being close to carriers of disease, so there must be an opening wedge through which the possessive entity can enter the personality of the victim. In those cases that I have personally looked into, I have found that the victims were all mediumistic to a degree to begin with, thus affording the first condition for successful possession—the physical setup of the victim's mind and body. But there are millions of people all over the world with such latent or overt possibilities and surely only a handful have suffered from possession.

The second condition, then, is an unconscious personality flaw, a weakness that allows a stronger possessive personality to exploit the victim. This flaw may be nothing more than fear of the unknown, fear of the future, or what have you. A positive, firm personality is not likely to fall victim to possession. The weakness may be caused by domestic problems, unhappiness, frustration, or professional problems so strong that they create a negative emotional field at all times. These are forms of what I call "intestinal dissension," turmoil within that the person cannot cope with. This negative field seems to give the invading force a magnetic pad onto which it can hold as if by suction. Some victims may even be unconsciously desirous of being possessed by a stronger force that will relieve them of their responsibilities. You would be surprised how many otherwise ordinary people have suppressed desires of being freed from duties of one kind or another in return for being willing slaves of some other, strong mind.

The third element necessary for true possession is the opportunity. Even if a mediumistic person torn by dissension is available, possession need not follow. But let us suppose that such a person exposes himself to psychic influences through trance, experimentations with table tipping and other forms of spirit communication, or is present in a location where an earthbound possessive personality is in evidence. All elements are present and the possession takes place.

Most of my readers will be familiar with the book and subsequent film *The Three Faces of Eve*, in which a subject found herself with three distinct personalities in one body, each personality diametrically opposed to what the other two stood for. It was then, and probably is now, the view among many psychiatrists that such triple-personality phenomena are nothing more than complicated forms of personality splits and that, in effect, all three faces of Eve were part of the original personality, operating as separate entities because of repressions and unfulfilled fantasies. Accordingly, we were shown how Eve's childhood memories and fears were behind one of the personalities. In the end, the treating psychiatrist succeeded in fusing the most desirable aspects of the three personalities into one single person, and Eve was returned to the doubtful blessings of being an average housewife. If the Eve case were a rare instance, it might be difficult to argue with this view, but unfortunately there are a number of such multiple-personality cases on record and the evidence for intervention by discarnate people from the outside is much too strong to be suppressed or regarded as doubtful.

Probably the best-known case in psychic research literature is the triple personality of Sally Beauchamps of Boston, a case investigated by Dr. Morton Prince in 1898. Three distinct personalities occupied the body of this young woman. When Prince finally managed to merge two of these extremes into a new, adjusted personality, a strong third personality unwilling to merge or leave, insisting that she was a spirit and not a splinter of the Beauchamps personality at all. Prince, using hypnotherapy, finally persuaded the unwanted guest to leave so that the young woman could lead a normal life.

Dr. William McDougall, a psychologist of renown who was familiar with this remarkable case, expressed the opinion that the Beauchamps case could be explained only by acknowledging that a separate psychic entity had somehow gained access to the body of Beauchamps. It is true that the young woman was physically weak at the time, and was filled with the frustrations and difficulties of her personal life. The Beauchamps case has been discussed more fully by Alson J. Smith in *The Three Sally Beauchamps*, but it suffices to say that it bears remarkable similarities to the Eve case. There, too, a strong and alien personality was expelled with considerable difficulty.

I came into close contact with such a case in the spring of 1961, when the Para-

psychology Foundation asked me to look into a strange case that had come its way. Since I had been known for my work with psychic possession cases, it was thought that I might perhaps shed some light on what would otherwise be just another story for the files, unresolved except perhaps for the pat answer the routine psychiatrist would have for it— one not necessarily corresponding with the facts. I knew at that time of the valuable and somewhat confidential work Eileen Garrett had done in hospitals and institutions for the insane, which she visited with the eminent psychiatrist Dr. Robert Laidlaw of New York to weed out cases of possession from mental cases. Because she is such a highly sensitive medium, she could readily spot the hangers-on around the bodies of the unfortunate victims and remove them through verbal commands.

The case brought to me involved Rita H. of Boston, who had been under treatment for a personality problem. She had described her state in a letter addressed to two people in public life, Bishop Fulton Sheen and Dr. Thomas Wyatt of Los Angeles. She hoped to find an understanding of her problem that she felt was lacking:

Due to a long, chronic illness, I became severely depressed. Then, in July 1959 I began to hear the voices of three people—two men and a woman. I cannot begin to describe the mysterious awe I felt to hear sentient human voices with no visible person present. To lie on my pillow at night and hear them, and realize that where once only I was there, now four separate minds inhabited my body, pent up in my mind and hearing my conscious thoughts. With the constant talk and confusion of thoughts, it was all I could do to maintain my sanity.

They told me they are people who have died and are, naturally, in a bodiless state, and that they heard my despairing thoughts and entered my mind to encourage me. They became trapped there in what they call the "aura" of my being and cannot release themselves. They fear too that the spirit has an affinity for the flesh. Many times we've been thrown into a near panic. In God's name, I don't know how to release them.

I struggled up from an unspeakable despair and physical exhaustion, and through God's help channeled my mind back into the outside world. I learned to read and concentrate again and block them from my conscious mind. I work full-time again and at a very demanding job and carry out my duties successfully. None of my employers, friends, or relatives know I hear 'voices.' I wish to spare them the misery and spare myself from derision.

I requested some sort of proof that these people really lived at one time. Rita H. eventually informed me that she had located the tombstone of at least one of them. This in itself is not absolute proof that outside personalities are trapped in the mind of the young woman. Miss H. also wrote to Ian Stevenson, professor of psychiatry at the University of Virginia, and to many other prominent researchers in the field of parapsychology. She has an eloquent way with words and her plea

sounded most convincing. If what she claims is true, many more discarnate human beings may be trapped in the minds of other evidently mediumistic persons, unable to free themselves from the self-imposed confinement.

I tried to hypnotize her but she would not take suggestion. This indicated that we were not dealing here with an extremely impressionable young woman. Far from it. The invasion might just be genuine, I thought, and if her illness and weakened physical state were the entrance wedge for some unattached earthbound spirits, she might well be telling the truth. Even if the names of the alleged invaders checked out as those of actual people who had once existed, it would not, in my estimation, eliminate at least the theoretical possibility of conscious or unconscious fraud.

Miss H. impressed me as a quiet, genuinely mystified person. I do not see how she would profit from any fraud since her job security and social standing were being jeopardized by her disclosures. A Boston physician later worked on the case in conjunction with a medium and I understand that they made some progress toward contacting the possessing people.

But if these invaders are, as I assume, less than sane minds, they will no more be able to help themselves than ghosts can get out from the entrapment of the place of their unhappy deaths. It is easier to force a ghost from a house than to evict an imprisoned spirit personality from within the mind of a living person!

Although the suggestion lies at hand, I do not consider the Rita H. case merely a question of unrecognized insanity. I did not hear the voices, but that does not prove they do not exist. What makes the Rita H. case different from the classical cases described earlier is the total lack of interest on the part of the invaders in remaining in, or using, the common body. They just want to get out. Also, the three alien personalities do not represent splinters of Miss H.'s own personality, nor are they materially different from her own or in any way like suppressed parts of her personality. They are just three bodiless people with personalities and desires of their own. The difficulty lies in our inability at present to prove their existence through apparatus capable of registering them as energy fields, or to exteriorate them as people through trance mediumship.

A far more sinister case came to my attention a few years ago. Miss H.'s plight is no bed of roses, but at least she is a rational individual, capable of limiting her possession to periods when her state cannot interfere with work or ordinary living habits. The other case I am about to report was not so well controlled. In fact, no happy solution is in sight. It concerns the wife of a prominent publishing executive whose brilliant career had included stints as a huntress in Africa, a stab or two at writing, and a good deal of painting. She had a social position of prominence, wit, and beauty. She was not ill in the physical sense when the chain of events I am about to report took place.

As far as I know, Mrs. K. did like a drink now and then, but she was neither an alcoholic nor given to deep depressions. Her physical and emotional states were reasonably good and no great problems existed in her pleasant life at the time of the incident. She had not the slightest interest in the occult; in fact, she derided all claims by believers as being mere superstition.

One day she was at the country house of a relative and, in a relaxed and somewhat expansive mood, agreed to take part in an after-dinner diversion her relative was fond of—the practice of table tipping to "raise the spirits." Mrs. K. entered the procedure in a skeptical and somewhat humorous frame of mind, more to please her hostess than out of honest curiosity or belief that it would work. The other two participants were her hostess and a woman friend who served as a kind of companion to that elderly woman.

Hardly had Mrs. K. placed her hands upon the table than she decided the whole thing was boring and got up. The ouija board was then brought out and Mrs. K.'s husband joined the group. The board seemed to concentrate all its activities on her, to the point where it frightened her and she did not wish to go on. But the hostess suggested that perhaps she ought to take out a pencil and paper, in case the spirits wished to write. Mrs. K. though this highly unlikely, but to please her relative, she took the pencil, placed it on the proffered paper, and waited. Suddenly the pencil, as if by its own volition, flew all over the paper, scribbling rapidly and drawing what appeared to be the distorted face of a young man, possibly insane. Around it, the writing read, in part, "I have killed the one I love," and the word killed was crossed out with great vehemence, tearing the paper. At this point, Mrs. K. rose from her chair and let out a wild scream so unlike herself that the others were filled with sheer terror at what had happened. Deeply in trance, Mrs. K. was unable to function rationally until some time later, still shaken by what appeared to be her first experience of involuntary trance—possession.

Not so skeptical anymore, she vowed never to tempt the uncanny again. But the door she had opened would not stay shut. She soon found her ordinary writing drifted off into hands other than her own and she became the writing instrument for a succession of discarnates who found in her a subject, a medium, through whom they could express themselves after long years of frustrating oblivion. These personalities included a parade of people from many periods, ranging from recently killed soldiers to the original builder of the house in which the K.s lived at the time, a man of the eighteenth century. But communications were often interrupted by the violent person who originally opened Mrs. K.'s psychic door, the murderer. He had been a painter and he now began to dominate Mrs. K.'s own artistry to the point where she became completely submerged in his violent style, so different from her own. She could not put a brush to canvas without his ever-present influence guiding it in his image.

This was followed a little later by the personality of an old crone who enjoyed physical violence. She frequently threw Mrs. K. to the floor unexpectedly and for no valid reason, thus causing many physical injuries and bruises. Taken to a leading hospital by her alarmed husband, Mrs. K. went through every conceivable test only to emerge with a clean bill of mental health. There just was no ordinary explanation for what was happening to her. The latest invader, apparently insane prior to her own death, was difficult to dislodge. A succession of psychiatrists sympathetic to parapsychology tried to help Mrs. K., but the door would not stay closed.

When I met her, she had already been through some of the vicious physical attacks. All I could do was try to induce the invading personality to let go. But you cannot reason with an insane mind, and the struggle was fierce. It took many months of intensive deep hypnosis to help her regain control. To make things even worse, Mrs. K.'s own life had taken on problems that had not existed earlier. A sense of frustration about her art and her writing, both of which had merit although they had not yet been publicly acknowledged, and an even deeper sense of self-destructiveness were gradually driving her to stronger doses of alcohol. The more she allowed this to happen, the more difficult it became to keep outside entities from slipping back in. Ultimately, she became so fascinated with her ability to serve as a medium that she devoted a great deal of time to her new talent. Instead of helping to close the psychic door, she kept it wide open to a succession of personalities who wished to write through her hands.

It became difficult to decide how much of this was genuine psychic communication and how much was the product of what I call "extending imagination," created by her own fertile and agile mind. Either way, it did not contribute to her health, which was rapidly failing. Even after she had been cured of overindulgence, her health did not improve. The damage to the body was already done. There is no question in my mind that all the early communications Mrs. K. received were genuine. In fact, I was able to prove the existence of some of the communicators through research at a time when Mrs. K. had no knowledge of these personalities. So many people tried to help Mrs. K. regain her health and drive out the invading entities possessing her that it is difficult to say who did what. But the melancholy truth is that in the end, it did not help, for Mrs. K. is today an invalid without any hope of great improvement in her condition. For a while I was successful in holding back the evil possessors, but when Mrs. K. failed in her desire to fight back, I could not help her any longer.

The various personalities manifesting themselves through her, whether in trance or through automatic writing, were in no way splinters of her own personality, nor did they resemble any facets of it. They were entire entities, mainly disturbed or evil, who had been drawn to Mrs. K. as a medium. Although a natural, Mrs. K. never knew how to control these invasions or to channel them where they could not hurt her.

There are a number of strange crimes on record in which apparently sane people go berserk and kill those closest to them. Recently a man in New Jersey returned home from work and for no reason at all shot and killed his wife and children. After he was apprehended, he could give no reason for his actions. He maintained that he had suddenly gone blank and remembered absolutely nothing from a

certain point on. Had someone else "operated" his body and committed the terrible crime? Had an evil discarnate with pent-up hostility somehow gotten in when the man returned home, tired, from a hard day's work? No judge or jury will accept such an explanation, and yet it may be true.

Other incidents of takeovers occur in bars and places where people consume alcoholic beverages. Because a person under the influence of alcohol may pass out, he could be taken over by one of the many discarnate personalities standing by for just such an opportunity. In the alcoholic state, there is a loosening of the ties between conscious and unconscious minds, a condition in which it is easier for the possessing entity to slip in and take over. The same danger applies to other forms of artificially weakened consciousness such as the various drugs, both medical and psychedelic, opiates, and barbiturates. Even astral projection can, under certain conditions, allow the takeover by outsiders of a person's physical body if the experimenter is not careful enough to suggest return to his own body prior to starting on the journey.

I have never found scientific evidence of the existence of a romantic world called "heaven" or a dreary place called "hell," inhabited respectively by winged creatures of great beauty and horned misfits with cloven hoofs. But I have found strong evidence of the existence of a nonphysical, spiritual world in which we continue as we were, the good still good and the evil ones just as bad as they were when the transition took place. This does not necessarily mean that they will not change eventually, but at first evil human beings become merely dead evil human beings and their destructive urges are not automatically canceled just because of the lack of a physical body.

On the contrary, this new state may even add frustrations to their already faulty characters, and their drives may become even more pronounced. Thus it seems that countless shady characters lurk about the living, ever ready to pounce on them and invade their bodies if given half a chance. Thereby hangs my watchword: if not given any chance, they are powerless to take over. If your own mental and physical health and positive approach to the thought processes are such that you are stronger than any potential invader no one will touch you. Possession, too, is a two-way street, and it can be avoided.

Obsession is the opposite of possession. Here it is not so much a matter of being invaded by an outsider, but of creating, within oneself, a force that clings to outside entities. Whereas possession is begun from the outside and is aided and abetted by the condition of the victim, obsession comes from the living person and directs itself toward outside forces and personalities, frequently discarnate.

A typical case of obsession would be that of the young woman who has made contact with a discarnate personality at a séance and proceeds to fall in love with him. She will gradually become obsessed with the idea of being united with him until the inevitable suicide occurs. This is a pattern that I have witnessed, although the suicide attempt in the case I refer to was unsuccessful. One might argue that this is an unhealthy, unnatural relation-

ship indicating an unbalanced mind, but it is not necessarily so.

The person in question was a highly intelligent individual who entered into this peculiar relationship of her own free will. Obsession is never within the confines of conventional behavior, but one may choose to remain outside that convention and still have a soul.

On occasion, bereavement will lead to obsession. A woman whose husband had died unexpectedly was so shaken by this separation that she could not and would not accept it. Both had been spiritualists in Europe, where the husband had been at work on an important book that would now remain unfinished unless the widow could get the needed information from him through séances and paranormal means. She became obsessed with the idea of finishing the book and did everything in her power to maintain contact with him. When she heard of my work, she implored me to allow her to come to any and all séances in the hope that her husband might be contacted. I explained that I don't hold séances but merely work with mediums investigating hauntings. On occasion I test and explore their paranormal abilities, but never for the purpose of gratifying the obsession, no matter how altruistic, of a single individual. Nevertheless, she kept asking me to keep her in mind if I heard of any séances. Her entire world revolved around this idea now and she neglected all other aspects of her existence, especially any attempt to rebuild her life with someone else or, at the very least, to find other interests to occupy her time.

There is still another kind of "stranger within," less obvious, certainly less dangerous and less common. Sometimes one meets a person who carries her own ghost, so to speak, with her. Ghosts do not travel, but there are people who have somehow attracted to themselves a personality from beyond who haunts them very much the way a ghost haunts a house. It is not possession nor is it obsession with the personality, for the victim usually wants nothing more fervently than to get rid of the unwanted follower.

The case in question concerns a young woman of Russian-Arabic parentage named Marika Bortin, who came to America from Europe a few years ago. She is an actress in motion pictures and on television, and she struck me as being well balanced and well adjusted. Anyone with her looks should have no romantic troubles and yet the difficulty she told me about did concern a man, but not a flesh-and-blood man. As a child, Bortin constantly predicted things that came true. She found herself lost in a London fog, unable to find her way. Suddenly the fifteen-year-old girl saw a light appear from nowhere and lead her home. It disappeared as soon as she reached her house.

Nothing unusual, in the psychic sense, happened to her until she spent some time in a hospital. A voice, seemingly out of nowhere, called her name. The following year she had her first experience with what she came to know as automatic writing. One day, while on the telephone and holding a pencil between her fingers, she suddenly felt her hand moving as if someone were guiding her arm. She knew she was not doing this herself. Many times since, a communica-

tor calling himself Ortez has written to her, through her. Especially at night she feels cold inside, there is a tenseness as if she were not alone, and her hand is forced to write.

We tried to see what Ortez had to say to *me*. "I am not dead," he wrote over and over when I started to explain what he was, if he was. One must be extremely careful not to confuse the creations of a person's own unconscious mind with what is a genuine hand from the Beyond. I remarked that the name Ortez sounded anything but Greek to me, although he claimed to be of that nationality. "I am more alive than you…I hate you!" he wrote in return. I said he might be Spanish or perhaps Puerto Rican. (In New York, being Puerto Rican is less desirable than being Greek.) There was anger and a futile outburst of frustration, but it sounded as if I had hit the nail on the head.

Psychiatrists will argue that Ortez, Greek or Spaniard, was a figment of Marika's own unconscious mind. They may be correct, but then again I am not convinced that they are. The reason for such a split-off personality was lacking, at least as far as I could tell. Bortin was doing well. She had love and success and did not need this talent to get attention from anyone. I told Ortez to leave her and threatened him in the most severe manner. It did not do much good. I often wonder if these automatic writers, if they are separate entities, are attracted by some unconscious desire or compassion within the victim. I have not heard from Bortin again, so I can only assume that Ortez has either withdrawn or Bortin has found life with Ortez acceptable enough not to fight him.

love beyond the grave

EVER SINCE THE FILM *GHOST* STIRRED THE imagination, if not the curiosity, of millions of people all over the world, the question of romantic ties beyond physical death has become something one can seriously discuss even in groups who would have laughed at such a possibility a scant ten years ago. But enough people saw this film to make it an all-time high income-producing movie, and questions about its validity from the general public are far more intense, more searching, more positive in tone, than, say, questions about the validity of Oliver Stone's film *JFK*.

Western society has been brainwashed for centuries by organized religion to let well enough alone—give onto the world what concerns your body, and give onto the church what concerns your soul, or whatever it is that happens to you when you die. Eastern people in some countries are less hostile to the notion of a tangible real hereafter, though not necessarily for scientific reasons. Religion assumes there is another world waiting when you leave this one, but it looks askance on any attempt by you directly to find out what it is like. Leaving that intelligence gathering and interpretation to the clergy is rarely helpful: at best it will give a partisan glimpse at that next dimension into which we all must pass; at worst, a distorted, even frightening view of what lies ahead.

We already have so much evidence, from scientifically valid sources, regarding the next state of existence, that one need not live one's life in ignorance and fear. To understand how love, romance, and sex can exist between people in the physical world and those who were, but are no longer, in it, one should first understand the nature of life itself. Only then do continuing communication and bonds with those on the Other Side make sense, and the nature of deep emotional relationships within the framework of the existing universe we know, will become clearer. It does not mean we will, or can, have all the answers, but we will be able, by examining our true nature, to deal with such incidents properly—neither with fear, nor with fanatic passion, but naturally, as each situation requires.

When one half of a couple passes out of the physical world, the half left behind will grieve, and eventually get over it, and even find another romantic partner. That is as it should be, though grieving for someone who has gone on is not helpful to either the one left behind, nor to the one who has gone on, as it will affect him or her adversely. Most often, attentions from the dead lover are not encouraged, that is, from the side of the living partner. Occasionally, the bond is still so strong that it is accepted, even desired, though this harbors great dangers in some cases, ranging from psychological damage to the possibility of induced possession.

An elderly Canadian woman had divorced her husband long before he died, but immediately after he was "over there" he started contacting her and making every effort to continue what he still perceived as a relationship. She had not wanted it before he died and wanted it even less afterward, but he persisted and caused her much anguish until we were able to break his hold on her psyche, at least to the extent that she was able to control his incursions.

When people pass over to the Other Side, nothing in their character changes immediately: their unfulfilled desires are as strong as before. They will try to get back to their usual surroundings, their old homes and impress their companions with their presence. Depending on the degree of the living person's psychic abilities, it will work well, badly, or not at all.

Mrs. J.H. is a housewife living in Maryland. At the time of the incidents I am about to report, her son, Richard, was seven and her daughter, Cheryl, six. Hers was a conventional marriage, until the tragic death of her husband, Frank. On September 3, he was locking up a restaurant where he was employed near Washington, D.C. Suddenly, two men entered by the rear door and shot him while attempting a robbery. For more than a year after the murder, no clue as to the murderers' identities was found by the police. Mrs. H. was still grieving over the sudden loss of her husband when something extraordinary took place in her home. Exactly one month to the day of his death, she happened to be in her living room when she saw a "wall of light" and something floated across the living room toward her. From it stepped the person of her late husband Frank. He seemed real to her, but somewhat transparent. Frightened, the widow turned on the lights and the apparition faded.

From that moment on, the house seemed to be alive with strange phenomena: knocks at the door that disclosed no one who could have caused them, the dog barking for no reason in the middle of the night, cats staring as if they were looking at a person in the room. Then one day the two children went into the bathroom and saw their dead father taking a shower! Needless to say, Mrs. H. was at a loss to explain that to them. The widow had placed all her late husband's clothes into an unused closet that was kept locked. She was the last one to go to bed at night and the first one to rise in the morning, and one morning she awoke to find Frank's shoes in the hallway; no one could have placed them there.

One day Mrs. H.'s mother, Mrs. D., who lives nearby, was washing clothes in her daughter's basement. When she approached the washer, she noticed that it was spotted with what appeared to be fresh blood. Immediately she and the widow searched the basement, looking for a possible leak in the ceiling to account for the blood, but they found nothing. Shortly afterward, a sister of the widow arrived to have lunch at the house. A fresh tablecloth was placed on the table. When the women started to clear the table after lunch, they noticed that under each dish there was a blood spot the size of a fifty-cent piece. Nothing they had eaten at lunch could possibly have accounted for such a stain.

But the widow's home was not the only place where manifestations took place. Her mother's home was close by, and one night a clock-radio alarm went off by itself in a room that had not been entered by anyone for months. It was the room belonging to Mrs. H.'s grandmother, who had been in the hospital for some time before. It became clear to Mrs. H. that her husband was trying to get in touch with her, since the phenomena continued at an unabated pace.

Three years after his death, two alarm clocks in the house went off at the same time, although they had not been set, and all the kitchen cabinets flew open by themselves. The late Frank H. appeared to his widow punctually on the third of each month, the day he was murdered, but the widow could not bring herself to address him and ask him what he wanted. Frightened, she turned

on the light, which caused him to fade away. In the middle of the night Mrs. H. would feel someone shake her shoulder, as if to wake her up. She recognized this touch as that of her late husband, for it had been his habit to wake her in just that manner.

Meanwhile his murderers were caught. Unfortunately, they got off lightly, one of the murderers with three years in prison, the other with ten. It seemed like a light sentence for having taken a man's life so deliberately.

Time went on, and the children were ten and eleven years of age, when Mrs. H. could no longer take the phenomena in the house and moved out. The house was rented to strangers, who are still living in it. They have had no experiences of an uncanny nature since, after all, Frank wants nothing from them.

As for the new house where Mrs. H. and her children live now, Frank has not put in an appearance as of yet. But there are occasional tappings on the wall, as if he still wanted to communicate with his wife. Mrs. H. wishes she could sleep in peace in the new home, but then she remembers how her late husband, who had been a believer in scientology, had assured her that when he died, he would be back.

The ghostly lover need not be half of a married couple, or even one of two people who used to live together without being married. Even a relationship that had been strong in life, at least on the part of one of the people involved, but had never been consummated, can cause a problem between the two worlds. When the desire to have a relationship is so strong, even after death, an attempt may yet be made to make it happen.

Grace Rivers was a secretary, and not given to hallucinations or emotional outbursts. I had spoken with her several times and always found her most reluctant to discuss what to her seemed incredible. It seemed that on weekends, Rivers and another secretary, named Juliet, were the houseguests of their employer, John Bergner, in Westbrook, Connecticut. Rivers was also a good friend of his, a man in his mid-fifties. She had joined the Bergner firm in 1948, six years after John Bergner had become the owner of a country house built in 1865.

Bergner liked to spend his weekends among his favorite employees, and sometimes asked some of the office boys as well as his two secretaries to come up to Connecticut with him. All was most idyllic until the early 1950s, when Bergner met an advertising man named Philip Mervin. This business relationship soon broadened into a social friendship, and before long Mervin was a steady and often self-invited houseguest in Westbrook.

At first, this did not disturb anyone, but when Mervin noticed the deep and growing friendship between Bergner and his right-hand girl, something akin to jealousy prompted him to interfere with this relationship at every turn. What made this triangle even more difficult for Mervin to bear was the apparent innocence with which Bergner treated Mervin's approaches. A feeling of dislike grew into hatred between Rivers and the intruder, but before it came to any open argument, the advertising man suddenly died of a heart attack at age fifty-one.

But that did not seem to be the end of

it. Soon after his demise, the Connecticut weekends were again interrupted, this time by strange noises no natural cause could account for. Most of the uncanny experiences were witnessed by both girls as well as by some of the office boys, who seemed frightened by it all. With the detachment of a good executive secretary, Rivers lists the phenomena:

Objects moving in space.

Stones hurled at us inside and outside the house.

Clanging of tools in the garage at night (when no one was there).

Washing machine starting up at 1:00 A.M., by itself.

Heavy footsteps, banging of doors, in the middle of the night.

Television sets turning themselves on and off at will.

A spoon constantly leaping out of a cutlery tray.

The feeling of a cold wind being swept over one.

And there was much more. When a priest was brought to the house to exorcise the ghost, things only got worse. Evidently the deceased had little regard for holy men. Juliet, the other secretary, brought her husband along. One night in 1962, when Juliet's husband slept in what was once the advertising man's favorite guest room, he heard clearly a series of knocks, as if someone were hitting the top of the bureau. Needless to say, her husband had been alone in the room, and he did not do the knocking. It became so bad that Grace Rivers no longer looked forward to those weekend invitations at her employer's country home. She feared them. It was then that she remembered, with terrifying suddenness, a remark the late Mervin had made to her fellow workers: "If anything ever happens to me and I die, I'm going to walk after those two girls the rest of their lives!" he had said. Rivers realized that he was keeping his word.

Her only hope was that the ghost of Mervin would someday be distracted by an earlier specter that was sharing the house with him. On several occasions, an old woman in black had been seen emerging from a side door of the house. A local man, sitting in front of the house during the weekdays when it was unoccupied—Bergner came up only on weekends—was wondering aloud to Rivers about the "old lady who claimed she occupied the back part of the house." He had encountered her on many occasions, always seeing her disappear into the house by that same, seldom-used, side door. One of the office boys invited by Bergner also saw her around 1:30 A.M. on a Sunday, when he stood outside the house, unable to go to sleep. When she saw him she said hello, and mentioned something about money, then disappeared into a field.

Grace Rivers looked into the background of the house and discovered that it had previously belonged to an aged man who lived there with his mother. When she died, he found money buried in the house, but he claimed his mother had hidden more money that he had never been able to locate. Evidently the ghost of his mother felt the same way about it, and was still searching. For that's how it is with ghosts sometimes—

they become forgetful about material things.

Romance beyond the grave can also involve a jealous lover who resents the "replacement" taking his or her place in the affections of the former mate, still enjoying physical life in all its glory. Such was the case with Sylvia W., who never thought a *menage a trois* could or should involve a ghost. Sylvia has been married twice and lived a full life. Since the age of eight she has had precognitive experiences, warnings, and feelings about impending events, many of which have come true, and psychic dreams. She has always accepted the importance of ESP in her life and never had any fears of the occult. But something happened in her life that had her stumped.

She had fallen in love with a widower, Albert, whose wife and infant daughter were killed in a motorcar accident in 1961. Albert's wife had had a premonition of the impending accident and had told him so. Moreover, three days after her death she appeared before him and assured him that she would always be with him and take care of him. Before her death she had requested that should she die he should not remarry. He did not promise this.

As soon as Albert had gotten over the shock of his wife's untimely death he began to mingle socially once again. Despite increased social activity he remained single. However, when he met Sylvia they became involved in a love relationship. They dated for about six months, and the first four months of their relationship were undisturbed and harmonious. But then strange things started to happen. Strange noises and movements occurred in her house and in his house. That was not surprising since they spent time in both. There were knockings on the door and when they opened it there was no one there. This happened mainly late at night. Then there were sounds of someone walking in the next room or heavy objects seemingly dropping to the floor. Upon investigation they found nothing to substantiate the noises. On occasion the blinds would open by themselves or a book would move of its own volition and open by itself to a certain page while the room in which this happened was closed off and no one had access to it. Apparently someone was trying to convey messages to Albert, for the books were marked at different passages. When they read one of the passages in a particular novel that had been left in a conspicuous spot so that they could not overlook it, they realized who was behind the phenomena. The passage in the book dealt with a female competitor who was domineering; about honest love, and about one partner being "from another world." And one passage referred to someone having "seen the light."

Fantastic as it seemed, they realized that the dead wife was trying to break up their romance from the beyond.

Sally S. lived in a nice section of Brooklyn, half an hour from Manhattan and, at the time of the happenings I am about to report, was semi-retired, working two days a week at her old job of secretary.

When Miss S. first moved into her Brooklyn apartment in May, it seemed nice and quiet. Then, on August 3, she had an unusual experience. It must have

been around 3:00 A.M. when she awoke with an uncanny feeling that she was not alone. In the semidarkness of her apartment, she looked around and had the distinct impression that there was an intruder in her place. She looked out into the room, and in the semidarkness saw what appeared to be a dark figure. It was a man, and though she could not make out any features, he seemed tall and as lifelike as any human intruder might be.

Thinking that it was best for her to play possum, she lay still and waited for the intruder to leave. Picture her shock and surprise when the figure approached her and started to touch her quilt cover. About fifteen minutes prior to this experience, she had awakened because she was cold, and had pulled the cover over herself. Thus she was very much awake when the "intruder" appeared to her. She lay still, trembling, watching his every move. Suddenly he vanished into thin air, and it was only then that Miss S. realized she wasn't dealing with any flesh-and-blood person, but a ghost.

A month later, again around 3:00 A.M., Miss S. awoke to see a white figure gliding back and forth in her room. This time she was sleepy, so she did not feel like doing much about it. However, when the figure came close to her bed, she stuck our her arm to touch it, and at that moment it dissolved into thin air. Wondering who the ghost might be, Miss S. had another opportunity to observe it in November, when around 6:00 A.M. she went into her kitchen to see the dark outline of a six-foot man standing in the archway between the kitchen and the dinette. She looked away for a moment, and then returned her gaze to the spot. The apparition was still there. Once more Miss S. closed her eyes and looked away, and when she returned her eyes to the spot, he was gone.

She decided to speak to her landlady about the incidents. No one had died in the house, nor had there been any tragedy to the best of her knowledge, the owner of the house assured her. As for a previous owner, she wouldn't know. Miss S. realized that it was her peculiar psychic talent that made the phenomena possible. For some time she had been able to predict the results of horse races with uncanny accuracy, getting somewhat of a reputation in this area. Even during her school days, she came up with answers she had not yet been taught. In April of the next year, Miss S. visited her sister and her husband in New Jersey. They had bought a house the year before, and knew nothing of its history. Sally was assigned a finished room in the attic. Shortly after 2:00 A.M., a ghost appeared to her in that room. But before she could make out any details, the figure vanished. By now Miss S. knew that she had a talent for such things, and preferred not to talk about them with her sister, a somewhat nervous person. But she kept wondering who the ghost at *her* house was.

Fourteen years earlier, a close friend named John had died. A year before, he had given her two fountain pens as gifts, and Miss S. had kept one at home, and used the other at her office. A year after her friend's death, she was using one of the pens in the office when the point broke. Because she couldn't use it any more, she put the pen into her desk drawer. Then she left the office for a few minutes. When she returned, she found a lovely, streamlined black pen on top of her desk. She immediately inquired whether any of the kids had left it there, but no one had, nor had anyone been near her desk. The pen was an expensive Mont Blanc, just the thing she needed. It made her wonder whether her late friend John had not presented her with it even from the beyond.

This belief was reinforced by an experience she had had on the first anniversary of his death when she heard his voice loud and clear calling her "sweetheart"— the name he had always used to address her, rather than her given name, Sally.

All this ran through her head fourteen years later, when she tried to come to terms with her ghostly experiences. Was the ghost someone who came with the house, someone who had been there before, or was it someone who somehow linked up with her?

Sally began to put two and two together. She was in the habit of leaving her feet outside her quilt cover because the room was warm with the heat on. However, in the course of the night, the temperature in the room fell; and frequently her feet became almost frostbitten as a result. One Saturday night in March, the same year she visited her sister, she was still awake, lying in bed around 11:00 P.M.. Her feet were sticking out of the quilt, as the temperature was still tolerable. Suddenly she felt a terrific tug on her quilt; it was first raised from above her ankles, and then pulled down to cover her feet. Yet she saw no one actually doing it.

Suddenly she remembered how her late friend John had been in the habit of covering her feet when she had fallen asleep after one of his visits with her. Evidently he was still concerned that Sally should not get cold feet, or worse, and had decided to watch over her in this manner.

A year after the first phenomena occurred she moved to Long Island, not because of her ghostly experiences, but because the neighborhood had become too noisy for her: ghosts she could stand, but human disturbances were too much.

Picture this: a healthy young medical doctor, Dr. Bill P., goes to Vietnam for military service. But then he dies, in the prime of his life. He is not prepared for the sudden change, and his vitality is still intact. He remembers a woman he fancied back home in America, and he contacts her. Only contact is not the word. He wants more.

I was brought into the case of psychic Edith Berger because the people who were handling it were frankly at wits' end. There was a fine medium, Betty Ritter, who in turn had been brought into the case by psychiatrist Dr. Nandor Fodor, who could no longer deal with it alone. He had been to the house in the company of Ritter, with whom I also had worked, and despite their visit and attempted exorcism, the phenomena continued. Ritter suggested that he get in touch with me and that I join the case.

Apparently, Edith Berger had known Dr. Bill P., a medical explorer, and had admired his work greatly. The day after his death abroad she discovered that her one-time suitor had attached himself to her and was physically forcing himself on her. The attacks, her mother explained, were so violent that she had to sleep in the same bed with her daughter for a

while. But it did not help. Even the mother felt the physical contact experienced through her daughter. The father of the young woman, a carpenter of Swedish extraction, had been highly skeptical of the entire matter, ascribing it to female hysteria. But even he had to admit that his daughter's behavior changed radically after the phenomena had begun. Berger had been far from tidy, and devoted to a prospective career as a singer, but had suddenly become the very model of tidiness and was interested only in being a nurse. Nursing was the profession that her late boyfriend had wanted her to pursue.

The discarnate doctor was constantly invading Edith's privacy. He expressed himself through her, and regulated her life. At times she would even assume his passing symptoms—those of the disease from which he had died. She showed evidence of suffering from malaria, exhibiting all the symptoms of it, yet when examined by a doctor, was found to be completely healthy. One might argue that such exhibitions could be of hysterical origin. Nevertheless, it is extraordinary to consider them in conjunction with all the other unusual personality changes that happened at the same time. Over and over, the dead doctor asked Edith to tell his mother that he was still alive. But how could she do this and not be labeled insane? In her somewhat simple, devoted way, Edith prayed for his release.

One day when she was praying for him, she felt a clutching sensation on her arm. Someone was close to her. A little later she went to bed. It was then that she heard his voice, speaking to her, "It is I, Bill." The indirect impressions, the personality changes, were followed by more direct attacks upon her. He wanted to be her lover as well. On one particularly amorous occasion, her mother reported that she saw a man's outline in the empty bed. Yet she knew that no man had slept with her daughter. Quickly, the mother grabbed a fly swatter and hit the outline in the bed. Once Edith wanted to put on her overcoat. As she turned around to pick it up, she saw her coat come toward her of its own volition as if someone were holding it for her to slip her arm into. Whenever she happened to be with other men, she felt the dead doctor close to her, kissing her, and complaining in a jealous voice that only she could hear.

On her first visit to the house, Betty Ritter immediately contacted the possessing personality and argued with him. It lessened doctor's hold upon Edith, but he stuck around, now filled with anger as well as love. That same night, Ritter awoke from a restless sleep to see a man standing next to her bed. He was stark naked and in a menacing mood. Evidently he had come to chase *her* away since the medium had tried to do the same thing to him early that evening. But Ritter was nonplussed. She prayed and asked her own "controls" for help. The naked man vanished. Several days later the medium saw the man again, this time fully clothed in a riding habit. She found out that he had been a great horseman, and that riding clothes were one of his favorite costumes. Even while Ritter was speaking to Edith Berger on the telephone, the impatient possessor started to pull Berger's hair in a most painful fashion, as if to prove that he was still very much around.

The possession continued since the doctor, who had died in the prime of life,

could not accept the separation from his physical body any more than the separation from his love. It was then that I was called into the case, and together with Dr. Fodor and Ritter, returned to the Berger home. This time the entity took over Ritter's unconscious mind almost immediately. Pointing a hand toward Edith, he yelled through the vocal apparatus of Ritter, "I shall not be pulled away from you. I won't go."

I began to reason with the entity, both rationally and emotionally, and eventually I must have gotten through to him. He broke down, crying, "I haven't been able to finish what I started," and spoke of his important medical work. After I had explained to him that he could continue his research on his side of life without possessing the physical body of his lady friend over here, he understood, and he promised not to trouble her any more. He only asked that he might from time to time be permitted to visit with her, and that I gladly allowed. Nothing further was heard from Edith Berger. I have changed the name of the doctor whose post-mortem sexual appetite would not stop, as he was—and is—a well-known personality.

To be sure, the majority of physical encounters between a discarnate and a living person are not exactly welcome or ideal in any sense. That is not to say that such relationships are not tangible in certain ways, and not just in the fertile imagination of the living partner. Then there are some cases where the incursion from beyond is not exactly sought, but quietly encouraged through prayer, meditation, and strong feelings of loneliness and a desire to have the physical relationship somehow continue.

But what I am about to report is none of the above. The parties involved did not know each other, or of each other, until they shared the same physical space. I thought I had laid to rest a young lady ghost in a Brooklyn College residence but the story was apparently not quite finished. Some time after my initial investigation, when I followed up on a report by four girls who lived in a flat in that house, I was contacted by some male students in great excitement: "Henny," as they had come to call the ghost, was apparently still active, and would I please do something about it.

Henny used to live in one of those old brownstone houses in a better section of Brooklyn. The house had been turned into a boarding house for students and professional people. Henny worked in a department store, having been unable to finish college. But she always had a great admiration for those who did, and dated many students, and even teachers, over the years. Henny had an extremely good figure, and an insatiable appetite for sex. Unfortunately, she also had a heart defect and died in her thirties. What had been her room at the boarding house was used by many others as time went on.

I don't know whether people had problems with her ghost until I heard about it, but a couple of Brooklyn College students called me in great excitement when Henny appeared to them. George, one of the two young fellows, had gone to bed in his room in that house when he was awakened in the night by a strange glow emanating from the ceiling. He checked it out and found no source for it. He decided to blame passing cars for it. He had hardly lain down again, when the glow became brighter and turned into the pulsating figure of a young woman, dressed in clothes of another era.

George sat up in bed and watched dumfounded, as the woman came toward him and began to stroke his head. He actually felt her caress though it seemed very cold and clammy. Half awake, George somehow thought she was one of the girls from the upper floors who was putting on a trick for him, but he really did not mind, especially as the girl took off her blouse and pressed her breasts against his chest. He could not help observing that her breasts were enormous and that her lips, touching his, were cold as ice. George does not remember any more than this: when he awoke the next day, he thought it had all been a sexy dream. He made light of it to his landlady, who was not at all amused by his graphic description of the girl's assets. "You wait here a moment," she demanded and rushed off to her own apartment. When she returned a moment later, she held a yellowed newspaper clipping in her hand. "Does that look anything like the woman you saw in your dream?" she asked. George took a look at the clipping. "Why, it's her," he replied. The clipping was the girl's obituary from over twenty years ago.

Since I had been asked to do something about poor Henny, I returned a week later with a good trance medium, Ethel Johnson Meyers, and we contacted Henny: the contact broke her obsession with the living, and she left, somewhat tearfully, but in peace.

When a close relationship of a romantic or sexual kind, preferably both together, comes to an end because one of the two participants passes out of the physical world, the continuance of that relationship is usually impossible for obvious reasons. But there are a number of instances where the obvious difficulties are being overcome by sheer passion and life force in the "dead" partner, proving once again that life does by no means end at death's door. For the surviving lover, this represents problems that need to be addressed. If the attentions from beyond the grave are welcome, or even encouraged actively, they will preempt any new relationship on the physical earth level.

But if the continuing romantic or sexual incursions by the "dead" partner continue and are not welcome because a new relationship has been formed by the surviving partner, there is need to deal with it in an appropriate way.

Sometimes this is difficult for the ghost, as he may be too strongly attached to feelings of guilt or revenge to let go. But eventually a combination of informative remarks by the parapsychologist and suggestions to call upon the dead person's family will pry him loose and send him out into the free world of spirit. Not many people have the proper ability or training to be good trance mediums. I have worked with Ethel Johnson Meyers, Sybil Leek, Betty Ritter, Trixie Allingham, and a few others, and I am constantly training young people in this difficult branch of true mediumship.

The proof of superior mediumship lies only in the results. If the alleged ghost, while possessing the medium's body, can give substantial information about his past, and if that information is checked out by me and found to be substantially correct the "channel of communication" has been a good one. In the majority of published cases, I have been able to prove that the knowledge obtained through a trance medium under my direction was unknown to the psychic person and could not have been obtained except by a qualified researcher such as myself, and even then with considerable effort.

Specific names, dates, and situations concerning the life of the ghost have been brought to me in this manner, and there is no doubt in my mind that the information emanated from the so-called ghost. The best mediums serve as channels without expressing or even holding explanatory views of their skills, leaving that to the parapsychologist.

Ghosts, then, are very real, and the range of those who may at one time or another observe them is wide. Anyone who sees or hears a ghostly phenomenon is by that very fact psychic. You do not have to be a professional medium to see a host, but you do have to be possessed of more than average ESP abilities to tune in on the refined vibrations or electromagnetic field that the human personality represents after it leaves the physical body. There are millions of such people in the world today, most of them not even aware of their particular talent.

ghosts, spirits, and hauntings

GHOSTS HAVE BEEN OBSERVED BY ONE OR MORE competent observers and where the likelihood of a recurrence of the phenomena still exists. There is no telling whether a casual visitor might have an experience. Ghosts do not appear on command, and even spending the night in a haunted house might produce nothing more than a stiff neck or the sniffles. Then again, one might walk into a haunted house unaware of that fact, and have an experience quite unexpectedly. While there are cases where a ghost has been observed "in the open"—at crossroads, in forests, at sea—generally, they are tied to the place of their demise and usually that involves a house or other building.

To the haunting entity, the ghost, time has stood still, and the events that caused the unfortunate condition the ghost is now in is still happening in its mind. There are thousands of verified cases of hauntings and ghosts in my research files and books, but some of the more interesting and current ones will serve here to illustrate the nature of the phenomenon. Never forget it is a fellow human being who is in difficulty, not a monster from a Hollywood film.

Authenticated cases of ghosts and hauntings are legion. Those familiar with my recent book *Ghosts* know that I have spent years investigating and resolving cases of this kind all over America and Europe. Ghosts and hauntings will continue to be created as long as human tragedies and emotional problems are created. It is part of the human race, and though ghosts and hauntings are exceptions from the norm of peaceful transition to the next world, those very exceptions are also part of human destiny.

224

Tied up at the pier in Baltimore and open to the public as a kind of floating museum is the proud U.S.F. *Constellation*, once the flagship of the American navy. Built in 1797 as the first man-of-war of the United States fleet, the ship was still in commission as late as World

Congress tried to decommission the U.S.F. *Constellation* several times and to pass her name on to a newer ship. But something would always happen to prevent this, or the new carrier of the name *Constellation* would become the victim of accidents. Gradually the old ship out-

The haunted frigate *Constellation* in Baltimore harbor.

War II. Part of its superstructure has recently been restored, and the timbers are only partially the original wood; otherwise nothing has been changed. This is important since the hauntings would not continue if most or all of the original material had been replaced.

lived her usefulness, and despite her heroic past, found herself forgotten at Newport, Rhode Island, where she was slowly falling into disrepair. Franklin Delano Roosevelt resurrected her from this ignominious position and recommissioned her as the flagship of the U.S.

Atlantic fleet in 1940, but funds to restore her were lacking, and the ship was towed to Boston. In 1953, a private committee of Baltimore citizens collected funds to get the ship home to Baltimore and restore her to her pristine glory. This has been done, and anyone visiting the *Constellation* at her Baltimore pier makes a small contribution to the maintenance of the old ship. Visitors are admitted, although no one is permitted to sleep aboard. Ever since I published the account of the ghostly happenings aboard the ship, people, out of curiosity, wanted to spend the night aboard. Since the ship is all wood, fire hazards exist, and the committee cannot permit anyone to stay on after dark. Frankly, I wouldn't if I were just a curious person, because two of the three resident ghosts aboard the U.S.F. *Constellation* are still there.

Those interested in the complete details of the hauntings might talk to the curator, Donald Stewart, of Baltimore. The first ghost is an old sailor, Neil Harvey, who keeps appearing to visitors wearing the uniform of bygone days. With the help of medium Sybil Leek I was able to pinpoint more accurately the other two haunting personalities. They are associated with the orlop deck below the main deck, and the area near where the gun emplacements used to be. The two haunting entities were closely associated with each other. One was the ship's captain, Thomas Truxtun. The other was a watchman who had fallen asleep on duty and in the cruel manner of the times had been condemned to death by the captain. Death was administered to the unfortunate one by his being strapped to a gun and blown to bits. The executed sailor is the other ghost, and Captain Truxtun's own feelings of guilt perhaps caused him to remain aboard.

Sybil Leek also felt the presence of a cabin boy who somehow had come to grief aboard ship, but she described that event as having happened at a later time, around 1822, whereas the events involving Captain Truxtun took place between 1795 and 1802. The man blown to bits, the unfortunate sailor, Neil Harvey, has been seen at various times by visitors to the ship who knew nothing whatsoever about the ghostly traditions attached to it.

A visit to the U.S.F. *Constellation* is a must if you are ever in the area. There is no need for an advance appointment, nor is it necessary to hide one's interest in the ghostly happenings aboard.

A GHOSTLY CONDUCTOR

Not all ghosts or hauntings are tied to buildings. There are haunted crossroads, haunted airports, and even haunted railroad crossings. One of the most famous of all such phenomena still exists at the railroad crossing near Maco, North Carolina, twelve miles west of Wilmington on the Atlantic Coast Line Railroad. Ever since 1867, an itinerant light has been observed by hundreds of people in the area, which could not be explained on natural grounds. Despite attempts by scientists to explain the light as part of swamp gas, reflected automobile headlights, or other natural origins, these explanations have not really answered the question.

I made an investigation of the phenomenon, and interviewed dozens of actual witnesses who had observed the light. There were several among them who had not only seen a light approach along the tracks where no light should be, but had actually observed that the light was inside an old railroad lantern; some had even heard the sound of an approaching train close by. The consensus seems to be that a ghostly personality appears at the Maco trestle holding a railroad lantern aloft as if to warn someone or something. This fits in with the tradition that a Joe Baldwin was behind the haunting period.

Baldwin was a conductor on what was then called the Wilmington, Manchester and Augusta Railroad, and he was riding in the end coach of a train one night in 1867. The coach somehow left the train and Baldwin grabbed a lantern in an effort to signal a passenger train that was following close. Unfortunately, the engineer of the train did not see the signal and a crash was the result. The only one to lose his life in the crash was Joe Baldwin: he was decapitated. The signal lantern was later found a distance from the track. There is no question in my mind that the surviving spirit of Baldwin—who, incidentally, is buried in a Roman Catholic cemetery near the tracks—is still trying to discharge what he considers his solemn duty. Unfortunately, he is not aware that no train is following him any more.

HAUNTED REHOBOTH RESORT

I received a telephone call from a woman who identified herself as Doris Armfield, inviting me to a house at Rehoboth, Massachusetts, where a poltergeist had taken up residence. I asked her to give me a detailed account of her experiences.

"My husband and I purchased the house around 1940. It was purported to be more than two hundred years old. We have never heard that it was haunted or that any violent death had occurred in it, but the legend has persisted that this was the house that had a fortune buried somewhere in a stone wall, and we treated this story as an old-time tale.

"We have had many odd happenings at the house during the years, but the noises heard in the kitchen are what concern me. The original house was a regular Cape Cod consisting of four rooms downstairs and an attic upstairs. One hundred years after the original house was built, a kitchen ell was added, consisting of the kitchen, a small room off the kitchen, and a large back hall. Our current postmaster in town lived in the house at one time and he added dormers upstairs. We put a porch along the ell. There is also a small barn used as a garage. These constitute the physical plan of the house. We own about 100 acres on both sides of the street.

"Shortly after we moved in, the first event happened. My husband and I were eating supper in the kitchen when a sound like an explosion made us both bound from our chairs. We found that a glass dish in the kitchen cupboard on the top shelf had shattered. We decided that maybe a change of temperature had made the dish break and left it at that. However, this noise had been the only one where we found physical evidence of breakage.

"About two years after this, my husband joined the navy in World War II and his aunt came to stay with me for a week or two. The first night as we sat down to supper in the kitchen, my dog Dusty sat beside my chair and suddenly he started to growl very deeply, the hackles rose on his back, he bared his teeth and scared me half to death, because I had never seen him do this unless he thought my husband or I was threatened. He was staring at an empty chair to my left, but I thought his growl meant someone was around the house. I went out and looked around, but no one was there.

"My aunt became frightened and swore that someone was sitting in that chair even though we couldn't see him. I banged the chair up and down and tried to put the dog's paws in the seat, but he was very upset. Then I tried to get him by the collar and pull him by the chair into the dining room, but I couldn't budge him.

"My aunt went home to her own house after a week or so and I lived alone in the house with the dog and some cats. One night I was reading in bed, with the dog at my feet. I reached up to turn off the bed lamp when I heard a tremendous crash and the sound of dishes banging, crashing, and shattering. I knew immediately that the dish cupboard in the kitchen had fallen loose from the wall and that it had hit the counter beneath it and just spewed all the hundreds of dishes across the floor and smashed them to smithereens. The dog and I flew into the kitchen, only to find everything was intact. I took a flashlight and went all over the house from cellar to attic, knowing all the while that the only big quantity of dishes were in that kitchen cupboard.

"We decided to make a three-room apartment upstairs for a girlfriend of ours who had lost her husband a few years before. She moved in, and the years went by, eighteen years, in fact. One evening at 5, she came home from work, and walked upstairs to her apartment. She had her foot on the last step when she just stood there unable to believe that horrible crashing and clattering of dishes being broken. Naturally, she expected to see the three-shelved kitchen cupboard torn away from the wall, figuring it had hit the counter beneath it, and that every dish had fallen, breaking and rolling along the floor. She stood there in amazement when she found nothing was disturbed.

"We went home the next weekend, and as we compared noises, we found we had both had the same impression of what had happened, and the noises were identical. This happened about two years ago.

"About two months ago, a neighbor and I were singing and playing the piano in the dining room, and were also tape recording our efforts. My husband was in the room behind the kitchen, and my sister was reading in the living room. At the end of a song we heard a crash of dishes or glasses and we all converged on the kitchen. I thought our Siamese cat had climbed onto a shelf on the hutch and possibly knocked off some plates. Once again we looked at one another and couldn't believe that nothing was broken. I then thought of the fact that the crash was on the tape, and we played it back and sure enough, we heard it loud and clear."

Immediately after I received Armfield's report, I telephoned her at her weekday residence in Connecticut. The house in Rehoboth, Massachusetts, where the uncanny phenomena had taken place, was a weekend retreat. I offered to come out to have a look at the house on my trip to Boston.

"Everything is quiet for the moment," she replied, "but you're welcome any-

time." Somehow the trip never occurred, and it was not until April 1965 that I finally got around to reaching the Armfields again. I have no staff to help me, and cases just pile up until I can get around to them. This time my note was answered by Doris's husband, Richard Armfield. His wife had died in January 1965. Under the circumstances, I decided not to trouble him, hoping that Mrs. Armfield herself might have discovered what or who it was who caused the uncanny noises in the Rehoboth house—from *her* side of the veil.

AMERICA'S MOST HAUNTED—THE WHALEY HOUSE, SAN DIEGO

The Whaley House, in a part of San Diego called Old Town, was originally built in 1857 as a two-story mansion by Thomas Whaley, a San Diego pioneer. It stands at the corner of San Diego Avenue and Harney Street and is a museum. It can be visited during daylight hours.

There are two stories connected by a staircase. Downstairs is a parlor, a music

room, a library, and in the annex, to the left of the entrance, there used to be the County Courthouse. At least one of the hauntings is connected with the courtroom. Upstairs are four bedrooms, tastefully furnished in the period during which the Whaley House was at its zenith—between 1860 and 1890. The house was restored by a group of citizens

The "most haunted" house in America—the Whaley House in San Diego, California.

in 1956. If it were not for them, there would now not be a Whaley House.

Numerous witnesses, visitors to the house and those serving as part-time guides or volunteers, have seen ghosts here. These include the figure of a woman in the courtroom; sounds of

observed by a number of people working in the house, and a baby has been heard crying. Strange lights, cool breezes, and cold spots have added to the atmosphere of haunting permeating the house. It is probably one of the most actively haunted mansions in the world.

Manifestations in the Whaley House caught on film by the staff.

footsteps in various parts of the house; windows opening by themselves in the upper part of the house despite the fact that strong bolts had been installed that could only be opened by someone on the inside; the figure of a man in a frock coat and pantaloons standing atop the stairs; organ music played in the courtroom where there is an organ although at the time no one was near it and the cover was closed; and a ghost dog has been seen scurrying down the hall toward the dining room. There is a black rocking chair upstairs that moves of its own volition at times, as if someone were sitting in it. A woman dressed in a green plaid gingham dress has been seen seated in one of the bedrooms upstairs. Smells include perfume and cigars. There is also a child ghost present, which has been

Despite my investigation with the help of Sybil Leek, arranged for by Regis Philbin, some of the apparitions have remained, and reports of continuing disturbances are still coming in to me. As far as I could ascertain through the trance session with Sybil, the ghosts include the builder of the house, Thomas Whaley, who had a just grievance against the city of San Diego, which probably has kept him tied to the house. He had put money into certain alterations so that he could sell the house to the county to be used as a courthouse. However, his contract was never executed and he was left holding the bag. Sybil also pinpointed a child ghost correctly, aged twelve, named Anna Belle, and named the lady ghost upstairs correctly Anna Lannay, Thomas Whaley's wife.

HAUNTS OF RINGWOOD MANOR

One of the most interesting haunted houses I ever visited is only an hour's drive from New York City, in northern New Jersey, not far from Saddle River. It is a manor house known locally as Ring-

result of the Revolutionary War, and the profits enabled Martin Ryerson, the late owner of Ringwood Manor, to rebuild it completely in 1807, tearing down the original house.

Ringwood Manor, New Jersey. The ghostly help does not measure up—yet.

wood Manor and it is considered one of the more important historical houses in New Jersey. Built on land purchased by the Ogden family in 1740, it originally was the home of the owners of a successful iron-smelting furnace. The area had many iron-smelting furnaces during the late colonial period, when this kind of business was profitable.

The main portion of the house dates back to 1762. Eventually, it became the property of Robert Erskine, the geographer of George Washington. The local iron business soared to great heights as a

However, after the iron business fell off in the 1830s, the house was sold to Peter Cooper and eventually passed to his son-in-law Abram S. Hewitt, one-time mayor of New York. Mrs. Hewitt changed the drab house into a mansion of fifty-one rooms, in the style of the early Victorian era. She moved various smaller buildings, already existing on the grounds, next to the main house, thereby giving it a somewhat offbeat appearance. In 1936, Erskine Hewitt left the estate to the State of New Jersey, and the mansion is now a museum that can be visited daily for a small fee. Not too many visitors come, since Ringwood Manor does not get the kind of attention some of the better-publicized national shrines attract.

I visited Ringwood Manor in the company of Ethel Johnson Meyers to follow up on persistent reports of haunt-

Waldron. He had heard footsteps when there was no one about, footsteps of two different people, indicating two entities. Doors that had been shut at night were found standing wide open in the morning when no one could have done it. The feeling of "presences" in various parts of the house persisted. There is a local tradition

The Conference House, Staten Island, New York. The ghosts of builder Christopher Billopp and of the slave girl he knifed to death in a rage are still trapped in this seventeenth-century mansion where a last-ditch conference between England's Lord Howe, and Benjamin Franklin and John Adams, could not avert the Revolutionary War after all.

ings in the old mansion. One of the chief witnesses to the ghostly goings-on was the superintendent of the manor, Alexander

that the ghost of Robert Erskine walks about with a lantern, but there is no evidence to substantiate this legend.

As a result of my investigation and Meyers's trance, I discovered that the restless one—at least, one of them—was a Jackson White, living at the house at one time. The Jackson Whites are said to be a mixture of Negro and Indian and Caucasian races. They are descendants of runaway slaves who settled in parts of New Jersey in the nineteenth century and lived among the hill folk.

The center of the hauntings seems to be what was once the area of Mrs. Erskine's bedroom, but all along the corridors both upstairs and downstairs there are spots where a sensitive person might experience chills or cold clammy feelings. I made contact with the surviving personality of Mrs. Erskine, as well as an unhappy servant whose name was Jeremiah, who complained bitterly about his mistress, who he claimed had mistreated him. The ghost lady whose manor we were visiting was not too pleased with our presence. Through the mouth of the medium in trance, she told us several times to get off her property.

THE INNER LIFE OF THE OCTAGON

One of the best-known monuments to Washington's past is the Octagon, the seat of the American Institute of Architects and a museum.

Originally built by Colonel John Tayloe in 1800 as his townhouse, the mansion stands in one of the most fashionable parts of Washington. The plot upon which it is built, at the corner of New York Avenue and Eighteenth Street, was originally surrounded by empty land, but today it forms the center of several

The Octagon, Washington, D.C., now the headquarters of the American Institute of Architects, once the temporary "White House" (in 1812) and still haunted.

avenues of mansions and expensive town-houses. There are three stories, it stands at the corner of two streets, and the building is octagon-shaped. The downstairs boasts a magnificent rotunda whence a staircase leads to the second and third stories. This staircase is the center of ghostly activities. Most of the reported phenomena took

in 1815. After the death of Mrs. Tayloe in 1855, the building passed into other hands. At first it was used as a school for girls, but as the immediate neighborhood deteriorated for a time, it became a slum building. It was rescued from that fate in 1899 when the American Institute of Architects took it over.

Left: From this balcony, Col. Tayloe's daughter jumped to her death because he disapproved of the man of her choice. This is the area of the haunting.

Right: The Octagon's "swinging chandelier": unseen hands keep moving it.

place on the second-floor landing near the banister, or on the third floor, which is not open to visitors. The entire building was overhauled once again to make it more attractive to the continuing influx of tourists who come not to look for a ghost but to visit a museum of renown and a historical landmark, for some of the greatest names in American history are connected with the Octagon.

Even while it was being constructed, General Washington spent time here, and during the British occupation of the capital and the subsequent construction of the White House, the Octagon served as a temporary residence to President Madison and his wife, Dolly, and he signed the peace treaty with Britain there

Ghostly phenomena have been reported as far back as the mid-nineteenth century. They have included reports of footsteps, the wailing of a female voice, and other uncanny signs of a human presence in the old mansion. There is a long list of rational, uncommitted observers who have experienced inexplicable things at the Octagon. One of the superintendents, Alric H. Clay, has on several occasions found the lights put on again after he had turned the switches off, and the doors wide open, after he had just locked them. Footsteps of a man and a woman have been heard repeatedly, especially on the third and second floors. A carpet at the bottom of the main staircase keeps flinging itself back when there

Above: The haunted stairway at the Octagon.

Right: This is the carpet at the Octagon where the girl landed and died. It keeps turning itself back this way night after night.

no one has made any attempt to exorcise the resident ghosts. From all indications, and a recent investigation with medium Ethel Meyers, I know that there are at least two entities still present at the Octagon.

One is the daughter of Colonel Tayloe, who committed suicide by jumping from the second-floor landing. Her body was found just where the carpet keeps flinging itself back of its own volition. The other must be the distraught father, Colonel Tayloe. It was his refusal to accept his daughter's choice of a husband that drove her to an untimely death. However, there may be a third ghost at the Octagon. During the British period, a young officer pursued one of the American servant girls, who also preferred to jump to her death rather than give in to his demands. We do not have her name, but visitors often report someone standing behind them on the upper floors. Those were the servants' quarters. The Tayloe girls would more likely be felt further below.

The Octagon is generally open to visitors. The American Institute of Architects is not especially fond of the notion that there might be other things among its exhibits than old manuscripts and artifacts. But I have no doubt that the hauntings at the Octagon continue.

is no one in the building. The chandeliers swing of their own volition at times. These phenomena may very well still occur since

THE HOUSE OF OCEAN-BORN MARY

If you ask the present owners of the "Ocean-Born Mary House" whether they have a ghost, they will deny it. They have had some bad experiences. On Halloween some youngsters mistake a haunting legend in a beautiful old house for

license to misbehave and throw rocks. Most people prefer to call it a museum, and the public is allowed to visit it most of the time for a small entrance fee. I have conducted several investigations because of the ghostly goings-on. I have worked with a local medium and with Sybil Leek, and there is no doubt that the surviving spirit of Mary Wallace, whose home this once was, is still present in the structure.

Mary is the ocean-born child who was befriended by a pirate, Don Pedro. Later in life he helped her build this house and in turn she permitted him to spend his old age as her pensioner. Unfortunately for Don Pedro, so the story goes, one of his men who had been disgruntled caught up with him, and in the ensuing fight Don Pedro was killed.

over by the spirit of Mary Wallace, who demanded to be heard through her. Frightened, she fled home to a Boston suburb. That night she awoke and, without being able to resist, drove her car all the way up to New Hampshire, still in her nightclothes.

I brought Mrs. A. back to Ocean-Born Mary's with me, in the daytime and wearing street clothes, and in trance Mary Wallace manifested. The gist of her communication through the medium was a concern for the proper maintenance of the old house and an almost

The Ocean-born Mary House in Henneker, New Hampshire, that Mary never left.

Allegedly his body lies underneath the fireplace, but there is no proof since the fireplace has never been dug up.

The place came to my attention when an amateur medium named L.A. asked my assistance in dealing with the phenomena she had encountered at the house. During a routine visit as a tourist, she had found herself practically taken

playful desire to be acknowledged and recognized. Subsequent to this visit I also drove up with Sybil Leek and attempted another trance session. Sybil managed to bring through a servant girl who had apparently met with foul play or was involved in it. At any rate, she must be the third resident ghost, in addition to Mary Wallace and her pirate friend.

There was also talk of buried treasure somewhere on the grounds. The directions were explicit and after Sybil came out of her trance we all went out and looked for the treasure underneath the stones behind the house. We did not dig, and treasures have a way of staying underground, especially after 250 years. While there may be some speculation about the reality of hidden treasure and possibly of the continued residence "in spirit" of the pirate, there is substantial evidence that the house is haunted by a woman greatly resembling the original owner.

A number of people have seen the tall, stately figure of Mary Wallace peering out of an upstairs window of the two-story structure. On one occasion, her intervention saved the house from burning to the ground. A heater had caught fire, but was smothered by unseen hands. The ghost has been described by one who saw her as "a lovely lady in her thirties with auburn-colored hair, smiling intensely and thoughtfully."

The house can be reached by car from Boston. It is worth a visit.

THE DEBUTANTE OF NOB HILL

On San Francisco's California Street, not far from the Fairmont Hotel, where the cable car stops, there is an intersection flanked by some of the oldest houses in San Francisco. It is here that the ghost of

Flora Sommerton walks. Gwen Hinzie saw her in 1967. She was riding up to California Street in a cable car in the company of a friend. Both women, looking out the window, noticed a strange girl

Nob Hill, San Francisco, where the ghost bride has been seen walking forlornly in her wedding gown.

walking up the street beside the cable car, wearing what appeared to be an odd dress for the time of day. The dress that Hinzie described was a kind of ballgown, and what was even more remarkable was the fact that the stranger seemed to walk right through people ahead of her. Others have noticed the lovely young girl seemingly walking straight ahead, as if she were trying to get away from something or someone down the hill.

This case concerned a San Francisco debutante, Flora Sommerton. A few hours before her scheduled debut, eighteen-year-old Flora disappeared from her mansion on Nob Hill, causing one of the major scandals of 1876. Her reason was that she did not care to marry the young man her parents had picked out for her. The girl was never found despite a huge reward offered for her return. Ever since her disappearance, rumors circulated that she had been seen here or there, but all turned out to be false. For the most part, these were feeble attempts at getting money from Flora's parents. However, as the years went by and the girl did not turn up, the family built a wall around themselves, and Flora was no longer discussed. The reward was withdrawn. No one who wanted to remain on good terms with the Sommertons dared mention Flora or ask if anything new about her had turned up.

The parents eventually accepted the medical theory that Flora's mind had snapped under the pressure of pre-wedding excitement. It was better to believe this version than to admit to themselves the real cause of Flora's panic. The man they had wanted her to marry was not the man she wanted. Afraid to face her parents in rebellion, she did the only thing she was capable of under the circumstances: she ran away. She did not even wait to change clothes, running up the hill in a ballgown. Flora's action was not premeditated but sudden, and in panic.

When the parents died, even the rumors of Flora's reappearance died out. It was not until much later that her name became once again newsworthy in her native city. Eventually, Flora died broke and ill in 1926, in a flophouse hotel in Butte, Montana. When found, she was dressed in a white ballgown of the 1880s. It was that same ballgown she was wearing when Mrs. Hinzie saw her ghost walking up Nob Hill with a determined look.

I cannot promise that in today's traffic anyone will notice the unusually clad young woman, but it is just possible that in the still of night and with great patience, a sensitive individual might feel her presence in the area. If you will slowly walk up and down the hill, starting at California Street, perhaps you will be one of the few.

NEW YORK CITY'S OLD MERCHANT'S HOUSE

At 29 East 4th Street in New York's Greenwich Village stands one of the few remaining brownstone houses that has preserved its original appearance completely. It was built in 1830. Untouched by the decay of the surrounding area, the house managed to survive the great changes of recent years.

The house became the property of Seabury Tredwell, a wealthy merchant in the hardware business, as soon as it was completed by its builder. It was convenient for his business.

The house is a federal-style building with windows opening onto 4th Street. Originally a lovely garden surrounded the house, but today the garden is gone. The entrance is particularly imposing, with two columns in classical style at the top of a few steps and wrought-iron lanterns adorning the door. There are three floors topped by an attic, and also a basement. Inside, the furniture is still of that period. There was a banister by Duncan Phyfe, and a fine staircase leading to the upper three stories. The downstairs was filled with fine furniture, some

to tradition, Tredwell did not take kindly to any suitor who seemed to want to marry one of his daughters for their financial status. This material served as the background for Henry James's *Washington Square*, which much later became a motion picture called *The Heiress*, and for a story of mine in *Gothic Ghosts*.

The main manifestations occurred in the kitchen on the ground floor in the rear of the house. But what used to be Gertrude's bedroom upstairs also has a presence in it from time to time. The ghost is that of a small elegant woman dressed in the finery of the mid-nineteenth century. That this is Gertrude herself is likely, since according to my psychic friend Ethel Johnson Meyers it was she who died tragically here. There had

The Old Merchant's House, New York City. Gitty (Gertrude) never left.

of it also by Duncan Phyfe, a rectangular piano that is still there, and in showcases along the walls one finds some of the costumes left behind.

The ghostly phenomena in the house center on Tredwell's three daughters: Phoebe, Sarah, and Gertrude. According

been an unwanted baby, followed by disapproval of her actions by her family. How much of this can be proven is doubtful, but a presence has been observed in the Old Merchant's House by several reliable witnesses, and no attempt has been made to exorcise her, since this was her home.

One need not dwell upon the ghostly manifestations, as far as the curator is concerned, since she may not be aware of them. But I suggest a visit to the kitchen area, the back bedroom upstairs, and Gertrude's front bedroom. It contains a small canopied bed, which according to at least one witness, is haunted.

One eerie story told about the Old Merchant's House concerns the fireplace on the third floor. Allegedly it cannot be photographed. I tried my luck with a very good camera while a photographer who was with me at the time also photographed the fireplace. Although the fireplace did appear on both pictures, there is a strange white area around it that cannot be accounted for.

The house is open to visitors at certain hours since it is now a museum maintained by a private group.

The showcase containing Gertrude's gown. It is the one in which she has been observed walking down the staircase from the upper floors.

THE FIFTH-AVENUE GHOST

Probably the most protracted investigation I have ever undertaken, and the most evidential case for the existence of ghosts, was the one that took me to 226 Fifth Avenue in New York. This address was once an elegant townhouse and later turned into an apartment house. At the time of my investigation in 1953, the top-floor apartment, a duplex, belonged to a Captain Davis, an explorer who was abroad much of the time.

Seven years later, the apartment house was shut down for repairs. For about two or three years it stood empty and began to look dismal. The area around this building is strictly commercial, and I thought it was only a matter of time before the building itself would be torn down to make room for a new skyscraper. Imagine my surprise when I recently passed the building: far from being torn down, it has been reconditioned, and though it is no longer an elegant townhouse, and has commercial tenants on each floor, at least its basic structure has been maintained, the outside cleaned up, and the stairs still lead up to the top-floor apartment that was once haunted.

Tenants of the top-floor apartment prior to Captain Davis included Richard Harding Davis and the actor Richard Mansfield. We have no record of whether they were disturbed by the resident ghost or not, but Captain Davis was. Thanks to an introduction by *Daily News* columnist Danton Walker, I was able to enter the case in conjunction with a group of fellow students then working at the headquarters of the Association for Research and Enlightenment. As a result of my investigation, I learned of a Confederate hero officer crossing lines in the midst of war to see his mistress.

General Samuel Edward McGowan, of McGowan's Brigade, is historically fully documented. There is no mention

evidential and filled with detailed knowledge of the Civil War that I do not doubt the harrowing account of McGowan's adventures in New York.

Separation and war being what it was, the general's lady love, Mignon

The "Fifth Avenue Ghost" is a Southern general, Samuel Edward McGowan, who crossed the lines and met an untimely end.

Far right: Lifetime portrait of Gen. McGowen.

of his ghostly captivity at 226 Fifth Avenue. To the official historian, he died later and lies buried in his hometown cemetery at Abbeyville, South Carolina. But the material coming through the medium Ethel Johnson Meyers was so

Guychone, of French Creole stock, had apparently taken up with another man, named Walter. Despite the fact that she loved the general and vice versa, and that they had had a baby from their union, a conflict arose. Walter showed up unexpectedly and strangled general McGowan. In order not to be charged with murder, he made it appear like suicide, and hanged the lifeless body of the Southern gentleman from the rafters in the little attic.

The most urgent need of the ghost—once he could communicate with us—was to set the record straight as to his suicide. Committing suicide was alien to the traditions of a gentleman officer, and McGowan was at great pains to explain that it was murder and not self-inflicted death. General McGowan is not there any longer, for he has communicated with me on numerous occa-

sions afterward from various places, something a true ghost cannot do, since ghosts are tied to the place where their tragedy has occurred until such time as they are freed from their emotional entanglements. But those wishing to visit this most famous of all my haunted houses can probably do so without even asking permission.

The house is open during business hours, and though the top-floor tenant may be somewhat surprised to have a stranger ring his bell or walk into his door, I leave it to the ingenuity and good sense of my readers to make up a suitable excuse.

SAINT MARK'S CHURCH

Saint Mark's, a Dutch reformed church, is one of the most famous landmarks in New York. It was built in 1799 on the site of an earlier chapel going back to Peter Stuyvesant, who was governor of New

York in 1660. Governor Stuyvesant, who became the legendary Father Knickerbocker, is buried in the crypt. The last member of his family died in 1953 and the crypt was sealed. One can see the

Saint-Mark's-in-the-Bowery, Greenwich Village, New York, is a church haunted by a remorseful woman parishioner and by Governor Peter Stuyvesant, who is buried in the crypt.

crypts across the street because they are half underground and half above ground, making the churchyard of Saint-Mark's-in-the Bowery a unique sight. The

had been removed, rebuilding on Saint-Mark's-in-the Bowery got started, and today it is again what it was before the fire. Built along neoclassical lines it

Clockwise from upper left:

Gov. Stuyvesant's seventeenth-century portrait in the nave of Saint Mark's.

The nave of Saint Mark's, where the ghostly woman parishioner has been observed.

A strange psychic photograph of the haunted nave of Saint Mark's.

Another picture of the nave, seemingly without the psychic emanations.

church suffered a fire, allegedly due to a cigarette left by a negligent worker working on the steeple restorations. Whether the fire was of natural origin or in some way connected with the paranormal goings-on in the church is debatable but as soon as the charred remains of the roof

stands in an area that is essentially an economically poor neighborhood. At one time this was not so. Around the church and the cemetery is a cast-iron fence and the church is open most of the time, although one should look at the schedule to see when visitors are permitted, since various neighborhood happenings such as concerts and meetings also use the church. When the church is open to the public, one need not get permission from anyone to visit it.

Saint Mark's boasts of three known ghosts. First there is a woman parishioner who has been observed by a number of reputable witnesses in the middle of the nave, staring at the altar. She has been described as a Victorian woman, pale and apparently unhappy. Who she is, no one seems to know. Another ghost has been observed on the balcony close to the magnificent organ. Several organists have had the uncanny feeling of being observed by someone they could not see. One of the men working in the church reported hearing footsteps coming up to the organ loft. He assumed that the organist had come to work early and got ready to welcome him when to his surprise the footsteps stopped and silence befell the organ loft. Needless to say, he did not see any organist. Finally, there are those who have heard the sounds of a man walking distinctly with a cane and it is thought that the limping ghost is none other than Peter Stuyvesant, who had a wooden leg and used a cane. His body, after all, lies in the crypt beneath the church.

Saint-Mark's-in-the-Bowery is easy to reach by bus or subway. It is advisable to go there during the daytime; it is generally closed at night.

PLEASE LEAVE—VINELAND, NEW JERSEY

Nancy, an attractive blonde, and her handsome husband Tom moved into the old farmhouse near Vineland, New Jersey, in summer 1975. Tom had been a captain in the air force when he and Nancy met and fell in love in her native Little Rock, Arkansas. After three years, Tom decided he wanted to leave his career as a pilot

The haunted house in Vineland, New Jersey. A previous owner does not want to let go.

and settle down on a farm. They returned to Tom's hometown of Vineland, where Tom got a job as the supervisor of a large food-processing company. The house had been built in 1906 by a family named Hauser who had owned it for many generations until Tom's father acquired it from the last Hauser nineteen years before. Sitting back a few hundred yards

from the road, the house has three stories and a delicate turn-of-the-century charm. There is a porch running the width of the front, and ample rooms for a growing family. Originally there were thirty-two acres to the surrounding farm but Tom and Nancy decided they needed only four acres to do their limited farming. Even though the house was run-down and would need a lot of repair, Tom and Nancy liked the quiet seclusion and decided to buy it from Tom's father and restore it to its former glory.

"The first time I walked into this house I felt something horrible had hap-

pened in it," Nancy explained to me. By the time the family had moved in Nancy had forgotten her initial apprehension about the house. But about four weeks later the first mysterious incident occurred. As Nancy explained it, "I was alone in the house with the children whom I had just put to bed. Suddenly I heard the sound of children laughing outside. I ran outside to look but didn't see anyone. I ran quickly back upstairs but my kids were safely in their beds, sound asleep, exactly where I'd left them."

That summer Nancy heard the sound of children laughing several times, always when her own were fast asleep. Then one day Nancy discovered her daughter Leslie Ann, then aged three and a half, engaged in lively conversation with an unseen friend. When asked what the friend looked like, the child seemed amazed her mother couldn't see her playmate herself. Convinced they had ghostly manifestations in the house, they decided to hold a séance with the help of a friend. After the séance the phenomenon of the unseen children ceased but something else happened—the gravestone incident.

"We found the gravestone when we cleared the land," Tom said. "We had to move it periodically to get it out of the way. We finally left it in the field about a hundred yards from the house. Suddenly the day after our séance it just decided to relocate itself right outside our back door. It seemed impossible—it would have taken four strong men to move that stone."

For some time Nancy had the uncanny feeling that Ella Hauser, the woman who had built the house, was "checking" on the new occupants. Tom had looked on the ghostly goings-on in a detached, clinical way, but when his tools started disappearing it was too much for even him.

Tom and Nancy were not the only ones who encountered the unknown. In August 1977, a babysitter, Nancy F., was putting the children to bed, when she heard someone going through the drawers downstairs. "She thought it was a prowler going for something," Nancy explained, "But when she finally went downstairs nothing had been touched." The night after the babysitter incident Nancy went downstairs to get a drink of water and found a 5-foot-10 man standing in her living room—at 3 in the morning. "He was wearing one of those khaki farmer's shirts and a pair of brown work pants. Everything was too big for the guy. I could tell he was an old man. I took one look and ran upstairs."

When I received their telephone call I immediately asked for additional details. It became clear to me that this was a classical case of haunting where structural changes, new owners, and new routines have upset someone who lived in the house and somehow remained in the atmosphere. As is my custom, I assembled the residence and a psychic I had brought with me into an informal circle in the kitchen. Together we asked Ella and whoever else might be "around" to please go away in peace and with our compassion—to enter those realms where they would be on their own. The atmosphere in the kitchen, which had felt heavy until now, seemed to lift.

When I talked to Nancy several weeks after my visit, all was well at the house. The house is privately owned and I doubt that the new owners are receiving visitors. But you can drive by it. Most people in Vineland know which one it is.

THE INFAMOUS AMITYVILLE

The night of Friday, November 13, 1974, six members of the DeFeo Family of Amityville, Long Island, were brutally murdered in their beds—one of the most horrifying and bizarre mass murders of recent memory.

The lone survivor of the crime, Ronald DeFeo, Jr., who had initially notified police, was soon after arrested and formally charged with the slayings. But there are aspects to the case that have never been satisfactorily resolved. When DeFeo got up in the middle of the night, took his gun, and murdered his entire family, that wasn't him who did it, he says, but something or someone who got inside his body and took over. I just couldn't stop, says DeFeo. Was DeFeo a suitable vehicle for spirit possession? The facts of my investigation strongly suggest it. DeFeo doesn't believe in anything supernatural. He doesn't understand what got into him. Did he massacre his family in cold blood, or under the influence of a power from beyond this dimension?

From the outset there were strange aspects to the case: no one seems to have heard the shots that killed six people; how was it that none of the victims resisted or ran out of the murderer's way? Did they not hear the shots either? At DeFeo's trial, two eminent psychiatrists differed sharply about the state of the murderer's sanity: Dr. Schwartz considers DeFeo psychotic at the time of the murder, while Dr. Zolan holds him fully responsible for what he did. Rumors to the effect that DeFeo had first drugged his family's food (which would have explained their seeming apathy) proved groundless. The mystery remained even though DeFeo's sentence was clear: twenty-five years to life on each of the six counts of murder in the second degree served consecutively—as if that mattered. Over and over DeFeo repeated the same story: yes, he had killed his family, and felt no remorse over it. But he didn't know why. Something had gotten inside his person and forced him to shoot, going from bedroom to bedroom at 3:00 A.M. and exterminating the same parents, brothers, and sisters he had lovingly embraced at a birthday party in the house a scant two months before the crime.

On January 15, 1977, I brought trance medium Ethel Johnson Meyers to the house on Ocean Avenue, along with a psychic photographer to investigate what was shaping up as a case of suspected possession. Though Meyers hadn't the slightest notion where she was or why I had brought her there, she immediately stated, "Whoever lives here is going to be the victim of all the anger... the blind fierceness... this is Indian burial ground, sacred to them." As she was gradually slipping into trance, I asked why the Indian spirits were so angry.

"A white person got to digging around and dug up a skeleton..." She described a long-jawed Indian whose influence she felt in the house.

"People get to fighting with each other and they don't why... they're driven to it because they are taken over by him." According to Meyers, the long-ago misdeed of a white settler is still being avenged, every white man on the spot is an enemy, and when a catalyst moves there, he becomes a perfect vehicle for possession, like Ronald DeFeo.

"I see a dark young man wandering around at night... like in a trance... goes berserk... a whole family is involved," the medium said and a shiver went up my spine. She had turned right into the terrible past of the house.

When the pictures taken by the psychic photographer were developed on the spot, some of them showed strange halos exactly where the bullets had struck. My camera jammed even though it had been working perfectly just before and was fine again the minute we left the house on Ocean Avenue, a house empty of life as we know it and yet filled with those who have died yet linger for they know not where to go.

All sorts of charlatans had been to the house, attracted by cheap publicity, until the new owners had enough. They knew all about the phenomena first-hand and eventually a best-selling book was based upon their experiences...embellished, enlarged, and elaborated upon. The real story was clear: 112 Ocean Avenue had been a psychically active location for perhaps two centuries. Phenomena ranging from footsteps and doors opening by themselves to the apparitions of figures that dissolve into thin air are well-attested poltergeist manifestations, phenomena observed in thousands of similar cases all over the world, grist for the mill of the parapsychologist who knows there is no such thing as the supernatural, only facets of human personality transcending the old boundaries of conventional psychology. DeFeo had painted a little room in the basement red, because the color pleased

When all the satanic fallout had settled, I decided to investigate with the result that the real Amityville story began to emerge. What happened at Amityville

Clockwise from upper left:

Amityville, Long Island. Séance photo of psychic material covering Holzer and entranced medium Ethel Johnson Meyers. The entity is an angry Indian chief whose burial ground is being disturbed.

Ethel Johnson Meyers falling into trance at Amityville.

Total trance, and the Indian chief speaks through the medium.

The Amityville house on Ocean Avenue: peaceful from the outside.

him. The room he used as a kind of tool shed. An eighteenth-century owner of the spot allegedly practiced witchcraft: add it all up, and enter the devil... DeFeo, Sr. was a devoutly religious man who believed the devil was in the house, but his son left the house the minute the priest his father had called moved in.

could have happened anywhere in the world where passions are spent and human lives terminated by violence. The residue of the great crime lingers on even as the vehicle of possession gropes for an explanation of its true status. Young DeFeo is not a believer in things that go bump in the night, nor does he fear either

God or the devil. But as he awaits still another interminable day in his cell at Dannemora Prison, Ronald DeFeo cannot help wondering about the stranger within, the force that made him commit impossible crimes. He could have killed his father in an argument perhaps, he concedes, but not his mother, not the children.

DeFeo may never get an answer he can live with, but he may yet see the day when some future owner of that house has his innings with the unknown. For that day will surely come. I've tried to exorcise the angry entity in the house and although I have frequently succeeded in such cases, so much accumulated residue of hatred is too powerful a reservoir to fade away. But in the end, we all get justice, one way or the other.

THE ASH LAWN ROCKING CHAIR

Not only houses are haunted; even furniture can be the recipient of ghostly attention. Not far from Castle Hill is one of America's most historical buildings, the country home once owned by James Monroe where he and Thomas Jefferson often exchanged conversation and also may have made some big political decisions. Today this is a modest cottage, rather than a big manor house, and it is well kept. It may be visited by tourists at certain hours, since it is considered a historical shrine. If any of my readers are in the area and feel like visiting Ash Lawn, I would suggest they do not mention ghosts too openly with the guides or caretakers.

Left: Ash Lawn, Virginia, home of President Monroe. The cottage is haunted.

Right: The chair Monroe used to sit in. It never stops rocking.

The ghostly goings-on center on a wooden rocking chair in the main room. This has been seen to rock without benefit of human hands. I don't know how many people have actually seen the chair rock, but Mrs. J. Massey, who lived in the area for many years, has said to me when I visited the place, "I will tell anyone and I have no objection to its being known, I've seen not once but time and time again the rocking chair rocking exactly as though someone were in it. My brother John has seen it too. Whenever we touched it, it would stop rocking."

This house, though small and cozy, was James Monroe's favorite house even after he moved to the bigger, which became his stately home later on. At Ash Lawn he could get away from his affairs of state, away from public attention, to discuss matters of great concern, with his friend Thomas Jefferson who lived only two miles away, at Monticello.

Who is the ghost in the rocking chair? Perhaps it is only a spirit, not an earth-bound ghost, a spirit who has become so attached to his former home and refuge from the affairs of state, that he still likes to sit now and then in his own rocking chair thinking things over.

LINCOLN'S ASSASSINS AND MARY SURRATT

Thirteen miles south of Washington, in a small town now called Clinton, but once known as Surrattville, stands an eighteenth-century building now used as a museum. Mary Surratt ran it as an inn at the time when the area was far enough removed from Washington to serve as a way station to those traveling south from the nation's capital. When business fell off Surratt leased the eighteenth-century

The haunted Surratt house in Clinton, Maryland. The Lincoln assassination was plotted here. The psychic impression of those meetings still clings to the atmosphere and has been heard by sensitive people.

tavern to John Lloyd and moved to Washington, where she ran a boarding house on H Street between Sixth and Seventh Streets. But she remained on close and friendly terms with her successor at the tavern at Surrattville, so that it was possible for her son John Surratt to use it as an occasional meeting place with friends. These friends included John Wilkes Booth, and the meetings eventually led to the plot to assassinate President Lincoln.

John Wilkes Booth slept here. The house once belonged to Mary Surratt, mother of one of his coconspirators, and was used as an inn.

After the murder, Booth escaped on horseback and made straight for the tavern. By prearrangement, he and an associate hid the guns they had with them in a cache in the floor of the tavern. Shortly after, he and the associate, David Herald, split up, and John Wilkes Booth continued his journey despite a broken foot. Eventually, he was discovered hiding at Garrett's barn and shot there.

The connection between Booth and the tavern was no longer public knowledge as the years went by. Some local people might have remembered it, but

the outside world had lost interest. At one time, the structure was acquired by John's brother, actor Edwin Booth, it appears. In the 1950s it passed into the hands of a local businessman named Mr. M. By now the village was known as Clinton, since the Surrattville name had been changed shortly after the infamous trial of Mary Surratt.

The hauntings observed here include the figure of a woman, thought to be the restless spirit of Mary Surratt, whose home this had been at one time. Strange men have been observed sitting on the back stairs when there was no one about but the occupants of the house. Muffled voices of a group of men talking in excited tones have also been reported, and seem to indicate that at the very least an imprint from the past has been preserved at the Surratt Tavern. Many meetings of the conspirators had taken place in the downstairs part of the building, and when I brought Sybil Leek to the tavern she immediately pointed out the site of the meetings, the place where the guns had been hidden, and, in trance, established communication with the former owner of the tavern, Edwin Booth.

Although the building is now a museum and open to visitors, one should first obtain permission from Mr. M. at his supermarket in Clinton, Maryland. Clinton is less than an hour's drive from downtown Washington. As far as I know there is no fee attached to a visit at Surratt Tavern. At the time when I made my investigation, Mr. M. had thought to sell the building to a museum or a historical trust, and by the time this appears in print, it may well have changed hands.

Anyone visiting the old tavern who is psychic might hear the same voices, or have some kind of psychic experience because the phenomena have not faded away, nor are they likely to, since no formal exorcism has ever been attempted there.

GHOSTS OF HELL'S KITCHEN

Hell's Kitchen is not an imaginary place in the devil's domain, but a somewhat rough neighborhood in the heart of New York City. It is never advisable to walk there alone in the middle of night, but in the daytime it is as reasonably safe as any part of a large city these days. What makes the entire area even more fascinating is the fact that it is one of the most historically active areas of New York, having been at one time, in revolutionary and colonial days, the uptown playground of the rich and important, such as the estate of Governor Clinton, whose house and gardens occupied a large area of what is now 44th Street through 46th Street, between Ninth Avenue and Eleventh Avenue.

Walking through the area today, one cannot be impressed by the beauty of the houses, for they are ordinary and frequently show their age without any grace. But a visitor to 420 West 46th Street might be in for a great surprise if he manages to go through the narrow door that separates it

from the street. This door leads to an open passage and a patio in back of the house. There he will find another house, connected to 420, marked 422Ω West 46th Street. This is Clinton Court, after

Clinton Court, Hell's Kitchen, Manhattan, used to be Gov. Clinton's carriage house during the colonial period. The yard has several specters.

Governor George Clinton, whose carriage house it once was. The ground was at one time used as a potter's field, the cemetery for the poor and the executed.

Consequently, there are "presences" here in various spots, remainders from New York's past, when this area was fairly far uptown.

When the British ruled New York, one of those buried here was a character known as "Old Moor," a sailor executed for mutiny. His ghost was the first phantom seen at this place. In the 1820s, when the house was still used as a carriage house for the estate of Governor Clinton and his family, Old Moor would appear

One day, one of the Clinton children, frightened by a real apparition, stumbled and fell to her death, becoming ghost number three. This child ghost was seen by Ruth Shaw, an artist who had rented the downstairs portion of the carriage house some years ago. All the hauntings are confined to that part of the building. The front, facing onto 46th Street, has never been affected.

I have held several investigations at this address, including one with Ethel

Two people fell to their deaths on these stairs when they observed earlier ghosts. To this day, Clinton Court is haunted.

and frighten people. One day he frightened the wife of a coachman, who fell down the winding stairs to her death. These very stairs leading from the upper story to the ground still exist, although a second staircase, farther to the rear, has since disappeared. The coachman's wife became ghost number two.

The ghostly legend of the house was so well known that the Clinton children played a private game called "Ghosts."

Johnson Meyers and another with Sybil Leek. I have also made a television film about it. Through Sybil, I met the ghost of a colonial officer named Walker at 422Ω West 46th Street. Enough personal information was received and checked out in regimental records to prove that such a man existed. The medium could not have known about it. He died in a duel.

There is a connection between this house and June Havoc's townhouse, two blocks away. The ground on which both houses stand was part of the same estate where Governor Clinton's mansion once stood. There may be other, undiscovered ghosts roaming the area, but the residents of the houses here are not likely to talk about them unless specifically asked. And it is not a wise thing to go around asking these people whether they have seen a ghost, because they are hardworking, generally poor people who need a ghost far less than they need proper employment.

While it is not difficult to walk into the courtyard of Clinton Court, as the house is still called, getting access to the two apartments is another matter. They are privately owned and do not look for visitors—especially not those who come for the ghosts rather than the flesh-and-blood people. Today the house is divided between two tenants. But since some of the phenomena have actually occurred outside the building, on the winding staircase, and in the courtyard, it is entirely possible that a sensitive individual might experience something outside the apartments.

HUNGRY LUCY

The well-known stage and screen actress June Havoc owned a townhouse in New York that stood in a very old part of town. Located on West 44th Street, near Ninth Avenue, this impressive Victorian townhouse was built over a hundred years ago and was originally the property of the Rodenberg family. It has four stories and at the time when it was built was considered one of the most elegant houses in the area. Today the area is known as Hell's Kitchen and considered less than desirable as a neighborhood. Eventually the house fell into disrepair but was restored to its original appearance both inside and outside by an architect in the 1950s. June Havoc acquired it in 1962 and rented the upper floors to various tenants but kept the

Left: The former home of actress June Havoc on 44th Street, Manhattan, has the ghost of "Hungry Lucy," who died of starvation and fever during the Revolutionary War.

Right: The kitchen where June Havoc heard the poltergeist-type noises asking only for attention.

downstairs apartment for herself. One reaches Havoc's apartment by a staircase up to the parlor floor.

Tenants never stayed long in that apartment but Havoc paid no attention at the time she moved in. Before long she noticed a number of things. There were strange tapping noises at various times of day and night and eventually they kept her from sleeping or concentrating on her work. This became particularly loud at 3:00 in the morning. At first she tried to find a logical explanation for the noises by calling in all sorts of workmen and experts to see whether the house was

On the first occasion we had the company of several distinguished observers, including newspaper columnist Earl Wilson and publicist Gail Benedict. As soon as Sybil had slipped into a trance state, during which her own personality was temporary absent while the alleged ghost was invited to speak through her, it became apparent that something dramatic had taken place in the house.

A young woman ghost calling herself Lucy manifested through the medium, crying out in pain of hunger and demanding food. During my questioning it appeared that "Hungry Lucy," as I later

One of two séances held by Holzer with medium Sybil Leek (center) and an anxious June Havoc looking on.

settling or whether there was something wrong with the pipes or the structure of the house. None of these things turned out to be true. When the noise became unbearable Havoc called on me to help her rid the house of whatever was causing the disturbances.

I paid the house two visits in the company of British medium Sybil Leek.

came to call her, had lived and died on the spot where the house now stands. Her death had been, according to her own testimony, due to a fever epidemic. She claimed to have lived in the year 1792. I then demanded to know why Lucy was still in the house, and what she was looking for. She explained she was waiting for her boyfriend, a soldier named Alfred. Since it is possible to check into the regiments of soldiers even several hundred years ago I asked what regiment her Alfred served in. Without hesitation Lucy replied, "Napier."

about Alfred, her boyfriend who had also died in the area. A second visit was arranged during which Sybil went into deep trance again. This time additional contacts were made with men who had

The following day we checked this out and discovered that Colonel Napier was the commanding officer of a regiment stationed in the grounds of Governor Clinton's estate. The land on which Havoc's house stood was part of that estate in 1792. Further, we found that a fever epidemic had occurred at that time and Colonel Napier had been shipped back to England because of illness. During the séance we convinced Lucy that there was no point in waiting around for her soldier any longer, and eventually she let go of her compulsion to stay on in the house. Soon she was slipping away and I left Havoc's apartment in the hopes that all would be quiet from then on.

However, this was not the case. It appears that while we had freed Lucy from the house, we had done nothing

Clockwise from upper left:

Sybil Leek examining the psychic atmosphere in June Havoc's house in Hell's Kitchen, Manhattan.

Suddenly, the floor becomes transparent as psychic material is superimposed on it, pointing at a presence in the area.

Even more, the floor takes on the appearance of a mirror.

lived and died in the area during the Revolutionary period and we were able to establish that these people had actually existed from comparing their names with entries in regimental and other historical records. We also addressed ourselves to Alfred imploring him to let go since his Lucy was now "on the other side of life," that is, no longer among the living. We should have done this at the same time we dispatched Lucy to her just reward. Unfortunately, Alfred failed to understand us and though the séance was otherwise successful, the noises continued sporadically. In 1969, June Havoc sold the house and with it relinquished her tenancy of the downstairs apartment. But I hear from people living in the house, now and again, that Alfred is still about.

THE HAUNTED CHURCH OF MILLVALE, PENNSYLVANIA

About an hour's drive from Pittsburgh, in the small town of Millvale, hard by the Allegheny River, stands an imposing stone church built at the turn of the last century. Positioned as it is on a bluff looking down toward the river, it seems somewhat out of place for so small a town as Millvale. Attached to the building is a school and rectory, and there is a clean efficiency about the entire complex. This is a Roman Catholic church, and the priests are all of Yugoslav background. Thus there is a peculiarity about the ritual, about the atmosphere inside the church, and about the men who serve here. The church is very large, and the altar is framed by original paintings in the Yugoslav style. They are the work of Maxim Hvatka, the celebrated Yugoslavian artist who worked in the early part of this century and who died a few years ago. Near the altar was a large eternal light—that is, an enclosed candle protected from drafts or other interference. This is important, since much of the phenomenon centers in this area and includes the blowing out of the eternal light by unknown causes.

Although the administrators of the church do not exactly cherish the notion that they have a ghost, there have been a number of witnesses who have seen a figure pass by the altar. The painter Hvatka saw the ghostly apparition while working on his frescoes. Chills, which could not be accounted for, were also noted in the immediate area of the eternal light. There is nothing concerning the present-day church that would account for the apparition of a figure at the altar. However, prior to the erection of the present church, a wooden church had stood on the same spot. It was Father Ranzinger who had built the wooden church, and who had devoted most of his life to that church and its flock. One night, the wooden church went up in flames. Father Ranzinger's life's work was destroyed. I suspect that it is his ghost that has been seen.

After a while I was able to convince the priest who had admitted me to the church that I meant no harm to the reputation and good name of the church and this order of priests, but that I was only interested in writing about natural psychic phenomena, which, after all, are part of God's world. Father X, as he insisted on being called, readily admitted that I was telling the truth and admitted that he, too, had had psychic experiences all his life. As we went on talking, he admitted that he had seen the ghost of the departed priest as had a painter who had been employed in the building to restore the magnificent frescoes put there years before. Strangely enough, the only one other than myself who wrote anything at all about the haunted church at Millvale was the Yugoslav author Louis Adamic, a self-confessed agnostic, a man who does not feel that there is any way to know that God exists.

As for the ghostly priest at the altar, he must still be there, roaming the church at will. In view of the difficulties of getting into the church in the first place, I was unable to bring a medium there to attempt a release of the unhappy priest. Thus, if you happen to be near Pittsburgh and feel like visiting the haunted church of Millvale, and if the time is just right, perhaps at dusk or at dawn, you may just encounter the restless ghost of Father Ranzinger. That is, if he hasn't long since faded away and come to peace with himself, as well he should.

The haunted church at Millvale, Pennsylvania. The ghost, still attached to it, believes he was responsible for a devastating fire that destroyed an earlier church on the spot. But he was not responsible.

In June 1696, Daniel Seabrook, aged twenty-six and a planter by profession, took his inheritance of eighty pounds sterling and bought 202 acres of property from his stepfather, Thomas Whitlock. For 250 years, this was a plantation in the hands of the Seabrook family, who worked the land and sailed their ships from the harbor. The "spy house" is probably one of the finest pieces of colonial architecture available for inspection in the eastern the bay area can be strong enough to take off the roof of a house. Every room has its own fireplace, as that was the only way in which colonial houses could be heated. The house, which is near Middletown, New Jersey, can be easily reached from New York City. It is kept by a group headed by curator Gertrude Neidlinger, helped by her historian brother, Travis Neidlinger, and as a museum it displays not only the furniture of the colonial

The revolutionary "spy house" in Middletown, New Jersey, is full of ghostly manifestations. No wonder, as it was smack between the lines.

United States, having been restored meticulously over the years. The house is built in the old manner, held together with wooden pegs. Handmade bricks are filled with clay mortar. The house has two stories and is painted white, and its sturdy construction points out that the winds in period but some of the implements of the whalers who were active in the nineteenth century. As an historical attraction, it is something that should not be missed by anyone, apart from ghostly connections.

One of the rooms in the house is dedicated to the period of the Battle of

Monmouth. This room, called the spy room by the British, for good reason, as we shall see, has copies of the documents kept in the Library of Congress in Washington, D.C., which are among General Washington's private papers.

In 1778, the English were marching through Middletown, pillaging and burning the village. Along the shoreline the Monmouth militia and the men who were working the whale boats got together to try to cut down the English shipping. General Washington asked for a patriot from Shoal Harbor, which was the name of the estate where the spy house was located, to help the American side fight the British. It turned out to be Corporal John Stillwell, who was given a telescope and instructions to spy on the British from a hill called Garrett's Hill, not far away, the highest point in the immediate area. The lines between British and Americans were intertwined and frequently crossed one another, and it was difficult for people to avoid crossing them at times. The assignment given to Corporal Stillwell was not easy, especially as some of his own relatives favored the other side in the war. Still, he was able to send messages to the militia, who were able to turn these messages into attacks on the British fleet. At that point, Stillwell observed there were 1,037 vessels in the fleet lying off the New Jersey coastline, at a time when the American forces had no navy at all. But the fisherman and their helpers on shore did well in this phase of the Revolutionary War. John Stillwell's son, Obadiah Stillwell, seventeen years old, served as message carrier from his father's observation point to the patriots.

Twenty-three naval battles were fought in the harbor after the battle of Monmouth. The success of the whaleboat operation was a stunning blow to the British fleet and a great embarrassment. Even daylight raids became so bold and successful that in one day two pilots were captured, upsetting the harbor shipping. Finally, the British gave the order to find the spy and end the rebel operation. The search party declared the Seabrook homestead as a spy house since they knew its owner, Major Seabrook, was a patriot. They did not realize that the real spy was John Stillwell, operating from Garrett's Hill. Nevertheless, they burned the spy house. It was later restored. Today, descendants of John Stillwell are among the society of friends of the museum, supporting it.

Gertrude Neidlinger turned to me for help with the several ghosts she felt in the house. Considering the history of the house, it is not surprising that there should be ghosts there. Neidlinger felt someone in the entrance room, whenever she has been alone in the house, especially at night. There is also a woman in white that comes down from the attic, walks along the hall and goes into what is called the blue and white room, and there tucks the covers into a crib or bed. Then she turns and goes out of sight. Neidlinger was not sure who she was, but thought she might have been the spirit of Mrs. Seabrook, who lived through the Revolutionary War in a particularly dangerous position, having relatives on both sides of the political fence.

In 1976, I brought Ingrid Beckman, my psychic friend, to the spy house, which is technically located in Keansburg, New Jersey, near Middletown. Ingrid knew nothing about the place, and as she walked about it, she immediately pointed out its ancient use as an outpost. While we were investigating the house, we clearly heard footsteps overhead where there was no one walking. Evidently, the ghosts knew of our arrival. Without knowing anything about the history of the house, Ingrid commented, "Down here around the fireplace I feel there are people planning strategy, worried about British ships." Then she continued, "This was to mobilize something like the minutemen, farming men who were to fight. This was a strategic point because it was the entry into New York."

I asked Ingrid to tell me whether she felt any ghosts, any residues of the past still in the house. When we went upstairs, Ingrid tuned into the past with a bang. "There's a woman here. She ties in with this house and something about spying, some kind of spying went on here." Then she added, "Somebody spied behind the American lines and brought back information." Upstairs near the window on the first-floor landing, Ingrid felt a man watching, waiting for someone to come his way.

Ingrid felt there was a man present who had committed an act of treason, a man who gave information back to the British. His name was Samuels. She felt that this man was hanged publicly. The people call him an ex-patriot. This is the entity, Ingrid said, who cannot leave his house out of remorse. Ingrid also asserted that the house was formerly used as a public house, an inn, when meetings took place here. The curator, Neidlinger, later confirmed this. Also, that among

the families living in the area, most of the members served in the patriot militia, but that there were occasional traitors, such as George Taylor. Colonel George Taylor might have been the man to whom Ingrid was referring. As for the man who was hanged, it would have been Captain Huddy, and he was hanged for having caused the death of Philip White. Captain Joshua Huddy had been unjustly accused of having caused the death of the patriot Philip White and despite his innocence was lynched by the patriots. Again, Ingrid had touched on something very real from history.

But the ghostly woman and the man who was hanged and the man who stared out the window onto the bay are not the only ghosts at the spy house. On the 4th of July, 1975, a group of local boys were in the house, in the blue and white room upstairs. Suddenly, the sewing-machine door opened by itself and the pedals worked themselves without benefit of human feet. One of the boys looked up, and in the mirror in the bureau, he could see a face with a long beard. Another boy looked down the hall and saw a figure with a tall black hat and a long beard and the sort of very full trousers that were worn in an earlier age. That was enough for them. They ran from the house and never went back.

One of the women who assists the curator, Mrs. L., refuses to do any typing in the upstairs room because the papers will not stand still. A draft seems to go by all the time and blow the papers to the floor even though the windows are closed. A Mrs. B. also saw the man with the beard standing at the top of the stairs wearing a black hat and dressed in the period of the late 1700s. He had large eyes, and seemed to be in his forties. He just stood there looking at her and she wouldn't pass him. Then he seemed to flash a light back and forth, a brilliant light like a flashlight. And there were footsteps all over the house at the same time. She could even hear the man breathe, yet he was a ghost!

GHOSTLY SUMMER THEATER AT THOUSAND OAKS, CALIFORNIA

Not far from Thousand Oaks, California, stands a simple wooden church, the Missionary Baptist Church. It is situated on a small bluff overlooking the freeway access road. This church is actually an old dairy barn remodeled, first into a theater, and later, when the theater people left, into now gain access to the church. There is also an attic, but the attic is so low that no one can stand up in it. This is of importance, since the observed hauntings seem to have emanated from that attic. Footsteps had been heard overhead by some of the Conejo Valley Players, when

The Missionary Baptist Church in Thousand Oaks, California, north of Los Angeles, was a summer theater years ago. An actor there came to an untimely end, and hasn't yet gotten used to that role.

the present church. (The original owner, a Goebel, sold it to the Conejo Valley Players, an amateur theatrical group.) There is a large door in front, and a smaller one in the rear, by which one can there was no one overhead. If there had been anyone standing in the attic, he would have had to have been no more than three feet tall. What was once the stage of the Conejo Valley Players is now the area of the altar. The minister of the Baptist church does not take kindly to psychic phenomena, so a visitor must make his own arrangements or walk into the church—for worship, as it were— and further such psychic impressions as he or she can without causing any stir.

The phenomena consisted mainly of a man's footsteps. Someone was pacing up and down in the attic. At first, no one paid any attention to it, trying to pretend the noise was not real. Eventually, members of the audience kept asking what the strange goings-on over their heads meant. Was there another auditorium there? Sometimes it sounded as if heavy objects such as furniture were being moved around. There was nothing of the kind in the attic.

One young girl, who had not been a member of the troupe for long, became almost hysterical and insisted that someone had been murdered in the building. Two women with psychic learnings could never enter the structure without immediately getting cold, clammy feelings. These feelings turned into terror when they attempted to go up into the attic, and, on hands and knees, look around for the cause of the strange noises. Hurriedly, they went down again. The noises continued, not only at night during actual performances, but even in the afternoons during rehearsals or casual visits.

Sybil Leek stuck her head into the attic immediately when we entered the barn. To her, that was the place of the haunting, although I had not told her anything whatever about the problem. She walked about the barn for a while, again poked her head into the attic, standing on a few steps leading up to it and then shook her head. She explained that the young man who had been murdered there would not leave.

The barn is no longer a theater, but a church. This does not seem to make the slightest difference to the ghost who lives in the past, his own past, that is, to whom the outside world does not exist. If you visit this barn, just ask for the barn by name and location and you may be rewarded with a psychic experience.

MORRIS-JUMEL MANSION—MANHATTAN

You wouldn't think that right in the heart of New York stands a magnificent Southern-style mansion with several ghosts in it. But there is such a building, now known as the Morris-Jumel mansion in Washington Heights, Manhattan, at the corner of 160th Street and Edgecombe Avenue. I've been to this mansion several times, twice as part of an investigation into the hauntings reported and several times more with friends, some of whom felt chilly and disturbed by the continuing presences in the building.

Built at the highest spot of Manhattan, originally called Harlem Heights, the mansion was erected by British-born Colonel Roger Morris, and in 1776, during the Revolutionary War, General George Washington made it his headquarters during the battle of Long Island. Later, when the fortunes of war changed, the British moved in again, and General Sir Henry Clinton stayed at the mansion.

From then on, the career of this magnificent building was checkered. At one point it served as an ordinary tavern called Calumet Hall. One day in 1810, a French wine merchant, Stephen Jumel, recently arrived on American shores, and his ambitious American-born wife passed

renovated the place and it soon became one of the showplaces of New York City.

There are four stories and a basement and the principal areas of psychic activity are the second and third floors as well as the balcony, which can be seen from a distance. It was on that balcony on January 19, 1964,

Clockwise from upper left:

The Morris-Jumel mansion in Washington Heights, Manhattan, is a colorful museum with several resi dent ghosts.

Madame Betsy Jumel, in this contemporary portrait, is one of them.

On this balcony, a group of schoolchildren saw a woman in a star-studded gown come out and shush them. That was Betsy Jumel, who did not care much for the noise.

Medium Ethel Johnson Meyers picking up Betsy's trail.

by and decided to buy the place on the spot. At that time the property included thirty-five acres of land surrounding it. Mrs. Jumel immediately refurbished and

that a small group of schoolchildren saw the ghost of Mrs. Jumel. It all happened when they were waiting to be let into the historical building. They had arrived a little early, and were becoming restless, when one of the children pointed to the balcony where a woman in a flimsy violet gown had just appeared. "Shush!" she said to the children, trying to calm them down. After that she receded into the room behind the balcony. It never occurred to the children until later that she had never opened the doors. When the curator, Mrs. C., arrived to let them in, they complained that they could have been in the house much sooner, and why didn't the woman on the balcony open up for them? There was no woman on the balcony as far as the curator was concerned. But soon she realized that she was presiding over a much-haunted house.

One flight up in what used to be Mrs. Jumel's own bedroom I held a séance with the help of Ethel Johnson Meyers, during which Stephen Jumel complained bitterly about being murdered by his own wife. He had fallen off a haywagon and hurt himself on a pitchfork, and a doctor had been summoned to attend to his wounds. As soon as the doctor had left Mrs. Jumel tore off the bandages and Stephen bled to death. I have tried to have his tomb reopened in a nearby cemetery but never received official permission to do so. The one-time vice president of the United States, Aaron Burr, political figure of the nineteenth century, was even then friendly with Mrs. Jumel. He married her and spent much time at the mansion. His presence has also been felt by many visitors.

As if having an angry victim of foul play in the house and perhaps the lingering spirit of Mrs. Jumel herself were not enough, there is also a young servant girl who became involved with one of the family and committed suicide by jumping out the window. She may be one of the ghosts, having been observed on the top floor where the servants' quarters were located. Since I conducted two "rescue" séances at the mansion during which Stephen Jumel had the opportunity to complain about his untimely death, I feel that he has been pacified and is no longer a resident of the Morris-Jumel mansion. But Mrs. Jumel and the servant girl may well still roam the corridors of the house where they once lived, the one in unusual splendor, the other in great anguish.

Not long ago a schoolteacher brought his class from a nearby school to visit the famed mansion. While the children were inspecting the lower two floors he dashed up to the top floor, being a history buff most eager to inspect the house from top to bottom. Picture his surprise when he was confronted by a Revolutionary soldier who had practically stepped out of a painting on the top floor! The teacher fainted on the spot, and was later revived.

Not so lucky was another teacher, who, having a history of heart disease, was frightened to death on one of the floors. But this is unusual: ghosts do not hurt people, and ghosts should not frighten people because they are, after all, only human beings in trouble with *themselves*.

The Morris-Jumel mansion can be visited every day until 4:00 P.M. It is maintained as a museum and there is no reservation necessary to visit. However, certain rooms of the upper floors have been closed off to the public, and whether for reasons of expediency or because of the continuing strong interests in ghosts, it is hard to say. The personnel serving in the mansion know nothing about the ghostly manifestations, so there is no point in questioning them about it.

STAGECOACH INN—CALIFORNIA

Not far from Ventura, at Thousand Oaks, a few yards back from the main road, stands an old stagecoach inn, now run as a museum; between 1952 and 1965, while in the process of being restored to its original appearance, it also served as a gift shop under the direction of a Mr. and Mrs. M., who had sensed the presence of a female ghost in the structure.

The house has nineteen rooms and an imposing frontage with columns running from the floor to the roof. There is a balcony in the central portion, and all

make room for the main road running through here. Nevertheless, its grandeur has not been affected by the move.

During the stagecoach days, bandits were active in this area. The inn had been erected because of the Butterfield Mail route, which was to have gone through the Conejo Valley on the way to Saint Louis. The Civil War halted this plan, and the routing was changed to go through the Santa Clara Valley.

I investigated the stagecoach inn with Gwen Hinzie and Sybil Leek. Upstairs to

The haunted Stagecoach Inn at Thousand Oaks, California.

windows have shutters, in the manner of the mid-nineteenth century. Surrounded by trees until a few years ago, it has been moved recently to a new position to

the left of the staircase Sybil noticed one of the particularly haunted rooms. She felt that a man named Pierre Devon was somehow connected with the building.

Since the structure was still in a state of disrepair, with building activities going on all around us, the task of walking up the stairs was not only a difficult one but also somewhat dangerous, for we could not be sure that the wooden structure would not collapse from our weight. We stepped gingerly. Sybil seemed to know just where to turn, as if she had been there before. Eventually, we ended up in a little room to the left of the stairwell. It must have been one of the smaller rooms, a "single" in today's terms.

Sybil complained of being cold all over. The man, Pierre Devon, had been killed in that room, she insisted, some-time between 1882 and 1889. She did not connect with the female ghost. However, several people living in the area have reported the presence of a tall stranger who could only be seen out of the corner of an eye, never for long. Pungent odors, perfume of a particularly heavy kind, also seem to waft in and out of the structure.

Like inns in general, this one may have more undiscovered ghosts hanging on to the spot. Life in nineteenth-century wayside inns does not compare favorably with life in today's Hilton. Some people going to these stagecoach inns for a night's rest never woke up to see another day.

THE BOATSMAN OF BLACK BASS INN, PENNSYLVANIA

When I decided to spend a quiet weekend to celebrate my birthday at the picturesque Logan Inn in New Hope, Pennsylvania, I had no idea that I was not just

The Black Bass Inn in Lumberville, Pennsylvania, has a restless boatsman who got into a fight with another canal boatsman and lost.

going to sleep in a haunted bedroom, but actually get two ghosts for the price of one!

The woman who communicated with my companion and me in the darkness of the silent January night via a flickering candle in room number 6 provided a heartwarming experience and one I can only hope helped the restless one get a better sense of still belonging to the house. Gwen Davis, the proprietor, assured me that the ghost is the mother of a former owner, who liked the place so much she never left.

Davis pointed me toward the Black Bass Inn in nearby Lumberville, an eighteenth-century pub, now a hotel right on the Delaware Canal. The place is filled with

Here is Holzer confronting
the specter, whose name,
incidentally, was also Hans
(photo by Rosemarie Khalil).

English antiques of the period and portraits of Kings Charles I and II and James II, proving that this was a Loyalist stronghold at one time. I went around the place with my camera, taking any number of photographs with fast color film in existing light. The story here concerned the ghost of a young man who made his living as a canal boatsman. Today, the canal is merely a curiosity for tourists, but in the nineteenth century, it was an active waterway for trade, bringing goods on barges down river. The canal, which winds around New Hope and some of the nearby towns, gives the area a charm all its own.

In the stone basement of the Black Bass, where the apparition had been seen by a number of people over the years, according to the current owner, Herbie Ward, I took some pictures and then asked my companion to take one of me. Picture my surprise when there appeared a white shape in the picture that cannot be reasonably explained as anything but the boatsman putting in a kind of appearance for me. The boatsman died in a violent argument with another boatsman. By the way, the name of the boatsman was Hans. Maybe he felt the two Hanses ought to get in touch?

Probably the most celebrated of British royal ghosts is the shade of unlucky Queen Anne Boleyn, the second wife of Henry VIII, who ended her days on the scaffold. Accused of infidelity, which was a form of treason in the sixteenth century, she had her head cut off despite protestations of her innocence. In retrospect, historians have established that she was speaking the truth. But at the time of her trial, it was a political matter to have her removed from the scene, and even her uncle, who sat in judgment of her as the trial judge, had no inclination to save her neck.

the Salt Tower within the confines of the Tower of London, a guard observed her ghost walking along headless, and he promptly fainted. The case is on record, and the man insisted over and over that he had not been drinking.

Perhaps he would have received a good deal of sympathy from Lieutenant Glynn, a member of the Royal Guard, who has stated, "I have seen the great Queen Elizabeth and recognized her, with her olive skin color, her fire-red hair, and her ugly dark teeth. There is no doubt about it in my mind." Although Elizabeth died a natural death at a ripe

The Tower of London has several ghosts, the best-known being Anne Boleyn (photo, British Tourist Authority).

Anne Boleyn's ghost has been reported in a number of places connected with her in her lifetime. There is her apparition at Hampton Court, attested to by a number of witnesses over the years, and even at Windsor Castle, where she is reported to have walked along the eastern parapet. At

old age, it is in the nature of ghosts that both the victims and the perpetrators of crimes sometimes becomes restless once they have left the physical body. In the case of good Queen Bess, there was plenty to be remorseful over. Although most observers assume Queen Elizabeth "walks" because of what she did to Mary Queen of Scots, I disagree. Mary had plotted against Elizabeth, and her execution was legal in terms of the times and conditions under which the events took place. If Queen Elizabeth I has anything to keep her restless, it would have to be found among the many lesser figures who owed their demise to her anger or cold cunning, including several ex-lovers.

Exactly as described in the popular English ballad, Anne Boleyn had been observed with "her 'ead tucked under," not only at the Tower of London, but also at Hever Castle, in Kent, where she was courted by King Henry VIII.

That the Tower ghosts were more than a legend can be seen by scanning two of the many accounts of ghostly encounters there. In 1864, Major General J. G. Dundas of the 60th Rifles was quartered in the Tower. Looking out the window from his quarters he noticed a guard below in the courtyard in front of the chamber where Anne Boleyn spent her last moments on earth. The guard

behaved strangely—he seemed to challenge something that, to the general, looked like a whitish female figure gliding toward the soldier. He charged right through the form, and then fainted. Only the general's testimony and corroboration saved the soldier from a long prison sentence at the court martial that took place as a consequence of his fainting while on duty. Those were stern times, remember.

In February 1957, a Welsh Guardsman on duty at the Tower reported seeing a ghost on the upper battlements of the Salt Tower on the anniversary of the execution of Lady Jane Grey, who died more than four hundred years ago after a reign as queen of only nine days. In the Church of Saint Peter ad Vincula, within the Tower compound, there have been reports of presences in the pews, like "a second shadow." Only a trance medium could ascertain the truthfulness of these reports. Perhaps I can smuggle one in the next time I'm in London. The Queen need never know.

THE DUEL OF GARRICK'S HEAD INN—BATH, ENGLAND

Three hours by car from London is the elegant resort city of Bath. Here, in Regency architectural wonderland, is an eighteenth-century inn called Garrick's Head Inn. At one time there was a connection between the inn and the theater next door, but the theater no longer exists. In the eighteenth century, the gambler Beau Nash owned this inn, which was then a gambling casino as well.

The downstairs bar looks like any other bar, divided between a large, dark

room where the customers sip their drinks, and a heavy wooden bar behind which the owner dispenses liquor and small talk. There is an upstairs with a window that, tradition says, is impossible to keep closed for some reason. The rooms upstairs are no longer used for guests, but are mainly storage rooms or private rooms of the owners.

At the time of my first visit to the Garrick's Head Inn it was owned by Bill Loud, who was a skeptic when he arrived in Bath. Within two months his skepticism was shattered by the phenomena he witnessed. The heavy till once took off by itself and smashed a chair. The noises of people walking was heard at night at a time when the place was entirely empty. He once walked into what he described as cobwebs and felt his head stroked by a

Nash, there had been an argument one night, and two men had words over a young woman. A duel followed. The winner was to take possession of the girl. One man was killed and the survivor rushed up the stairs to claim his prize. The girl, who had started to flee when she saw him win, was not agreeable, and when she heard

The Garrick Head Inn in Bath, England (Somerset), has the ghost of an unlucky girl gambled away by her boyfriend. The owner saw a heavy cash register take off by its own volition, standing behind the bar.

gentle hand. He also smelled perfume when he was entirely alone in the cellar. A reporter from a Bristol newspaper who spent the night at the inn also vouched for the authenticity of the footsteps and strange noises.

Finally the owner decided to dig into the past of the building, and discovered that there have been incidents that could well be the basis for the haunting. During the ownership of gambling king Beau

him coming, barricaded herself in the upstairs room and hanged herself.

Whether you will see or hear the lady ghost at the Garrick's Head Inn is a matter of individual ability to communicate with the psychic world. It also depends upon the hours of the night you go there, for the Garrick's Head Inn is noisy in the early part of the evening when it is filled with people looking for spirits in the bottle rather than the more ethereal kind.

LONGLEAT PALACE—SOMERSET, ENGLAND

In the west of England, and not far from the city of Bath, stands the huge country house Longleat, ancestral seat of the Marquess of Bath. From a distance this white building looks majestic and much like a fairy-tale palace. There are swans in some

dining facilities on the grounds. The ordinary tourist comes for that and the magnificent art in the house. Very few people think of ghosts when visiting Longleat. However, if you wish to see the so-called haunted areas, it would be wiser

Longleat Palace, Somerset, England, is the favorite haunt of Sir Thomas Thynne, whose wife had him murdered on the highway (photo, British Tourist Authority).

of the ponds in the large park for which Longleat was famous. As with so many large estates, the owners had to go public to defray the expense of keeping the place in order and pay taxes. Visitors are not only permitted; they are actively encouraged to come. There are extra attractions, such as a zoo with many lions, and

to write ahead of time and ask for a special tour. Some of these spots are on the regular tourist route for all visitors, and some are in the private portion of Longleat.

By 1580 the main portion of the house was already in existence, but it was later added to and finally rebuilt in the seventeenth century, when it achieved its current appearance. The original owner was Sir John Thynne, a financier to the royal family, who had acquired the property during a period of stress in English history.

He and his successors managed to amass a fortune in fine art and fill Longleat with it from ground floor to the roof.

There are three sets of ghosts at Longleat. In the red library the apparition of

Above: The Red Library at Longleat is where the ghost of Sir Thomas has been seen.

Right: The haunted corridor at Longleat.

a scholarly-looking man wearing a high collar and the costume of the sixteenth century has been seen. He is believed to be the builder of Longleat, Sir John Thynne. He may be kept roaming the corridors for personal reasons connected with the acquisition of the property.

Upstairs is a haunted corridor with a long narrow passage paralleling the bedrooms. It is here that the ghost of Louisa Carteret, one of the women in the Bath family, has been repeatedly observed. She has every reason, it appears, to be there. On one occasion she was discovered with a lover by the second Viscount Weymouth, one of Lord Bath's ancestors. A duel was fought by the viscount, and the intruder was killed. Since the viscount had the power of justice in his domain, there was no need for any inquest. The body of the intruder was hurriedly buried in the cellar. A few years ago, when the present Lord Bath was putting in a boiler, the skeleton of the unfortunate lover was accidentally discovered and removed. But Lady Louisa was forever seen looking for her lost lover, and for all I know she may be looking for him still.

Finally, there is a man of the seventeenth century who has been observed in some of the reception rooms downstairs. According to British medium Trixie Allingham, with whom I worked at Longleat, this is the restless ghost of Sir Thomas Thynne, another of Lord Bath's ancestors. Sir Thomas had the misfortune of being betrayed by his wife, it appeared, whose lover had hired two assassins to murder the husband. This event took place on the high road, where the murderers stopped a coach bringing Sir Thomas home, dragged him out and killed him. As sometimes happens with ghosts, he was drawn back to where his emotions were, his home, and apparently he cannot find peace because of the tragic events.

With so many ghosts at Longleat, the chances of running into one or the other are considerably higher than if only an occasional specter were to appear at certain times. But don't expect Longleat ghosts to wait upon you just because you paid your entrance fee or had lunch downstairs in the cafeteria. If you can wrangle a personal introduction to Lord Bath, and a private tour into the non-tourist areas, perhaps you might experience some of the things I have been talking about.

SALISBURY HALL—SAINT ALBANS, HERTFORDSHIRE

About an hour from London, in the direction of Saint Albans, Hertfordshire, stands a moderate-size manor house, Salisbury Hall. The area was settled at a very early period in British history, and within a few miles the Roman city of Verulamium stood, and Roman artifacts are frequently dug out of the soil in and around Salisbury Hall. Another noteworthy event was the battle of Barnet, during which the hall was a fortified strongpoint. Many soldiers died in and around the house, and swords and bones have been found in the moat and garden.

The ground floor of the manor contains several smaller rooms and a very large and impressive room called the crown chamber, with a fireplace on one side. Next to the fireplace is a door and beyond it a staircase leading to the upper floor. The area near this staircase is the spot where a number of witnesses have seen the ghost of Nell Gwyn, favorite of Charles II. It may strike some readers as curious that a ghost can appear in more than one location, but Nell Gwyn apparently was partially free and allowed herself to be drawn back to two places connected with her emotional life. Both her city apartment at 69 Dean Street and this country place held deep and precious memories for her, and it is therefore conceivable that she could have been seen at various times in both places. There was no doubt about the identity of the apparition that had been described by Sir Winston Churchill's stepfather, Cornwallis-West. Less illustrious observers have also seen her.

But in addition to the wraith of Nell, there is the ghost of a Cavalier who haunts the upstairs part of the hall. At one time there was an additional wing to the building, which no longer exists. It is in the corridor leading to that nonexistent wing that the cavalier has been observed. In one of the rooms at the end of the corridor, the cavalier is said to have committed suicide when being pursued by soldiers of Oliver Cromwell. He apparently carried some valuable documents on him and did not want to have them fall into the hands of his pursuers; nor did he want to be tortured into telling them anything of value.

This was at the height of the Civil War in England, when the Cavaliers—or partisans of the Royalists—were hotly pursued by the parliamentary soldiers, also known as Roundheads. Although the suicide took place in the 1640s, the footsteps of the ghostly cavalier can still be heard on occasion at Salisbury Hall.

Salisbury Hall belongs to Walter Goldsmith, who lives there with his wife and children. He is an artist by profession but has lately turned the hall into a part-time tourist attraction on certain days of the week. Since he has spent great sums of money to restore the manor from the state of disrepair in which he bought it, one can hardly blame him for the modest fee of admission required for a visit. Goldsmith will gladly point out the haunted spots and discuss psychic phenomena without denying their reality, especially in his house.

BLOODY HALL—SAWSTON HALL, ENGLAND

A short distance from the great English university town of Cambridge, off the main road, lies Sawston Hall, a Catholic stronghold that has been in the Huddleston family for many generations. It is an imposing gray stone structure, three stories high and surrounded by a lovely garden. It is so secluded that it is sometimes hard to locate unless one knows exactly where to turn off the main road. Inside, the great hall is a major accomplishment of Tudor architecture, and there are many large rooms, bedrooms, and galleries. Its size lies somewhere between the great houses of royalty and the baronial estates that dot the English countryside by the hundreds. Sawston Hall can be visited by the public on certain days and by prearrangement. The man to contact is Major A.C. Eyre, nephew of the late Captain Huddleston, who manages the estate.

The principal personality associated with Sawston Hall is Queen Mary Tudor, sometimes called Bloody Mary. She rebuilt Sawston Hall after her enemies had burned it down. Her favorite room was a drawing room with a virginal, a sixteenth-century musical instrument. From the drawing room, one goes through a corridor called the Little Gallery, and a paneled bedroom, into the Tapestry Bedroom, which is named for a large set of Flemish tapestries on the wall, depicting the life of King Solomon. In the center of this room is a four-poster in which Queen Mary allegedly slept. In the wall behind the bed is a door through which her ghost is said to have appeared on several occasions. Behind that door lies a passage leading to a so-called priest's hole, a secret hiding place where Catholic priests were hidden during the turbulent times of the religious wars in the sixteenth century. Whenever Protestant raiders came, the priests would hide themselves in these prearranged hiding places, which were well supplied with air, water, and food. As soon as everything was clear, the priests would reemerge to join the Catholic household.

A number of people who have slept in what is called Queen Mary's room, in the four-poster, have reported uncanny experiences. It is always the same story: three knocks at the door, then the door opens by itself and a gray form slowly floats across the room and disappears into the tapestry. Many have heard the virginal play soft music when there was no one in the drawing room. It is a fact that the young Princess Mary was expert at this instrument, and on numerous occasions was asked to play in order to show off her musical talents.

In 1553, Princess Mary was living in Norfolk when her half-brother Edward VI died. The duke of Northumberland,

duke of Northumberland to lure her to London where he could dispose of her. When Mary reached Sawston Hall on her way to the capital, she received word of the real situation. She immediately fled back to Norfolk. When they discovered that their prey had escaped, the troops of the duke of Northumberland were enraged and set fire to Sawston Hall. Looking back on the smoldering ruins of Sawston Hall, Mary said to John Huddleston that she would build him a greater hall than ever, once she came to the throne.

Sawston Hall, Cambridge, boasts a haunted bedroom where Mary Tudor—Bloody Mary—was hidden from her enemies prior to her taking power. Mary's ghost seems drawn back to this safe haven, as people sleeping in her bed report seeing her.

who then dominated the English government, did not want her to succeed to the throne, but wanted instead to have a member of his own family rule England. A false message was sent to Mary, purporting to come from her ailing brother Edward. It was a trap set for her by the

Not much later she kept her word, and Sawston Hall is the building created during the reign of Mary Tudor. It is not surprising that her spirit should be drawn back to a place that actually saved her life at one time, where she found more love than at any other place in England. Mary Tudor was herself a Catholic, as were the Huddlestons, and thus Sawston Hall does represent the kind of emotional tie I have found to be necessary for ghostly manifestation.

Visitors to the hall may not encounter the ghost of Mary Tudor, but one never knows. There are also other presences in this ancient house, but they seem to be concentrated in the upstairs part. The great hall, the Little Gallery, and Mary's bedroom are all the domain of "the gray lady."

THE MONKS OF WINCHESTER CATHEDRAL— SOUTHERN ENGLAND

I wanted to investigate hauntings at Winchester Cathedral. I had heard that a number of witnesses had observed ghostly monks walking in the aisles of this church, where no monks have actually walked since the 1500s. During the dissolution of the monasteries upon orders of Henry VIII, monks and abbots were abused and occasionally executed or murdered, especially when they resisted the orders driving them from their customary places. Here at Winchester, so close to the capital, the order was strictly enforced and the ghostly monks seen by a number of witnesses may have had some unfinished business.

I discovered that I was not the first man to obtain psychic photographs in this place. According to a dispatch of the *Newark Evening News* of September 9, 1958, an amateur photographer, T. L. Taylor, was visiting the ancient cathedral with his family. Taylor, who was then forty-two years old, an electrical engineer, was on a sightseeing tour without the slightest interest or knowledge of the supernormal. He took a number of pictures in the choir area—the same area where my ghostly monks appeared—in late 1957. With him at the time was Mrs. Taylor and his sixteen-year-old daughter, Valerie. Incidentally, none of them observed any ghostly goings-on.

The first exposure turned out to be a normal view of the choir chairs, but on the following picture—perhaps taken from a slightly different angle—there appeared in these same empty chairs thirteen human figures dressed in what appeared to be medieval costumes. When the film and prints came back from the lab, Taylor was aghast. As a technician he knew that his camera could not take double exposures accidentally—just as mine can't—because of a locking mechanism, and the manufacturer of the film confirmed to him upon inquiry that the film was in no way faulty and the "ghosts" could not be explained through some form of error in manufacture of film or developing. Satisfied that he had somehow obtained some supernormal material, Taylor turned the results over to the Lewisham Psychic Research Society, where they presumably still are.

Catherine, my ex-wife, and I walked up to the choir area and I began to take black-and-white photographs, exposing two seconds for each picture. The high content of moisture in the atmosphere may have had some bearing on the supernormal results. On other occasions I have found that moist air is a better psychic conductor than dry air. After I had exposed the entire roll of eleven pictures in various directions, but from the same area, we returned to our car, still ignorant. Since all my psychic photography is unexpected and purely accidental, no thoughts of what might turn up filled my mind at the time. I was merely taking

here not with one identical picture of a monk exposed somehow three times as he moved about but with three slightly different figures, one of which looks sideways, while the other two are caught from the rear. I was puzzled by the apparent lack of

Winchester Cathedral in southern England was turned into a Protestant church by Henry VIII, who got rid of the monks forcefully. A row of ghost monks, nevertheless, has been observed by several witnesses, not to mention Holzer's camera.

photographs of the cathedral because people had observed ghosts in it. Only later did I discover that someone else had also obtained photographs of ghosts there.

Upon developing and printing, it became immediately clear that I had caught the cowled, hooded figures of three monks walking in the aisle. On close inspection it is clear that we are dealing

height on the part of these figures and wondered if sixteenth-century men were that much smaller than we are. But on examination of the records I discovered that the stone floor of the cathedral was raised a hundred years after the last monks had been driven out from Winchester. Thus the figures caught here are walking on what to them must be the original floor.

Jubilant, I took these two photographs, along with other less spectacular ones, to Eileen Garrett, at the same time showing her my camera and how it worked. She listened quietly and then admitted that perhaps there had been a breakthrough after

HOW THIS PICTURE WAS OBTAINED

TIME: September 15, 1964, 11:00 A.M.

PLACE: Winchester Cathedral, England, main nave, area of the choir chairs

LIGHT CONDITIONS: Overcast skies (rain) producing flat daylight through overhead

But in another part of the choir area, no ghosts manifest.

all. She knew me well enough to know that any possibility of fraud on my part was out of the question, and the evidence before her eyes together with the circumstances of its production, was such that no one with normal eyesight could deny they were human figures—figures that should not, and could not, appear on the negatives, but that nevertheless did do just that.

church windows, but no direct light, no artificial light source of any kind, and no reflecting surfaces of any kind within the area photographed.

CAMERA: Super Ikonta B. Zeiss, frequently examined for faults by the Zeiss workshop in New York, and found in perfect working order.

FILM: Agfa Record Isopan 120, from fresh

pack purchased at Fotoshop, New York. Camera loaded in subdued light.

EXPOSURE: Two seconds with camera resting on firm surface, i.e., wooden back of choir chair. Exposures were taken at that time in four different directions from the same vantage point.

OPERATOR: Hans Holzer, in the presence of Mrs. Holzer. Otherwise, entire nave of church deserted.

DEVELOPING AND PRINTING: Kodak of London, professional department.

THE MONKS OF AETNA SPRINGS—SAINT HELENA, CALFORNIA

In 1963, Dr. Andrew von Salza had gone on vacation at the popular northern Californian resort of Aetna Springs, near Saint Helena, where a large golf course was among the attractions. A camera buff, he struck up an acquaintance with the resort's owner, one George Heibel, who had a stereo camera, which then was the latest in unusual photographic equipment, although they are now a bit passé. A stereo camera gives an "in-depth" view of a scene, which is due to its taking two pictures simultaneously. This was a Wollensack, and the two men decided to try for some good shots on the golf course. It was midafternoon on a sunny day in late summer, so they set the lens at F/16, and exposed 1/250 of a second, using daytime color film with a rating of 160 ASA. After taking a number of shots, Heibel, it appeared, allowed von Salza to use the camera and take two more pictures. What they saw was just a golf course, the area in which they were standing being empty. When the film came back from the laboratory they were in for a big surprise, for although most of the roll showed just the golf course, the two pictures taken by von Salza with Heibel's camera were quite different.

Two different views of a group of robed monks appeared seemingly out of nowhere, perhaps eight or ten figures in all, and on one of the pictures surrounded by what appeared to be flames. One can clearly see the lighted candles they carry in their hands, and the expression of grim determination upon their faces. The white robes seemed to indicate that these men were of the Dominican order. As I reported in my book *Ghosts of the Golden West*, I was able to bring British medium Sybil Leek to this area in 1966, and through deep trance establish the dramatic narrative of these monks. Later, I corroborated the account through research, showing that these were the ghosts of sixteenth-century dissidents who had defended the rights of native Indians against the ruling church, and had therefore been condemned and burned.

These photographs are the first and only psychic stereo pictures taken, and one can only marvel at the clarity and frightening realism with which the tormented souls of the monks have manifested themselves on film. When Heibel saw the pictures he wanted no part of the whole story. It upset him to such a degree that he gave von Salza his valuable stereo camera as a gift.

Even more impressive are
two photographs taken by
Dr. Andrew von Salza on an
empty golf course at Aetna
Springs in northern California, a somewhat forgotten
summer resort now. These
were the Franciscan monks
who tried to improve the lot
of native Indian slave workers, but instead got done in
by fire set here by the
Dominicans acting on orders
of the Spanish Inquisition
(photographs by Andrew
von Salza, M.D.).

On subsequent visits the doctor tried in vain to draw Heibel into conversation about the incident with the monks. Finally he learned from a local parish priest that monks had come to this area in the distant past even though there were no missions established here. The friars, it would seem, stayed only a short time and disappeared for unknown reasons. I received a final note concerning the transparent monks of Aetna Springs in September 1966. Von Salza had again gone back to his favorite holiday resort only to discover that the golf course was being torn up. Evidently the place was being remodeled. Still unyielding on the subject, the owner refused to discuss it. But as my expedition in 1966 resulted in a direct contact with the monks, I am sure they are no longer earthbound there, anyway.

HOW THESE PICTURES WERE OBTAINED

TIME: Late summer 1963. Afternoon.

PLACE: The golf course at Aetna Springs, Saint Helena, California.

LIGHT CONDITIONS: Bright, sunny.

CAMERA: Wollensack stereo camera.

FILM: Color stereo film, daytime, 160 ASA.

EXPOSURE: ½₅₀ second at F/16.

OPERATOR: Dr. Andrew von Salza, with Heibel's camera.

DEVELOPING: San Francisco photography shop.

KILKEA CASTLE, IRELAND

From a distance, Ireland's Kilkea Castle looks the very image of an Irish castle.

Kilkea Castle, Ireland, has a haunted room connected with the execution of a stable boy who had eyes for the lord's daughter.

dows that give it a massive and fortified appearance, Kilkea Castle is one of the

Turreted, gray, proud, sticking up from the landscape with narrow and tall win-

most comfortable tourist hotels in present-day Ireland. Anyone may go there by making a reservation with the genial host, Dr. William Cade. The castle is about an hour and a half by car from Dublin, in the middle of fertile farmlands. There are beautiful walks all around it, and the grounds are filled with brooks, old trees, and meadows, populated by a large number of cows.

Kilkea was built in 1180 by an Anglo-Norman knight, Sir Walter de Riddleford, and is said to be the oldest inhabited castle in Ireland, although I have seen this claim put forward in regard to several places. Let there be no mistake: the inside has been modified and little of the original castle remains. But the haunting is still there.

The castle has four floors, not counting cellars and roof. The rooms are of varying sizes and kinds. The haunted area is actually what must have been the servants' quarters at one time, and is reached through a narrow passage in the northern section of the castle. The room is just large enough for one person, and if you should want to sleep in it, you had better make a reservation way ahead of time. All you need to do is ask Cade for the haunted room. He will understand.

The story of the haunting goes back to the early Middle Ages. Apparently one of the beautiful daughters of an early owner fell in love with a stableboy. Her proud father disapproved and threatened to kill them both if they continued their association. One night, the father found the young man in his daughter's room. In the struggle that followed the boy was killed, but we are not told whether the girl was killed. But it is the boy's ghost that apparently still roams the corridors, trying to get his sweetheart back.

In the course of rebuilding, this room became part of the servants' quarters. A number of people have reported uncanny feelings in the area. The owner of Kilkea, though skeptical, has admitted to witnessing doors opening by themselves for no apparent reason. Locally, the Wizard Earl is blamed for the happenings at Kilkea Castle, and there is even a legend about him. Apparently to please his lady fair, the earl transformed himself into a bird and sat on her shoulder. But he had not counted on the presence of the castle cat, who leaped up and ate the bird. The legend continues that the earl and his companions still ride at night and will eventually return from the beyond to "put things right in Ireland"—if that is necessary. The legend does not say what happened to the cat.

SKRYNE CASTLE, IRELAND

James Reynolds first mentioned Skryne Castle in *More Ghosts in Irish Houses*, and I reported my visit there in *The Lively Ghosts of Ireland*. The castle is not far from renowned Tara, ancient capital of Ireland—or what remains of it, which is nothing more than a few hills, since Tara was built entirely of wood. But it is an easy ride from Dublin and one can combine a visit to Tara with a short stay at Skryne Castle.

Built in 1172, the ancient house fell into disrepair and was not rebuilt until early in the nineteenth century. Today it looks much more like a Victorian country home than an ancient castle. The walls are covered with ivy and the root is surmounted by a small tower and turret in the fashion of the Victorian age. This style was popular when builders fancied themselves the romantic successors to the castle builders of the Middle Ages and liked to imitate what they thought was the proper style of the twelfth century, but which is nothing more than a nineteenth-century imitation.

renting it out for wedding parties and such. It is therefore semiprivate—or rather, semipublic—and one can make arrangements for a visit by telephoning ahead, although we took a chance and drove up, asking for permission to enter when we arrived.

The upstairs salon to the right of the staircase is the one Sybil Leek felt to be the most haunted. There were several layers of ghostly happenings in the atmosphere, she explained—one having to do

At Skryne Castle, Ireland, Sybil Leek vividly relived the murder of a young woman by her lover. The hauntings never ceased.

Still, Skryne is an imposing building, especially when one drives up from the village and sees it looming behind the ancient trees on both sides of the driveway. Apparently the present owners use the house for catering now and again,

with a courier arriving at the house half dead and unable to save himself. That one goes back to the Middle Ages. Sybil received the impression that the man spoke of the Finn, a term that meant nothing to me at the time. But I discovered later that the *fianna* were a group of nobles who had rebelled against the high king Cairbre around A.D. 597, and that a battle had been fought between the rebels and the king at the foot of Skryne Castle.

The specter in the house was female, and, according to Leek, her name was something like "Mathilda." According to Reynolds, the girl's name was Lilith Palmerston, and the tragedy that ended her life happened in 1740 when the house was owned by Sir Bromley Casway. Lilith was his beautiful ward, and during her long stay at Skryne Castle the young girl

unwanted suitor. The night before their planned departure for Dublin Sellers got wind of their intent, broke into Skryne Castle, entered the girl's room and strangled her. He was hanged for his crime at Galway City.

It is the girl's unhappy presence that has been felt on many occasions by those who have slept in what used to be her room. One man saw what he thought was a nun, who dissolved before his very eyes. A Mrs. Riley, who often worked in Skryne Castle, had heard footsteps, when no one was walking.

Sybil Leek, the medium, outside Skryne Castle.

met a young man named Phelim Sellers, who lived not far from Skryne. He fell in love with Lilith, but she was unable to return his feelings. Finally Sir Bromley decided to take his beautiful ward back to Dublin to escape the attentions of the

If you are in the vicinity, call upon the owner, whose name is Nichols. Better yet, drop a line ahead of time. The Irish are hospitable, but they do like to know whom to expect. Exceptions are made only for ghosts.

The fortified castle at Wolfsegg, Bavaria, is now state property and can be visited only through the kindness and permission of its owner. It used to be one of the few privately owned fortresses in the world, and thereby hangs a tale.

The late Georg Rauchenberger, a painter and the official guardian of monuments for the province of the Upper Palatinate, which is part of the state of Bavaria, purchased this ancient fortress with his own savings. Since he was the man who passes on monies to be spent by the state for the restoration of ancient monuments in the province, he had a particularly touchy situation on his hands, for he could not allow any funds to be diverted to his own castle. Consequently, every penny spent upon the restoration of this medieval fortress came from his own pocket. Over the years he had gradually restored this relic of the past

In a desolate area near Regensburg, Germany, the twelfth-century fortress called Wolfsegg has a resident ghost: a noble lady unjustly accused of infidelity and killed by her husband. The accusers were his enemies, but that did not save the wife.

into a livable, if primitive, medieval fortress. He put in some of the missing wooden floors, and turned the clock back to the eleventh century in every respect.

which the fortress perches made attack difficult.

Wolfsegg never fell to an enemy, and even the formidable Swedes, who besieged

Wolfsegg in all its glory: it was never conquered.

Two persons, so far, can sleep comfortably in the large fortress, but as it is still in the process of being restored, it will be a long time before it can compare with some of the tourist attractions under state control. Nevertheless, small groups of interested visitors have been admitted most days of the week for a guided tour through the Hall of Knights and other parts of the fortress.

Because of the proximity of the River Danube, the fortress at Wolfsegg was always of some importance. It rises majestically out of the valley to the equivalent of four or five modern stories. Constructed for defense, its thick bulky walls are forbidding, the small windows high up to discourage aggressors The hill upon

it for a long time during the Thirty Years' War, had to give up. Built in 1028, Wolfsegg belonged to several noble Bavarian families and was always directly or indirectly involved in the intricate dynastic struggles between the various lines of the Wittelsbachs, who ruled Bavaria until 1918. Many of the masters of Wolfsegg made a living by being *Raubritter*—robber barons. The area had an unsavory reputation even as early as the twelfth century.

The walls are thick and the living quarters located well above ground. The Knights Hall on the third floor is reached by a broad staircase, and one flight down is also a lookout tower that has been restored as if it were in the sixteenth century. In the inner court is a wooden gallery running along part of the wall (at one time this gallery covered the entire length of the wall). The lower stories have not yet been fully restored or even explored.

Georg Rauchenberger had heard uncanny noises, footsteps, and experienced cold drafts at various times in vari-

The restored room at Wolfsegg, where manifestations have taken place.

had become the innocent victim of a political plot. The legend of the beautiful ghost at Wolfsegg had existed prior to our arrival on the scene. Apparently, greedy relatives of a fourteenth-century owner of Wolfsegg had decided to take over the property, then of considerable value, by

ous parts of the fortress. The late Therese Pielmeier, wife of the custodian, saw a whitish form in the yard, full of luminescence, and she heard various unexplained noises. On one occasion, Rauchenberger saw a young woman coming in with a small group of visitors, and when he turned to speak to her she disappeared.

I held a séance at Wolfsegg with a Viennese woman, Edith Riedl, who served as my medium. Through the trance mediumship of Riedl, I was able to trace the terrible story of a triple murder involving a beautiful woman, once the wife of a Wolfsegg baron, who

trapping the young wife of the owner with another man. The husband, told of the rendezvous, arrived in time to see the two lovers together, killed both of them, and was in turn murdered by his cunning relatives.

The portrait of the unlucky lady of Wolfsegg hangs in one of the corridors, the work of the father of the current owner, who painted her from impressions received while visiting the castle. Although I was able to make contact with the atmosphere surrounding the "white woman" of Wolfsegg, and to shed light upon a hitherto unknown Renaissance tragedy, it is entirely possible that the restless baroness still roams the corridors to find recognition and to prove her innocence to the world.

One reaches Wolfsegg on secondary roads in about a half hour's drive from Regensburg, and it is situated near a small and primitive village, northwest of the city on the north side of the Danube River. There is only one inn in this village, and staying overnight, as I once did, is not recommended.

This is a remote and strange area of Germany, despite the comparative nearness of the city of Regensburg. By the way, Regensburg is sometimes called Ratisbon, and is the center of one of the few remaining strongly Celtic areas in Germany.

ERNEGG CASTLE—AUSTRIA

Among the unusual and little-known attractions of Austria are some of the privately owned castles now taking guests for a night or two. The appointments in most of these places are simple, if not sometimes ghostly legends. Ernegg is on a country road leading south from the Danube. One leaves on the main road from Vienna and drives in the direction of Ybbs, the nearest large town. Ernegg is

Austria's Ernegg, an Auersberg castle and now a country pension, has the unfortunate ghost of a young man who got too friendly with one of the count's daughters.

primitive, but what the places lack in Hilton-type comfort they more than make up for in romantic atmosphere and about two hours' drive from Vienna, and clearly visible from a distance as one approaches.

The castle belongs to Prince Auers-berg, and is now operated as a pension where one can stay a day or a week with the calm surroundings of the countryside and the forest as prime attractions. The food is simple and good; the prices are modest; and the manager speaks excellent English. Those wishing to visit Ernegg

small town of Stein am Forst. It is an imposing Renaissance structure built of white stone in a style reminiscent of northern Italian castles. There are three stories and an inner courtyard of pergo-las, allowing one to walk even if it is rain-ing. The many arches of this courtyard give the building elegance, even though

Ernegg's magnificent Renais-sance courtyard. The ghost has been observed here.

need only address themselves to Direktor, Schloss Ernegg bei Ybbs, Oberösterreich, or Upper Austria. Most of the guests at Ernegg are people from some of the cen-tral Austrian cities, or a few Viennese who like unusual places.

Ernegg Castle sits on a hill looking down into the valley and toward the

the rooms are simple. All rooms are indi-vidually heated by the peculiarly Aus-trian, tall tile-covered stoves that must be filled early in the morning and again late at night to provide the necessary heat.

The main area of the alleged haunt-ing of Ernegg is to be found in what is now the apartment of the owners. Even this part of the castle is available to guests during certain parts of the year when the owners are away. It is best to ask the director for the rooms where the ghostly lovers allegedly have been seen.

The story goes that a young man was courting one of the Auersberg daughters. Since he was only a servant in the castle, Prince Auersberg disapproved. On one occasion the young man was found in a part of the castle where he had no business,

and was consequently arrested. In the manner of the late Middle Ages, he was summarily executed by the castle owner, who had full jurisdiction over all those who lived under his roof. The ghost of this unfortunate groom is said to haunt that part of the castle now used by the family.

Whether a sensitive visitor will pick up this imprint from the past, or perhaps some other impression, is anyone's guess, but Ernegg definitely warrants a visit.

THE LOVERS OF MAYERLING—VIENNA

The majority of tourists visiting the Imperial Castle in Vienna are shown the sumptuous reception rooms, the state-

rooms, the treasuries, both worldly and religious, but never the haunted areas of the castle. It remained for me to redis-

Vienna's Imperial Castle. The only ghost actually observed appeared in the old section.

cover these areas, much to the amazement of the castle officials. They had never been told of the haunted areas. The castle was the ancient seat of Austria's

was discontinued and the area became part of the castle. But a ghostly monk has been seen in the area from time to time, walking the dark corridors connecting

Mayerling, former hunting lodge of the murdered Crown Prince Rudolf (now a Carmelite monastery), and the locked door to Rudolf's private apartment at the Imperial Castle, where he and his lady-love Mary Vetsera met frequently.

emperors, and before that of the Holy Roman Emperors. The building goes back to the beginning of the Middle Ages, but there are many additions. The major portion of the "Old Castle" of Vienna came into existence after 1400. The thirteenth- and fourteenth-century wing is called "Schweizerhof," or Swiss court.

Walking up to the second floor of this tract, or portion, of the castle, one finds oneself in an area where the walls are two to three yards thick. Here was a small monastery of the Capuchin friars, for the personal use of members of the Imperial family only. Later this monastery

this ancient portion of the castle with the more modern sections.

A short walk from the Capuchin monastery area of the castle lies a section I have written about and that is connected with the tragedy of Crown Prince Rudolf and his love Mary Vetsera. Rudolf and Mary met at the Imperial Castle time and again. There is a staircase leading up from the first to the second floor, which Mary must have used to gain access to Rudolf's apartment. After the tragedy, in the late 1880s, the stairwell nearby was walled up, the door nailed shut, and a heavy closet moved against it to cover any trace of a connecting link between the two floors at this point. Between the two staircases lies the area where the whitish figure of a woman has been observed by a number of witnesses. This figure

appeared shortly after the tragedy at Mayerling. Apparently, the figure comes up the stairs from the lower floor, glides along the corridor, and disappears toward Rudolf's apartment.

It is not surprising that Mary should still be attracted to this part of the Imperial Castle, where she lived through some of her happiest moments. Mayerling held only tragedy for her. The Imperial Castle is always available to tourists, but to see the areas just described it is perhaps wisest to ask for permission or at least for a guide to come along. One addresses oneself to the administrator of the castle, or "Burghauptmann."

At the spot where the stairs reach the corridor is now a *marterl*, a peculiarly Austrian Madonna encased in glass and

meant to be a miniature shrine for those who wish to pray en route to their destinations. Why the holy picture was placed at this point no one seems to know, but

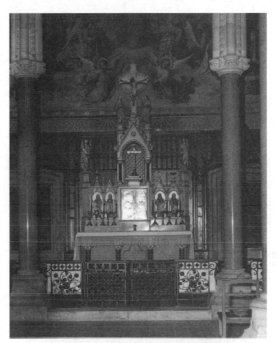

it seems of relatively recent origin and may well be linked up with the tragedy of Mary Vetsera.

Clockwise from upper left:

Until Holzer had it opened, the apartment and door had been locked since the tragedy in 1889.

The altar in the Carmelite monastery where the murders of Rudolf and Mary occurred.

The sacred memorial near the lovers' apartment in the Imperial Castle.

On the spot where Rudolf's bed once stood is now this Madonna.

Those who wish to visit Mayerling as well can do so. One of the photographs taken by me at Mayerling does show a ghostly presence. It is male and may well link up with the death of Crown Prince Rudolf. Whether it is the unhappy prince, or perhaps one of his remorseful murderers, or someone else, is not clear. At any rate, Mayerling is now a Carmelite monastery and can be reached by road in about half an hour from Vienna. It can be visited freely, although there is no one to take one behind the principal chapel. This is hardly necessary, since the chapel represents the heart of the tragedy. Prior to being turned into a chapel, the area was divided into two floors, the lower being the reception hall of what was then a hunting lodge, with the upper story having been the bedroom in which the two lovers died. The emperor Franz Joseph, upon hearing the terrible news, ordered the transformation of his son's hunting lodge into a strict Carmelite monastery.

evidence for psychic healing

P SYCHIC HEALING IS AS OLD AS MANKIND. IT is the treatment of ailments, both physical and mental, by the powers of the spirit, or by forces that man has not yet recognized as being physical in the ordinary sense. Much of the early psychic healing was done mainly by priests or lay priests, and it was thought necessary to surround the application of such healing with a certain mystery to strengthen the patient's belief in it, and thus strengthen his will to get well.

To this day, it makes a great deal of difference whether a sick person trusts his doctor. Faith cannot move mountains, but it can surely rally the body's own defense mechanisms.

In psychic healing, no medicines of any kind are used, and it is not necessary that the patient be a believer for the cure to work. Certainly faith helps   and also strengthens the resistance to disease—but true psychic healing, which is often instantaneous or nearly so, does not require such state of mind on the part of the subject. There are several kinds of what in England is often referred to as "unorthodox healing"—as if there were an orthodox death and an unorthodox one—depending on the method used.

Spiritualism, which is essentially a religion—or a cult, if you wish—calls it *spiritual healing* and claims that God works through the hands of the healer as he touches the body of the patient.

Harry Edwards, who has cured thousands by the mere laying on of hands, falls into this category. Of course, he has had failures, too, but the fact that he has had successes in large numbers is the more remarkable fact. Some traditional physicians like to explain such cures by speaking of unexpected remissions. But many of the diseases that have been helped by healers like Edwards, the Brazilian miracle healer Arrigo, or the latest Philippine psychic surgeons are not the kind that disappear by themselves.

The nonspiritualist healer refers to his craft as psychic healing in that it utilizes some force present in his body to destroy disease in another person's aura and body.

The theory behind this is that when the healer concentrates his psychic energies in his hands and lightly moves them above the affected area of a sick person's body, he "burns out" the diseased portion of the aura or magnetic field. Health energy then rushes in to fill the gap, and the moment the inner body is restored to perfect health, the parallel outer body cannot help but fall in line. The disease clears up almost at once or as fast as the cells can keep pace with the orders from the etheric within.

I know this works and it works principally among people possessed of great magnetism or power of personality—people whose life force seems very strong, so strong that they can spare some of it to heal less fortunate human beings. In a modest sort of way I have been able to heal an aching joint or a headache or two. I merely concentrate my thought energies on the afflicted area and pass gently over it with my hands, without touching it. If the patient responds properly, he will report a hot sensation in the affected part, far beyond the normal bodily warmth emanating from a hand passing an inch away.

Dr. John Myers, the great photography medium, is also a fine healer. I have seen testimonials from people who had been given up by orthodox doctors only to be rescued at death's door by Myers. The energy streaming from him has shrunk tumors and has restored health to a number of people in recent years. Myers reports on this in his writings, but the statements from his cured patients speak even louder. He has never charged a penny for his service.

Another successful practitioner is the London healer Fricker, who runs two clinics around the clock. He has achieved remarkable cures. Fricker is not a spiritualist, but religious in his orientation. He feels that God is working directly through him. Be this as it may, he has cured people who were not helped elsewhere. I have had a session with Fricker for a minor but incurable ear ailment I have had for many years. One session is hard enough to hope for cure, but I did have an odd sensation when he placed his hands over my ears. It was as though a strong electrical current were flowing from them into my head. Great warmth seemed to come from them and I felt relaxed and a bit numb. The ear noises were slightly less loud for a day or two, and then they returned. But something did happen, and I am sure that Fricker would eventually have succeeded if I had been available for more sessions.

Many people who are otherwise not in the least interested in ESP or psychic phenomena may have the gift of healing and not realize it until someone tells them of the strange sensations experienced when their hands were put on them or passed above them. Just like other forms of the extra sense, the power to heal can be increased through use. Once recognized, the gift should be used often.

Fricker was a disbeliever before he went to a healer not long ago. There he was told that he, too, had the gift of healing. Skeptical, he did not do anything about it until an emergency occurred and a girl in his shop became ill. With no doctor on hand, Fricker put his hands on her and she recovered.

Probably the greatest healer of modern times was psychic Edgar Cayce. Several books have been written about this remarkable man. Gina Cerminara's *Many Mansions* and Thomas Sugrue's *There Is a River* are the best of the books about Cayce. Jess Stearn, in his book *The Sleeping Prophet,* also writes with much insight and compassion about the man. The Association for Research and Enlightenment (ARE), which is also referred to as the Cayce Foundation, has a curriculum of lectures in Virginia Beach and at its New York branch dealing not only with Cayce's work as a healing medium, but with his even more remarkable readings of people's past incarnations.

A little-educated photographer by profession, Cayce knew none of the answers to anyone's problems when he was awake. But in trance, ostensibly asleep, he was taken over by experts in medicine who could instantly diagnose a person's illness at a distance, prescribe the proper remedy, and *never fail.*

From these astounding cures by the thousands, Cayce went to predictions about world conditions in the future—one of the less pleasant ones being the destruction of parts of California and New York City.

Cayce's trance statements were all carefully written down by his followers and are available in published form for anyone to study. As for the reincarnation aspects of his work, they may well be as authentic as his other accomplishments, but they are more difficult to prove in the conventional scientific sense.

To give briefly even a rudimentary account of the remarkable powers of Edgar Cayce would be to do an injustice to his memory and the foundation now practicing so much of what he preached, for Cayce was a deeply religious man who

thought that God had given him his unique gift to help the suffering. The facts are readily available for those who wish to study them, but Cayce, unfortunately, is no longer healing the sick.

To heal oneself psychically, one must learn to let go of the outer world so that the inner world may come to the fore and take over, at least temporarily, the functions of life. A broken leg may not be easily healed by psychic energy, but many other ailments can be. In fact, I am convinced that disease is a state of disharmony inflicted on a person either by himself or indirectly by others. Even then, he is to blame for allowing such conditions to persist. Bacteria and viruses exist, but they are always present in the human system. Could it not be that these latent disease causers are impotent while the personality maintains in the body a proper physical, mental, and spiritual balance?

If this delicate balance is upset by wrongful thinking, negative emotions—ranging from fear and anxiety to hatred and destructiveness, from frustration to depression and boredom—the body must fall ill. Conversely, proper thought will restore the state of good health. This brings us to the great question of this age—the art of proper thinking. It is nothing less than the key to happiness, health, and success in all spheres of human life.

A thought is an electromagnetic impulse, a small piece of energy created in the mind (not the brain) of a human being, which carries an image—visual or auditory or an idea. If the thought is merely created for the creator himself ("I was just thinking") the impulse may go out from the mind in every direction and possibly be caught by any receiving mind close enough to catch it. By "close enough" I do not mean only physically close, but also emotionally close.

For example: let us say that you think of a beautiful red rose, because you happen to like red roses. They mean pleasure to you, and thinking of them is a sensation that pleases you. Someone standing next to you might suddenly say, "I like red roses, don't you?" or something to that effect. He may not even be aware that the thought did not originate with him and that he was merely verbalizing something that came drifting into his unconscious. Or again, a loved one far away may suddenly have a thought of red roses while also thinking of you. She may write you about it and on checking the time the idea came to her mind, you will find that it coincides with your original thought about the red roses. This is telepathic communication. It may be possible because of physical or emotional closeness. But without the existence of the thought process, telepathy could not exist. We could not communicate with each other or even with ourselves.

Nothing becomes real until we think it is real. By themselves, objects, or even other people, have no reality for us. They do not exist as far as we are concerned until we formulate a thought of them. At the same time, anything we can express in thought is *real* whether it actually exists in the physical, material sense or not.

This is why, in the thought world into which we all pass after death, life is so much more real than in the material world. Over there, as you think, so you are. If you think you are young and handsome,

that is how you are, not only to yourself, seen through your own etheric eyes, but to others looking at you with theirs.

Thoughts originating in the mind are a true creative process colored by emotional connotations. They are made up of electrically charged molecules that travel outward the moment they are put outward as a "thought." They keep traveling, indefinitely, but on the way gradually lose potency, since radiation from the original thought keeps going out in all directions, and thus ultimately the thought will become weaker and weaker as it travels farther and farther.

If a thought is created and directed specifically at another mind with the desire that the other person receive it, such a thought is much stronger and less likely to stray all over the map. If the receiver is attuned—that is, emotionally fit to receive—thought transfer will take place directly. This may even be successful if the receiver is asleep and the thought is implanted in his unconscious mind. It is clear that the discipline of the sender is most important, and such thought discipline can be attained by proper training and by proper attitudes.

Some scientists still refer to the brain as the seat of *thought creation,* which it assuredly is not. The brain is merely the transformer, the switchboard, and the storing house of thought impulses both sent out and received. It is the mind that operates and controls the brain; the mind is the real place of origin for the thought process. Even animals have minds, for they have as yet not attained our degree of evolution.

It is a moot question whether God created man in one fell swoop or whether man slowly climbed from the monkey state. In either case man is a divine creation, as is all of nature in its miraculous way. Even the intricate biochemical processes that have caused life as we know it are a miracle. To attempt to formulate the exact theological truth is not my purpose. I do know that the power in man is *thought,* and only thought.

Granted that we cannot all be brilliant and that human personality varies greatly, I maintain that any normal, reasonably well-balanced human being can influence his own life by *proper thinking.* Not only can illness be reduced to the natural processes of aging, but healing depends largely on the frame of mind of the one to be healed—not a state of belief, but of optimism in all matters. The trick in self-healing, even in so small a matter as a cold, is to suggest to your own body that it rally and drive out the invaders, function properly, and enjoy the healthy life it is capable of. This power to suggest to your body, even to parts of your body, works. I have seen it work. Verbalizing a problem is no mumbo jumbo. It is a realistic process with tangible results if properly carried out in a positive state of mind. By that I mean that trying it while thinking that it might not work is as bad as not doing it at all. You must be honestly convinced that it will work, and work for you it will.

But cure of many illnesses, especially the large group of *psychosomatic* illnesses—those caused by emotional and mental processes and only exteriorized by the physical body—is merely the beginning of practical use for thought power. In the material world, most people face superiors or business partners of one kind or another at various times in their lives.

To help themselves reach a successful conclusion of such meetings, proper thought images should be set up ahead of time. By thinking that one will bring the other person around to one's own views—be it to do with a sale, employment, partnership, or what have you—one need only set up a thought pattern showing that what one desires has already happened. Then, when the confrontation occurs, quietly repeat the thought while awaiting the outcome. It does not always work, but it works enough to be worth trying. When it fails to work, a contrary thought pattern may be at work in the mind of the other person, stronger than yours and thus able to set your desires aside. But you lose nothing in trying and may gain everything by assuming that it will work.

Words are the key instruments to action. Thoughts are the souls of words. Disciplining your thoughts so that they will always remain in constructive channels is achieved by maintaining a firm grip on your own mind.

Try not to allow negative emotions, such as hatred, destructiveness, envy, jealousy, or depression to enter and clutter a clear mind. They do nothing for you except salve the ego, and ego is nature's way of putting you on guard. When you find yourself feeding the ego with false pride or with self-pity because of failure, it is time to pull back and do some actively constructive thinking instead—for it uses up energy, too, and leads absolutely nowhere.

When you're turned down in some enterprise, beware of feeling: (a) self-pity, (b) hatred for the one who turned you down, or (c) a sense of frustration that you cover by changing the direction of your drive. Instead, analyze why you have failed *this time*, regroup your mental forces, and come back for another day as soon as you can with the firm and unaltered conviction that you will ultimately win.

Fear and anxiety are sure to defeat any project. Fear is the absence of necessary information, and anxiety is the state in which fears are allowed to dominate your life. You, the individual, are fully and solely responsible for bringing them on. Your own faulty thought processes have allowed these bad idea patterns to slip into your healthy mind.

Once you recognize your own guilt in permitting this, you have won half the battle. *Anything you bring on, you can also take away.* Repeat this to yourself a few times and you will realize how quickly you can act. Command your mind to cast out the fearful thoughts and replace them with fresh thoughts of self-assertion and confidence. Then plan again, and this time you may be the winner.

Your own state of mind is as much recognized by those you deal with as if it were written all over your face. Thoughts form a person's atmosphere—the aura that surrounds him, and anyone even slightly sensitive can feel it if he is uncertain or apprehensive. These negative thoughts communicate themselves to the other person and help defeat you. By the same token, positive, confident thoughts of accomplishment also come across between you and the other man and may well help you win him over to your way of thinking.

MIND OVER MATTER - HEALING METHODS

The basic difference between conventional medicine and the various forms of psychic healing has been summed up recently by Dr. William McGarey, a medical doctor who heads the Edgar Cayce Clinic in Phoenix, where treatments according to Cayce are available. "The way Cayce looks at it," McGarey explained to me, "a person is first of all a spiritual being and manifests, through mind, as a material being. The spirit creates and the physical body is the result. But in medicine we think of structure: a man has liver disease, or lung disease. The way Cayce sees it is that one of the forces within the body has become unbalanced with the other forces."

If one is to grasp the significance of seemingly impossible cures, one has to accept the duality of man as the rational basis. A physical body on the outside, but a finer, inner or etheric body underneath, the real *persona*, the soul, if you wish. Psychic healing is always holistic: the entire person is healed, body and etheric body; one without the other cannot be treated.

There are a number of healing processes in currently accepted medical practice. First, there is *psychic healing* proper. Here the healer draws energy from his physical body mainly from the two solar plexus in back of the stomach and at the top of the head, where ganglia of nerves come together. This energy is then channeled through his hands and applied to the *aura* of the patient. A good healer notices a discolored aura (the magnetic field extending somewhat beyond the physical body). Discoloration indicates illness. By placing his energy into the troubled areas of the aural, the healer displaces the diseased particles and momentarily creates a vacuum. Into this vacuum, healthy electrically charged particles rush to fill the gap in the aura, and instant healing is the result, since the physical body must fall in line with its inner, etheric counterpart.

This type of psychic healer—either a man or a woman, sometimes even a youngster, for the gift plays no favorites—rarely touches the patient's skin. The healing takes place at the periphery of the aura, where it is most sensitive. Healing may take place whether the patient believes in it or not. It is a purely mechanical process and its success depends on the healer's ability to draw enough of his life force into his hands to effect the healing. Psychic healers who are spiritualists prefer to attribute their success to the intervention of spirit controls, but I find that some nonspiritualists and even some atheists have remarkable results.

Physical healing, the second kind of unorthodox treatment, consists in the touching of the body in the afflicted areas. This laying on of hands has been practiced by many religions, and even today it is at least symbolically part of church ritual. Although the prime force in this kind of treatment is still the psychic energy of the healer, a positive attitude toward it on the part of the patient is helpful, and when the healer is also a priest or minister, religious faith enters the process to some extent.

Hypnotherapy as a form of psychic healing is a method in which the patient undergoes deep hypnosis so that he or she may effect self-healing. The healer first explores emotional conflicts within the patient, removes them, and replaces them with positive, helpful suggestions. By placing such low-key commands into the unconscious mind of the patient, the hypnotic suggestions help the patient overcome his ailments, using his own psychic energies in the process.

Faith healing is often confused in the public's mind with psychic healing. But it has little in common with it. In faith healing everything depends on three elements. First, the afflicted person must have a religious belief in the power of healing (and intercession of divine forces), the more fanatical the better. Second, the patient must have unlimited confidence in the healer from whom he expects the miracle. Third, a large audience, the larger the better, is a must for the faith healing to succeed.

The late Katherine Kuhlman is a prime example of the acclaimed faith healer. She was a slight, gentle woman whose appearance belied her fervor on the platform. Thousands say they have been cured in her meetings, and thousands more always awaited her appearance in their areas with great eagerness. Mrs. Kuhlman herself disclaimed any healing powers, always putting it forth as a work of God and taking no credit for the cures.

Successful faith healings are not necessarily the result of religious belief alone. In invoking spiritual guidance, the faith healer unleashes within himself psychic forces that are utilized to heal the sick; the expectant state in which the usually desperate patient finds himself, often to the point of hysteria, spurs his own healing powers to higher performance, so the result may be spontaneous cure. It seems to me that the available energies from a religiously oriented crowd, working in unison as it were, would furnish the energies to burn out diseased areas of a person's aura and allow the healthy aura particles to flow in and straighten out the etheric body.

Occasionally, faith healing can work without an audience. Rabbi Friedlander of the Bronx, New York, is a healer of some renown. He is the eleventh generation of a family of Hasidic rabbis that believe in possession and other forms of psychic phenomena. The number of those who have been healed by the "miracle rabbi" include Cecile Diamond, aged fourteen, who suffered from inflammation of the brain. According to physicians, Cecile had only one chance in a hundred of survival. Rabbi Solomon Friedlander saw her in the hospital, placed an amulet in her hand and prayed. The child felt better the following day and left the hospital soon after, completely cured.

Whether this effect is achieved by intellectual means, or by the invocation of divine powers is really beside the point. The fact remains that religious healing works often enough to make it a responsible form of unorthodox healing.

PSYCHIC HEALERS

Probably the world's most famous psychic healer was England's Harry Edwards. Edwards heard the call at a spiritualist séance when he was told by the medium that he should use his gifts for psychic healing. Soon after he developed trance mediumship and realized that he had been chosen as an instrument to manifest healing from the spirit world. He is convinced that his spirit guides are Dr. Louis Pasteur and Lord Lister, but he attributes the essence of his powers to God.

Edwards was a heavy-set, physical type oozing with robust health. Even in his eighties, he worked, assisted by four other healers, Ray and Joan Branch, and George and Olive Burton, and each healer specialized in one particular part of the human body. The majority of Harry Edwards' work was done at a sanctuary at Shere, Surrey, England, where he used the early morning hours to meditate and tune in on the power he would use during the day.

From time to time Edwards undertook mass healing services at London's Albert Hall or Royal Festival Hall, places large enough to hold several thousand people at one time. He welcomed the spotlight of press, radio, and television and had an impressive record of actual healings performed in the glare of precisely such spotlights. Crippled individuals stepped up and explained their affliction to the healer. He then made some passes over them or touched their bodies, at the same time praying for divine assistance. Not infrequently, the healing was instantaneous and the crippled person, unable to walk before, in many instances, walked off the platform briskly—cured. At other times, several consultations or healing sessions were necessary.

One of the first cases Edwards worked on involved a neighbor named Gladys Cudd, a teenager dying of consumption. Edwards placed his hand on her head and asked for healing. At that point he became conscious of a power flow through him. His body felt alive with energy, which flowed down through his arms and from there into the patient. Something within him made him tell the girl's mother that she would be up and well within three days; the physician had told the mother that her daughter was about to die.

That same afternoon, the high fever which she had long been suffering from was gone from the girl. The following day she vomited large quantities of a red substance and started to take food again as if she were not suffering from any deadly disease. Two days later she was up and about, cured. For a while Edwards kept in touch with his patient through absent healing correspondence; then he lost track of her. Over the years she married and raised a family. In 1970 she paid the healer a surprise visit at his shrine in Shere to inform him that she was about to become a healer herself, opening a center for healing the sick in Devonshire, England.

There are far too few outstanding healers in America today, but one of the most unusual healers I have met is Betty Dye, a housewife, living near Atlanta, Georgia. She is mother of several children and the wife of a slight, soft-spoken man who works for one of the major oil companies, and a medium. Not just a woman with a prophetic vision of the world to come—and a fine record of past predictions come true—Betty Dye has the power of spiritual healing. Gradually, as she became more and more aware of her psychic powers, principally through predictions and involvement in various cases of murder or mysterious disappearances, she also developed her powers as a psychic healer. Thus, after much consultation as to the direction her developments should take, and perhaps also influenced by the fact that the spiritualist churches seem to offer protection from the law

enforcement authorities who still look askance at psychics in some parts of the world, Betty Dye became a spiritualist minister and member of the association. However, as Dye herself is fully aware, membership in a spiritualist association does not have anything to do with her ability as a healer. "Please get the idea across very firmly," she told me during one of our meetings in Atlanta, "that healers do not have to be ordained ministers, church deacons, or special ones within the church. They are surely not the only ones God gives the healing power to." To Betty Dye, who comes from a devout Southern Baptist background, the power to heal stems directly from God.

But what about her record?

James Douglas DePass of Atlanta, an author and officer of the local chapter of the Theosophical Society, consulted Betty Dye. In response, Dye went into a state of trance during which one of her controls, who identified himself as a medical doctor in physical life, diagnosed DePass's ailment as being connected to the stomach. Betty Dye had not been told anything about the visitor's problem. Speaking through the medium, but in a voice of his own, the doctor from beyond then placed Dye's hands on DePass's stomach. Whereas DePass had been in continual pain right up to his arrival (he suffered from unexplained stomach trouble and nausea) the pains left immediately after the treatment. He walked out a well man, free from further pain in the days to come.

Betty Dye feels that the power comes directly from her spirit guides and the thoughts and word expressed by her during trance are merely filtered through her as a vehicle. The voice speaking through her at such times is that of a man who has far greater knowledge and vocabulary that she has in her ordinary condition.

Mrs. Floyd Cummings, of East Point, Georgia, came to Dye in a state of abject fear: her doctor had told her she had a growth in her throat, and surgery was necessary. This is how Cummings relates it: "My doctor found a growth in my throat. He made an appointment with a specialist to perform surgery and remove the growth. Before going to the specialist, however, I went to see Betty Dye, and she gave me a treatment. During the treatment I experienced a wonderful feeling of healing, cleansing, and extreme heat coming from the hands of Mrs. Dye while in trance. Several days later I went to the specialist. When he examined my throat, the growth was gone. It has not returned."

Dye is one of perhaps a dozen reputable psychic healers in this country who have been gaining a reputation of helping where conventional medicine can't. But it is the earmark of the reliable psychic healer to have a potential patient get a regular medical checkup first.

I knew John Myers for twenty years before he died in May, 1972. He was one of the great mediums—and great healers—of all time. The cases Myers cured number several hundred, and they are on record.

Perhaps the most outstanding of his cases was also his first important one: Myers' meeting with the American businessman, R. L. Parish, who was suffering from a chronic sciatic condition as well as from near-blindness without hope of cure. He had been sent to Myers as a last resort. Within a few days after Myers' application of healing, the pain from the sciatic nerve had ceased and for the first time in years Parish was also able to see without glasses.

Many years later Mr. Parish's wife was injured in an automobile accident during a snowstorm. In the hospital, she was examined by the family doctor, Donald Richie, M.D. The examination showed multiple bilateral rib fractures, hemorrhaging into the right side of the chest cavity, partial collapse of the right lung, and a fracture of the right shoulder. John Myers, who was then in Mexico, rushed back to New York, to be at the bedside of his friend's wife. He requested fifteen minutes alone with the patient. The second day after the healer's visit, Mrs. Parish was out of bed. On the eleventh day, she left the hospital. Dr. Richie stated at the time that "no medical explanation for a recovery in six days from injuries that would have taken even a young, active person three to four weeks' time can be offered."

Interestingly, Myers was able to heal himself, something few psychic healers can do. In 1957, he suffered a serious hemorrhage and was rushed to Medical Arts Hospital in New York in the middle of the night. His personal physician, Dr. Karl Fischach, examined him and discovered a growth over the right kidney. Several cancer experts examined Myers, and biopsies were taken to determine whether or not the growth was malignant. The unanimous verdict was that an immediate operation was imperative, that any delay might prove to be fatal.

John Myers steadfastly refused, and informed his doctors he would do for himself what he had often done for others.

He remained in the hospital for one week for observation, and concentrated on his own healing. The cancer disappeared at the end of the week, never to return.

The following year, Myers came down with an acute inflammation of the appendix, a condition that can be fatal if not immediately attended to. Again, Myers refused an operation: two hours later, all pain had ceased and an examination revealed that the inflammation had completely disappeared. Myers had his appendix to the end of his long life.

A former musician from Brooklyn seems well on his way to walk in John Myers's footsteps. Dean Kraft does "touch healing" with amazing results, and frequent cures. He works with medical doctors and often goes into hospitals to minister to patients with their doctors' approval.

Kraft discovered his supernormal abilities by accident in November 1972. He was driving home from work when he heard a strange clicking sound and found the doors locked though he had not touched the appropriate buttons. He asked, more as a joke than seriously, if there were spirits present, and to his amazement received an answer in a sort of code of clicks! At the time he was working in a music shop and together with his boss, he perfected this code until he could actually communicate with "them."

One day, he heard the sound of an automobile crash outside the shop. He rushed to the street and found a woman on the pavement who had been badly hurt. Something told him to hold her in his hands until an ambulance came to take her to the hospital. Later, when he drove home, the unseen communicators told him, via the "click code," "Tonight your hands were used for healing." He did not understand the message, but when he checked on the woman's condition, the hospital told him she was on the critical list and would undergo surgery in the morning. Placing a telephone call the next day to find out how she was doing after the surgery, he was shocked to hear she had been discharged. Somehow her injuries had "healed themselves during the early hours of the morning," he was told.

He freely admits he does not always succeed with patients. Half the patients he sees are referred to him by doctors. Frequently, he has a doctor present when he gives treatments. He starts by slightly darkening the room, then proceeds to touch the patient's head and neck gently; during this stage of the treatment, Kraft feels he is "charging up his batteries." The healing takes about five minutes, but afterward Kraft has to rest for a while because it takes a lot of energy out of him, he claims. He has had particular success with psoriasis, tumors, and some forms of cancer, and he likes to do laboratory work to find out more about his amazing powers himself.

These powers have worked seeming miracles at times. There was the time he was called to the North Shore Community Hospital, where a patient was dying of colon cancer. Kraft saw him a couple of times. The man is still alive. He has cured another man who had leukemia; Kraft saw him two days in a row, and saved him. A judge who suffered from an incurable arthritic condition in his knees and back called on Kraft for help. After a few treatments, the pains left the judge and they have never returned.

Kraft insists on checking up on his patients after he treats them, to make sure the cure is permanent. He also teaches his methods, claiming that others can acquire his ability, too. Dr. Michael Smith of Lincoln Hospital, Bronx, New York, has been using Kraft's method successfully. So has neurologist Dr. Gabriel Rubin. Psychiatrist Abraham Weinberg of New York considers psychic healing as demonstrated by Dean Kraft "a valuable adjunct" to medical treatment.

The Israeli healer Ze'ev Kolman might be the greatest paranormal healer of this age. He has cured cancer and heart disease, permanently, and treated people with such serious illnesses as multiple sclerosis and even paralysis. Kolman uses bio-energetic, or "life force" power, by passing his palms over the body of the patient. He has also been quite successful with absent healing via the telephone, in one case curing a woman in Japan with ten long-distance sessions. The exploits of Kolman are well documented with medical reports and laboratory statements, backing up his cures. The true story of Kolman is in my book *The Secret of Healing/The Powers of the Healer Ze'ev Kolman.*

The number of gifted healers among us seem to be on the increase. They come from every imaginable background and from every walk of life. Consider, for example, healer John Scudder, a former aeronautical engineer turned Spiritualist minister, who discovered he had the gift of healing the sick. The list of his successful cases is impressive indeed.

The New York Times of September 5, 1993 reported the work of a registered nurse turned healer, by the name of Judy Wicker, who lives in new York City. Wicker calls herself a metaphysician, but what she really does is healing, using meditation to induce it. Considering that meditation is really a form of self-induced altered state of consciousness, during which energies can be made available for healing purposes more easily, we seem to be dealing with the same energy source all healers use.

Maria Cooper Janis, the daughter of the late Gary Cooper, has for years studied healers and psychics, and is herself a healer with considerable success in "absent healing," and meditation is used to "tune in" on a patient at a distance.

A German man named George Rieder is reported to have "x-ray eyes" which allow him to diagnose a patient by looking at him or her. Rieder claims to have discovered his gift through a spirit guide; he heals the etheric body, not the physical counterpart, which then falls in line with it. Cancer, even AIDS, are illnesses he has dealt with and is willing to deal with. Reider ran into trouble in Austria, where the local medical association accused him of quackery: but the healer had ample proof that he had indeed been successful in the treatment of cancer patients and the matter was dropped.

It is important to know how healing works, and the various forms it takes, because physicians are by no means the only ones who can help the sick. Many ordinary people who are psychic also possess psychic healing powers, and use them. This should be encouraged so long as there is a balance between conventional medical checkups and healing. Use the best of both worlds!

THIRTEEN
reincarnation and past lives

ONE OF THE MOST DIFFICULT TASKS IN parapsychology is to be able to differentiate between a psychic experience and true *reincarnation memories*. With seemingly highly evidential cases pointing to reincarnation as the only explanation, there is still the possibility that this knowledge comes not from the person's own former-life memory, but from another person whose communication from the Other Side is the true source of that knowledge.

From my own experience and the large number of cases I have personally investigated over the years, I have learned that reincarnation memories usually (but not exclusively) occur in people who possess no psychic abilities whatever either prior to the reincarnation memory, or after having realized it. But there are exceptions; it is possible for psychic persons, whether amateur or professional medium, to have reincarnation memories separate from their psychic gifts—but this is rare. The majority of my verified reincarnation cases involve people without any psychic abilities or interest in the subject.

In the Orient, reincarnation is much more accepted as a matter of fact because so many Eastern religions have incorporated this concept into their dogma. There are also passages in the Christian teachings that hint at reincarnation, and the question of whether Christ is the reincarnated prophet Elijah is only an extension of the older Hebrew idea that Elijah might be Moses come back to earth. In Tibet, the idea of reincarnation has also been a practical way of government. The Dalai Lama is always reincarnated in a child, and it is the often difficult job of the priests to locate the child into which the previous Dalai Lama has chosen to reincarnate. By delicate signs, and perhaps guided by the discarnate one himself—though that would indicate he isn't reincarnated after all—they do manage to find a young successor and groom him for priesthood.

In some African societies, the reincarnated spirits of the ancestors also play major roles in government. This concept can be found in the native Haitian religion called voodoo, which is nothing like the popular conception—or rather, misconception—of it.

In America, I have found two basically honest approaches to reincarnation. One is the painstaking and very difficult approach that includes verification. To my mind, this is the only valid approach if it is proof that we want and not wishful thinking. The other, which is unfortunately far more popular, is uncritical, wallowing in fanciful worlds that may well have existed, for I can no more prove that they *didn't* than the believers can prove that they did or do. I am speaking of the past-life readings that certain mediums will do for anyone willing to pay the price of their "research." The only life readings perhaps having some basis in fact are those undertaken by the renowned psychic Edgar Cayce. The reason I feel this way about life readings, all nicely recorded at the Virginia Beach Headquarters of the Association for Research and Enlightenment, is that other aspects of Cayce's mediumship have been proved to be accurate and truly outstanding.

But there are readers who will tell you that you were so-and-so in ancient Egypt or some other fanciful clime. Very rarely were you a commoner. Not infrequently did you consort with Cleo herself, or with other well-known historical figures. Ah, and the reason you are attracted to your present mate is that you were wed once before, some centuries ago. The strange thing is that all this may be perfectly true, and certainly, this type of material may be verifiable if the proper safeguards are used. If the reader has no access to such information and appears to be less than an Egyptologist, and if the said reader comes up with names and events that are checked out later and found to be correct, we would at least have some corroboration that such people and events actually existed.

It still remains to find proof for a link between them and the subject of the life reading. I am not attacking the idea of tracing back evidence for reincarnation. In fact, I am in favor of a concerted effort in this direction. But I am against unproven or unprovable information being sold to gullible people who then enjoy the luxury of an ancient tradition without benefit or proof. Only when something turns up that is not readily accessible to the medium and is independently corroborated do we have a genuine case for reincarnation. Such a case was reported from London by Reuters:

An Indian expert on the supernatural today meets little twin sisters who, parents believe, have returned from the dead.

He is Hemendra Banerjee, director of the Department of Parapsychology at Rajasthan, whose work for twelve years has centered on the theory of reincarnation—rebirth.

Banerjee will meet seven-year-old twins Jennifer and Gillian Pollack, whose parents believe they are reincarnations of their two previous children, Jacqueline, six, and Joanne, 11, who died in a road accident eight years ago.

Jennifer and Gillian carry a scar and birthmark in identical spots to similar marks on the dead children.

The parents claim they have heard the twins discussing details of the fatal crash—which happened before they were born.

Their handwriting, speech and mannerisms are similar to the dead children, Mr. and Mrs. Pollock claim.

In an earlier case in his native India, Professor H. N. Banerjee reports the amazing story of a boy, Munesh, who seemed to have memory of a man who lived and died in the village of Itarni. He was tested by parapsychologists, who concluded that they had a genuine case of, as they like to call it, extra-cerebral memory. In an article in the May 1966 issue of *Fate* magazine, Banerjee gives a full account of the boy's experiences and his ability to lead researchers to his former home, recognize relatives of his previous incarnation, and otherwise prove beyond the shadow of a doubt that he was the man who died of a fever in 1951.

In essence, the boy claimed to be the reincarnated Bhajan Singh, and finally his parents agreed to test the claim by bringing him to the dead man's family. If a wife could not recognize her own husband—even reborn in a little boy—then who could? Fearful of an imposter, the widow drew the boy aside. "Let me know some specific event in our life so that I may believe that you are my husband reborn," she said. Without hesitating, Munesh replied, "When I returned to Itarni after taking my intermediate examination in Agra, I found a quarrel had taken place between you and my mother.

I beat you with the churning stick that broke and cut your arm."

He also told the astonished widow, Ayodhya Devi, of intimate conjugal affairs, which in India are strongly secret between husband and wife. Hearing of these things that no one else could have known, she was convinced and asked that the child go with them to Itarni. Finding the proper house without difficulty or hesitation, the boy astonished the two families even further by the uncanny way in which he was able to recognize people and conditions, although he had never been there or met them before.

Munesh then walked around the house and farm, recalling incidents and things he remembered vividly. He took all the curious people to the attic, an unusual feature for a house in Itarni, telling them eagerly that it had been his room, that here he had taken his wife the day they were married, and here, at the age of twenty-one, he had breathed his last breath. On the way to the room where Bhajan Singh had kept his books, the boy asked his "wife," "Where is the sari I bought you from Agra?" Ayodhya Devi was startled. No one else had known about it.

The number of such cases is not as large as, say, the number of plausible ghost cases, and by "plausible," I mean recent, observed by competent witnesses, and properly researched by people qualified to do so. That the number of hauntings meeting these standards is very large we will see later on.

Reincarnation material is not as spectacular and consequently does not command as much attention as the appearance of a ghost. My position is the same here as in the case of so-called unidentified flying objects. If 90 percent of all reports have ordinary explanations and 10 percent don't that is 10 percent too many for comfort. If only a handful of solidly substantiated cases of reincarnation exist where no alternate explanation is possible we have a scientific case for its existence. It is on this basis, I believe, that Dr. Stevenson has been able to proceed, and though he must be regarded as something of a specialist in this field, he is not the only one delving into it on a serious scientific basis.

The cases of recognition and verification are by no means happening only in India, traditionally a country friendly to the idea of karma and rebirth. They have happened in England, where a child vividly recalled freezing to death with her father in a hut in the country. The facts bore this out, yet the child could not have known them. They are happening elsewhere, too. The question arises of whether we can always separate legitimate evidence for reincarnation from, say, a child's psychic ability, or the use of a young person by a discarnate entity to express unfulfilled desires. If possession of the body and speech apparatus by a person who has died would be the explanation, the child would show evidence of deep trance. But all the reports I have read on veridical reincarnation show nothing of the kind. The child is fully awake and normal—except for the insistence that he or she is someone else.

One classical case involved a young girl in India, who was born almost at the exact moment a charwoman died in far-off Spain. When the child reached the age of speech, she insisted that she was a Spanish charwoman and had to be about her job. A name was given, and eventually the case was investigated and traced back to Spain, where the identity of the newly born woman was established. What is more, the child never became normal in the ordinary sense but continued the life and memories of her former existence!

Sometimes the memory of a previous existence is not as clear-cut as one would like. If the philosophies of the East are correct, it is not supposed to be a clear memory. The whole concept of karma postulates the fresh start from incarnation to incarnation until the soul has reached a satisfactory level of consciousness, when no further return to a bodily existence is necessary. During each incarnation, certain experiences are undergone and the person is tested for either advancement up the ladder of spiritual development or down toward a more earthbound existence. This is the basic structure of the Eastern belief in reincarnation. It is not a scientific fact at all, but no one can prove that it is fallacious, either.

Memories of one incarnation, one life, are supposed to be wiped out completely prior to commencement of the next journey in the body, but there seem to be a limited number of cases where the system does not work too well. Nature is basically perfect, but as we will see with ghosts, deviations from the norm do crop up. There is a much larger number of experiences generally classified as *déjà vu* experiences by orthodox psychiatry. It is the uncanny feeling of having been there before or, upon meeting a stranger for the first time, getting the impression that you have met him before, somewhere, sometime, but do not know where or when.

There is hardly a person alive who has not had this sensation at one time or another in a vague sort of way. Again, orthodox psychiatry has explained this as opening the wrong memory door in one's consciousness. It tells us that in these cases, we press the wrong button. Instead of pushing the button marked "never saw him before," we press the one marked "I've met him before." But psychiatry does not tell us why we do this, or how. Since the reaction is practically instantaneous, I venture to say it is not up to us to press anything at all. Rather, the radiation, or whatever, emanating from the stranger instantly brings back something from our unconscious past. If this is so, it may well be that we have all been reincarnated, perhaps more than once, but cannot recall these vestigial memories beyond an automatic reaction when something or someone out of a past life pops up in our present one. That's about all The Law allows us to know about past lives. This is the reincarnation view and it may well be correct, although we must probe much deeper into this comparatively new field of inquiry before reaching conclusions.

On the other hand, there are numerous cases on record where a person will suddenly see and hear a scene take place in his conscious life that he knows, at that instant, he has seen and heard before. Parapsychologists offer an alternate explanation to reincarnation in such cases. They feel that the subject has had a precognitive experience, either in the dream state or in the waking state, but so

quickly that he has instantly forgotten the impression. When the experience takes place in reality, he suddenly remembers having seen it sometime before, and it all comes back to him. In most cases, we cannot prove that the subject had such a psychic impression, a premonition, or other precognitive experience, because he neglected to write it down, or to report it to a competent witness. Quite naturally so, since he did not pay attention to it at the time it occurred—if it occurred.

Barry Bingham, a distinguished newspaper editor, was for some years at the helm of the *Louisville Courier-Journal & Times*. He put his own *déjà vu* experiences into an article that he published in his newspaper on September 1, 1963. I met Bingham through Lord Christopher Thynne, son of the Marquess of Bath, when I visited Longleat in quest of ghosts a few years ago. Bingham had had interest in psychic matters for some time, but there is nothing like a first-hand experience:

"Several times in my life, I have had a curious and arresting experience. I have felt that everything I was seeing and hearing had been seen and heard before, and that I knew exactly what was going to happen next. My own most memorable experience with *déjà vu* occurred a good many years ago, but I recall it with abnormal exactness. I had had at that time a recurrent dream over a period of several months. In it, I found myself approaching a very tall and beautiful building that stood in an open space of green grass. The scene was always bathed in the serene light of a morning that follows a rainy night, when the world looks newly washed and limpidly pure. I knew, in the way we know things in dreams, that the earth had just undergone some vast cataclysm, and that the band of people I was about to join were the sole survivors of the human race come together to make a plan for the future. The men and women I saw as I neared them were not familiar to me. They were not sad, or ill, or distraught, but wrapped in a kind of mute ecstasy as they moved toward the majestic doors of the edifice.

"Then one day, I found myself in front of Salisbury Cathedral in England for the first time in my life. Suddenly, I stood stock-still to breathe. This ancient church, waiting for me so quietly in its setting of dewy greensward, was the building of my dream in every detail. I knew the soaring line of the spires, the intricate carving of the doorway, the very feel of the stones under my feet. It was as though I had spent year upon year of my life in that very spot. Stumbling into the church, still dazed and awed by my experience, I moved up the aisle and sat down for a moment to rest and gather my wits. As I raised my eyes, I saw directly before me the cenotaph of Robert Bingham, a remote collateral ancestor of whom I had read. He was the bishop of that see for seventeen years. He was the man who passed across that very spot of ground, over and over again each day. He was the man who knew that scene, so new to outward experience, as he knew the palm of his own hand. But Bishop Bingham died in 1246, and was laid to his rest seven long centuries ago."

This case is particularly interesting, as it offers two possible avenues of explanation. Since an ancestor of the subject is involved, could this not be a matter of *psychic communication,* or was Barry

Bingham actually a person living at the time of the event he experienced, perhaps even his own ancestor? We can only state that Bingham has had an extraordinary psychic experience. I was at Salisbury in the summer of 1966 because of this experience and also because someone else had managed to photograph what appears to be a ghostly manifestation in the old church. Since I have no emotional ties to Salisbury, nothing unusual was felt by me. But I have been to the Scottish Highlands and felt terribly sure I have lived there before. No facts, just a feeling.

So it goes with *déjà vu.* You cannot always pin it down, but to dismiss it lightly is like closing the door on what I consider one of the most intriguing chapters in the history of man. I often hear from people with these "having-been-there-before" experiences, and I am always eager to follow up on them so that some day we may safely link the living with their former incarnations to a point where science will accept the evidence as true.

Mrs. Frank lives in Macon, Georgia, with her husband. On a European trip by the couple as part of a group tour, they found themselves in Florence, Italy, for the first time. Suddenly, Mrs. Frank broke away from the group and insisted on walking through an elaborate iron gate of a palazzo across the street they were on. Nothing could stop her, and, for that matter, Mrs. Frank later described her experience as one of utter compulsion to enter that house at all cost, because she once lived there in another lifetime. Having done so, her emotions becalmed themselves and she returned once more to the others. Apparently there had been the need for her to acknowledge and be aware of her previous existence. The question remains, what made her come to that house, to Florence, in the first place?

The cases I am responsible for are all from the West, which disproves a popularly held belief that reincarnation is something only people in the East accept as true.

The case of Pamela Wollenberg—a young girl from upstate Illinois who had recurrent dreams about Scotland in the year 1600 and two names that she did not understand at all, Ruthven and Gowrie, and the words "I lept"—I have always considered my best case, proving the validity of reincarnation for everyone though only some can recall prior lives.

Wollenberg's case, which I investigated for many months, including using hypnotic regression and local research in Scotland, led to a plethora of detailed information about a person in the Scotland of 1600 of whom she could not possibly have known. The Ruthven family name was linked to the Gowrie name as part of the family name, and the year 1600 was the date when the two Gowrie brothers had been involved in a conspiracy to kidnap the young king James VI. The lady Gowrie had "leaped" from one tower of the castle to another, to escape her mother's pursuit when a young man had shared her chamber that night. None of this material was easily found by me and none of it would have been accessible to Wollenberg.

I have since realized that detailed and evidential reincarnation material does surface only when the prior life had been violently terminated or in some manner cut short or unfulfilled. When I taped a pilot for a proposed television program in Cleveland some years ago, a group practicing "suggestive regression" under the control and guidance of a professional esoteric group leader caught my attention and we proceeded to watch a session. Each of the dozen or so participants, all of them women, went into a meditative state first, presumably to tap their deeper levels of consciousness including past-life memories. Each in turn spoke up and told me who they had been before. At least two of the women were sure they had been Egyptians, but the young woman who assured me that she was Isadora Duncan in a previous life, and the Queen of Sheba, Solomon's lover, in the person of a Cleveland housewife, particularly interested me. I realized that it was her harmless fantasy, and knew of at least two other Isadora Duncans in other cities myself, so I did not even attempt a serious investigation. But what little I saw and heard made it clear to me that these two nice women did not know the personalities they claimed to have been in a previous life very well at all.

People who wish to believe that they lived before as people markedly different from (and probably more interesting than) their present circumstances are welcome to their dreams. Where I feel less charitable is when I am confronted by an increasing number of casual practitioners giving past-life readings at a price. None of them uses professional hypnotic regression to see whether there is any memory of a possible previous incarnation; they prefer to do their readings intuitively and generally in terms that are incapable of verification in books or records. A particularly crass case dealt with a woman who had been complaining of pains in her wrists and feet. She had not been able to get a medical explanation that satisfied her (such as arthritis or rheumatism or tension) but met a young woman who had the right answer, apparently: those pains were due to crucifixion at the time of Jesus! With that, the pains seemed to cease, or at least, recede, from the patient's attention.

PAST-LIFE READERS AND OTHER FADS

Dr. William Yaney, an eminent psychiatrist in Beverly Hills, California, who includes reincarnation trauma in his treatment of patients, with the help of a good trance medium as his assistant, told one male patient that the terrible pains in his legs were due to his having lost his legs in another lifetime. The patient accepted the explanation, and learned to live with his problem. But unless there are specific data, such as names, dates, and places given, the past-life material, even when it turns out to be beneficial to the patient, is rarely more than just another psychological trick.

Past lives are sometimes blamed for something done in this life that would otherwise be socially unacceptable. A publisher of esoteric materials and tapes of renown divorced his wife when he met another young woman he fancied immediately; they had been together in another lifetime, and needed to resume in this one!

What is one to do to avoid being taken in by past-life readers, who may well believe fully in their work and its

authenticity? There aren't that many conscious frauds among them, but quite a few self-deluded people, and even they, on occasion, help a client, though not in the way they think. On the other hand, if an honest quest for truth is what you are looking for, certain precautions in dealing with such practitioners are inevitable. To begin with, never talk about yourself or what you think you were in a prior life. Don't answer questions by the reader along these lines, either. If the reader tells you of an existence in another life, insist on details: when, where, what name. Chances are, the reader will do one of two things: make them up to sound substantial; or tell you, sorry, I don't get those details. Either way, take everything you are told with a big grain of salt.

Acceptable past-life evidence is always possible. But in all the years of my practice in parapsychology, I have found that such material is almost never searched out deliberately in the hope of finding something. Instead, the signs suggesting that regressive hypnosis might have positive results must be present before this ought to be undertaken, and done by a professionally trained person, not a housewife or saleswoman turned past-life reader by her own volition. These signs are possible recurrent dreams that are well recalled on awakening; extended *déjà vu* experiences in a place the percipient has not been before and that contain particulars regarding the previous connection; and knowledge or ability in a field not acquired consciously in this lifetime, such as a foreign language, or technical knowledge, or "memories" of places and situations one is not familiar with in normal life, and has had no access to through books, newspapers, television, and so on.

If you observe these signposts carefully, pursuing the quest for evidence of past lives can be stimulating and worthwhile. We all have lived before, but the majority do not have conscious knowledge of it in this lifetime. Those who do, or are able to recall under regression, are nearly always people whose previous lives came to abrupt or violent ends, at least as far as my own records show. It appears that we all reincarnate, but each case is different as to the periods in between lives, and the frequency of return. While we all come back to other lives, only those whose lives had been somehow irregular seem to get a sort of bonus in memory, by being able to recall snatches of their past lives, either directly, through recurrent dreams, or through hypnotic regression.

For one person to "see" the past lives of another is strictly a psychic ability and does not necessarily involve the person in some sort of joint reincarnation memory. A popular notion persists that people reincarnate together in groups, sometimes changing social positions in the process as a matter of learning spiritual values, but the evidence for group reincarnation does not seem to be strong and not as scientifically evidential as is the material on the basic facts of the validity of reincarnation. I should also add that no evidence whatever points toward the notion of transmigration that humans have lived before as animals, which is part of East Indian belief systems.

Certain paranormal practices or beliefs occur in cycles. After World War I, the bereaved frequented spiritualist séances in droves, in the hopes that their loved ones would talk with them from the Great Beyond. And sometimes, they did. Fraud was easily detected if the alleged communicator could not be properly identified by the relative or friend at the séances. To this day, a certain amount of material coming through in spiritualist churches is valid. The proof lies always in the specific nature of the material or message, and if only generalities are obtained, buyer beware.

Channelling is another fad that has come about of late and is still with us, though some of the people purporting to practice it haven't the vaguest idea of what it is. Until a few years ago, channeling meant very little to the average esoteric seeker, and nothing at all to the uncommitted outsider. There is a human condition commonly called "trance mediumship," or dissociation of personality. In this condition, an alleged exterior or foreign personality uses the physical body, the "apparatus" of a medium, to speak with the living.

Depending on exact and individual circumstances, such as background, education of the medium, test conditions, and supervision of the experiment, this material will be regarded as veridical or not. Among researchers are those who reject any notion, regardless of evidence pointing in that direction. Other researchers, including myself, interpret the authenticity of such phenomena strictly on the basis of results: if the material obtained through a trance medium is accurate in terms of later verification, unknown or inaccessible to the medium at the time of the experiment, and sufficiently precise and detailed, any reasonable researcher will accept it as prima facie evidence in the absence of any strong evidence to the contrary.

Trance mediums are rare; why, I don't know, except that perhaps because the work seems to be strenuous in physical terms. No one who has worked for many years with "physical mediums" (which includes trance mediums as well as that even rarer phenomenon, ectoplastic manifestations) will doubt that the medium undergoes extreme stress while working, and no actress can fake what transpires in front of the experienced researcher.

Then along came the channelers. On the surface they looked and acted like trance mediums. They closed their eyes or rolled them dramatically before going into their particular state. Shortly thereafter a voice pretending to be someone other than the channeler would speak to the audience or client.

With a trance medium, any researcher worth his scientific salt will demand identification of the alleged communicator. Usually, he gets it fairly quickly, if only in halting sentences. The researcher will then proceed to have a dialogue with the spirit entity, using the trance medium as a kind of telephone, and elicit as much detailed and personal information as he is able to, in order to verify it later on. Not so with the channeler: attempts at questioning these "entities" as to personal background, or even real names, either lead to platitudes about the high level of their mission, or fantasy names and circumstances that cannot be verified, or if they sound as if they might be capable of scientific verification, and this is attempted, they will invariably turn out to be incapable of being traced in any known records.

What makes the channeler run is twofold: on the one hand, an eager audience of followers supplies energies feeding the ego (and often also money); on the other hand, an otherwise ordinary personality uses deeper levels of consciousness to act out fantasies satisfying an otherwise neglected craving within that personality. Some conventional psychiatrists and psychologists will dismiss the channeling phenomenon, along with older, more religiously tinged "speaking in tongues" as merely an aberration of the mind. One can scarcely blame them, since their medical training has never allowed the postulation of the spirit component in human life. As Otto Sauerbruch, a German surgeon, stated years ago, "I cut up a body, and I don't find the spirit, ergo, there is no spirit."

There is an enormous body of evidence in the annals of reputable research societies that human personality does survive the dissolution of the *physical body*—the outer shell, as it were. The channeler couldn't care less about scientists or scientific evidence. In metaphysics, belief is everything, after all. Channeling has become not only big business, including not only in-person seminars where the faithful gather, at a stiff price, and are allowed to partake of the often questionable pearls of wisdom dropping from the lips of their channeler, but also audiotapes, books, magazines, and more seminars, where people seek the counsel of the channeling entity in solving their personal problems.

Perhaps the kingpin of them all is a crafty lady using the name J. Z. Knight and claiming to be the spokeswoman (channel) for one Ramtha, whom she has characterized as a native of India who "lived 35,000 years ago." Anyone familiar with Indo-Germanic language roots will know that the name Ramtha (really, Ramatha) could not have existed 35,000 years ago, as the people whose language may have contained that term were still unborn in what some 15,000 to 20,000 years *later* became known as the Pamir plateau, north of India. Much of the style used by Knight in her "Ramtha" personality reminds one of Edgar Cayce, the granddaddy of trance communication, whom dozens of would-be mediums have claimed as their inspiration, if not actual communicator. And just as with the Cayce material, eager groups of followers are gathering all these readings and trying to interpret them in such a way that they present a new, world-shaking approach to life. Nothing could be further from the truth. Any fairly intelligent person, with a smattering of psychology and religious orientation, could come up with similar advice. You don't have to be 35,000 years old to do it.

But let us assume for the moment that there really was an entity, a real person long deceased, speaking through Knight, as some of the so-called guides do with many reputable trance mediums. Would it not be sensible to establish that we are hearing from an "enlightened one", (as Ramtha repeatedly calls himself), who actually lived at one time in a place on this planet? If we can't find his name listed in a directory, could he not enlighten us with specific detailed knowledge? Assuming for the moment that some illustrious historical figures chose to

manifest through a channeler, would it not be likely that their personalities, their characters, their styles would somehow come through, even if it is in English?

I recall one of my earliest cases, when the late medium and researcher Eileen Garrett accompanied me and *Daily News* columnist Danton Walker to his pre-Revolutionary house in the Ramapo hills. There Eileen slipped into a deep trance and became the vehicle for a badly wounded, suffering soldier of Polish origin who told us his terrible story, haltingly and piecemeal, including his name and the people he had been with. The authenticity of this voice was incredible: the name and circumstances also checked out. More recently, the clairvoyant and trance medium Yolana Lassaw, who often works with police on unsolved crimes, accompanied a detective of the New York Police and me to the site of a grisly murder that had not been solved. In sudden, deep trance, Yolana, who knew absolutely nothing of the case or where we had taken her, spoke with the voice of the actual victim, pointing the finger at one of the suspects the police needed more information on!

Anyone with a gift for turning a clever phrase can claim to be channeling some exotic long-ago personality or "Master." Not every "ascended master" is a figment of the imagination. But *some kind of evidence* should be required before accepting the communication as genuine and as something external to the channeler or medium. Years ago, Ethel Johnson Meyers, one of the finest trance mediums we have had in America, who had worked with me on dozens of hauntings and brought through amazing evidence of a detailed nature, fell into a deep trance during one of our many sittings. It so happened that astrologer Charles Jayne was present. A personality not at all sounding like Ethel spoke through her, greeting the astrologer and engaging in an hour's worth of technical conversation about the exact position and orbits of certain planets, including ones not yet discovered in our solar system. That had been Jayne's specialty, and after the session was over, he went ahead and verified the material given him by the communicator, who had freely given his name, Kamaraya, and the approximate time of his life on earth. Even that name is correct for the period and country of origin, something the medium would scarcely have known; her training was in music.

The alleged communicator from the "Great Beyond" should identify himself in some manner subject to verification, if not by individual name, then by authentic knowledge of the period and place claimed by the communicators.

It is possible that some of the channeled pseudo-wisdom is helpful to people listening. Dianetics and EST, though widely attacked as highly questionable, may have helped some people with problems. But the occasional benefits of channeling in some cases where the material fits a preexisting need that the participant does not want to address in a more conventional manner should not be misinterpreted as validating the method employed here. True deep trance is a psychic phenomenon that in the right hands can be very helpful both as a scientific tool of inquiry into the nature of man, and as a vital link between our world and the next one. Channelers are not part of this.

Next to channeling, "past lives" is very popular right now, and again we have both the real and the patently imaginary. I have hypnotically regressed dozens of subjects when recurrent dreams or genuine *déjà vu* experiences seemed to suggest there might be unresolved issues from the past and often found evidential material through this process, which only works when there is residue because of unfinished business, sudden death, or some other unusual situation in a past existence. It does not work at all as a way of finding out who you were before, just so you can tell your friends.

Jerry Lee, a psychic, also does past-life work in this simplistic manner, but the odd thing is, people get satisfaction from such unsubstantiated bits of information about themselves in previous lives. Often, the past-life practitioner is a good psychic and picks up information about a client in that way, but rarely are there names, dates, or other details furnished that can be substantiated in the usual and proper research way.

Naturally, I am always curious about my own past lives—after all, there might be an explanation of why I am having so many problems in this one! To test this, I will gladly allow practitioners to try to get me that valuable information. Once, when I was in Hollywood, I met psychic Kebrina Kinkaid, who was as pretty to look at as she was successful in telling people about their past lives. She came to see me and told me to visualize a door, then open that door (in my mind) and tell her what I saw. She wasn't about to tell me what my past lives were and I was really disappointed, but decided to do as told. I described a fanciful life in medieval

Florence, and she assured me that that was true. Naturally, I had made it all up.

Reincarnation and past lives are too important an element in our understanding of our existence in this world to be trifled with. The sooner the lines are drawn between what is proper scientific evidence (and it exists) and fashionable and often irresponsible make-believe, the better.

319

psychic tools: ouija boards, tarot cards, and crystal balls

Once the province of gypsy fortune-tellers, crystal balls are actually concentration tools allowing a psychic to exteriorize visions; there is even a technical term for it, *scrying*. Ouija boards have become avail able in toy stores and novelty catalogs, and the tarot deck can be ordered from a fully illustrated catalog of at least fifty different kinds of cards.

But how do these tools relate to the psychic ability? Probably one of the most common questions asked of me is what I think of ouija boards. More people seem to be using them these days than ever before, and their numbers definitely are far greater than the tarot-card decks or crystal balls in use at the present time among occult aficionados.

A ouija board is nothing more than a flat piece of wood, square, rectangular, or circular, upon which the alphabet, numerals one to nine, and the words "yes," "no," and "maybe" have been written. In conjunction with the board, people use a pointer made from plastic materials or wood. The pointer is large enough to place two hands upon. Some variations of this instrument have a pencil stuck through them. The *planchette* is an older version of the ouija board and was popular in the late nineteenth century. It, too, relies upon the movement of a pointer guided by at least one hand.

The term "ouija" is nothing more than a combination of the words *oui* and *ja*, which mean "yes" in French and German, respectively, and it refers to the two prominent questions asked of the alleged operator of the board as to certain personal problems, yes or no. The board has no special properties. Neither has the pointer. When one or more persons, preferably two, operate the pointer placed upon the board, electromagnetic energies flow from the bodies of the users into the board. Not unlike the membrane of a telephone, the energy then produces certain results. It may be, as with table tipping, crackling sounds due to the static electrical energy present or, more frequently, it may move the pointer about the board. Those who scoff at all psychic communications hold that the pointer is being moved across the board by the hands of those who operate the gadget. This is true, but the impetus for the movement may come from other sources.

It is my conviction that in the majority of cases the unconscious mind of the person operating the pointer is responsible for the information obtained from it. This does not make the operation fraudulent by any means, but it does make it a simple extension tool of natural ESP. In a small number of cases external entities seem to be working through the hands of those who operate the pointer. The proof lies in the information obtained in these cases, which was found to be alien to the people working the board or to anyone else in the vicinity, and was of such a precise nature that it could not be attributed to guesswork or coincidence, yet was independently verified afterward.

Sometimes people with genuine hauntings in their houses attempt to find out what the cause of the phenomena is. They purchase a ouija board and try to make contact with the "hung-up" entity in the house. This is not recommended because a ghost, if genuine, is in no position to correspond rationally with the owner of the house, especially as he may be in conflict with the owner. Frequently unintelligible material, even words without meaning, comes through the ouija board.

Some people have attributed these utterances to elementals or mentally incompetent spirits. More likely they are attempts by the unconscious of the sitter to exteriorize some undeveloped ideas. It should be remembered that the unconscious mind is free of all logical constraint and is sometimes childish, even immoral, and capable of extemporizing material even in invented languages. The ouija board has been used widely by people in need of personal guidance in lieu of consulting the nearest astrologer or fortune-teller. Again, if answers received through this means could be known to the person asking the questions at the time, we must attribute them to the "tapping of the unconscious" of the sitter or sitters. There is nothing wrong with that, and information may be gleaned in this manner that is ordinarily hidden in the person or persons involved. In this way, the board helps unlock deeply felt emotions or information.

But the ouija board is not a toy. I find the idea that this instrument is being sold in large quantities to children and young people, and for that matter, to older people as well, objectionable. I find it unhealthy because it suggests that communication with the dead is a nice game that should be played by everyone. I find it unacceptable because there are occasional incidents involving a ouija board that are filled with danger. Should an operator be capable of deep-trance mediumship and not be aware of it, if he uses a ouija board, he may well trigger the latent mediumship in himself. As a result, unwanted entities may take over, and if the person involved is not familiar with the techniques of controlling such invasions, all kinds of psychotic states may result.

While this is a rare possibility, it has nevertheless occurred. I spent several years assisting a New York woman, the wife of a prominent publisher, who had used the ouija board as a lark while on vacation with relatives. More to please her aged aunt and companion than out of any belief that it would really work, my friend found herself taken over by an unscrupulous and evil entity. It turned out that she had somehow been contacted by the departed spirit of a murderer who had found an entry wedge at that time and at that place into the physical world through the mediumship of my friend. Because of this careless "parlor game," my friend was possessed by this and other entities drawn to her, and her involuntary mediumship continued for a long time after. As a matter of fact, there had been latent traces of alcoholism, which, together with the overpowering influences of negative personalities, were too much for her frail personality. I cannot condone the indiscriminatory advertising of ouija boards without precautionary instructions, at the least; in particular, I find it offensive when mentalists, that is, stage entertainers, advertise such devices as harmless, when they may not be.

As for veridical material obtained through the use of the ouija board, this occurs occasionally also, and would probably occur by any other means of mediumship as well. The board is merely one of several devices that induces this state of consciousness and should not be confused with any kind of channel or actual probing device. Several years ago I sat with medium Ethel Johnson Meyers on her insistence that we try our hands at a ouija board, which at that time I looked at with jaundiced eyes. During that particular session a personality claiming to be a deceased soldier who had parachuted to his death in the Philippines during

World War II manifested itself and gave the name of his parents and the circumstances of his death. To my surprise, I discovered that he had had parents where he had indicated and the communication was apparently genuine. This was even more surprising as neither Meyers nor I had any knowledge of the person beforehand and there seemed to be no particular significance for his "coming through" to us except that we had opened a channel of communication for him.

John H. Steinmeyer, Jr., is an underwriter for a large life insurance company, holds a degree in economics and sociology with a minor in chemistry and biology, and has spent many years selling scientific apparatus to university medical research laboratories. He has had a marked interest in parapsychology for many years and might have followed it professionally if he had had the chance. Among other experimental attempts, he has devoted many hours to the ouija board, together with his wife and other combinations of about thirty persons during one year. Significant results were obtained only when his wife and he operated the board together. He submits a particularly interesting example in his report to me:

"My cousin Harry Classen, whom I rarely see, since he lives in Atlanta, stopped in to see us several months ago. My former wife and I were working the ouija board when he arrived with his wife. We knew only that he had been to Beaufort, South Carolina, that day. We continued with the ouija board and shortly afterward received a message for 'Harry' from Fred. We assumed that this referred to Harry's stepfather, Fred Huddelmeier, who died two years ago. There were eight people in the room at the time and a third party took notes of what came through the board. The first four lines were random words without significance, followed by just groups of letters, but then the name 'Jack' was repeated several times. Following it came a word spelled differently several times although similar, something like 'polotic.' At the time I felt the board was attempting to write 'political' and I felt a slightly conscious effort on my part to help it spell correctly. Then the word 'land' repeated itself several times, followed by 'a land Edith asked about lies between a jambled marsh estate. Jack is crooked. Edith finds a happy life here.'

"Following the above message we asked Harry if it made any sense to him at all. He was obviously disturbed and told us he had gone to Beaufort for the sole purpose of settling some legal matters relating to property his mother, Edith, deceased about six months, had left at the time of her death. The realtor had a similar-sounding name. Neither my wife nor I had ever heard the name. Also, significant to Harry was the fact that he vividly recalled that his stepfather, Fred, had disliked the man intensely and had on more than one occasion stated that he was dishonest. To conclude, about a month later Harry told us that he had just been to Savannah to sign some legal papers connected with this property. In the interim, a title search had been required and they learned that an estate had once stood on part of this property, which is now covered by marshland. Harry had not known this at the time we received the message from Fred."

Lest there be any misgivings, the reference to the real estate man which referred to the opinion of him is entirely that of the late Fred Huddelmeier, and not the author's, who has no opinion one way or the other. Steinmeyer adds that the spelling in this message was very bad; for instance, the word "asked" was spelled "asced" and the real estate man's name was slightly misspelled. The communicator, Fred Huddelmeier, had been born and educated in Germany and had never attended an American school. He spoke with a decided accent, often used incorrect grammar, and probably spelled English poorly. Steinmeyer goes on to report another veridical experience with the ouija board:

"About eight months ago my wife and I were working the ouija board with about fifteen people present. Among them were two young marines visiting from Parris Island. We had met them only a short time before and knew nothing of their personal lives. A message came through for 'Bob.' We knew both were named Bob so I asked for a last name. It spelled 'Bearce.' I asked who the message was from and the board spelled 'Frances.' I asked Bob if he knew anyone named Frances and he replied that he did, so I quickly cautioned him not to say anything else that could possibly influence the message. We then asked for the message. It replied, 'Be a good boy.' Because I am basically a doubter, I asked Frances if she could tell us something neither I nor my wife could possibly know. She replied with the word 'escort.' This made little sense so I asked, 'Escort where?' The reply was 'home.' I asked, 'Home from where?' Reply, 'California.' I then asked. 'When?' The reply was, '1955.' At this point we all noticed that Bob was visibly shaken. He had never seen a ouija board in his life, knew nothing about it, and obviously knew we knew nothing of what it said. He actually appeared near fainting so I stopped and asked if he could explain. In 1954 he was a child of about ten years when he moved from Pennsylvania to California. He had an aunt named Frances, who was now deceased. In 1955 she escorted him on a trip from California back to Pennsylvania. Bob said he had not been thinking about any of this at the time we got the message."

A very critical observer might think that this material, although entirely correct and of a very privy nature, could nevertheless have been drawn from the unconscious mind of Bob, since he knew of an aunt named Frances and the circumstances that were described in the message. This would presuppose that a ouija board can draw upon past memories, no matter how hidden in a person's unconscious mind, and bring them to the surface at will. It would also assume that the sitter's personality could detach part of itself to operate the ouija board and reply to its own questions. All this is theoretically possible, but not very likely.

In the view of the late bishop James Pike, a good scientist must always take the most plausible hypothesis if there are several presented. But so long as material obtained through a ouija board or similar device is known to anyone present in the room, whether consciously or unconsciously, whether of current interest or forgotten, that shadow of a doubt must remain. Only when something is communicated through the ouija board that is unknown to all present and is checked out and found to be correct, or if a statement is made that becomes objective reality only after the session has ended, can we be completely sure that a genuine communication between a discarnate personality and living people has taken place.

Steinmeyer evidently had strong leanings toward absolute proof in science. He, too, demanded some sort of evidence that the material couldn't have been drawn from the unconscious of those present. Of the considerable volume of messages received by him and his group, ten messages were considered to have significance in an evidential way. A communicator calling himself Sir Thomas Richards gave them a message almost every time they had a session. One day in the summer of 1968, the communicator was asked to give some sort of proof that he was not just part of the unconscious of the six or seven people present but a real, separate entity. He replied immediately, saying that there would soon be great floods that would send thousands of people fleeing. Not satisfied with such a statement, Steinmeyer demanded to know where. The communicator replied, "Texas." About two weeks later a hurricane hit Texas and sent thousands fleeing, just as forecast by the entity on the ouija board.

Steinmeyer states, "Certainly, I am not psychic in the sense of the persons about whom you write, but it is significant to me that on numerous occasions during the past ten years when I followed a strong hunch, almost a compulsion at times, to call on an account not on my original itinerary, I found that it was the most important call of the day or perhaps day of the year, and that I could not have made the call on a more appropriate day. I was top man in a sales force of more than sixty salesmen, and have often felt any success I had was due to feelings such as the foregoing, and the fortunate consequences of such insights, which were seemingly beyond my natural abilities at times."

Mrs. D. Thompson of Missouri has had ESP experiences of various kinds all her life. In 1966, her father suffered a severe heart attack and had to be hospitalized. During one of the occasions when she kept her father company in the hospital, Thompson had a flash vision of a funeral scene in a cemetery and she knew then that it was her father's funeral she was seeing. Although this filled her with anxiety, her father recovered, and the following summer, when the family met again, her vision had been all but forgotten.

To wile away the time, the brothers and sisters of the family decided to play with a ouija board, and the board came up with some pretty weird things that shook them up. Thompson recalled when the board was asked where her father had been born. At the time of this question, the father was not in the house. To every-

one's surprise, the communicator working the board replied, "Pineyville." They all laughed because they knew that he had been born in Doe Run. When her father returned home, she asked him about it and to her amazement he became very angry and told her to put the "damn fool thing" away.

But the funeral scene she had envisioned the year before came to pass. The day she and her brothers and sisters were coming home from the cemetery after burying their father, someone mentioned the incident with the ouija board and how strange it was that the communicator mentioned the wrong birthplace for her father. At this, an aunt of Thompson's, an elder sister of her father's, said that shortly after he had been born the area was incorporated into the town of Doe Run. However, it had been unofficially called Pineyville by residents. Since Thompson's father had not been present during the particular ouija-board session when the information about Pineyville came through the board, and since that information was unknown to all those present at the time, there remains the inescapable conclusion that this information was communicated to them from an outside source working the ouija board, not from any of the unconscious minds of those present.

A well-read person in the psychic field, familiar with the various phases of ESP, should have no difficulty using the board without undue risks, although to exclude self-delusion, it is wise to look at any information obtained in this manner in the light of what has just been said. If any of the information is known to those present, it should not be regarded as fully evidential. Should material be obtained that is unknown to all present and subsequently verified additional material could be taken with a degree of acceptance and the ouija board may then be an opening wedge for psychic communications.

As for the actual use of the board, it should be remembered that the hands of the operators do move the indicator, the pointer, but do so allegedly under guidance from either the unconscious of the operators or an external source, possibly a spirit personality. It is therefore important to rest the hands as lightly as possible on the instrument, to exert no force whatsoever, and to learn to yield to even the slightest nudge received through one's nervous and muscular apparatus. It is helpful to exclude all conscious thoughts to the degree one is able to do so. Resting the fingertips rather than the entire palm of the hand on the instrument and yielding to even the slightest sense of movement will produce the best results. Under no circumstances should one push or move the indicator consciously or deliberately. Fraud in this case is pure self-delusion, not likely to yield any results at all.

Closely related to the ouija board is the talent known as *automatic writing*. Here the person endeavoring communication with an external source allows the pen or pencil to be guided by that source. The hand holding the pen or pencil lightly on paper, ready to follow the slightest movement without resistance, is similar to the hand resting on the indicator on the ouija board. There is one marked difference between the two methods of communication and that is the character of

the handwriting, which may or may not be recognized as belonging to a deceased person. As a matter of fact, one of the evidential elements in automatic writing is recognition of the handwriting as belonging to another individual.

Handwriting can be imitated, of course, especially in a case where the alleged communicator is known to the automatic writer; knowledge of that person's handwriting is likely to exist at least on the unconscious level. Nevertheless, graphologists and handwriting experts can usually tell whether a handwriting is a clever copy or the "real thing", especially if sufficient samples are at hand. In addition to being guided, as it were, by an unseen hand, the automatic writer receives information and impulses to write down sentences faster than he ordinarily would be able to do. One of the earmarks of genuine automatic writing is the tremendous speed with which dictation takes place. But here, too, the proof lies not only in the appearance of the writing, the lack of time to make up the sentences being written, but also in the nature of the information being transmitted. If any of it is known to the writer, whether consciously or unconsciously, it should be discounted as of evidential value.

If, on the other hand, there are detailed and privy items of information contained in such scripts, it is entirely possible that an authentic communication between a discarnate and a living person is taking place. Much rarer is automatic communication of this kind between two living people, but there are instances of that also on record. Just as with the ouija board, there are some inherent dangers in automatic writing. If the automatist is a deep-trance medium and is not aware of that particular talent, unscrupulous entities may use the opening wedge of the automatic writing to enter the unconscious of the writer and possess him. Automatic writing is generally done alone. In most cases, illegible scribblings are the initial indication that an outside entity is about to possess the hand of the automatic writer. After a while, the scribbled letters take on the shape of words, although many of the first words thus transmitted may be meaningless. Eventually, the sentences become more concise and the misspellings disappear unless, of course, misspelling was part of the character of the communicator.

Automatic writing has its place among genuine ESP communications. When it turns into a crutch upon which a person leans to avoid the realities of physical life it loses its innocent aspects. In some cases, the automatic writer becomes a willing and uncritical instrument of the alleged communicator, submerging his own personality under the will of the automatic partner, doing his bidding, and living only for the next session with the unseen communicator. In other cases, automatic writing is followed by a more sophisticated form of communication, such as an apparition or an auditory phenomenon. As with ouija boards, the majority of automatic material can be explained on the basis of tapping the unconscious of the writer, but perhaps 20 percent of the material scientifically evaluated by psychic research societies or parapsychologists such as myself seem to indicate a genuine communication with a deceased individual.

The late New York columnist Danton Walker, a man with much ESP in his makeup but forever cautious about it, related to me his surprise when he received a compelling automatic communication from a man who claimed to have been killed during the Russian-Japanese War of 1905. The man identified himself as a Russian officer, gave his full name and other details that Danton Walker, with a newspaperman's nose for detail, was able to verify. Why this Russian officer should pick on Danton to tell his story, the columnist never understood. Possibly it happened because Danton was the only newspaperman around who was also mediumistic. For anyone to be able to do automatic writing, or rather to receive automatic writing, the person has to have a fair degree of developed ESP. It is ESP that makes the communication possible, and that is what is at work in this unusual partnership between a living and a deceased individual.

Other tools useful with ESP communications include the crystal ball, tarot cards, coffee grounds, and tea leaves. All of them serve merely as concentration points, and have no ESP qualities of their own.

In the case of the *crystal ball,* the ability to focus one's attention in a narrow channel and eventually perceive visual imprints is called *scrying.* Scrying is a talent some people possess to the exclusion of all other ESP talents. Those easily given to vertigo or headaches should not attempt it. The proverbial crystal ball, so dear to the heart of newspaper cartoonists whenever they draw an alleged medium or gypsy fortune-teller, is actually nothing more than a smooth piece of glass, or, in some cases, natural crystal, which captures a light beam in such a manner that it reduces the outside world to insignificance for the observer. By thus eliminating external disturbances, the scryer is able to tune in on his own unconscious mind and obtain veridical material from it.

Even the colloquial expression that one's crystal ball may be cloudy, meaning that one does not foresee the future, has basis in fact. Whenever the channel of communication is not open, the crystal will not divulge any information and the glass remains unimpressed. But we must remember that the vision does not actually exist in the crystal or on its glass surface, but is only reflected by the unconscious mind of the scryer. Those who wish to try crystal-ball gazing or scrying may do so by placing their crystal balls on a firm, preferably dark, surface, ridding themselves of as many diverting objects as possible, and placing themselves in a receptive mood, preferably in a quiet and not too brightly lit room. Concentrating their gaze upon the surface of the crystal, they will eventually "see" scenes taking place upon the surface. This exercise should be undertaken daily but not for more than fifteen minutes at any one time in order not to cause eyestrain or headaches. If the experimenter is capable of scrying, results should be obtained within a week.

Tarot cards could be discussed for volumes at a time, so deep is the symbolic meaning of each and every card in the deck. Originally a medieval device to divine the future, the cards are based upon ancient designs, although there doesn't seem to be any record that the ancients actually used tarot cards as such. They are more definitely established as being in wide use in Europe from the early sixteenth century onward, although they may have been used in the Orient even before then. Tarot cards contain coded and pictorialized information about various aspects of human nature. A person consulting the tarot is, in effect, consulting his own unconscious. The cards merely allow him to follow certain guidelines in which he confides.

There are various ways to consult the tarot, depending upon the number of cards used and the number or extent of the desired readings. Best known is the Scottish, or Tree of Life, method, so called from the origin and appearance of the layout. Professional tarot readers may spend up to an hour laying out various combinations of cards, asking the person to be read to shuffle them repeatedly and eventually to draw at random a set number of cards from the deck for the reader to interpret. By touching the deck of cards repeatedly, the person to be read gives the psychic reader a great deal of psychometric material as well as his personal selection of cards, which may or may not indicate a link with fate and karma in the way the subject selects his cards.

More than anything else, it is the power of ESP in the psychic reader that permits him to speak freely about the subject, especially when the subject is unknown to him. The cards are secondary; in a way, they open up the flood gates of ESP within the reader because he so believes and because he is stimulated by the rich symbolism of the cards. I doubt that anyone without significant traces of ESP in his makeup can give a satisfactory tarot reading. Countless tarot decks have been sold as toys or as parlor games, but only those who have some ESP can use them to advantage. Anyone wishing to familiarize himself with the method of using the tarot cards should consult books on the subject by Edward Waite or Eden Gray.

Coffee-grounds and *tea-leaf readings,* so dear to gypsy fortune-tellers, are similar to tarot readings in that the pattern into which coffee grounds fall or tea leaves organize themselves when the liquid has been drained stimulate certain reactions in the psychic reader. If the reader sees an image in the dregs, he does so in much the same manner as a subject will see various images in inkblots during a Rorschach test, a well-known standby of psychiatrists. There is nothing supernatural or even remotely psychic in either coffee grounds or tea leaves by themselves. The result of such readings depends entirely upon the reader, and if he derives much stimulation from looking at coffee grounds and tea leaves, he will be a satisfactory reader. Two or more people looking at the coffee grounds or tea leaves may get entirely different impressions from them because, objectively, the grounds and leaves do not take on the shape of anything pertaining to the future. It is all in the eye of the beholder.

It should therefore be remembered that ESP does not depend on any psychic tool or inducer, and that it is an inherent part of a person's makeup and can be enhanced whether or not tools are being used. Some of the devices now being offered on the market or in popular magazines as being useful to develop ESP are nothing more than commercial ways of romanticizing a most interesting subject. Other than the ESP test kit now in use at the New York Institute of Technology, where I teach parapsychology, or kits or sets in use at Duke University, psychic tools, even sophisticated-looking tools, have little value and should be treated more as objects of amusement.

how to develop your psychic gift

I S THERE ANY TRAINING WE CAN USE TO ENHANCE our ability to foretell the future? People who have had some indication of this talent would naturally be more likely to be able to do something about increasing it than those who come to it cold. But the technique to be used is much the same in either case. Basically, it consists of a state of watchfulness toward any indication, no matter how slight, that a premonition is about to take place. Nothing must be ignored; everything should be written down and, if possible, reputable witnesses should be alerted as to the nature of the premonition as soon as it is received. If possible, one should write oneself a letter concerning the experience and mail it by registered mail to oneself, thus permitting the postmark to act as a guarantee concerning the time element of the prediction.

As to increasing one's ability to have premonitory experiences, the attitude should be one of acceptance, regardless of whether the material to be obtained is pleasant or unpleasant. Absence of fear and a certain objectivity concerning the material are equally necessary. Morally, one is required to pass on whatever information is received, whether it is good or bad. If specific information concerning the future is wanted, there are certain inducing agents that may work. If the subject is someone other than oneself, perhaps a photograph or the person's name written in clear letters on a piece of paper may serve as a concentration point. Having visualized the subject or object of the search into the future, one settles back in as relaxed a state as possible and concentrates upon the subject or object. In this respect, the process resembles meditation except that a precise channeling is taking place. Tangent thoughts should be dismissed, and the mind, if wandering off, should be disciplined to stick to the topic at hand.

How can facts that are not in existence at the time they are being described by a person with ESP, and how can people who may not have been born yet at the time when someone describes and names them, be squared with the conventional view concerning the sequence of events and the time-space continuum? The past is followed by the present, which in turn is followed by the future. The sequence cannot be reversed, nor can anyone jump from the past into the future without dwelling in the present.

Against this view stand thousands of verified cases where people have foreseen future events in great detail long before these events became objective reality without having any clues as to the events themselves. Thousands of cases, which do not allow an alternate explanation of either coincidence or vagueness or guesswork, are available to serious researchers in the files of reputable research societies. Foretelling the future in detail is not an isolated instance of some extraordinarily gifted individual; it is a fairly common occurrence among many types of people, young and old, rich and poor, living in almost every country on earth. It has occurred in the past, and it continues to occur daily. It is a natural part of human personality that some people can foresee future events. It is not the same with everyone, to be sure, but allowing for degrees of perfection, the ability to break through the time and space barrier is inherent in the nature of man.

If you wish to develop a potential ESP capability, you can do so by suggesting to your unconscious that the dream state be utilized to expand consciousness, and to begin receiving material from external sources as well as from your own unconscious, to be brought to the surface and remembered upon awakening. Eventually, if you do this on a regular basis, you will have ESP experiences that increase with time as you continue this technique.

Much was made some years ago of devices connected with earphones placed below the pillow so that the sleeper would be subjected to a low-keyed voice repeating certain words over and over. But learning in one's sleep has never been very successful. While it is true that in single cases suggestion made in this manner may reach the unconscious level exactly the way a human voice would, the method fails to work once the sleeper has reached the deeper levels of sleep and begins to dream.

According to Dr. Stanley Krippner of the Maimonides Hospital Dream Laboratory in Brooklyn, New York, the sleep state now called REM, meaning "rapid eye movement" state, is the period in which most remembered dreaming takes place. Dr. Wilse B. Webb, a research psychologist at the University of Florida, says that an average of thirty-five sleep-stage changes take place during a single night, indicating quite a bit of wandering about by the dreamer in comparatively short periods. Of course, the number of dreams remembered upon awakening is a mere fraction of those that have actually occurred in the course of a night. As research initiated by Krippner continues, more is being learned concerning the nature of REM episodes during sleep. It appears that the rapid eye movement episodes occur at fairly regular intervals, primarily during the last third of the night, according to researchers Dr. W. C. Dement and Nathaniel Kleitman. They have also found that REM sleep occurs even in the daytime, not just during nighttime sleep.

One of the best works dealing with sleep and dreams has been published by Harper. Called *The Sleep Book,* and written by Shirley Motter Linde and Louis M. Savery, the book has put together various theories concerning sleep and dreams and deals with the subject in language understandable to the layman, which most dream books do not. The authors report that 65 percent of ESP experiences reported to the Institute for Parapsychology in Durham, North Carolina, occurred during the dream state. "If you find as you keep track of your dreams that you have premonitions of events to come or seem to pick up other people's thoughts, do not become alarmed; accept these experiences as an enhancement of your life, and use the dreams in whatever positive ways that suggest themselves," say the authors.

Why do *some* such dreams not come true as dreamed? Who is to say when the cutoff date is for such dream material? Many of the dreams concerning catastrophes and so on may yet become objective reality in the future. Finally, where the cutoff date has already occurred because of the nature of the particular dream, it may well be that the dream was a warning dream to begin with, and the results had somehow been aborted. Certainly, there is a fraction of dreams that are false to begin with, and should be explained not on paranormal grounds but as expressions of a symbolic or strictly personal nature.

If you wish to determine whether you (and others) have basic ESP capabilities, sit in the same room but at least two yards distant from other people. At a given signal, concentrate *lightly* on any numeral between one and ten. For about thirty seconds, hold the thought of that numeral and visualize it being written on a piece of paper at the same time. Close your eyes when you do this, then open them and look directly at the proposed receiver of your message. Pause for a moment, then do the same thing with another numeral until you have done it with five different numerals. At the same time, the proposed receiver has been instructed to write down whatever numeral he gets mentally.

When the experiment is completed, compare notes, since you yourself have also written down the sequence of numerals to be broadcast mind to mind. We find that two out of five is not unusual, three out of five may occur, and four out of five is most unusual. Frequently, the sequence of numerals broadcast may be inverted or numerals may be received out of sequence. I have already explained earlier in this book that this is due to the fact that telepathy works in a non-time, nonspace dimension where all things, all thoughts, coexist simultaneously.

Testing for ESP capabilities with images, sentences, or visualizations of thoughts: the same method as in test number one is to be employed, except that an entire sentence is being broadcast or a visual concept is being sent out.

Make sentences short, though, and visual concepts fairly simple, as it may be difficult to hold the thought of a complicated image or a very long sentence for the time required for it to be received.

(A) First sentence (image) broadcast
(B) Second sentence (image) broadcast
(C) Third sentence (image) broadcast

RESULT:

(A) First sentence (image) received
1. completely 2. partially 3. not at all

(B) Second sentence (image) received
1. completely 2. partially 3. not at all

(C) Third sentence (image) received
1. completely 2. partially 3. not at all

great american mediums of the past and present

S O YOU THINK THE BEST MEDIUMS LIVE IN England? Or that ghosts are usually found in British castles, rattling chains and bemoaning their sad fate? Both assumptions would be erroneous. Ghosts can occur everywhere in the world, from past times to the very present, and some of the best mediums lived and worked in America. I know, because I was privileged to work with them in my investigations.

Often called "the dean" of mediums, the late Carolyn Chapman, a true Southern lady from the Carolinas, was for many years the oldest practicing medium and clairvoyant in New York. For a long time she saw her clients at a tidy apartment in the Ansonia, a landmark building on Broadway and 73rd Street. Later, she moved to a modern flat on East 34th Street, where she worked until dying at a very old age.

Carolyn Chapman was essentially an old-fashioned reader who worked exclusively for private clients. Many of the predictions she made to me over the years came to pass. But it was the unexpected visit of Dr. Andrew von Salza, a rejuvenation specialist in Los Angeles, who had come along with a woman client that threw Chapman for a loop. The doctor routinely took Chapman's photograph with a Polaroid camera, because he thought she was an interesting-looking woman. Picture his and her surprise when a man appeared standing next to the medium! "Oh, how nice," Chapman exclaimed, matter-of-factly, though very surprised, "that's my late husband paying me a visit."

Chapman had no use for generalities. When I first met her in 1960, she told me that my mother, Martha, was present, and that it was her anniversary: as a matter of fact, the sitting was on November 3, my late mother's birthday. She then went on to give me greetings "from John who went out suddenly and didn't tell the truth"; John Latouche, my dear friend, died of a sudden heart attack, and only after his death did it become known that someone else owned his house and certain rights.

Ethel Johnson Meyers, who died in her nineties, was a long-time friend and collaborator of mine in many cases. Originally an opera singer in her native San Francisco, later a vaudeville performer jointly with her first husband, Albert,

work, and gradually it became her main occupation. She saw clients individually, and had weekly "development" circles at her studio on the ground floor of her Sherman Square apartment on West 73rd Street, a large room dominated by a grand piano and an array of intertwining plants. Never willing to limit herself to deep-trance mediumship, which she was

Carolyn Chapman,
"the dean of mediums."

also an artist, she eventually moved to New York and became a much sought-after vocal coach. It was not until she contemplated suicide following her husband's death and his unexpected intervention from the spirit world, that Ethel became interested in psychic matters. Eventually, she added mediumship to her

very good at, or clairvoyant readings, which she did for her clients, Ethel "sat" for direct voice phenomena, with her circle, and eventually achieved that phase of mediumship as well. She sometimes accompanied me in the dead of night in quest of hauntings, getting into deep trance quickly and regardless of circumstances, and always delivering the spiritual goods. There are very few like Ethel, because true deep-trance mediums are rare.

Once I took Ethel on a case involving murder, a case the police were unable to solve. We deliberately took a detour so that she would not know where the house we were going to was located. But the moment we stopped the car, Ethel said, "What's the pianist doing here?" What pianist, I wanted to know. "Rubinstein!" Well, the case we were about to work on was the murder of financier Serge Rubinstein. But to voice-teacher-cum-medium Ethel, the name Rubinstein had to be the pianist, of course!

The late Sybil Leek, originally trained as a journalist and working for years as a

was her faith, not her profession. But her unusual psychic powers soon led her to seek out my assistance and we worked and traveled together many times, both in America and in Europe. She was also a gifted author with many books to her credit and eventually moved to Florida, where she died. Leek accompanied me and Regis Philbin to California's most haunted house, the Whaley House in San Diego.

There she identified one of the resident ghosts as "Ann Lannay": sure enough, as I later discovered, Anna Lannay was the maiden name of the wife of Thomas Whaley, the man who built the house. In a still officially unresolved murder case of a prominent actress who died in 1958, Sybil correctly identified the full name of

The entranced medium
Ethel Johnson Meyers at
Poughkeepsie Christ Church,
with Holzer.

documentary producer in her native England, is perhaps better known for her often publicized involvement with "the old religion," Wicca, or witchcraft, which

the young man who had been dating her, who to this day remains a suspect in the case. Though he has an alibi given him by a friend, he was never arrested and charged. How would Sybil, newly arrived from England, know such things?

Betty Ritter, née Betty Rogers, was an Italian-American from Pennsylvania with a great gift at clairvoyance and psychometry. I met her at a "blind" assembly in New York many years ago, where she and Ethel Meyers were to be introduced to an interested professional audience of investigators and researchers. Ritter picked me

Otto Stransky was a composer; his wife, Alice had by then long turned gray—though from his memory, I suppose, she would always be his blonde!

Taken by me to a house in Greenwich Village, she correctly identified it as having once been Mayor Jimmy Walker's hideaway.

Carolyn, Ethel, Sybil, and Betty are now on the Other Side, where they must be

Hans Holzer with Sybil Leek at haunted West townhouse, Ireland.

out of the audience and informed me that an uncle of mine wished to be acknowledged. I demanded details, and she said, "His name is Otto, he was into music, and he had a blond wife named Alice." I was flabbergasted. My late uncle

regarded as very special people, which they were and are.

One more observation, based on many years of exploring this field: the reason that some psychic readers get part of the future but not all, or at different times than the sitter would like, is because a higher order of things wants us to know only what is good for us to know at any given time in our lives—no more, no less. And that is as it should be.

Testing psychics is part of my work. I am an academic parapsychologist, and I go on evidence, and evidence alone. No one is 100 percent accurate. But even 50 percent accuracy is far beyond coincidence or accident—a copout explanation often offered by outsider skeptics who do not study the evidence themselves.

There may be some as yet unsung psychic heroes or heroines waiting to be discovered and tested, but for now the big four are Yolana Lassaw, Rosanna Rogers, Marisa Anderson, and Judy Hoffman. In a class by herself is New York's Kathleen Karter.

Yolana Lassaw, a New York psychic and medium, has a waiting list of would-be clients longer than the mayor has of complainants. But she gets around to most of them. Living in a building called *Le Triomphe* in New York, she triumphs more often than not. Yolana discovered her gift to "see things before they happened" when still a housewife working a few odd jobs. She can be reached at (212) 308-0836.

When I took her in hand with rigorous training, it was all news to her. Now she is usually right on target. Not always. No one's perfect. But if anyone among psychics is close to it, it is Yolana.

Some of her predictions have been listed in earlier chapters.

As Yolana is the top trance medium and clairvoyant in America today, so Rosanna Rogers of Cleveland is the most accurate interpreter of the ancient tarot.

Rosanna Rogers was born in Austria and brought up in Germany, where she attended high school at the Convent of the Sisters of Saint Francis in Pirmasens, and college at the Convent of San Lioba, in Freiburg. She lives in a colorful house

Betty Ritter in New York.

in one of Cleveland's quiet districts, at 13214 Svec Avenue, and has her own local cable television program. People from many parts of the world keep reaching out to her for predictions, which she bases on a unique tarot card deck that she has designed.

Rosanna is no ordinary fortune-teller: she is precise and firm with her predictions. A woman whose name I know but who wants it kept private came to consult

Rosanna in the summer of 1987 during a civic fair. Her husband at the time was in prison on what she knew to be a false accusation, and she had no hope of seeing him exonerated, so she had decided to sell their apartment building. But the psychic, who had never seen the

Christmas came and her husband was still in jail. But suddenly, the case took an unexpected turn, and the appellate court freed the man. They celebrated the following Christmas together... a year late, maybe, but then psychics can't be right all the time... or can they?

Clockwise from upper left:

Yolana Lassaw, best American deep-trance medium today.

Rosanna Rogers of Cleveland, Ohio, best American tarot reader.

Marisa Anderson, four-star psychic.

Spiritualist medium and psychic Kathleen Karter, New York.

woman before, told her not to sell it, because her husband would be home in time for them to share a Christmas celebration.

Rosanna has many clients in the greater New York area, which she visits from time to time. She also does a good deal of her work on the telephone. She is probably the best tarot-card reader in America, and excellent in matters of a personal nature. She can be reached at (216) 751-1651.

Pittsburgh-born Judy Hoffman told her therapist of a dream in which she saw "a U.S. Air plane taking off to Pittsburgh, not fully repaired," and she saw a ball of fire and a crash. That was on August 2, 1994, confirmed by the entry in her therapist's diary. The crash took place September 30, 1994.

Judy Hoffman is an excellent reader using ordinary playing cards as induction tools. She has told a Florida hotel executive the exact date when her divorce would occur, who her next husband would be, and the exact date of this new marriage proposal. She told a client that she would meet a man named Mike during a sports activity, and that he would be wearing a uniform. A little later the client met a marine named Mike while in a swimming pool! Judy can be reached at (212) 534-6279.

Marisa Anderson is more accurate on telephone readings than in person. She has foreseen airplane crashes and was able to warn clients not to take a certain flight, which saved their lives. She pinpointed the exact day that I would receive an offer regarding a film project, and she was right on target.

A client who was looking to buy a used car was told not to worry, someone she already knew would soon offer her a car, which the psychic described in detail. Two weeks later she was offered just such a car by the mother of a friend. Marisa is also an excellent diagnostician with both humans and pets. She can be reached at (914) 725-8871, or P.O. 904, Scarsdale, NY 10530.

Finally, the very reliable medium Kathleen Karter, in New York, a very spiritual person. (212) 663-7434.

the psychic way of life

AFTER A LIFETIME SPENT IN THE PURSUIT of paranormal experiences, and searching for a system into which they all fit, I have learned a great deal about how it all works. But I have yet to discover, and perhaps never will, what force put all this into existence. In parapsychology, there are two schools of thought, one comfortable and limited, and one puzzling and wide in scope.

Limiting one's findings and areas of research to all that could comfortably be explained on the basis of human ability, notably extrasensory perception, required no acceptance of anything beyond the known world, though it opened new aspects of man's own nature to further research. On the other hand, extending the area of inquiry into areas usually reserved for religion, and thus speculation, belief, and faith, would of necessity lead to answers not possible under the first method.

Combining scientific methods of inquiry with an open-minded approach to everything yet to be discovered about life and life beyond, is the only honest way of dealing with those areas of human experience.

At such moments I look past my own successful career and knowledge, way past the temporary—and the temporal—questions mankind faces every day, into a kind of mental telescope focused on what lies "out there," way out there. I am fortunate in having had a good education, to have acquired knowledge of this universe from many angles, and to be gifted with a keen sense of perception that does not allow for easy answers or closed doors.

Through 124 published books, through newspaper and magazine articles, through television appearances and film, through theater and lectures and meetings and interviews, over the years, I have pointed to the frontiers of the mind and what lies beyond them. I have found some opposition, largely from those who were comfortable within the confines of their convictions and structures, afraid of new and upsetting knowledge that might conceivably rob them of their sense of composure and complacency. But I have also found tremendous interest from the majority of people I have met or reached out to through the media, people who find my postulations and the evidence presented both challenging and reassuring to them. These are people in all walks of life, all ages, all socioeconomic groups. What they have in common is a healthy curiosity about themselves and their place in the universe and the hint of some important answers to age-old questions about the nature of man and our universe.

At a time when it was almost ludicrous to do so, I stepped forward and wrote about the psychic evidence that man survives the dissolution of the physical body, about another dimension into which we all pass—but from the point of view of science, not religion. Belief had nothing to do with it, reasonable evidence obtained under scientifically valid conditions, through observation or experimentation, were and are, my tools.

I brought together a small group of dedicated scientists, doctors, and researchers with a similar outlook to try to establish a center that would deal with the question of life after death, reincarnation evidence, the nature of ESP and psychic experiences, spontaneous phenomena, and unorthodox healing, in a relaxed, scientific yet positive atmosphere, for maximum results, and a better understanding of how all this works. Inevitably, my path soon led to other areas crying for reasonable answers, areas beyond human experience and this planet. In a jungle of half-truths and outright delusion, I tried to isolate the hard facts and dispose of the reports and people who were projecting false images of this research, thus impeding our progress. But after I had published a successful book dealing with extraterrestrial incursions of our planet, and after examining even more cases coming to my attention after the book had been published, I came to the conviction that many of these reported incidents were true. The implication of human-like life existing on other planets circling other suns was inescapable, and it became another important question to be resolved by humanity.

Lacking major official interest, and finding little private support, I turned to my own resources to find ways of doing this necessary work, by creating television series, motion pictures, plays, and musicals, as well as more books and magazine stories, to touch upon these matters in popular ways, capable of generating profits large enough to be put into the service of my greater agenda.

Various theories are being offered by the best astronomers regarding the birth of the universe—from the Big Bang to gradual development from gaseous matter, congealing under the influence of some form of energy—and the theories keep changing because they do not address the fundamental problem: if "the universe"—the grand total of all that exists in space, known to us or not—is finite, and has boundaries, what exists "beyond" the universe? What begins where the universe ends?

Clearly, this is an impossible question to answer with our knowledge and scientific tools of today. But let us assume there is no universe, no heavenly bodies at all, just black, empty space without anything whatever in it—a vast nothingness without beginning or end. Only "nothing" can get away with that: anything that is "something" needs to be defined in some way as to appearance, size, extension.

The late "prophet" Edgar Cayce—and many psychic researchers as well—have stated that the "inner body," that is, the so-called spirit, creates and controls the physical, outer body, and thus all illness needs to be dealt with by dealing with that finer, inner body first. Even orthodox medicine acknowledges the power of the mind over purely physical manifestations. But what is "mind" other than human energy directed in specific paths? As we know through Einstein's work, energy and matter are interrelated, and actually represent different ends of the same scale—energy turning into matter under certain conditions, and vice-versa.

The "spiritual" universe, being an energy field, could conceivably also "manifest," a denser layer called matter, over long stretches of what we have come to call "time." But being composed only of energy, being a field, it cannot have boundaries as we understand the meaning of this term: only a potential, which may either increase or decrease depending upon the activities of this power reservoir. Thus, the "spiritual" universe would lie outside the space-time continuum, even though it does occupy "space": this factor it has in common with the vast nothingness of empty space—both are truly infinite.

But when this "spiritual" universe proceeds to manifest a physical counterpart, that universe becomes finite to the extent of its creation and development: the "expanding universe" theory then fits. What remains unanswered, perhaps forever by its very nature, is the question of what, or who, put this development into motion, and who, or what, so appointed that authority. There may well exist laws in the universe we do not know or understand, under which these developments occur naturally. On the other hand, the hard evidence for what we have come to call "life after death" in the vernacular is mounting, and the existence of a dimension beyond our physical world is no longer questioned by serious researchers who are familiar with the facts.

Thus, the borderline between pure scientific inquiry and the spiritual existence, even religion, is becoming increasingly blurred—until, perhaps, the two paths merge into one. That Other Side of life is neither supernatural nor haphazard. But who or what arranged all this? Who is in charge? And who appointed that "person" in the first place, if it is a person?

The answer is not here yet and may well never come. But I do know that there is "law and order" in that universe, just as there is here in its physical counterpart.

index